THE BRIDGESTONE IRISH FOOD GUIDE

The Bridgestone

IRISH FOOD GUIDE

JOHN McKENNA - SALLY McKENNA

ESTRAGON PRESS

FIRST PUBLISHED IN 2004

BY ESTRAGON PRESS

DURRUS

COUNTY CORK

© ESTRAGON PRESS

TEXT © JOHN & SALLY McKENNA

THE MORAL RIGHT OF THE AUTHORS

HAS BEEN ASSERTED

ISBN 1 874076 58 8

PRINTED IN SPAIN BY GRAPHYCEMS

WRITTEN BY JOHN McKENNA

CONTRIBUTING EDITORS:

EAMON BARRETT

ORLA BRODERICK

ELIZABETH FIELD

CLAIRE GOODWILLIE

LESLIE WILLIAMS

CAROLINE WORKMAN

PUBLISHER: SALLY McKENNA

EDITOR: JUDITH CASEY

ART DIRECTION BY NICK CANN

COVER PHOTOS BY MIKE O'TOOLE

ILLUSTRATIONS BY AOIFE WASSER

WEB: FLUIDEDGE.IE

FOR

FIONA CORBETT
KEVIN SHERIDAN
SEAMUS SHERIDAN

"... and in that moment the story of the land melts in our mouths." (K. Sheridan, F. Corbett *Seilide*)

THE AUTHORS WOULD LIKE

TO THANK

Sarah Bates, Fiona Burke,

Josette Cadoret,

Nick Cann, Des Collins,

Colm Conyngham,

Dr Denis Cotter,

Margie Deverell, Frieda Forde,

Sile Ginnane, Eoghan Harris,

George Lane,

Lelia McKenna,

Frank McKevitt, Mike O'Toole,

Miguel Sancho,

Hugh Stancliffe, Ann Marie Tobin

Bridgestone is the world's largest tyre and rubber company.

● Founded in Japan in 1931, it currently employs over 100,000 people in Europe, Asia and America and its products are sold in more than 150 countries. Its European plants are situated in France, Spain, Italy, Poland and Turkey.

● Bridgestone manufacture tyres for a wide variety of vehicles from passenger cars and motorcycles, trucks and buses to giant earthmovers and aircraft.

● Many new cars are fitted with Bridgestone tyres during manufacture, including Ford, Toyota, Volkswagen, Mercedes and BMW. Ferrari and Porsche are also fitted with Bridgestone performance tyres as original equipment.

● Bridgestone commercial vehicle tyres enjoy a worldwide reputation for durability and its aircraft tyres are used by more than 100 airlines.

● In Formula 1 Bridgestone supply tyres to leading teams and drivers, including Ferrari and Michael Schumacher. Technology developed in the sport has led to increased performance and safety in Bridgestone's road tyres.

BRIDGESTONE TYRES

● Bridgestone tyres are distributed in Ireland by Bridgestone Ireland Ltd, a subsidiary of the multinational Bridgestone Corporation. A wide range of tyres is stocked in its 70,000 square foot central warehouse and its staff provide sales, technical and delivery services all over Ireland.

● Bridgestone tyres are available from First Stop Tyre Centres and tyre dealers throughout Ireland.

FOR FURTHER INFORMATION:

BRIDGESTONE IRELAND LTD
10 Fingal Bay Business Park
Balbriggan
County Dublin

Tel: + 353 1 841 0000
Fax: + 353 1 841 5245

websites:
www.bridgestone-eu.com
www.firststop-eu.com

• In the final chapter of his autobiography *California Dish*, entitled *Long Live the Revolution*, the American chef Jeremiah Tower reflects on the culinary changes that rang through his career. Tower concludes with a simple but stunning thought: "Supplier, chef and restaurant customer could change completely the culinary scene of a locality in just twenty years".

• Do note the authority of that statement: this trilogy of players "could change completely the culinary scene of a locality", and note the time frame: no more than two decades.

• Well, fifteen years after the publication of our first book on Irish food, and with five years having elapsed since the last time the *Bridgestone Irish Food Guide* appeared in a single volume, maybe we should take stock, and ask how far our own revolution in culinary terms has advanced. Have things changed completely, or changed at all? What is the culinary scene of the little locality that is the island of Ireland?

• The most fundamental change that has occurred has been the creation of a class of creative artisan producers, and just as important has been the respect and status afforded them by their customers. Fifteen years ago, "artisan" was virtually a term of abuse. At a meeting in the Department of Agriculture back in 1989, a civil servant scoffed loudly at the suggestion that Government use its resources to assist artisan production. "Those people aren't even making it at home, never mind abroad! Why should we help them?" he barked, revealing all the tortured intellectual and cultural confusion of what we came to call "The Kerrygold Syndrome", that curious belief that Irish foods could only be sold as mass-market, low-value, single-branded products. No room for specialisation, for added value, for signature foods. No chance for regional flavours, individual creativity, no possibility of creating and encouraging world-class tastes.

• Fifteen years later, and this situation, this belief, has changed completely. Of course, there are doubtless still many civil servants who do their shopping in discount supermarkets controlled by multinational companies, and who thereby enjoy a modern lifestyle and diet. But, there are others, now, who shop at farmers' markets, and who know the names of the people who make the foods they buy. They know where the foods they eat are produced and reared, and they respect the craft of artisanship, and celebrate its creativity.

• For what the markets and the artisans have given us is simple: the luxury of choice. Real choice, meaningful choice. The choice of cheeses made with raw milk. The choice of wild fish instead of farmed fish. The choice of organically grown foods. The chance to buy the meat of animals raised in harmony with the environment. Real choice. Meaningful choice. The chance to behave like an adult who understands and appreciates that making a purchase at the apex of the food chain is a complex business, and that in making the right choices we can behave nobly, and demonstrate our respect for the mystically miraculous complexity of the foods we want to enjoy.

• The artisans have won the moral victory for real food over the last fifteen years. No civil servant or departmental scientist can take this victory from them, or deny any longer that they have achieved it. It is in this way that we have seen how a creative, respectful and sympathetic attitude to our food "could change completely the culinary scene of a locality", as Jeremiah Tower puts it. There is a new attitude to what Irish food actually is, an attitude documented in this book.

• The battle may be won, but the war, of course, is never-ending. The achievements of the artisan class over the last fifteen years have been enormous. But we believe that during the next five years the artisans – the cheesemakers, the fish smokers, bakers, growers, creative chefs and, above all, the customers – will become even more significant, powerful and respected. For we all have a taste for freedom now, the freedom of real choice, and we have the knowledge of all the good that making the right choice can achieve. Long live the Revolution.

John and Sally McKenna
Durrus, West Cork, July 2004

Several years ago, the writer Eliot Coleman, writing in *Mother Earth News*, proposed a post-organic term for food based on the Greek word *authentes* – "one who does things for him or herself". To merit an Authentic designation, Coleman argued, the food should be sold by the person or family who made and produced it: "local, seller-grown, and fresh" was how Coleman saw his new term being applied.

Authentic

● We like Mr Coleman's way of thinking, and a designation which focuses on the creative fusion that brings about a foodstuff seems to us to have very many merits. It also fits neatly within the dynamic context of the artisans working in farmers' markets in Ireland. And so we have created a symbol for **Authentic** food, and producers.

To celebrate the creativity of chefs, wine merchants, and other producers of food, we have created the award of being **On Top of their Game**, that creative peak when a certain magic can happen.

Being **Worth a Detour** means exactly what it says: these are people and places worth going out of your way to explore.

● Shops, producers and restaurants that are featured in the Bridgestone Guide often display our plaques and logos. These are carefully monitored and represent true quality. In a world of too much choice, we hope these awards will help you to find the best in Ireland.

• The Bridgestone Irish Food Guide is arranged alphabetically, by county so it begins with County Carlow, which is followed by County Cavan, and so on.

• Within the counties the towns are once again listed alphabetically.

• This system varies in Counties Cork and Dublin where the city centres and county regions are listed separately.

• Northern Ireland is listed at the end of the book as a separate entity. Note that this is a sterling currency area, though the euro is often accepted, particularly in the border areas.

• In the fifteen years since we began writing about Irish food, we have seen one major change in the way information is passed on to the customer — this is the use of websites.

• *Websites are a tool in which places can bring the most up-to-date information right onto your desk, often including a booking service, and shopping on-line service.*

• *Accordingly, our first preference has been to list a website, and this listing works interactively with our own website, www.bridgestoneguides.com, which acts as a portal for the addresses of all the best food and hospitality industries in Ireland. Check out this website for up-to-date changes and information about food and hospitality in Ireland.*

• Obviously not every establishment has a website — indeed many small food industries have yet to make this leap. Where this is the case we have always given contact telephone numbers. In addition to this we have indicated whether a restaurant is a day-time restaurant, or a restaurant which opens for dinner in the evening, or both.

• We have omitted detailed listings of prices and opening times, because these change regularly, and an out-of-date listing is not a helpful listing.

• Where we know that an establishment does not take credit cards this is indicated in the text, but very many places do take credit cards, particularly the Visa, Access/Master group.

• Many of the places featured in this book are only open during the summer season, which means that they can be closed for any given length of time between October and March. Many others change their opening times during winter. It is always advisable to check the website or telephone in advance if you are using this book in the countryside, out of season.

• Finally, we greatly appreciate receiving reports, suggestions and criticisms from readers, and would like to thank those who have written in the past, whose opinions are of enormous assistance to us when considering which entries finally make it into this book.

www.bridgestoneguides.com

CONTENTS

County Carlow

Slaney wild salmon, micro-brewery stout,
Borris honey . . .

Bagenalstown

Guesthouse
● **Kilgraney House**

Here is the sort of distinctive individuals that Brian Leech
and Martin Marley, creators of Kilgraney
House, prove themselves to be. Their
marmalade, made for the breakfast table
in the beautiful Kilgraney, is not simply
the standard Seville orange you will
encounter everywhere: it is Seville orange
and passionfruit, the tartly bitter-sweet potion flecked with
the tiny black seeds of the passionfruit.
That's the way these guys think; they are always looking for
a new way of doing things, searching for a distinctive, individualistic way of doing things, whether it is decorating a
room in the house or an apartment in the grounds, or making marmalade. They take nothing for granted, and that is
what makes Kilgraney such a special place: their individuality
causes you, the guest, to look de novo at what you might
otherwise have taken for granted. Such perspicuity has
made Kilgraney one of the cult addresses, famed for its
style, its cooking — sorrel roasted breast of chicken; home-
smoked duck and noodle salad; Slaney salmon in nori and
wasabi; dark chocolate mousse cake with home-made
honey and lavender ice cream — and its magical spirit.
(Bryan Leech & Martin Marley, Bagenalstown
☎ 059-977 5283 www.kilgraneyhouse.com)

Borris

Honey
● **Bearna Honey**

Kilgraney House use this pure Irish honey from the
Fitzgerald's bees, to make their honey and lavender ice
cream. Always look out for local honeys in Ireland, as they
can be wonderfully distinctive and surprisingly different. The
secret to finding the real ones, and not imported honeys
that are bottled here, is to find the beekeeper's name on
the jar. (Borris ☎ 059-977 3122)

Carlow

Guesthouse
● Barrowville Townhouse

Randal and Marie Dempsey's handsome house is hidden by a tall wall, just as the road to Kilkenny snakes out of Carlow town. Its location, and its sense of privacy means that one can be a stone's throw from the centre of town, and yet feel well away from it all. It's a nice sense of escape which the Dempseys, with their assured professionalism in the people business, complement with their efficient charm and hospitality. (Randal & Marie Dempsey, Kilkenny Rd, Carlow ☎ 059-914 3324
www.barrowvillehouse.com)

Butchers Shop
● Bosco's

Mary King O'Connell's excellent butcher's shop is one of the stars of Carlow town, an institution based on good meat, and good service. The service is as important as the quality of the meat, and it means that shopping in Bosco's is always a treat, something to be enjoyed, a shop to be treasured. (Mary King O'Connell, 132 Tullow St, Carlow ☎ 059-913 1093)

Brewery
● Carlow Craft Brewery

For our money, O'Hara's stout, made by the Carlow Brewing Company, is the greatest contemporary drink made in Ireland, the equal of Power's Gold Label whiskey and Barry's Classic Blend tea. Hoppy, tart, smoky, smooth, it is a drink to fall in love with, and a drink that will make you fall out of love with any other stout, which in comparison are drab, dilute and compromised.

On top of their game

From the start, Seamus and Eamon O'Hara and brewer Brendan Flanagan have stuck with their trio of brews — Curim Gold wheat beer and Molings red ale are the partners of O'Hara's stout — and having gotten it all right at the start they have simply stuck to producing their beers with enviable consistency. Food lovers should not miss the chance to drink these brews with food, for their liveliness and character means they are superb with cooked foods, and especially with farmhouse cheeses: a bottle of O'Hara's, a wedge of raw milk Durrus farmhouse cheese, and it does- n't get any better than that. (The Goods Store, Station Rd, Carlow ☎ 059-913 4356 www.carlowbrewing.com)

Café Bar
● Lennon's Café Bar

"Lennon's is a great, contemporary pub." So writes Diana Henry in her splendid *The Gastro-Pub Cookbook.* Significantly, Ms Henry points out that "The staff are proud of the place", and that is a true and telling remark about the crew in Sinead Byrne's stylish, hip and yet somehow modest gastro-pub: they are indeed proud of the room, of their work, of the food, and they really do their very best. That sense of energy, of pleasure in their craft, lifts Lennon's far above the norm. This isn't pub food; this is gastro-pub food.

What they do, they do very well indeed, from the breads ("among the best you'll find in a country where good bak- ing is valued" says Diana Henry) to the funky soups — Caribbean pepperpot, Cashel Blue, bacon and courgette — to the terrific sandwiches — char-grilled chicken with red pepper mayo; fresh salmon with herb mayo — to the ace mains — loin of pork with cider sauce; perfect cod in beer batter; bacon with parsley sauce — and culminating in desserts that bestow grandeur on classics such as banoffee pie or Katriona's lovely apple crumble. A great, contempo- rary gastro-pub. (Sinead Byrne, 121 Tullow St, Carlow ☎ 059-913 1575 lennonscafebar@eircom.net — Open for food day-time)

Cult Choice Stout

In twenty years time, Ireland will no longer be syn- onymous with Guinness, that popular dark drink crafted and drafted by Diageo. Ireland will, instead, be synonymous with O'Hara's Stout, and Carlow will be a place of pilgrimage for beer lovers who cherish the respectful brewing which is the trademark of the Carlow Brewing Company.

Leighlinbridge

Restaurant & Guesthouse
● The Lord Bagenal Inn

James and Mary Kehoe's restaurant and bar with rooms is
one of the most popular local destinations you can find anywhere in Ireland, and on Sunday lunchtimes in particular it
can seem as if the entire county has turned up for lunch
and is happily waiting in the huge queue. Such success can
put the kitchen under pressure at times, so it's best to see
the LB at its best on quieter days, when there is more
space and time to enjoy the classic comfort food which has
made their reputation. Mr Kehoe is an intensely self-critical
man always working on new projects to improve the LB,
and this energy — and his commitment to the local community — powers along this hugely successful enterprise.
Above all, don't miss studying and enjoying two elements of
the LB that show Mr Kehoe's superb good taste: the brilliant art collection with its superb concentration of modern
Irish painting, and the only-wonderful wine list. (James &
Mary Kehoe, Leighlinbridge ☎ 059-972 1668
www.lordbagenal.com — Open Lunch and Dinner)

Tullow

Herb Garden
● Cottage Garden Herbs

Michelle Power is much-respected as a herb grower and for
her chilli jellies and the very, very fine pickled tomatilloes.
Her newest venture is the very exciting Boozeberries,
where fresh fruits are immersed in alcohol, designed to be
served in a shot glass. Rich in vibrant colour and powerful
in alcohol, these are a great new concept. Don't miss 'em.
(Ballyconnell Lodge, Ballyconnell, Tullow
☎ 059-915 6312 www.cottagegardenherbs.ie)

Butcher's Shop
● Laz Murphy

Laz's shop is highly respected in the region for top-class
meats and skilful charcuterie. (Laz Murphy, Church St, Tullow
☎ 059-9151316)

County Cavan

goat's cheese, hard and soft, boiled boxty, sausages,
black and white pudding, Thornhill ducks...

Bailieboro

Farmhouse Cheese
● **Boilie Cheese**

Just because you will find Boilie in every chill
cabinet in every shop in Ireland, don't make
the mistake of taking the Brodie family's
cheese for granted: Boilie is a star. Its ubiq-
uity might suggest it is another over-
processed factory product, but in fact this is
an artisan-orientated soft cheese. It may be big in
production terms, but nothing has altered with Boilie ever
since it became that most unusual sport-of-nature: an artisan food that crossed over into the mass-market. We love
the soft orbs of goat's milk cheeses in particular, whether
on breakfast toast or used in a gazillion other ways. Every
fridge needs a jar of Boilie, simple as that.
(Bailieboro ☎ 042-966 6848 www.ryefield.com)

Wholefoods & Café
● **Planet Earth**

Diane Crook's wholefood shop in pretty Bailieboro has
developed to include a café, and it's a lovely space, bright,
lively, energised, an invaluable stop. (Lower Main St,
Bailieboro ☎ 042-966 5490)

Belturbet

Farmhouse Cheese
● **Corleggy Farmhouse Cheese**

Almost 20 years on in her career, and Silke Cropp remains
a pioneering artisan. Amongst the first of the
farmhouse cheesemakers in Ireland, she has
pioneered direct contact with her customers via farmers' markets. Today she
pioneers the use of raw milk in cheesemaking, and in tandem she pioneers the production of a range of cheeses from a variety of raw milks,
something of a contrast with the standard Irish farmhouse
practice of only producing a single cheese.

Her trio of cheeses are the much-loved Corleggy, whose small pillboxes of pale white goat's milk cheeses are well-known. There is also Drumlin, made with raw cow's milk, and most recently Creeny, made with raw sheep's milk, a cheese usually matured to about four months, at which stage it is close in style to a Pecorino.

The Corleggy Three are as quirky, idiosyncratic and enigmatic as their maker, beautifully individual, always satisfying cheeses, a vision of the artisan Arcadia.

(Silke Cropp, Corleggy, Belturbet ☎ 049-952 2930 www.corleggy.com)

Blacklion

Restaurant with Rooms

● MacNean Bistro

Neven Maguire's career has had many fairy-tale aspects to it so far. A man from a remote hamlet, in an overlooked county, who goes on to become not just the best-known chef in Ireland, but also one of the most respected modern cooks, it all seems to be a little bit too-good-to-be-true.

On top of their game

But, the simple fact is that Maguire's success has been founded on sheer hard work. Truth be told, he has the careers of half-a-dozen men: cook, restaurateur, teacher, author, television performer, and public figure, and quite how he balances them, well we simply don't know. He is a disciplined guy. He has to be.

That discipline is best seen, thankfully, in his cooking. Eating the tasting menu in the charmingly simple room of the MacNean, one is struck by just how well Maguire can orchestrate and counterpoint an entire armada of flavours: scallops wrapped in Fermanagh black bacon; pork belly with celeriac and apple rémoulade; rabbit stuffed with black pudding with Madeira; roast loin of lamb with confit shoulder, and then those extraordinary desserts: roasted banana with chocolate croquettes; warm raspberry shortcake with crème anglaise; baked figs in crème de cassis. On the right evening, it can be nothing less than perfection: perfectly cooked, balanced, understood, and stonking value at that. Despite such precocious accomplishment, we believe the best of Neven Maguire is yet to come. (Blacklion ☎ 071-985 3022 — Open Dinner & Sun Lunch)

Duck and Geese Farm
● Thornhill Ducks

Ken Moffat's game birds are rare in Ireland in being known by a brand name: Thornhill is as fine a signature of quality as you will find. You can buy these superb ducks from the farm, and you will find them also in local butcher's shops. In the MacNean Bistro, Neven Maguire has always made a speciality of the Thornhill birds, whilst Jean Campbell of the excellent Bay Tree Company, in Leitrim, uses the duck livers for her pâtés. In particular, do consider the fine geese Ken raises for the Christmas table. (Thornhill Farm, Thornhill, Blacklion, ☎ 071-985 3044 thornhillfarm@eircom.net)

Cult Choice Boxty

Boiled boxty — known as a Hurly — is a product that is almost unknown in neighbouring counties. Whilst the west of Ireland would know pan-cooked boxty, and the North would have their fadge, boiled boxty is a treat that comes solely from Cavan. Raw and cooked potatoes are first boiled together, then sliced, and fried in a delicious Cavan fusion of starchy doughiness.

Cavan

Butcher
● Barry John Crowe

You would expect a young butcher with a name like Barry John to make a pork and leek sausage, and indeed BJ Crowe does just that, and in two sizes, and he has won prizes for the pork and leek, what's more. Barry John is a talent to watch: his sausages are very fine, and his black and white puddings are even better. The sausages have 75% pork, with beef flank used in the beef, onion and tomato banger, a rarity amongst butchers in this country. We shall be hearing a lot more of BJ Crowe. (2 Connolly St, Cavan ☎ 049-436 2671)

Pub & Off Licence
● Blessings

There is a good selection of wines in the off licence of this handsome pub. (92 Pearse St, Cavan ☎ 049-433 1138)

Cloverhill

Restaurant with Rooms
● Olde Post Inn

Tara and Gearoid have carved out a mighty reputation in double-quick time in the pretty Olde Post Inn. The rooms are comfy and commodious, the restaurant is comfortable, and Mr Lynch is a formidable cook with considerable ambitions and considerable skills. He does all the cheffy stuff beloved of young cooks, such as bacon and cabbage terrine, prawns in ketaffi pastry, the signature Coq Hardi chicken breast stuffed with potato, apple, bacon and herbs, or tempura of sea bass, and if sometimes the technique eclipses the taste, you can forgive it anytime for the sheer challenge and excitement the cooking promises. Amongst the clutch of young talents now cooking in, and re-animating, the culinary culture of the Borderlands, The Olde Post shines brightly. (Tara McCann & Gearoid Lynch, Cloverhill, Butler's Bridge ☎ 047-55555 www.theoldpostinn.com — Open Dinner and Sun Lunch)

Killeshandra

Boxty
● Drummully Boxty

The Farrelly family have been making Drummully Boxty since 1984, using a recipe from mother Nan. This is an unmissible product for fans of the arcane, with history in each mouthful — and delicious with it. The texture of the little barrel of boxties, which are sold in local shops, comes from a mixture of cooked and raw potato, boiled together, then fried. (Paul Farrelly, Drummully, Killeshandra ☎ 049-433 4626)

Virginia

Sauces
● Jill's Country Shop

Jill Wright makes fine sauces using real, fresh ingredients, and her pasta vegetable sauces can also be used in casseroles. (Ballaghanea, Virginia ☎ 049-854 8234)

County Clare

smoked salmon, territorial-style farmhouse cheese,
soft goat's cheese, local bakeries, preserves, honey...

Ballina

Restaurant
Restaurant
● **The Cherry Tree**

Harry McKeogh's smart, modern restaurant, right at the
water's edge of the River Shannon, is County
Clare's outstanding destination. With his
more-than-able head chef, Mark
Anderson, leading a cutting-edge kitchen
crew, McKeogh's food is smart, sincere,
and compellingly delicious; the Cherry
Tree menus presenting a road map of both
the region and its very best producers and growers.
There is spring roll of Carrigaholt crabmeat;
Castletownbere John Dory with sauce gazpacho; west coast
lobster with lobster froth; Comeragh Mountain spring lamb
with a ragoût of artichokes, wild mushrooms and asparagus.
The palpable sense of creative excitement that animates
this kitchen makes for one of the very best Irish restaurants, a shining light of modern, original Irish cooking, and
the gracious service by local staff has just the right note of
familiarity. Both vegetarians and vegans should note that the
Cherry Tree offers many dishes without meat or dairy
products that are just as excitingly creative as everything
else. (Harry McKeogh, Lakeside, Ballina, Killaloe ☎ 061-375688
— Open Dinner)

Ballynacally

Farmhouse Cheese
● **Bluebell Falls Goat's Cheese**

This delicious, fresh, soft goat's milk cheese is one of the
stars of the west coast, made and distributed by Paul Keane,
and it packs a mighty wallop of flavour despite being sold
very young. Fantastic for salads and grilled goat's cheese
dishes. You will find it in good delicatessens and wholefood
shops on the West Coast. (Paul Keane, Ballynacally ☎ 065-
683 8024)

Ballyvaughan

Farmhouse Cheese and other produce
● Aillwee Cave

The Aillwee Cave tour is one of few organised tourist jun-
kets we would recommend, a genuinely impressive under-
ground excursion, so do sign up for it. But, the main reason
to go to the Cave is to buy Ben Johnson's excellent Burren
Gold cheeses straight from the shop. You won't find them
anywhere else, except occasionally in the Limerick market,
and indeed it's a pity they aren't more widely distributed,
for these are impressively well-fashioned Gouda-style
cheeses, packed with sweet toffee-like flavours. There are
also lots of other interesting foods and, if you are lucky,
they may well have some of their charcoal for sale, which is
the finest we have ever used. It is made from their carefully
managed hazel copse, just another impressive scheme from
this dynamic organisation. (Aillwee Cave, Ballyvaughan
☎ 065-707 7036 www.aillweecave.ie — Open day-time)

Cafe
● An Fear Gorta

The tea room of your dreams is a pretty thatched cottage
hard by the harbour in pretty Ballyvaughan. Catherine
O'Donoghue's lovely tea room is one of those rare places
where time seems to stand still as you enjoy tea and cake
and scones, a place of charming civility and impish bohemi-
anism that could only be found in County Clare. Open in
high summer only. (Catherine O'Donoghue, Pier Road,
Ballyvaughan ☎ 065-707 7023 — Open day-time)

Shop
● Burren Fine Food & Wine

Cathleen Connole's sweet little wine and gift shop is just
outside Ballyvaughan as you head towards Corkscrew Hill,
and for anyone renting a cottage near the village, this selection of wines at excellent prices will be a godsend. Their
relationship with Galway's Noblevine means that the wines
are imported directly, so value is very keen. Nice gifts, nice
hampers, including a North Clare Hamper, and a Burren
Hamper, and do drop in for teas, coffees and light lunches.
(Corkscrew Hill Road, Ballyvaughan ☎ 065-707 7046
www.burrenwines.ie)

Cult Choice A County Clare Hamper

The foods of County Clare are singular and delicious, ranging from smoked foods, fine preserves, to a superb range of cheeses. A number of shops put these splendid foods together in Hampers, which is an ideal opportunity to discover these foods in a special way. Recommended Hamper providers include the Burren Smokehouse, Ennis Gourmet Store and Burren Fine Food and Wine.

Restaurant & Accommodation
● Holywell Italian Café

Holywell is a godsend. It looks like a celestial deity dropped it out of the sky, onto the hill above Ballyvaughan, having lifted it from its natural home in the Tyrol. But thank heavens it's here, for Sibylle and Wolfgang Dietl's restaurant, which is also a language school and accommodation, is a pure beaut. The vegetarian menu couldn't be simpler: four starters such as soup of pasta e fagioli or salad caprese; seven pasta dishes, five styles of pizza, then some cakes and ice creams for dessert. It is ruddy food — think Austrian more than Italian — but it is deliciously agrestic and impressive, and the whole concept is a real sport of nature, a one-off, as radical and simple as other visionary addresses such as Island Cottage or Fishy Fishy Café.

We had the bruschetta, with all manner of toppings, and then green ravioli with tomato sauce, and of course we couldn't manage the enormous portions, but we still had to try their brilliant ice creams: strawberry; blackberry; vanilla; honey; coffee and toffee. Great service, lovely wines, including a light red which is specially bottled for them, and a darling new address, so book a room and bring the family. (Sibylle and Wolfgang Dietl, Newtown, Ballyvaughan ☎ 065-707 7322 www.holywell.net — Open Lunch & Dinner)

Bar
● O'Loclainn's Bar

You can lock us in Peter O'Loghlen's tiny, never-changing
bar and throw away the key and we won't protest a jot: this
is one of our favourite bars anywhere in Ireland, and their
capacious and intriguing selection of whiskeys is enough to
mesmerise a man even before he has had a drop to drink. If
you want to explore the world of uisce beatha in all its
multifarious glory, then Ballyvaughan is your destination.
Don't miss O'Loclainn's at any cost. (Peter O'Loghlen,
Ballyvaughan ☎ 065-707 7006)

Shop
● The Village Stores

Sheila McGannon's well-stocked little local supermarket is
especially important if you are self-catering and want to discover local specialities. (Ballyvaughan ☎ 065-707 7181)

Carron

Café
● The Burren Perfumery

It is worth making a detour to buy the special, organic
Burren perfumery products made by Sadie Chowen and
Edward Briggs. Their aromatherapy range is especially covetable, but everything they make is natural and artistically
conceived and executed. The BP is also a great place to go
for coffee, cakes and bakes and soups and sandwiches, all
served in their organic tea rooms at the Perfumery, and follow lunch then with a spin around the organic herb garden.
Bliss. (Carron ☎ 065-708 9102 www.burrenperfumery.com
— Open day-time)

Pub
● Cassidy's Croide na Boirne

This old R.I.C. barracks overlook the largest turlough in
Ireland, right in the centre of the Burren, and to sip a pint
whilst admiring the extraordinary views is a balmy pleasure.
They serve simple, good food that is very family-friendly,
and it's a great spot to kick back if you have been trekking
or cycling. (Carron ☎ 065-708 9109 www.cassidyspub.com —
Food served day-time and early-evening)

Corofin

Country House
● Clifden House

Jim and Bernadette Robson's country house is splendidly
dishevelled, beautifully located, down by Lake Inchiquin, and
if you can abandon yourself to the Bohemian naturalism of
Clifden, you will likely fall in love with it. It's not for those
who want 5-star, but it is for those who want a little bit of
wild-side civility and good craic. (Jim and Bernadette
Robson, Corofin ☎ 065-683 7692
www.clifdenhouse-countyclare.ie)

Restaurant
● Le Catelinais

You will find it difficult to get a table early in the evening in
the pretty, cosy Le Catelinais, for their early bird menus
offer great value for some really excellent cooking – Galway
Bay mussels with white wine, shallots and garlic; Tournafulla
black and white puddings with champ and mustard sauce (a
Burren walker's starter if ever there was one); excellent sirloin with parsnip chips; good braised lamb shank.
The à la carte is also well priced, and there is real style in a
dish of turbot with stir-fried vegetables. Good sticky toffee
pudding, or a fine almond and pear tart with Bailey's custard
make for satisfying puddings, and only some poor coffee
lowers the otherwise strictly observed standards of fine
fresh cooking and smart presentation. The Lloyd Webber-
Westlife juxtaposition on the stereo is pleasingly ironic, for
a little while. (Síobháin O'Connor & Yanne Lecathelinais,
Market St, Corofin ☎ 065-683 7425 — Open Dinner)

Cratloe

Farmhouse Cheese
● Cratloe Hills Sheep's Cheese

Look out for the mature Cratloe, sold as a tiny, mustard-
golden orb of cheese, and use it as you would a Parmesan,
grating the golden goodness of Sean and Deirdre
Fitzgerald's fine sheep's milk cheese onto anything and
everything, from polenta to creamy potato gratins. (Sean
and Deirdre Fitzgerald, Cratloe ☎ 061-357185)

Doolin

Preserves
● The Clare Jam Company

David and Vera Muir's pristine preserves company produces delicious jams, marmalades and chutneys using old-fashioned methods of hand pouring, and open pot boiling. You can find their preserves through County Clare, and they also have a shop selling their entire range, including rhubarb and ginger, blackberry and Port, whiskey marmalade, peach chutney and a great strawberry jam. A visit to the shop, just 2km from the Cliffs of Moher, is a must: just smell those jams bubbling away, aah! (Lough North, Doolin, ☎ 065-707 4778 christinemuir@eircom.net)

Restaurant & Guesthouse
● Cullinan's Restaurant & Guest House

Cullinan's is one of those quiet, modest County Clare success stories; a destination address for locals who enjoy James Cullinan's good seafood cookery, and for holidaymakers who want to sample the fizzle of lovely Doolin and who like the attractive, good-value accommodation in the house. Good, fresh seafood is the house speciality. (James & Carol Cullinan, Doolin ☎ 065-707 4183 www.cullinansdoolin.com)

Café
● Doolin Café

This ageless, cottagey-style room is always a nicely laid-back spot in which to enjoy a bowl of good seafood chowder and some excellent brown bread, and to get a fix of the Bohemian, laid-back zeitgeist that is so particular to, and pervasive in, Doolin. (Niall Sheedy & Deirdre Clancy, Doolin ☎ 065-707 4795 — Open day-time)

Restaurant
● Doolin Crafts Gallery & Restaurant

One of County Clare's most enduring destinations, the Crafts Gallery has been twinning gorgeous crafts with good home-baking from Mary Grey for more than 20 years. Mary concentrates on soups, salads, fresh baking and sandwiches, and the sharp, choice aesthetic of the gallery is shared by the restaurant. (Ballyvoe, Doolin ☎ 065-707 4309 www.doolincrafts.com — Open day-time)

Doonbeg

Wine Importer
● Doonbeg Wine Imports

John and Dan Mulhall started Doonbeg Wine Imports as a hobby, but it has steadily grown into a business, supplying local restaurants, shops and private customers. They concentrate on France, and in particular regions such as the Loire Valley, though recently the list has grown to reach as far south as the Languedoc, as far north as Alsace, and even a few interlopers from Australia have appeared. Wines such as the Domaine de Riaux Pouilly Fumé deliver great typicity, with notes of green apple and smoke, whilst wines sourced from co-operatives such as Cellier du Beaujardin are modest, correct and extremely enjoyable. Doonbeg is also a company from which one can source older vintages: a 1997 Anjou Villages such as Domaine Fardeau shows how even relatively simple, inexpensive country wines from the Loire will age with great grace. (Doonbeg ☎ 065-905 5334)

Gastro Pub
● Morrissey's Pub

April arrives and Hugh McNally and the crew gear up for another season of knocking everyone sideways with good seafood and good cheer at the lovely Morrissey's. Prawns in garlic butter, fillet of salmon, scampi in golden crumbs, open smoked salmon sandwich, and there is even a sirloin steak for those who have strayed from the sea of piscine faithfulness. Everything is done simply and well and with no little style. Food lovers who enjoy tracing culinary family trees might like to know that Jenny McNally of this tribe is the cook at the splendiferous Coast, in Tramore, County Waterford, proving that good cooking runs in the blood. (Hugh McNally, Doonbeg ☎ 065-905 5304 hughmcnally@hotmail.com)

Ennis

Shop
● Ennis Gourmet Store

There are always lovely new discoveries to be made in Ann Leyden's tiny and crammed-to-the-rafters shop: last time we were in here, we picked up some of Tibo's Inis coffee, homeroasted in Ennis using Monte Redondo Tarrazú beans: demon stuff, and Fair Trade as well. Don't miss the lunchtime salads and sandwiches, and that fine hit of Java Republic coffee will wake you up at breakfast-time. (Anne Leyden & David Lasblaye, 1 Barrack St, Ennis ☎ 065-684 3314, gourmetstore@eircom.net)

Café
● **Henry's**

You can't miss Henry's, a big, glass-fronted room at the far end of the Abbey Street car park that looks like an insurance office. And you shouldn't miss those good New York-style hot sandwiches and the fine ice cream. They also now open on occasional evenings so you can hang out over a sundae on a Saturday night, but the real attraction here is the pizzas, especially their fine St Tola goat's cheese pizza which is a star. Salads are unreliable, but staff are realiably friendly, and it's a rockin' spot at lunchtime. (Henry Benagh, Abbey Street Car Park, Ennis ☎ 065-682 2848 — Open day-time & weekend Dinner)

Ennis Saturday Market...

Ennis is very supportive of the Saturday market, much in line with the progressive attitude of Clare County Council, which in March 2004 repealed a by-law that prevented anyone selling untrimmed vegetables with dirt, clay or soil on them.

Unfortunately, they also built a multi-storey car park smack in the centre of where the traders ply their wares, which doesn't do much for atmosphere or footfall. Nevertheless, there are good things here early in the morning: the Real Olive Co (of course); excellent breads and cakes from Kelly and Vi of Limerick's Sunflower bakery; great sweet delights from Galway's Gourmet Tart Co; and fantastic organic produce from Kelvin Frost of Drumminalough Organics, everything from asparagus to bushy raspberry plants to potatoes, chutneys, jams and jellies. Look out also for the lovely garden plants and herbs from the Rainbow Organic Nursery.

Traiteur
● The Food Emporium

T.J. McGuinness's traiteur sails ever onwards, producing good food-to-go from a talented young crew who relish their work. It's always a nice, understated, almost-domestic spot to take a simple lunch or some coffee and good scones, and if you have to feed a convocation of cardinals or somesuch, then Mr McGuinness is your only man. (TJ McGuinness and Brenda Deering, 8-9 Francis St, Ennis ☎ 065-682 0554)

Café
● Glor

This attractive, light, modern space offers a good value lunch or cool coffee spot, open daily in Ennis' theatre venue, Glor. (Friar's Walk, Ennis ☎ 065-684 3103 — Open Lunch)

Butcher
● Derek Molloy

Look out for the dry-cured bacon sold in Molloy's tiny wee butcher's shop in the centre of town: it's especially good, boiled for dinner, with some cabbage cooked in the bacon water as you roast the bacon to finish it. And how lovely to see a traditional butcher's shop, offering skilled charcuterie and polite service, thriving right smack in the centre of lovely Ennis. (Abbey St, Ennis ☎ 065-682 3296)

Hotel
● The Old Ground Hotel

The Old Ground is one of the most celebrated of Ireland's traditional town-centre coaching hotels and has maintained impressive standards for decades. The Town Hall Café is its funky, young bistro (see opposite). (O'Connell St, Ennis ☎ 065-682 8127 www.flynnhotels.com)

Wholefood Shop
● Open Sesame

This excellent wholefood shop has long been one of the vital addresses in Ennis, and unlike many shops that avoid dealing with fresh and local produce, Open Sesame is where you will find lots of good local things. (35 Parnell St, Ennis ☎ 065-682 1480 opensesame@eircom.net)

Restaurant
● **The Town Hall Café**

The smart THC is the locals' first choice for informal, modern, bistro-style cooking in a modish, stylish room: braised shank of lamb; good prawns in filo; grilled goat's cheese with salad. It's not original, but it is done with style and an energetic charm. (O'Connell St, Ennis ☎ 065-682 8127 — Open Lunch & Dinner)

Wine
● **The Wine Buff**

Just down from the corner with Abbey St, the Wine Buff is the Ennis outlet of the growing franchise of shops started by Bordeaux-resident Paddy O'Flynn. The WB chain has quickly grown to six separate outlets. Bordeaux is, wisely, their focus, but not the classed growths or other trophy wines that you will find here. Instead, O'Flynn and his crew hunt for out-of-the-way marques, and they find them with a vengeance: check out the much-lauded Chateau Fauconnerie, and don't miss the terrific value offered by wines such as Marquis de Beaulieu, a crisp white wine that is a steal, or Chateau Haut Marin Bordeax Sec. There are also wines from Alsace and the Languedoc, as well as a small offering from Spain and Italy. (Paddy O'Flynn, 4 Francis St, Ennis ☎ 065-684 2082 www.thewinebuff.com)

Ennistymon

Restaurant with Rooms
● **Byrne's Restaurant & Townhouse**

Richard and Mary Byrne's handsome restaurant with rooms in the centre of pretty Ennistymon is a comfortable, spacious place, with some nicely achieved modern cooking – spinach and blue cheese soup; crab claws with lemon and garlic cream; oven-baked turbot with basil and goat's cheese mash; cod in Parma ham with oregano and chilli, and classic desserts such as crème brûlée and tiramisu are right on the money in terms of taste and texture.
Service is personable and relaxed, the music is always well-chosen, and value for money is keen, especially for the early evening menus which are very popular with the local audience. (Main St, Ennistymon ☎ 065-707 1080 byrnesennistymon@eircom.net)

Farmhouse Cheese
● Mount Callan Cheddar

Lucy Hayes' cloth-bound mature cheddar-style cheese is one of the newer arrivals on the artisan cheesemaking scene, and one of the most assured, raw-milk cheeses you can find. The cheese has a rich, lactic pungency and a long, mellow aftertaste that speaks of utterly skilful cheesemaking, with flavours and scents gloriously commingled, and the texture and colour are beautifully achieved. Mount Callan is one of the finest and most exciting of the new Irish cheeses. (Michael and Lucy Hayes, Drinagh, Ennistymon ☎ 065-707 2008 mtcallan@oceanfree.net mlhayes@esatclear.ie)

Bakery
● Unglert's Bakery

A charming little village bakery in lovely Ennistymon, Unglert's has nice, quirky breads and good, sweet, sticky things that kids just adore. Whatever else you do in Ennistymon, and wherever else you go, you simply must visit Unglert's. (Mr Unglert, Ennistymon ☎ 065-707 1217)

Inagh

Brewery
● The Biddy Early Brewery

Niall Garvey's pub and craft brewery was the pioneer amongst craft brewers in Ireland, and the original trio of brews – the formidable Black Biddy stout, the sweet ale Red Biddy and the Pilsener-style White Biddy – have now been joined by Real Biddy, a cask-conditioned ale. These brews are

refreshing, distinctive and pleasingly refulgent, with bog myrtle and carrageen moss used to fine the beers and to give them body. Do not, under any circumstance, miss a visit to the colourful brew pub when heading through Inagh, and do look out for the BE brews in other local pubs. Your good health! (Niall Garvey, Inagh, Ennis ☎ 065-683 6742 www.beb.ie)

Farmhouse Cheese
● St Tola Goat's Cheese

Siobhan ni Ghairbhith continues the noble craft of the great
St. Tola goat's milk cheeses, with the same
patient care and conscientiousness that
marked the cheesemaking career of her
predecessors, Meg and Derrick Gordon. To
see the artisan skills begun by the Gordons
developed and expanded by Siobhan is bliss
for food lovers, the continuation of craft, of culture, of culinary skills. All of the cheeses are superb, from the magnificent St. Tola log, to the small crottins of fresh cheese, to the
St. Tola preserved in oil, to the hard cheeses. All of them will
improve your table, and improve your life. (Siobhan ni
Ghairbhith, Inagh ☎ 065-683 6633 www.st-tola.ie)

Kilfenora

Gastro Pub
● Vaughan's Pub

Vaughan's is famous for great music sessions, but it is also a
pub that is serious about its food, so you can expect much
more than the average level of food served in country pubs,
and there are real, artisan, country flavours to be enjoyed in
their cooking: cottage pie, wild salmon, crab salad and their
famous chowder. (The Vaughan family, Kilfenora
☎ 065-708 8004 www.vaughanspub.com)

Kilkee

Bistro and Shop
● The Pantry & Bakery

During the summer season, it seems that Imelda Bourke
and her hard-working team feed every holidaymaker in
Kilkee. Sometimes, the situation in this bustling bistro is akin
to bedlam, and hungry families line up to order bumper
portions of tasty cooking. Around the corner in the shop, it
can be just as crazy and chaotic, as Mums and Dads pick up
huge amounts of good foods – buttery scones; fresh pots of
jam, cooked chickens, creamy gratins, dreamy creamy cakes
– to take away. It's only brilliant, and make sure to take a

walk around by the waterfront to buy some sea vegetables and winkles. And in the summertime, do note that there is a farmers' market in the town on Sundays. (Imelda Bourke, O'Curry St, Kilkee ☎ 065-905 6576)

Kilnaboy

B&B
● Fergus View

Mary Kelleher's traditional B&B is home to good hospitality and good cooking, and its location makes an excellent base for anyone planning to explore the beauty of the Burren. (Kilnaboy, Corofin ☎ 065-683 7606 deckell@indigo.ie)

Cult Choice St Tola
Darina Allen uses it to stuff courgette blossoms; Ger Foote serves it herbed with chargrilled chicken; Paul Rankin bakes it with roast beetroot and a walnut vinaigrette.

Farmhouse Cheese
● Poulcoin Cheese

Anneliese Bartelink's gouda-style cheeses are difficult to find, but it is worth the effort of hunting them down wherever you may find them in the locality, for they express the great skill of this singular cheesemaker. (Hunt it down in local shops and B&Bs)

Kilrush

Bakery
● Considine's Bakery

Considine's is one of the few old-style bakeries and shops left in Ireland; places where you will find old fashioned breads such as cob loaves. Just across the street is a tiny wine shop, Gemma's Wines Direct, so why not make a picnic? (Francis St, Kilrush ☎ 065-905 1095)

Lahinch

Restaurant
● Barrtra

Paul and Theresa O'Brien's delightful seaside cottage restaurant is one of the County Clare veterans, having started in the business back in the late 1980's. But, to see this vivacious pair at work, cooking and ferrying their seafood specialities — sushi nori with mackerel; prawns with lemongrass, ginger, chilli and garlic; seabass with orange and ginger; baked hake with crab — you would think they had just opened their doors. Barrtra has always kept the zeitgeist, always kept its sense of democratic generosity and great hospitality. Paul and Theresa O'Brien, Barrtra, Lahinch ☎ 065-708 1280 barrtra@hotmail.com — Open Dinner)

Farmhouse Cheese
● Kilshanny Cheese

Peter Nibbering is one of the stalwarts of the Limerick market, where he sells the various Kilshanny cheeses at a cracking rate on Saturday mornings. Made with raw cow's milk, these are expertly made, accessible and enjoyable cheeses, some flavoured with cumin, nettles and garlic. Demand is such that the cheeses are often sold when very young, but if you can get your hands on a mature cheese, then relish the fudgy, satisfying mineral richness that raw milk, and patient, practised cheesemaking, offers. (Peter Nibbering, Derry House, Kilshanny ☎ 065-707 1228)

Guesthouse
● Moy House

Perched high on the hill overlooking the Atlantic ocean, just at the edge of Lahinch, Moy House is a romantic, almost-cinematic, destination – this is a rather special house. And, thanks to manageress Bernie Merry, it is also extremely well-run. The attention to detail shown in their bathrooms, for instance, packed with potions, unguents, lotions and what-have-you, makes taking a bath a Sybaritic pleasure, and the informal elegance of the house and the cooking further congratulates this pleasure. (Antoin O'Looney, Lahinch ☎ 065-708 2800 www.moyhouse.com)

Liscannor

Pub & Wine Specialist
● Egan's

Patrick Egan's cult pub is a great spot for a summertime
pint, and wine lovers also come here to source Patrick's
favourite clarets, which range from modest estates to wal-
let-busting superwines. Quixotic and splendidly surreal.
(Liscannor ☎ 065-81784)

Lisdoonvarna

Smokehouse
● The Burren Smokehouse

This busy shop is a little bit of Avoca Handweavers for the
west. Peter and Brigitta Curtin are a dynamic
couple, and over the last 15 years they have
produced superb smoked fish, and steadily
improved their fine visitors' centre, which
adjoins the smokehouse, and which is full of
interesting things to buy, from excellent foods to
good crafts and other covetable essentials for your well-
chosen lifestyle. The smoked fish is particularly fine, and
their delivery service through their smart website is speedy
and reliable. (Lisdoonvarna ☎ 065-707 4432
www.burrensmokehouse.ie)

Miltown Malbay

Restaurant
● The Black Oak

It's often difficult to get a table at Tom and Bernie Hatton's
ever-popular Black Oak, such is the clamour for their cooking, which marries extraordinary value-for-money with
rock-solid reliability.
Punchy starters, such as tempura tiger prawns with the
unusual alliance of pear and Roquefort salad with chilli barbecue sauce, or very fine crab cakes with a smart horseradish and cucumber cream, set the tenor of considered,
flavourful modern cooking. Their touch with meat dishes,
such as mint and mustard crusted lamb, or a very fine sir-

loin with red wine and onion confit, can't be faulted. Old stagers such as French onion soup, or old-fashioned roast duckling, are cooked with care and accomplishment, and lush desserts like hazelnut meringue with blackcurrant sorbet or artery-threatening triple chocolate Kahlua torte bring dinner to a rich, rousing conclusion.

Friendly service from local staff, and the stonking energy of a room packed with regular customers, help one to overlook the rather suburban decor, whilst those who get lucky and get a table in the front room can expect to be mesmerised by the views out across the sea. (Bernie & Tom Hamilton, Rineen, Miltown Malbay ☎ 065-708 4403 — Open Dinner)

Mountshannon

Cafe
● Rob's An Cúpan Caife

Rob's is a nice spot in the centre of cute Mountshannon to take a break, and have some decent coffee and a scone in a comfy room. During the summer Rob's will be packed with boating holidaymakers, taking a break from lazing on the lake, who love the relaxed familiarity offered by the friendly cooking, and who especially cherish the long, lazy weekend breakfasts. Charming and simple. (Robert McDonagh, Main St, Mountshannon ☎ 061-927275 — Open day-time)

Tulla

Restaurant
● Flapper's Restaurant

Patricia McInerney is a smashing cook, whose modest, soulful food is pure delight — fresh salmon with white bean ragoût; rack of lamb with colcannon; skewered monkfish with lime and ginger; barbary duck with turnip purée. The food is expertly executed, but it never shows off; it simply delivers pure flavours and pleasure. Lunchtimes see this small, smart set of rooms packed out with locals, whilst the weekend dinners see the cooking at its expressive, enjoyable zenith. Value for money in Flapper's is only excellent. (Patricia and Jim McInerney, Main St, Tulla ☎ 065-683 5711 — Open Lunch and Weekend Dinner)

10 GREAT
IRISH COOKBOOKS

1

DARINA ALLEN
BALLYMALOE COOKERY COURSE

2

MYRTLE ALLEN
THE BALLYMALOE COOK BOOK

3

HUGO ARNOLD
AVOCA CAFÉ COOKBOOK

4

DENIS COTTER
CAFE PARADISO COOKBOOK

5

PAUL FLYNN
IRISH ADVENTURE WITH FOOD

6

ELGY GILLESPIE
YOU SAY POTATO

7

NEVEN MAGUIRE
NEVEN COOKS

8

PAUL & JEANNE RANKIN
GOURMET IRELAND

9

JANE RUSSELL
IRISH FARMHOUSE CHEESE RECIPES

10

REGINA SEXTON
LITTLE HISTORY OF IRISH FOOD

County Cork

farmhouse cheese, farmhouse butter, blood puddings, drisheen, milk, buttermilk, tea, oatmeal, shrimps, corned beef, cured meat...

Cork City Centre

Bakery
● Arbutus Bread

Here are the two things you need to know about Declan Ryan's artisan bakery. Firstly, Mr Ryan bakes the best loaves you can eat in Ireland. Secondly, you will not find these loaves for sale in shops: they are sold via farmers' markets and in the English Market. Declan Ryan has bucked the system everywhichway, and his achievement is considerable. Of course, even before he set about mastering the business of artisan, sourdough baking, he had made Arbutus Lodge of Montenotte one of the most significant and successful desti-nation restaurants in Ireland. To have created a new career, and to have done so to such exacting standards for a sec-ond time, is an extraordinary accomplishment, and places Mr Ryan as one of the most pivotal food people in Ireland. The loaves are dreamy perfection, slowly proved, carefully minded, bread that seems to emerge from TLC as much as sheer skill. This is as good as Irish artisanship gets. (Rathdene, Montenotte ☎ 021-450 1113 arbutus@iol.ie Available at markets in Cork, Bantry, Clonakilty, Kenmare, Macroom and Midleton)

On top of their game

Tea
● Barry's Tea

You will find the Barry's blends of tea everywhere, from Adrigole to Zingerman's in Ann Arbor, USA, but don't ever make the mistake of taking these great teas for granted; they are ubiquitous because of their superb quality, especial-ly the Classic Blend leaf tea and the sachets of Earl Grey. It's principally African teas that are used in the blends, and the skilfulness, assurance and consistency of the Barry's teas is simply outstanding: they make life better. (Kinsale Road, Cork ☎ 021-491 5000 www.barrystea.ie)

Café
● **Café Gusto**

The best coffee in town (we know everyone claims that, but it's simply true of Gusto) and a small range of good quality and consistent wraps and sandwiches to eat in, take out or have delivered. (3 Washington St, Cork ☎ 021-425 4446 www.cafegusto.com)

Restaurant
● **Café Paradiso**

Denis Cotter and Bridget Healy's seminal restaurant has become so successful and so celebrated that we are entirely at ease with its achievements. But, we should not lose sight of just what an extraordinarily radical place and concept Café Paradiso actually is. After all, if you never use meat or meat products in your cooking, yet 90% of your customers are carnivores, you are overturning entire notions of what running a restaurant involves, along with notions of what people expect when they go out to eat.

On top of their game

Like another radical of an earlier age, Ballymaloe's Myrtle Allen, what Healy and Cotter did was to first of all answer a personal need – to express themselves through cooking and running a restaurant – before they probably adverted to what it was their customers might want. But, so complete and true was their vision, that we all bought into CP, on their terms. We wanted what they cooked, and we wanted it served the way they served it, and any other ideas of personal preference were secondary: we wanted their art, and that is what CP has delivered now for 10 years.

As with any great artists, Cotter and Healy have refined and reformulated their work. The cooking has become more abstract, more personal, the service and style has become simpler, more original. This is no mean feat: for most people, running a restaurant means doing the same thing time and again, in order that you can be consistent. CP doesn't do that: this restaurant works like a continuous improvisation. The cooking is sui generis: oyster mushrooms in sage and cider cream with a potato, parsnip and wild rice cake; goat's cheese, roasted tomato and pinenut charlotte with grilled polenta; ravioli of pinenuts, currants and sheep's cheese in a lemon-thyme cream. Special cooking; special place. (Lancaster Quay, Cork ☎ 021-427 7939 www.cafeparadiso.ie — Open Lunch & Dinner)

Ice Cream
● Collin's Ice Cream

Tom and Anne Collins's lovely range of ice creams has remained one of the best-kept Cork secrets for far too long, for these are excellent ices, beautifully made, with true fruit flavours – and they are always pleasing. Look out for them in good Cork shops and supermarkets. (Castlewhite, Waterfall, Cork ☎ 021-434 2050)

Restaurant
● Crawford Gallery Café

Isaac Allen cooks beautiful food in the Crawford, food that espouses the Ballymaloe ethos of care in the sourcing, and love in the cooking. As such, this sympathetic and delicious food is the perfect match for the genial, gentlemanly, erudite ambience of the Gallery Café itself, for there is elegance on the plate – a gratin of clams; chicken with butter and leeks; fresh fish from Ballycotton, lovely cakes and bakes – and there is elegance all around you in this tall, fine room. Any time you find yourself in the Crawford is a time to give thanks and praise for the good things created by talented people. (Emmet Place, Cork ☎ 021-427 4415 www.ballymaloe.ie/crawfordcafe/crawford.htm — Open Lunch)

Chocolates
● Eve Chocolate Shop

Chocolates – and jelly bellies – are all you will find in Eve St Leger's lovely chocolate shop, a child's dream destination. Huh, to hell with the kids: this is a dream destination for any food lover, a small, cosy, delirious sweetie shop that feeds not just our sweet tooth, but also feeds our fantasies. Eve is what a chocolate shop should be: undiluted; distinct; specialist; artisan.

The Corkies – that unbelievable mixture of savoury, salty nut and sweet caramel with chocolate which simply has no equivalent in the chocolate world – are perhaps Ms St Leger's most significant signature creation, but the crunchies are ace; the Easter eggs are fab; the special treats for Valentine's day and Xmas are a treat and a tonic. (College Commercial Park, Magazine Road, Cork ☎ 021-434 7781)

A Pizza Cork...

As you might expect of a sun-loving, fun-loving Mediterranean people, Cork citizens have a taste for good pizza...

• *Ciao Ciao*, on Washington Street, serve a decent range of pizzas in the evening, and show their real strengths when it comes to cooking a soft egg on a pizza (not easy), and their clever judgement of chilli seasoning.

• *Fast Al's* on Paradise Place serves way-to-go! pizza slices à la Napoli or New York. This is a tiny shop, serving only two or three different types of pizza, depending on which Fast Al has made. We don't know whether his name's Al, nor does his accent make it clear if he is from Cork, the 'States or Monaghan, but he is a very likable man, proud of making his own dough by hand, and proud of his pizza. He offers pesto, chillies or black pepper as garnishes. The pizza is crisp on the bottom, but soft and chewy above, and folds easily, which is bang on the button with the guidelines being laid down in Italy for Napoli pizza. Al is open until 6pm daily, then re-opens from 9.30pm-3.30am on Fridays and Saturdays. He has a food mixer but doesn't like what it does to his dough.

• Across the road, in *Pizza Republic*, you can get more studiously and self-consciously Milano-style restaurant pizza, with carefully chosen Italian wines and funky atmosphere.

• The old timers of Cork pizza has to be *Bully's Restaurant* of Paul Street, and elsewhere, who have been making crisp-based pizza, using Italian flour, for yonks now, and many consider them to be the best. (☎ 021-427 3555)

Restaurant
● The Farmgate

Kay Harte's café, up the stairs in the centre of the English Market, remains as reliable a destination for good cooking as it has ever been. They cook the foods of the market that ranges on all the counters and stalls below them – corned beef, lamb stews, tripe and drisheen, smashing tarts with farmhouse cheeses – and they cook them with patient,

CORK - Co. CORK (CITY)

maternal, respectful care. The dining room splits into a busy
self-service counter, and the restaurant, which is an oasis of
calm, in the midst of all the bustle of the market. (Old
English Market, Princess St, Cork ☎ 021-427 8134 — Open
Lunch)

Brew Pub
● **Franciscan Well Brew Pub**

There are good, distinctive brews down here on North
Mall, though the Franciscan Well isn't the grooviest pub in
the city. The Franciscan wheat beer is their trump card,
though the smoothness of the Shandon stout is pleasing
and real. Well worth any beer lover's time. (14b North Mall,
Cork ☎ 021-439 3434)

Wines & Spirit Shop
● **Galvin's Wines & Spirits**

There are four branches of the Galvin's chain of wine shops
dotted around Cork city: Washington Street, Watercourse
Road, Douglas Road and Bandon Road. They are well-
designed, pleasingly timeless shops, and the range of wines
is impressive, with good bargains often prompting one to
walk in and check out what is on special offer.
(Washington St, Cork ☎ 021-427 6314)

B&B
● **Garnish House**

Hansi Lucey's handsome B&B is one of the great Cork
addresses, with maternal attention paid to everything and
everyone. The breakfasts are a legend, and that moment
when you arrive and that scent of freshly baked breads and
cakes hits you is one of those great moments of your life.
Pure darling, nothing less. (Western Road, Cork
☎ 021-427 5111 www.garnish.ie)

Restaurant
● **Les Gourmandises**

We have enjoyed some perfect cooking from Patrick Kiely
in Les Gourmandises, food so fine that it makes us regret all
the more the fact that this is not a great room. But the
cooking is pure and precise: duck confit with glazed shallots,
olives and thyme; sirloin with pommes fondant and braised
carrots; benchmark chicken with tomato concasse and
olives and capers, seasoned with lemon zest and clove, a

THE BRIDGESTONE IRISH FOOD GUIDE   49

dish that had us scribble Perfect! in our notebook. Lunch is a very popular time, whilst dinner has a trio of choices for starters and main, with three desserts and cheeses. If they can get the room right, the Kielys could shoot for the stars. (Pat and Soizic Kiely, 17 Cook St, Cork ☎ 021-425 1959 www.lesgourmandises.ie — Open Lunch & Dinner)

Hotel
● Hayfield Manor

"It is a wonderful place and the staff could not have been nicer to us." Well, that's a pretty succinct and adept summary from a friend of the pleasures of Hayfield Manor. It's an elegantly luxurious address, quietly tucked away in the midst of the university zone, and a calm expertise reigns throughout. (Hayfield Manor Hotel, Perrott Avenue, College Rd, Cork☎ 021-484 5900 www.hayfieldmanor.ie)

Café
● Idaho Café

Idaho is one of those places that, if it didn't exist, you would simply have to invent it, because once you discover it, you can't live without it. A tiny room on the corner of the street, it is permanently packed with happy people enjoying delicious cooking: risotto with bacon and basil; blackened chicken salad; shepherdess pie; crispy duck quesadilla. Children love it, adults love it, they love it for breakfast time, for lunchtime, for afternoon tea time. Last time we were in, it was for a sausage sandwich and a cup of coffee early in the morning, and everything was as delightful as it always is. Outside, on the street, a man was playing "Bohemian Rhapsody" on an upright piano (we're not making this up). Surrealism may have died out elsewhere, but it is alive and well in Cork, thank heavens. And Idaho, this simple, masterful place for good food served with utter charm, is alive and well also. (Mairéad & Richard Jacobs, 19 Caroline St, Cork ☎ 021-427 6376 — Open Day-time)

Restaurant
● Isaac's

Canice Sharkey and Michael Ryan's northside room is handsome, whilst the cooking is modern and efficient in the bistro style: tagliatelle with red pepper sauce; king prawns with chilli; sirloin with béarnaise. (48 MacCurtain St, Cork ☎ 021-450 3805 isaacs@iol.ie — Open Lunch & Dinner)

10 ARTISAN
RAW MILK CHEESES

1
BAYLOUGH
Co TIPPERARY

2
BEENOSKEE
Co KERRY

3
BELLINGHAM BLUE
Co LOUTH

4
CORLEGGY
Co CAVAN

5
DESMOND
Co CORK

6
DURRUS
Co CORK

7
MAIGHEAN
Co TIPPERARY

8
MOUNT CALLAN
Co CLARE

9
ST GALL
Co CORK

10
ST TOLA
Co CLARE

Restaurant

● The Ivory Tower Gastrological Restaurant

If the chaotic maelstrom of foods and sounds and senses that is the Ivory Tower gets to you, then you will reckon every other restaurant is tame and compromised by comparison. If it doesn't get to you, you will hate it. That's how it is with Seamus O'Connell's Ivory Tower: either you feel you are in an ivory tower, or a dungeon.

We would love it if the room was a little smarter and the housekeeping was sharper, but we can forgive anything when the cooking is as original as this. Mr Soul Food is a culinary polymath, making connections with foods, finding affinity with ingredients and cooking up concepts others wouldn't, or couldn't, even dream about.

Some of the signature dishes are now well-known, but they are never cooked the same way twice: the Crozier soufflé served in an artichoke; the warm duck salad; the celebrated carpaccio of wood pigeon; the venison with chocolate. Provocative, erratic, utterly exotic. (Exchange Buildings, Princes St, Cork ☎ 021-427 4665 — Open Dinner)

Restaurant

● Jacobs on the Mall

Mercy Fenton is one of those cooks who, despite being responsible for some of the finest food cooked in the country, remains little known outside of Cork culinary circles. These days, Ms Fenton directs the cooking in Jacob's in her position as front-of-house, a role in which she demonstrates the same quiet power that was always evident in her kitchen work.

We need only a single word to describe her style of food: harmonious. Other cooks would take a selection of ingredients that don't appear to belong together – roast monkfish, grilled polenta, flat mushrooms, buttered celery and a tarragon cream – and be unable to make any manner of harmony with them. Ms Fenton makes these unlikely ingredients sing like a choir with perfect pitch, and that is her signature, her brilliance: she finds harmonies with her chosen dishes that others would never appreciate or be able to combine and conjure. You would eat such food in a Nissen hut, but Jacob's is also a great room, with great service, and really great value. (30a South Mall, Cork ☎ 021-425 1530 jacobsonthemall@eircom.net — Open Lunch & Dinner)

Restaurant
● Jacques

Let us salute and celebrate 25 years of good food, for that
is what Jacque and Eithne of Jacques restaurant have given
to Cork city. Maternal, delicious, moreish cooking, quietly
and competently delivered for a quarter of a century: the
great Jacques antipasti; scallops with shallot purée and
Gubbeen bacon; their classic duck with potato and apricot
stuffing; aubergine with almonds and Ardsallagh goat's
cheese; winter fruit bread and butter pudding. They source
well, they cook carefully, they serve with charm and skill,
and the ambience is cool and modern and comfortable.
What a fabulous institution, a restaurant that is part of the
culture of the city. (Jacque & Eithne Barry, 9a Phoenix St,
Cork ☎ 021-427 7387 — Open Lunch & Dinner)

Chipper
● Jackie Lennox

Lennox's is a legend, especially with generations of Cork
students for whom it has been a home-from-home. The
chips are only great, the staff are only great. Great, like. (137
Bandon Road, Cork ☎ 021-431 6118)

Coffee Roasters
● Maher's Coffee

Only in Cork would you find a little one-off coffee roaster
shop such as Maher's, suppliers of good roasts to the city
for years and years. The Italian roast remains our favourite,
but all the blends are good, and the shop is charming and
petite. (25 Oliver Plunkett St, Cork ☎ 021-427 0008)

Restaurant
● Nash 19

Claire Nash's ever-busy restaurant is a simple, self-service
room where the cooking does all the talking, and the cooking here talks loudly. The food is as well-focused as that
served at Avoca, and like Avoca it shows care, solid sourcing. Order their homemade burger, for instance, and you
also buy into some delicious balsamic caramelised onions,
crunchy, real coleslaw, and excellent crispy, thin fries: a cliché
re-animated into a classic. (19 Princes St, Cork
☎ 021-427 0880 — Open Day-time)

Wholefood shop, bakery and café
● Natural Foods

NF has been one of the key addresses in Cork for 20 years, thanks largely to its particularly fine wholefood baking. The shop is also a great source of wholefoods and organic produce. Look out for the cherry bracks and the vegetarian baps. (Wendy Byrne, 26 Paul St, Cork ☎ 021-427 7244)

Wine Merchant
● O'Donovan's

Gary O'Donovan has quietly and firmly powered the number of O'Donovan's shops into double figures, with the units dotted all around the city and as far afield as Midleton, a Munster echo of what the rapidly-expanding O'Brien's chain has been doing in Leinster. These are good shops with a good range right across the wine globe and right across the price bracket. The shop in Ballincollig is their flagship store, and O'Donovan's is an ambitious bunch, a company to watch. (St Patrick's Woollen Mills, Douglas ☎ 021-436 4799: also at Ballincollig; Bishopstown; Blackpool; Summerhill; Oliver Plunkett Street; Shandon Street; Main St, Midleton; and Riversdale, Midleton)

Butcher
● O'Flynn's

Simon and John O'Flynn's famous butcher's shop in the centre of town is one of the country's great butcher's, home to great service from kindly staff – the sort of service you only get in Cork – and to excellent charcuterie. O'Flynn's is one of the very few shops where you get a true sense of the creative and culinary potential of charcuterie, for the brothers think not simply like butchers, but like cooks: they create their recipes with an end in sight, with a vision of how the beef or the lamb or the sausages will be cooked and used and enjoyed. Creative charcuterie, that's what you get in O'Flynn's. (36 Marlborough St, Cork ☎ 021-427 5685)

Wholefood Shop and Self Service Restaurant
● The Quay Co-Op

The ground floor of the Quay is devoted to a particularly fine shop that mixes choice organics with good wholefoods. There are wines, fruit and vegetables, and an in-house bakery cooking gluten-free, dairy-free, wheat-free, yeast-free and sugar-free loaves. Upstairs, there is a popular self-service vegetarian café. (24 Sullivans Quay, Cork, ☎ 021-431 7026 www.quaycoop.com — Open Day-time & early Evening)

Restaurant
● Star Anise

In a room just on the north of the river from which many others have come and gone, Star Anise has hung on and created a following for some seriously nice cooking. They get the essentials right; the room sparkles, the water jugs are iced and primed, service is sharp, and the cooking is creative: crab and salmon cakes with Caesar salad; their signature dish of lamb baked in filo, and there are always smart vegetarian choices. If ingredients were sourced with a little more care, everything in SA could effortlessly trade up another notch. (4 Bridge St, Cork ☎ 021-455 1635 — Open Lunch & Dinner)

Soup and Sandwich Bar
● Wildways

Moira Roche's organic soup and sandwich bar is a great destination for a quick bite at any time, and the punky, funky, up-for-it staff give the room a great buzz and great energy. Stylish, enigmatic, and a real corker. (21 Princess St, Cork ☎ 021-427 2199 www.wildways.net)

Wine Merchant
● The Wine Buff

With companion shops trading in Clonmel, Ennis, Limerick, Tralee and Galway, the Wine Buff has quickly moved to be a player in Ireland's wine market. Their USP is simple: founder Paddy O'Flynn lives in Bordeaux, from where he sources wines from smaller chateaux and less well-known zones. This can throw up wines that are extremely fine, and extremely fine value. Whites, such as Marquis de Beaulieu 2002, or Chateau Haut Maurin 2002, are superbly drinkable wines for less than a tenner, and have character and nuance. Red wines, such as Chateau La Fauconnerie, have won great acclaim. You get, in short, the sort of wines the French themselves would drink at dinnertime, and if you think wines should be quirky, modest, fun and suitable for everyday enjoyment, then the Wine Buff wines will ring your bell. The shops are staffed by helpful buffs.(4 Washington St, Cork ☎ 021-425 1668 www.thewinebuff.com)

The Coal Quay Market

There are ambitious plans for 2005 to develop
the Coal Quay Market with a target of
around 25 stalls, but at the present time
it's a quirky collection of powerful
individuals: *Caroline Robinson*, (Parkmore,
Templemartin, Co Cork
☎ 021-733 0178), one of the powerhouses behind farmers' markets, will be selling her vegetables; *Mark Hosford*
(☎ 087-635 1954 kellyandmark@eircom.net) will have his
enigmatic collation of great Cork county specialities from
the best artisans; *Dockrell Organics* (Adrienne Dockrell
☎ 021-438 4963) will have local organic crops and herbs
as well as some imported organic produce, and there will
also be organics from Eugene Walsh's *Gleann na
Smaointe Permaculture Farm* (Ballygarvan, ☎ 021-
484 0862). If Olga and Peter Ireson from *Knockatee
Organic Dairy* (☎ 064-84236) are there, don't miss their
incredible Jersey butter and the best buttermilk you can
buy, and look out for sweet things from *Sorcha's Kitchen*
and from *Noreen Webster* (☎ 087-9198905), and hummus
and home-made dressings from *Amanda Mellett* (☎ 021-
497 5332).

The English Market

You could live a lifetime in Cork and never
need any shopping destination other than
the English Market. Everything you could
possibly need is here, from champagne to
turbot, organics to exotics, drisheen to tripe,
mutton to the most magnificent bread in the country.

· *The Alternative Bread Company's* speciality is a very
moreish walnut bread, but there are lots of other funky
flavours and textures in their extensive range of healthy,
real breads. (☎ 021-489 7787)

· So, you have just got your hot new copy of Aussie cookery queen Kylie Kwong's fab cookery book, *Heart and Soul* and you ask yourself: but where can I find all this queer culinary gear so I can cook Kylie's recipes? The answer is: *Mr Bell's*. Every exotic, of howsoever remote a provenance, is here, and there is a lot more besides. And the clutter and clamour of the stalls feels just right as you hunt down the Kikkoman's, the shiitake, the galangal and the bird's eye chillis. Ace. (Driss Belmajdoub, ☎ 021-488 5333)

· *Michael Bresnan's* is one of the best butcher's shops, and it's invaluable not just for superb beef and lamb, but for stuff like sweetbreads, tongue, oxtails, hearts and all the precious stuff that has the best flavour. The meat is from their own farm and slaughter house. Just around the corner, Mr Bresnan's sister, Catherine O'Mahoney, has equally fine produce. (☎ 021-427 1119)

· Billy Forrester's wine company *Bubble Brothers* does have a specialisation in champagnes, but the shop has much, much more to offer also, with a well-chosen and genuinely eclectic list of wines, and service and the e-mail newsletters show a very focused, hip organisation. Do keep an eye out for their seasonal hamper offers which marry excellent foods and wines from the Market. (☎ 021-455 2252 www.bubblebrothers.com)

· Mary Rose Daly takes the art of coffee very seriously, and also brews excellent Clive McCabe teas in *Café Central*. Sit down and enjoy the bustle of the market. (☎ 021-427 1999)

· *The Garden* always has something intriguing amidst its array of organic vegetables and extensive dried and pre-served fruit and nuts (need brazil nuts? dried papaya? — you'll find it here), and its expansion into two bays of the market shows how Donal O'Callaghaan has amassed an appreciative audience over the last few years. (Donal O'Callaghan, ☎ 021-427 2368)

THE CORK CITY MARKETS

· Joe Hegarty's patisserie, *Heaven's Cake*, is elegant and decadently enjoyable, he's a patissier of fine cakes, who can also turn his hand to savoury things, so grab a beef and redcurrant pie or a pie of smoked bacon, pineapple and pecorino before they sell out, which they inevitably do. (☎ 021-422 2775)

· Sean and Josephine Calder-Pott's *Iago* has long been a exemplary beacon of quality, selling the very best cheeses, fine home-made pasta, sauces and sundries, all impeccably sourced and sold with metropolitan style. (☎ 021-427 7047)

· Ken Barrett's *Meat Centre* is a somewhat unprepossessing stall, but is home to that rarest of modern foods: mutton. Boiled mutton and caper sauce: now you're talking. Quite how we have lost the taste for mutton we don't understand, so the Meat Centre is a journey of discovery to forgotten tastes. Ken reckons he simply has an ability to select a good animal for slaughter: "The Lord never gave me the gift of brains but he gave me the gift of knowing animals," says Mr Barrett. Fans of curious cuts should also note that *Cathleen Noonan* sells pig's feet from her stall and that other particular market speciality buttered eggs are available from *Moynihans*, near the entrance to the market. (☎ 021-427 7085)

· The O'Connell brothers – Pat and Paul – of *O'Connell's Fishmongers*, are the superstars of the market, known via television and the print media throughout the food-loving world. No celebrity worth his or her salt would dare to visit Cork without having their picture taken with Pat O'Connell. For ordinary decent folk, O'Connell's is the finest fish shop in the country, and in this regard O'Connell's has no peers: everything here is tip-top, first-class, 24-carat, fish and shellfish so supremely fresh that they can turn a novice cook into a master cuisinier. O'Connell's is where you realise just how vital food is to the heartbeat of the city. (☎ 021-427 6380 www.koconnellsfish.com)

· Isobel Sheridan's *On The Pig's Back* stall is where you will find Declan Ryan's Arbutus Breads, unanimously regarded as the finest loaves baked in the country. Grab a few of these, and some of their home-made pàtés, terrines, excellent cheeses in excellent condition and lots of superb foods, sold with great panache by an ace crew. Here you will get lunchtime sandwiches, and some choice speciality products from Ireland and France. Confit of duck rubs shoulders with Gee's Jams, The Scullery Preserves, and Mary Burns' Adrahan Lullaby. Another pivotal stall in this market. (☎ 021-427 9232 www.onthepigsback.ie)

· Marc O'Mahoney's *The Organic Shop* has every manner of organics your heart could desire, including soups, yogurts, cans, dried foods, vegetables – if it's organic, you'll find it here. Of particular interest is the range of well butchered organic meats sold in the adjacent organic butchers, with a lot of the meat being sourced from Marc's farm. (☎ 021-427 9419)

· The dynamism of the *The Real Olive Co.* gets bigger and better all the time, opening up markets with confident dignity. Woe betide any county council to stand in the way of Toby Simmonds and his dream of re-establishing market rights to producers all around Ireland. This stall is Olive Co HQ, with a flourishing sandwich bar next door. More power to them. (☎ 021-427 0842)

· Tripe and drisheen, the local blood pudding made with sheep's blood and as refulgently reminiscent of a farmyard as a great red Burgundy wine, is what they sell at *Stephen O'Reilly's* stall. Now, when did you ever think you would see drisheen compared to a Romanee-Conti? Whilst we are at it, cook the tripe Lyonnaise style, and drink a cool young Beaujolais cru with it. Or a bottle of stout. You can often taste these particular Cork specialities upstairs in *The Farmgate Cafe* —see page 48 for details of this market restaurant. (Stephen O'Reilly ☎ 021-496 6397)

Cork City Outskirts

Ballincollig

Butcher
● Michael O'Crulaoi

Michael O'Crulaoi is an ambitious and skilled young
butcher. In just a few years, he has powered
this shop into its position as the pre-emi-
nent food destination in the fast-growing
suburb of Ballincollig, and the planned opening of a new deli just beside the store shows a
man who is still moving as fast as he can.

O'Crulaoi's expertise comes from the experience and appli-
cation of generations of butchers and farmers, and his meat
is simply superb, both beef and lamb. The prepared meats
section is also extremely well-achieved, and their cooked
foods are clamorously popular – somedays there are so
many people in here buying cooked lunches and dinners
that it seems that no one in Ballincollig cooks anymore. A
great shop. (Ballincollig ☎ 021-487 1205)

Blarney

Guesthouse
● Ashlee Lodge

Anne O'Leary's hip, luxurious B&B is one of those houses
that brings people back time and again. And it's not just visitors to Blarney, but even visitors to Cork who come back
for the spiffingly luxurious rooms, for Ashlee is really closer
to a 5-star hotel than any manner of guesthouse, and there
is even a hot tub and a sauna. (Tower, Blarney ☎ 021-438
5346 www.ashleelodge.com)

Gastro Pub
● Blair's Inn

Good home cooking from Anne Blair is the attraction in
the pretty Blair's Inn. Baked ham with cabbage; lamb with
cider; Irish stew; corned beef with parsley sauce are some
of the well-executed traditional dishes, but the kitchen can

also show its form with more modern ideas. Friendly, cosy, intimate.(Cloghroe, Blarney ☎ 021-438 1470 www.blairsinn.ie — Open Lunch & Dinner)

B&B with Restaurant
● Phelan's Woodview House

Billie Phelan has won high regard for his cooking in Phelan's, and whilst the style of the house doesn't match the style of the cooking, it's a valuable place to know in popular Blarney. (Tweedmount, Blarney ☎ 021-438 5197 — Open Dinner)

Carrigaline

Country Market
● Carrigaline Country Market

Famed throughout the length and breadth of the country as one of the finest country markets in existence, Carrigaline is unmissable for great local produce and a vibrant community atmosphere. (Carrigaline GAA Pavilion, Fridays 9.30am)

Farmhouse Cheese
● Carrigaline Farmhouse Cheese

Pat and Eilis O'Regan's gentle, mild, handmade Carrigaline cheeses are friendly, direct and quite delicious farmhouse cheeses, and are today amongst the most enduring of Ireland's artisan foods. The limestone content of the pastures on which the Carrigaline Friesians graze gives the cheese a distinctiveness that is always pleasing. (The Rock, Carrigaline ☎ 021-437 2856 http://carrigalinecheese.com)

Restaurant
● Gregory's Restaurant

Gregory Dawson's popular neighbourhood restaurant has a decade of experience under its belt by now, but the light, food, and the energetic buzz and the value remain youthful and always enjoyable. (Main St, Carrigaline ☎ 021-437 1512 — Open dinner, Sun lunch)

Wine Wholesaler
● Karwig's Wines

Chances are that you will get lost trying to find your way to Joe Karwig's shop, but do persevere, and when you finally arrive, you will see that it has been worth the hassle of getting hopelessly lost. Joe's selection of wines is only great: personal, reliable, the choice of a wine merchant who respects the craftmanship found in wines by winemakers such as Winzer von Erbach, Burklin-Wolf, Barone Cornacchia, Avignonesi and some chirpy, quirky new arrivals from the New World. (Kilnagleary, Carrigaline ☎ 021-437 2864 www.karwigwines.ie)

Chocolates
● O'Conaill Chocolate

Casey O'Conaill's chocolate company has been a dynamic mover and shaker in recent times, steadily upgrading their list and their packaging, making their presence felt in farmers' markets, and they have now dipped a toe into the city culture by opening O'Conaill's Chocolateers on French Church Street. This chocolate co. is one hot ticket right now. (Church Rd, Carrigaline ☎ 021-437 3407)

Crosshaven

Bagel Café
● Milis Café

Mags Curtin made her name as the renowned patissier in Café Paradiso, where she created droolsome delicacies for almost a decade. Ms Curtin has now moved closer to the sea to open Milis (pronounced millish: life is sweet, don't you know). Here you will find Mags' great signature handmade bagels – we like 'em toasted and smeared with cream cheese, and of course a brunch of scrambled eggs achieves transcendence with a Milis bagel – along with lovely soups, a daily pasta dish, sandwiches, and home-churned ice creams, all signed with a signature of artisan excellence. (Crosshaven ☎ 021-483 3735 — Open Day-time)

Douglas

Traiteur
● Liam Bresnan

A brother of Michael Bresnan, terrific butcher in the Cork Market, Liam sells quality meat from their shared farm. (Douglas Village Shopping Centre, 021-489 1009)

Traiteur
● Billy Mackesy's Douglas Village Foods

Aeons ago, Billy Mackesy was a high-profile chef in
Ballinhassig. Today, he is a high-profile chef operating a hugely successful traiteur's shop in Douglas, a tiny room
crammed with fridges and freezers packed with food-to-go.
There is everything from a very fine, very smooth chicken
liver pâté, to navarin of lamb, quiches to petits fours to
fresh pasta with mushroom sauce. The shop is perpetually
jammed, and the white-coated staff whirl around the place
stocking up and serving like it's a Monsieur Hulot movie. (1
Tramway Terrace, Douglas ☎ 021-489 0060)

Fish and Chips
● KC's Fish & Chip Shop

Wes Crawford and his crew work hard to dispel the notion
that every chipper is the same, so they use fresh ingredients
and imagination, rather than just pulling stuff out of a
freezer and bathing it in hot oil. (Douglas, Cork
☎ 021-436 1418)

Restaurant
● Lovett's

Niamh Lovett heads up the restaurant whilst Marie Harding
heads up the kitchens, and this pair of sparky women have
kept the long-running Lovett's operating smooth as a die
since they assumed control. Ms Lovett is a fine cook, another of Cork's invaluable female keepers of the kitchen.
(Church Lane, Douglas ☎ 021-429 4909 — Open Lunch
and Dinner)

Rochestown

Traiteur
● Cinnamon Cottage

CC is a splendid neighbourhood deli: check out their fine
salads, good breads; packs of Ted Browne's crab meat, and
there is also an extensive range of cooked meals-to-go. The
choice is only excellent: making up your mind and deciding
just what you feel like eating is the only difficult bit!
Cinnamon is a great address to know about if you are having a big family gathering: let them do the cooking!
(Monastery Rd, Rochestown ☎ 021-489 4922)

East Cork

Ballycotton

Restaurant
● **Grapefruit Moon**

Ivan Whelan and Jean Manning have made GM into a sure-fire East Cork destination, a sparky, astute and fun place in which to enjoy Mr Whelan's snappy cooking and Ms Manning's brilliant service.

Mr Whelan bases his cooking on fish from the bay, but he also likes to ring the seasonal changes: November menus will see partridge with walnut stuffing, and wild venison with apple and parsnip purée, whilst in summer the food has a lovely light zing: heritage tomato and basil soup; John Dory with Mediterranean salsa; cod with crab beurre blanc. The wine list has grown into one of the best – and best written – that you will find in the county, and this restaurant is purring and powering ahead. (Main St, Ballycotton, ☎ 021-464 6646 — Open Dinner)

Carrigtwohill

Farmhouse Cheese
● **Ardsallagh Goat's Cheese**

Don't miss Jane Murphy selling her splendid goat's cheeses at the Midleton Market: we love the fresh cheeses, and the extra-matured cheese which you can only get from the cheese-maker herself. Mrs Murphy has recently begun creating really exciting variations of fresh cheeses with sweet things – bilberry, oats and honey, to name just two of the first experiments – which are already proving a big hit with food lovers who want to create the equivalent of the traditional savoury, instead of a conventional sweet course. Now that sounds like just the thing to welcome the pitcher of port as dinner winds down to a wonderful conclusion. There is also a very good Ardsallagh goat's milk yogurt which is quite widely available and which has a tart, pleasing bite to it. (Woodstock, Carrigtwohill ☎ 021-488 2336)

Cloyne

Counry House
● Barnabrow House

Geraldine O'Brien's fashionably stylish country house has
become a favourite for small, elegant, bespoke weddings.
(Geraldine O'Brien, Cloyne, Midleton 021-465 2534
www.barnabrowhouse.ie — Open Dinner & Sun Lunch))

Deli & Bakery
● Cuddigan's Foodstore

The former premises of Micheal Cuddigan's legendary
butcher's shop has kept its name, in tribute to the man, but
has morphed into a funky little deli and bakery that specialises in breads and sweet baking. In addition, there are
lots of handmade foods in the fridge: breast of chicken in
white wine and mushroom sauce; seafood chowder; cottage
pie; gratin dauphinoise. It's a friendly shop, and a keen crew
are running it. (Cloyne ☎ 021-465 2762)

Cobh

Wines & Spirit Shop
● Belvelly Smokehouse

Frank Hederman is one of the supreme artisans of the age.
Whether he is smoking some eel, or making
a smoked mackerel pâté, or making a
dressing for his smoked mussels, his
instinct for distinctive flavours and textures is unerring. His salmon is utterly individualistic, the use of beech wood making for
an effect that is milder than when oak is used, and it's an
addictive elixir of tastes that has won enormous admiration:
if you order the smoked salmon in Rick Stein's Seafood
Restaurant in Padstow, Cornwall, then it is Frank
Hederman's smoked salmon that you will be served. Rick
Stein knows his stuff. There is nothing to choose between
the various varieties of smoked fish, from sprats to mackerel to mussels to salmon to eel: each is as fine as the others,
each is as distinctive as the others. Belvelly Smokehouse
shows artisanship and epicureanism working hand in hand,
giving cutting-edge flavours, yet extracting these flavours
through time-honoured technique. (Cobh ☎ 021-481 1089)

Killeagh

B&B with Restaurant
● Ballymakeigh House

Margaret Browne's celebrated B&B, up on the hill just east
of Killeagh, has the woman of the house firmly in control of
the kitchen and sending forth excellent breakfasts, and comforting dinners that you hope never stop: Ballymakeigh
steak with horseradish and a fiery pepper sauce; chicken
stuffed with smoked salmon mousse; collops of monkfish
with red pepper sauce. Mrs Browne enjoys the challenge of
the kitchen, and there is a mischievous creativity to be
enjoyed in her cooking. (Killeagh, Youghal ☎ 024-95184
ballymakeigh@eircom.net www.ballymakeighhouse.com)

Midleton

Fishmonger
● Ballycotton Seafood

This fine wet fish shop always gives the shopper inspiration,
with its excellent selection of fish and shellfish of pristine
freshness. The fish shop has spawned an associated industry
of value-added products. (46 Main St, Midleton
☎ 021-461 3122 www.ballycottonseafood.com)

Restaurant
● The Farmgate

Marog O'Brien's restaurant is home to yet another of those
formidably talented and dedicated women who are Les
Mères of County Cork, a tribe of female cooks whose defi-
ant, anti-fashionable, timeless style of maternal food has
been the bedrock on which Cork's culinary culture has
been created over the last 30 years. Women like Marog are
alephs of the food culture, cooks whose work shines a light
on all the myriad aspects of Cork's eating life. In her simple
dish of roast duck, for instance, you can see and taste how
Cork cooks have no need of the fashions of food, simply
because they have travelled far beyond them. They understand their ingredients and choose them with care and
respect, they understand their culinary techniques, and they
know how to cook food that has sustenance and savour.
Ace. (Coolbawn, Midleton ☎ 021-463 2771 — Open Lunch
and weekend Dinner)

Honey
● Glenanore Apiaries
The bees from Michael Woulfe's apiaries feast on sycamore, hawthorn, clover and blackberry blossoms, and produce wonderfully runny honey which you can buy in the local butchers' shops, in Killeagh Pharmacy, as well as the Ballymaloe Cookery School and the must-visit Carewswood Garden Centre. (Railway House, Midleton ☎ 021-463 1011)

Restaurant
● O'Donovan's
This splendid restaurant remains a local secret, but we don't reckon that can last much longer. We have enjoyed splendid, unpretentious and true cooking from chef Ian Cronin: accurate and unmessed-with Caesar salad; beautiful cassoulet of lamb's tongues (one of our faves); a super Ballycotton chowder; Barbary duck with a beetroot and horseradish tapenade, the sort of historically well under-stood and well-executed relish that shows how much Mr Cronin thinks about his work. Pat O'Donovan fronts the restaurant with genial patience, and value for money is exceptional. (58 Main St, Midleton ☎ 021-463 1255 — Open Lunch & Dinner)

Wholefood Shop
● Well & Good
Jill Bell's wholefood shop is a haven for local growers and producers who respect the kindred, inquisitive spirit that animates Ms Bell. A founding member of the Cork Free Choice Consumer group, here you can buy vegetables from Ballyroe Organics as well as many other things to make you well and good. (Broderick St, Midleton ☎ 021-463 3499)

Cult Choice Corkies

Eve St Leger's Corkies are the most quixotic sweet thing you can eat: they are sweet — milk chocolate – yet they are also somewhat salty — dark caramel, nuts — so there is a double hit when you bite into them. Amazing.

Midleton farmers' market

The jamboree of good things that makes up the Saturday Midleton market is a joy to behold. The chutzpah and confidence of the traders, and their strong sense of camaraderie, might suggest that the Midleton market has been here for years. But, in fact, it only began trading with a bunch of local growers, producers and artisans in 2000. Since then, it has been unstoppable, with local people turning up to the car park just at the top of the town to buy local foods from local people every weelend of the year. Already, the Midleton market has inspired competition – there is a new market now in Douglas village, just on the edge of Cork, and further markets have begun in Fermoy, and further east in Dungarvan and Waterford. For the market has shown how a new archetype of behaviour for artisans, where you produce and then sell direct to the customer via a market pitch, and don't waste time dealing with suprmarkets, is the new way to success. Just as importantly, such a way of working is a vital barometer of the health of a community: community spirit is what you find at the Midleton market, a vital social cohesion that comes from local people working with local people. All that, and loads of great food.

(www.midletonfarmersmarket.com)

· *Dan Ahern*: Dan's chickens are reared slowly, slowly on grass and have a genuine free-range life. The beef from the farm at Ballysimon is grass-fed, and matured for three weeks, and everything is certified organic. (☎ 021-463 1058/086-163 9258)

· *Arbutus Breads*: superlative sourdoughs from Declan Ryan's bespoke Cork city bakery: but just make sure to get to the market early or there will be none of these amazing loaves left. (☎ 021-450 1113/ 086-251 3919)

· *Ardsallagh*: Jane Murphy's splendid Ardsallagh stall will have rarities such as smoked and aged Ardsallagh goat's cheese. (☎ 021-488 2336)

· *Helen Ahern & Ted Murphy*: hand-made, home-made cakes, jams, scones, as well as vegetables & shrubs.

· *Ballintubber Farm*: David and Siobhan Barry bring the produce of Ballintubber Farm, where they also have a farm shop (open on Friday afternoons 4pm-7pm). Look out for peas in the pod, romanesco, good purple sprouting broccoli, and there are plants for those who want to grow their own. (☎ 086-823 8187/021-488 3034)

· *Ballymaloe Gardens*: Darina Allen can walk it as well as talk it, so the Ballymaloe gardens stall is a treasure trove of exotics and good local things produced to pristine perfection by the team at Ballymaloe under Susan Turner. If they have their fresh tomatillos, snap 'em up. Roisin Allen and Elenor Herlihy help man the stall. (☎ 021-464 6785)

· *Belvelly Smokehouse*: Frank Hederman's stall is where you get lunch sorted: smashing fish pâtés to begin (eaten with Arbutus breads) then smoked mackerel, or else smoked mussels to be paired with some fresh pasta and some sauvignon blanc. Life is good. (☎ 021-481 1089)

· *Fiona Burke*: Fiona is one of the great Cork marketeers, known most of all for selling artisan Irish and French cheeses, but look out also for country butters and other precious foods. (☎ 026-43537)

· *Frances and Keith Burns*: sell vegetables and fruit, as well as flowers, shrubs and plants. (☎ 024-95234)

· *Caitriona Daunt*: Catriona will have exceptional quality organic fruit and vegetables, both Irish produced and imported, and there are teas, blueberry tonic and other good things. (☎ 086-362 2918/021-454 6718)

· *Glenribben Organics:* excellent organic vegetables, brought from Waterford by Tim York. (☎ 058-54860)

· *Just Organic*: Deirdre Hilliard uses organic ingredients to make her soups, pasta sauces, pestos and lasagnes. (☎ 021-481 2367)

· *Margaret Keane*: Margaret will have nice vegetarian tarts and pizzas, and soups, pâté and hummus. (☎ 021-450 6231/086-606 6231)

· *For The Love of Food*: everything made by Clodagh McKenna for her For the Love of Food company is of superb quality, and that chicken liver pâté is so sensationally luxurious it should be made illegal. (☎ 023-54587/087 683 1602)

· *O'Conaill Chocolate*: Casey O'Conaill has powered his artisan chocolate company into overdrive in the last few years, so pick up some handsome, tasty chocs. (☎ 021-437 3407)

· *Wendy England & Mary O'Connell*: good free-range eggs as well as fine cakes made with them, also scones, breads and preserves. (☎ 058-59358/024-98121)

· *Ann Murphy & Kate O'Donovan:* head here for excellent marinades, chutneys and preserves, and to grab a much-needed hot dog grilled by Kate. (☎ 087-638 5595/087-235 0632)

· *Willie Scannell:* queue up to buy your floury Home Guard, British Queens, Kerrs Pinks and Golden Wonders as Willie brings the earlies and the late cropping spuds up from the farm at Ballytrasna. (☎ 021-464 6924/086-830 3625)

· *Brian Cott & Chris Cashman: Tempting Treats* is what Brian and Chris bake up, and all the breads, cakes and pastries are made with real butter and choice ingredients. (☎ 021-463 0123)

Shanagarry

Restaurant and Country House

● **Ballymaloe House**

Myrtle Allen has reached four score years, and her legendary Ballymaloe House, with Hazel and Rory Allen mastering the show out front, has never felt as focused and as generously individualistic as it does today. From the house itself, with Rory O'Connell having slowly and steadily brought his signature style to bear on the food, through to the fantastic shop with its sparkling café, Ballymaloe has a spring in its step that is exhilarating. As a country house, it is sui generis: not simply the first, not simply the best, but simply Ballymaloe.

The cooking is poised and delicious, classic country cooking that is modest and wise: hot oysters with beurre blanc and cucumbers; mousseline of Jerusalem artichokes with leek and saffron; East Cork beef with aïoli and straw potatoes; loin of bacon with spiced cranberries. The trueness of the cooking lies with the trueness of the flavours. (Shanagarry ☎ 021-465 2531 www.ballymaloe.com — Open Lunch & Dinner)

Kitchen Shop and Café

● **Ballymaloe Shop & Café at the End of the Shop**

In the café of Wendy Whelan's Ballymaloe shop, the cooking is simply and sparkily delicious: a Midleton Market plate — an ode to Belvelly superlative smoked fish; goat's cheese, potato and mint tart; mackerel open sandwich, and the sweet baking is just smashing. Make sure to buy some of the aged Imokilly cheddar to bring home; this is the only place where you will find it.

The cooking utensils, furniture and kitchenware of the shop are selected with a fastidious eye, and are simply irresistible. Everything from the arcane to the simply trendy is piled on the wooden tables. There are great knives, all sorts of baking equipment, as well as covetable pottery and glass. Don't miss the little wooden butter pats to shape butterballs which always grace the Ballymaloe breakfast tables. (Ballymaloe Shop, Ballymaloe House, Shanagarry ☎ 021-465 2032 — Open Day-time)

Cookery School

● Ballymaloe Cookery School & Gardens

Darina Allen's cookery school, and the beautiful gardens which surround the school, are the fruits of hard graft and a dedicated, holistic vision. Mrs Allen will explain that when students start at the school, they are first brought to plant a seed in the gardens, and then to nurture their emerging food over the ensuing months. Others will teach you how to cook; Ballymaloe will teach you how to cook, but it will also teach you how to think about cooking and about food, what it means, what it represents, what culture it enshrines and expresses. For those taking the popular shorter cours- es, the teaching is excellent and effective, and Ballymaloe is the sort of place where you will make friends, and will make friends for life. The gardens are a must-visit, the shop at the school is packed with delectables. (Shanagarry ☎ 021- 464 6785 www.cookingisfun.ie)

Craft Shop

● Stephen Pearce Emporium

This fine big emporium, scarcely a stone's throw from the Ballymaloe School is perhaps the best place to see the com- plete range of Stephen Pearce's beautiful pottery in all its tactile, irresistible glory. This pottery endows every meal with an aesthetic aura. (Shanagarry ☎ 021-464 6807 www.stephenpearce.com)

Whitegate

Butcher

● Day's of Whitegate

Tucked in at the back of the Spar supermarket in the centre of the village, Kevin Day's butcher's shop may appear unpre- possessing — okay, it may appear incredibly unpre- possessing — but there is nothing unprepossessing about the quality of meat reared and prepared by this fine butch- er. We make a detour down the peninsula just to buy meat from Mr Day, us and hordes of others who cherish the skills and the care of this excellent artisan butcher. There is nothing fancy about his work: you are here for sweet, herby beef, sweet, grassy lamb, good quality pork, and top quality meat from Mr Day's farm is what you will get. (Whitegate ☎ 021-466 1223)

Youghal

Restaurant and Guesthouse
● Aherne's

The supreme professionals of the town, the Fitzgibbon family's restaurant with rooms and bars is so rock-solid and competent that you could trust these guys with your life. But don't imagine that such competency implies complacency: not a bit of it. The brothers Fitzgibbon and their wives run this place with the energy and zip of youngsters, and the cooking has an assured élan that you can never tire of, thanks to the fact that every detail of a dinner, from a starter of rock oysters through to a fine salad and onto some John Dory with a shellfish risotto with vegetables and then a slice of lemon tart, everything is simply tickety-boo. Delicious food, calm cooking, and perhaps that adjective calm explains why Aherne's works so well: it's a calm place, a calming place, and it's always a treat to be back here, being well looked after. (163 North Main St, Youghal ☎ 024-92424 www.ahernes.com — Open Lunch & Dinner)

Country House
● Glenally House

An old house with a new sensibility is what you will find in Fred and Herta Rigney's Glenally House. "People want a surprise when they go somewhere, they want a difference, they want to be invigorated," say Fred and Herta, and that is what this lovely house offers, the challenge of new design in an old framework. It works superbly, creating comfort and challenge, and with good cooking to look forward to at dinner. (Copperalley, Youghal ☎ 024-91623 www.glenally.com)

Cult Choice Power's Gold Label

They distill many fine whiskeys in Irish Distillers, but for us the finest is the elegantly torchy Powers Gold Label, a drink which fuses the complexities of pot-still characteristics, and delivers them at a fantastic price. Leavened with a little cold water, the flavours are narcotic, slightly dangerous, always alluring. www.whiskeytours.ie

North Cork

Castlelyons

Country House
● **Ballyvolane**

Ballyvolane is one of the great country houses, run with calm expertise and a comforting modesty by Justin and Jenny Greene. It works because it colludes with our mental image of what a country house should offer; ageless grace; a slight eccentricity; great good cheer with our fellow guests, and fabulous cooking. Put all these things together – as they do in Ballyvolane – and what you create is that country house magic in all its singular glory. (Castlelyons, Fermoy ☎ 025-36349 www.ballyvolanehouse.ie)

Charleville

Farmhouse Cheese
● **Clonmore Goat's Cheese**

Tom Biggane's goat's cheese is a cult success, with the cheesemaker barely able to keep up with demand for this fine goat's cheese. It's only made with summer pasture milk, which is pasteurised at the lowest possible temperature. It's then released after about two months, though Mr Biggane reckons another month sees it getting even better, and if allowed even longer on an affineur's shelf then the sweet, nutty flavours become even more pronounced. Look for the cheese in Sheridan's, Manning's, Iago and other good shops. (Newtown, Charleville ☎ 063-70490)

Coolea

Farmhouse Cheese
● **Coolea Farmhouse Cheese**

Dick Willems is the second-generation cheesemaker of the superb Coolea, a Gouda-style cheese made in large four- and eight-kilo waxed rounds. Mr Willems uses only summer milk, flavours some of the cheese with cumin, and then ages the Coolea for between six to 24 months. When young, the grassy and herbaceous taste of the young curd has a volatile and lovely sour-sweet assortment of tastes, and when aged for a couple of years it becomes mustardy, fudgey, yet never dry or crumbly, with a massively robust and lengthy aftertaste. Coolea is one of those cheeses that seems to be a total food, making it incredibly satisfying and enjoyable whatever the occasion. (Coolea ☎ 026-45204)

Doneraile

Mushroom Grower
● Forest Mushrooms

Fran and Jim Fraser produce the most exotic mushrooms you can find in Ireland, grown on wood substrates without using chemicals. Anyone in the restaurant business should know about their king oyster, beech oyster, shiitake, nameko and golden mushrooms. Unique. (Doneraile ☎ 022-24105)

Fermoy

Restaurant
● La Bigoudenne

This simple and pretty room on the main strip of Fermoy is home to the gently pastoral style of French cooking that is the signature of Noelle and Rodolphe Semeria. They are well known for the delicious crêpes which are the speciality of their Breton homeland, but we also admire the serene and modest evening cooking, when the menu opens out to allow Rodolphe to show what he can do.
(28 McCurtain St, Fermoy ☎ 025-32832 — Open Lunch & Dinner)

Farmhouse Cheese
● Fermoy Natural Cheeses

On their farm just outside Fermoy, Frank and Gudrun Shinnick make the hard cheese St Gall, one of the most explosively flavoured of Irish raw milk cheeses, with mustardy, peppery and grainy flavour notes packed into a dense curd. Just as individual is their lovely St. Brigid, a beautiful, sweet and alluring cheese with a semi-soft curd and a pinkish washed-rind exterior that has notes of walnuts and wild mushrooms: smashing! Most recently, they have introduced and had a great success with two soft cheeses, Caois Dubh and Caois Ruadh, the latter being sold when only three weeks old. You will find these fresh cheeses for sale at the Nano Nagle market and also in some good delis. This is a very promising and very skilful cheesemaking operation. (Strawhall, Fermoy ☎ 025-31310 gudrun1@eircom.net)

Café

● Munchies

Bring the children to this popular spot up the town in Fermoy, and your lunch will feed not just yourself but your entire tribe also. The portions are gargantuan, so alongside your fries there will be some bacon mash, and some coleslaw, and a mass of vegetables and fruits and whatnot. Friendly service makes for lots of happy, and very well-fed, locals. (Lower Patrick St, Fermoy ☎ 025-33653)

Kanturk

Farmhouse Cheese and Milk

● Ardrahan Farmhouse Cheese

Mary Burns' farmhouse cheese is one of the best-known and best-loved amongst the Irish farmhouse cheeses, largely thanks to a powerful, milky-mustardy flavour in the curd that is quite addictive. The explanation for this power-fully lactic concentration is simple: the Ardrahan herd graze on great, rich, tradition-al Munster pastures. A small amount of the cheese is also smoked. Mary's latest venture has been Ardrahan Lullaby, a divine morning milk from the herd, which is pasteurised but not homogenised, so rich cream sits afloat the milk. Being morning milk, the Lullaby has higher levels of melatonin, which is what helps us all to sleep: insomniacs pay atten-tion! It's a brilliant food that children adore, and that adults need. (Ardrahan, Kanturk ☎ 029-78099 www.ardrahancheese.ie)

Country House
● Assolas Country House

Joe and Hazel Bourke's country house is elegant in every
way. Elegantly proportioned, elegantly posi-
tioned, elegantly decorated, and with Mrs
Bourke's supremely elegant food to complete a most gracious enterprise.
Mrs Bourke is, for us, one of the very best
cooks, with a style so profound and so simple that
it is genuinely iconoclastic. She does the very minimum to
her foods. No pyrotechnics. No conceit. Simply a focus on
getting the purest flavours from her products. It is an easy
thing to say that, but it is difficult to do it in practice. Yet do
it is the very thing that Hazel Bourke does. Reciting the
dishes – salad of Kenmare mussels and catriona potatoes;
brill with a crust of garden herbs; goat's cheese wrapped in
sorrel leaves; Kanturk lamb with mint pesto – gives no hint
of just how singular Mrs Bourke's cooking actually is: it is
like no one else's work. One of the great cooks, and one of
the great houses. Note: there is now a Saturday Kanturk
market, selling Hazel's produce, and good things from North
Cork. (Kanturk ☎ 029-50015 www.assolas.com)

Butcher
● Jack McCarthy

Jack McCarthy is a superbly skilled butcher, a charcutier
with a wild, artisanal imagination. Just try that whiskey-cured
bacon for an amazing treat, or any one of those dozen varieties of sausage – they even make a plum and mulled wine
sausage for Christmas! – or that excellent Angus and
Hereford beef, from Michael Daly of Dysert.
"We are very traditional," Mr McCarthy explains, and hal-
lelujah for that, but there is more than tradition here: there
is tradition and a respect for tradition, and both are married with a creative imagination. Put them together and Mr
McCarthy has created a destination address for charcuterie
that is as good as it gets. (Main St, Kanturk ☎ 029-50178)

Pub with Restaurant
● The Vintage

The Vintage is well-known as a good stop for a lunchtime
sandwich and a bowl of soup, and it's a well-run, popular
pub near to the bridge. (O'Brien St, Kanturk ☎ 029-50549)

Macroom

Farmhouse Cheese
● Carraig Goat's Cheese

One of the ironies about Aart Versloot's Carraig goat's cheese has been the fact that is has always been one of the best Irish cheeses, and also probably the most difficult cheese to actually get your hands on.

Well guess what? It is now even more difficult to get your hands on a piece of Carraig, for production has diminished even further as Mr Versloot takes things easy as the years roll gently by him. That much may have changed, but what hasn't changed is the fact that Carraig is a superb farmhouse cheese, with a meticulously fashioned curd that is flinty, mineral-rich, complex and hugely pleasing. To get a taste of this rarest gem, you will need to look carefully in and around the Bantry wholefood shops in summertime and, who knows, your luck might just be in. (Ballingeary ☎ 026-47126)

Organic Chickens
● Coolroe Farm

Michael and Noelle Murray produce the most delicious, organically-reared chickens, birds bursting with flavoursome flesh, birds that roast with crisply flavoursome skin, and a nice gelatinous richness to make a decent gravy.

The birds can be as much as 100 days old before slaughter, so there is lots of time for the flavour to develop. Cook one of the Coolroe birds and the nobility of the chicken in the pot is re-born. Michael also has plans to rear some organic Angus beef. Visitors are welcome to the farm to buy chickens, whether fresh or frozen. (Kilmichael, Macroom ☎ 026-49961)

Hotel
● Creedon's Hotel

Joe Creedon's hotel is the sort of place that brings a smile to your heart. Hospitable and deeply cultured hospitality are joined here by some lovely traditional cooking which is done just right: friends will call you up to tell you just how fine the bacon and cabbage and the clovey-apple tart are. (Inchigeelagh, nr Macroom ☎ 026-45288)

Cult Choice Preserves

Every country house has a secret, and for many of the best houses that secret is super-duper home-made preserves, pickles and other potions. In Longueville House, bring home armfuls of William O'Callaghan's jams and dressings. In Assolas House, Hazel Bourke makes splendiferous pre-serves with fruit from the walled garden.

Preserves

● Folláin

Peadar O'Lionáird's Folláin jams and preserves are well-known in West Cork and further afield, and a new range of low-sugar jams has just been launched. Their latest star turn is a very fine hot Mexican salsa, whilst their chutney is the quintessential relish for the perfect ploughman's. (Cuil Aodha, Maghchromtha ☎ 026-45288 follaineircom.net)

Oatmeal

● Macroom Oatmeal

Donal Creedon believes that the secret of good oatmeal is how you roast the grain. Most people steam the grain, but Mr Creedon reckons the per-fect way to create great porridge is via roasting, as this intensifies the taste, rather than diluting it as steaming does. Roasting on the traditional cast-iron plate in the mill also adds a smoky, nutty element, making the flavour more complex.

Mr Creedon knows what he is talking about, for Walton's Mills in Macroom has been in production since the early 1800's, and has always enjoyed a stellar reputation for its porridge oats. Today, the oats are still hand-roasted, before they are shelled and ground, with Mr Creedon judging their readiness simply by sight and smell. The result of this hist-ory, this patience, and this ancient, artisan skill is one of the most singular Irish foods, an oatmeal so good that it deserves to be blessed every morning with the Northern Irish way of anointing the porridge: with a splash of good Irish whiskey. The Mill also produces a rich, coarse whole-meal flour which is splendid for breadmaking. (Kanturk ☎ 029-50015)

The Blackwater Valley
farmers' market

· The market is held every second Saturday at the Nano Nagle Centre, when the Blackwater Valley community gets together to meet and to trade.

· Look out for the fresh cheeses made by Gudrun and Frank Shinnick of Fermoy Natural Cheeses, who will also have their splendid St Gall and St Brigid cheeses for sale.

· The Nano Nagle Centre themselves will have organic vegetables as well as their fine eggs and meat.

· There is lots of baking from Betty Corry, Deirdre Owens, Elizabeth Brosnan and Julie Lucey.

· John Thornton of Doneraile has pottery.

· Geraldine Bass will have smoked salmon from the Mill Bank Smokehouse.

· Mary and Tom O'Shea of Lavally Lower will have their honey and honey products.

· The North Cork organic group will have their vegetables, as will Alan Slone and Adrienne Dockrell.

· There are fair-trade products, Blue Moon aromatherapy products, recycled stationery and recycled crafts, and flowers and crafts and even a smoothie or a juice to quench the thirst.

· The Nano Nagle Centre, Ballygriffin, Mallow. (Contact Mary Sleeman ☎ 022-25270)

Mallow

Country House
● Longueville House

The refurbishment of their beautiful Victorian conservatory
has gifted Longueville House with what has
to be the most romantic dining room in
the entire country. Softly lit, swathed in
drapes, it is intimate and tactile, and as
such it is the perfect setting for William
O'Callaghan's extraordinary cooking. The cooking is extraordinary because whilst it is convoluted and
pyrotechical in execution, is is serene to eat. William
O'Callaghan knows where to apply all the grace notes —
the cooking juices of tripe and oxtail scented with tansy; a
prune and black stout relish for wild rabbit pâté; a sorrel
pesto for carpaccio of Blackwater salmon; a stuffed courgette flower with darne of halibut; beer ice cream with a
vanilla poached pear. This is some of the best cooking in
Europe, a cuisine that speaks of the land, the river, the place.
(Mallow ☎ 022-47156 www.longuevillehouse.ie — Open
Dinner & Lunch for groups)

Butcher
● The Meat Centre

Denis McCarthy's is a busy butcher's shop on the Main
Street of Mallow, and is known locally as The Meat Centre.
Good beef and lamb are their trademark, and service is
helpful and informed. (41 Bank Place, Mallow ☎ 022-21923)

Market & Free Range Eggs
● Nano Nagle Centre

The fine market held every second Saturday at the Nano
Nagle Centre – it's near the switch-back bridge on the
Fermoy-Mallow road – has grown out of the North Cork
Organic Group, and there will be up to 20 excellent stall-
holders here, so look out for local specialities such as the
centre's own eggs – also sold in The Garden in the English
Market in Cork city – and for local fresh cheeses from
Fermoy Natural Cheeses amongst many other treats. The
sisters of the Centre also produce organic vegetables, beef
and lamb. (Sister Miriam Therese McGillis, Ballygriffin,
Mallow. Contact Sister Mary Kelliher at ☎ 022-26411)

Mitchelstown

Delicatessen
● O'Callaghan's

"Survived since 1988" it says proudly over the door of
O'Callaghan's, but Pat and Mary have done more than survive, they have prospered since 1988, and done so thanks to
real cooking, real baking, and a great deal of care and consideration for their customers – they have a complete
range of gluten-free foods which they prepare, for instance,
and with all the other good things it makes O'Callaghan's a
one-stop shop. The shop and restaurant have a lovely, timeless feel, and service is maternal and delightful: "Will you
have some cream with that?", they ask when you order
your rhubarb tart and tea. Ah, sure we will. (19 Lr Cork St,
Mitchelstown ☎ 025-24657 ocalhansdeli@eircom.net —
Open day-time)

Whitechurch

Farmhouse Cheese
● Hegarty's Farmhouse Cheddar

Dan and John Hegarty milk 80 cows, and in addition to
making a fine cheddar cheese – some of
which is matured for up to 30 months –
they also make superb fruit yogurts, using
fruit from Sunnyside fruit farm in
Rathcormac. Flavoured with apple, rhubarb
and strawberry, these are real beauts, with a
whopping 25% fruit, and a very low sugar content. The
Hegarty's cheddar is cloth-bound, made with pasteurised
milk, and is usually released after about 14 months, and it
has all the gentle, subtle flavour notes of a good cheddar
cheese. The brothers are always working out new ideas, the
latest of which is a planned blue-veined cheddar cheese.
(Dan & John Hegarty, Ballinvarrig, Whitechurch
☎ 021-488 4238)

West Cork

Ballydehob

Restaurant
● Annie's

Annie Barry's restaurant is one of the West Cork institutions, beloved by visitors who begin the evening with a
drink or two in Julia and Nell Levis' unmissable bar, across
the street, and then whoop it up royally with the hearty
comfort cooking – lamb's kidneys on toast; duck liver pâté
with Cumberland sauce; fillet steak with peppercorns and
brandy; brill and sole stuffed with crabmeat – in this
roistering space. (Main St, Ballydehob ☎ 028-37292 —
Open Dinner)

Wholefoood Shop and Café
● Hudson's

Gill Hudson's excellent wholefood shop has all the best
West Cork specialities and is an excellent source of organic
vegetables. The wraps and other lunchtime foods prepared
in the café of the shop are particularly tasty, imaginative and
enjoyable. (Main St, Ballydehob ☎ 028-37565 — Open day-
time)

Free-range Ducks
● Skeaghanore Ducks

Eugene and Helena Hickey's ducks, duck breasts and duck
legs can be found in all the best West Cork shops and
supermarkets. Food lovers should note that the fashion for
duck breast means that the duck legs are sold at very keen
prices, so there has never been a better time to make that
duck leg stew with olives you've been thinking about. Note,
they also have geese for sale at Christmas. (Skeaghanore,
Ballydehob ☎ 028-37428 skeaghanoreduck@eircom.net)

Preserves
● Sonia's Inner Pickle

Sonia Bower's pickles are a world away from most other
Irish condiments. These are fiery, fun combinations, closer in
spirit to the complex pickles of India and the Caribbean
than the quotidian Irish versions. The aubergine and green

pepper pickle is masterly, the chilli and ginger a fiery treat, the roasted red pepper and garlic a toasty indulgence. Sonia also sells chilli sauces with different global styles. Find them at Clon on Thurs, Bantry on Fairday, Schull on Sunday, and Douglas on Saturday. (Ballydehob ☎ 086-313 1362)

Delicatessen and Café
● West Cork Gourmet Store

Lunch in Joanne Cassidy's shop is a treat: some rich, fresh potato and leek soup to warm the soul, then a fine tapas plate that features three local salamis, olives, quince paste; semi-dried tomatoes; pickled chillis, stuffed vine leaves, a veritable cornucopia of good things. The shelves are similarly crowded with handsome foods, and the extensive range of oriental ingredients means WCGS is where you head to when curries and noodles are on the menu. Joanne also stocks a choice selection of wines. (Staball Hill, Ballydehob ☎ 028-37781 — Open day-time)

Baltimore

Farmhouse Cheese
● Ardagh Castle Goat's Cheese

This pale white goat's cheese is only found in West Cork markets and is well worth hunting down. Judy Watton's cheese is hard and ever so slightly crumbly, and the finish is smooth and the aftertaste very pleasing. (Ardagh South, Baltimore ☎ 028-20547)

Restaurant
● The Customs House

Consider this: the menu in Susan Holland and Ian Parr's restaurant appears to rarely change: mixed selection of fish to start; brandade de morue in piquillo pepper; sole meunière; red mullet with tapenade mash; brill with salmoriglio; duck with red wine sauce; tarte tatin; crème brûlée; blackcurrant sorbet with orange macaroon.

Then consider this: Ms Holland never cooks any of these dishes in the same way twice. You could turn up here five nights on the trot, order the fish tasting plate, then the brill with salmoriglio, and every evening it would be slightly different, there would be a different point of focus with the dishes, a different emphasis, a varied sense of colour and articulation. Just as a great musician will never play the same sonata in exactly the same way, so Susan Holland plays variations on her favourite themes. For us, that is the pinnacle of cooking as art, and that is what Ms Holland and Mr Parr achieve in The Customs House: cooking as art. You would pay a fortune for this food, but, democrats and ascetic aesthetes that they are, they offer it at outstanding value for money. (Baltimore ☎ 028-20200)

Café and Gardens
● **Glebe House**

Jean and Peter Perry's beautiful gardens and gallery are one of the highlights of West Cork, and they now have a small daytime café, where you can enjoy good baking and salads, grown right outside the window in their organic garden. (Glebe Gardens, Baltimore ☎ 028-20232 www.glebegardens.com — Open Day-time)

Self-Catering Accommodation
● **Inish Beg**

The Bridgestone Guides don't traditionally do self-catering accommodation, but Paul and Georgie Keane's houses on the beautiful Inish Beg estate are no ordinary houses. A food lover's idea of sheer bliss would be to rent one of these utterly lovely houses for a week, then shop all around West Cork and turn the week into a self-catering feast, buying all the best foods from the local shops and markets. This is an idyllic place, and you not only need a spell here, you deserve it. (Inish Beg, Baltimore ☎ 028-21745 www.inishbeg.com)

Restaurant
● **The Mews**

Lucy Carey's restaurant is a pretty, gentle room, romantic in nature thanks to the carefully arranged aesthetic of art works, flowers and candlelight that Ms Carey orchestrates with enviable skill. Classic dishes such as rack of lamb with redcurrant jus, or fillet steak with honeyed shallots, mix it with spring rolls or oriental vegetable parcels that have a nice modern edge. (Baltimore ☎ 028 - 20390)

Hostel
● Rolf's

West Cork locals love the fact that Rolf's – a mixture of restaurant, hostel and self-catering which is just up the hill of Baltimore – stays open when everyone else has shut up shop. They also like the fact that the cooking here is solid and true. (Baltimore ☎ 028-20289 www.rolfsholidays.com — Open Lunch & Dinner)

B&B
● The Slipway

Wilmie Owen's charming B&B is just across the road from the sea, and it's a delightful destination as a base for Baltimore and West Cork. Breakfasts are particularly fine. (The Cove, Baltimore ☎ 028-20134 www.theslipway.com)

Bandon

Butcher
● Carey's Butchers

Martin Carey's butcher's shop is one of the key destinations for West Cork food lovers, for this butcher is one of the most skilful and imaginative charcutiers at work in Ireland today. It's not just the quality of the beef and lamb and pork and chickens: his USP lies in the beautiful presentation of all the foods he sells, whether it is the highly-regarded sausages, or the prepared meats, or the T-bones which are a particular speciality. Mr Carey is an outstanding butcher: progressive, creative, imaginative, and the quality of service in the shop is second-to-none. (82 South Main St, Bandon ☎ 023-42017)

On top of their game

Pâtés and Terrines
● Clodagh McKenna's 'For The Love of Food'

Clodagh McKenna makes a delicious range of pâtés (chicken liver with smoked Gubbeen bacon or caramelised onions) and terrines (terrine of Caherbeg Pork, studded with hazelnuts and spiced apple) which are sold in the various markets around West Cork. And you can finish the meal with either her scrummy Onion Jam or Spicy Apple Chutney. (Watergate St, Bandon ☎ 023-54587)

Smoked Fish
● **Shorescape Seafoods**

Richard Fitzgerald's company now has a stall in the English Market in Cork which sells their complete range of smoked fish, and you will also see their foods in many shops and supermarkets. Look out for his fine smoked trout – a TLT (trout, lettuce and tomato sandwich) is a real humdinger of a dish when made with the Shorescape fish. (Brewery Food Centre, Bandon ☎ 087-280 9368)

Shop
● **URRU**

Urru is the finest shop to have opened in Ireland in the last five years. The sort of painstaking care Ruth Healy brings to her work can be seen in her reply to the question: "What coffee do you serve?". Most people say: Java Republic, or Illy, or whatever. Ruth says: "Sumatran Lingtong". Wow! Style and content elide blissfully here: the best foods from the best artisans, great wines, fantastic lunchtime sandwiches, and beautiful books and essentials in a gorgeously comfortable store show an utterly expert eye. Urru makes life better for us all, and it is an essential stop for any food lover. And the name? URban/RUral. Now you know. (The Mill, McSwiney Quay ☎ 023-54731 www.urru.ie)

Bantry

Fishmonger
● **Central Fish Market**

Colman and Ann-Marie's shop is one of the country's best places to buy fresh fish. The quality of the wet fish they source is superb, and it is always beautifully prepared and presented. Every town should have a fish shop as fine as the Central: lucky old Bantry. (New St, Bantry ☎ 027-53714)

Ecology Centre
● **Coomhola Salmon Trust**

Mark Boyden's Coomhola salmon trust is a remarkable educational resource, which explores and explains the habitat of the wild salmon, and thereby examines the ecology of our rivers and our environment. (Coomhola Salmon Trust, Bantry ☎ 027-50453 streamscapes@eircom.net www.streamscapes.org)

Café

● Chubb's Fine Food

Charlotte Chubb is the pastry queen of West Cork. Everything she makes and bakes in her little shop and café on the Glengarriff Road is good, but the pies are quite exceptional, and worth a detour all on their own. Genuine pork pies, fantastic pasties, and an especially fine chicken pie show a skilful cook with a real signature. There are excellent foods sourced from Sheridan's and Peter Ward, and it's a darling place to take coffee, after you have browsed the country collectables in their quaint little antique shop. (Glengarriff Rd, Bantry ☎ 027-53872 — Open Day-time)

Organic Growing Supplies

● Fruit Hill Farm

Manfred Wandel's Fruit Hill Farm supplies the most covetable bespoke garden tools, as well as an extensive range of ecological requisites for anyone planning to grow vegetables, or just to have a happy, healthy, garden. The quality of everything Mr Wandel sells is simply superlative. (Bantry ☎ 027-50710 www.fruithillfarm.com)

Nursery

● Future Forests

This pioneering nursery was the source of the plantspeople behind Mary Reynolds Gold Medal-winning garden in Chelsea. The building alone, made of wood from the forests, is worth the visit. When here you will find one of the most exciting selections of plants in the country, specialising in native trees, including many fruit trees and hedgerows. (Kealkill, Bantry ☎ 027-66176 www.futureforests.net)

Knifemaker

● Hand-Crafted Knives

Rory Conner's knives are the work of a real craftsman, and it is fitting that this skilled artisan should be a member of the West Cork Craft and Design Guild. This is knifemaking as art: high-tech processes and materials are allied with traditional, time-patient skills to produce the most singular range of knives and cutlery that are future heirlooms, things of beauty and a joy to use. Mr Conner's newest range of table cutlery, in particular, shows a wild imagination at its zenith. (Ballylickey, Bantry ☎ 027-50032 handcraftedknives@eircom.net)

B&B and Restaurant
● Larchwood House

Whilst many people find the domestic-style of the dining room at Larchwood not to their taste, no one disagrees about the efficacy and seriousness of Sheila Vaughan's cooking. Mrs Vaughan's cooking is imaginative and polished, especially her signature soups, such as lettuce and rhubarb, or carrot, peach and paprika, and main courses and desserts are bumper in size and flavour. Larchwood is also well known for its splendid gardens, part of the West Cork garden trail. (Pearsons Bridge, Bantry ☎ 027-66181 — Open for accommodation and Dinner)

Shop
● Manning's Emporium

Val Manning was one of the pioneering supporters of artisan foods in Ireland, and today he remains as committed to the cause of artisanship, done in the most practical way via his Emporium in the centre of Ballylickey. Mr Manning's annual midsummer food fairs are unmissable events, but anytime you pay a visit to the shop is a chance to get engaged with the West Cork culinary culture. (Ballylickey, Bantry ☎ 027-50456)

Willow Baskets and Produce
● Maughnasily Organic Farm

Martin and Yvonne O'Flynn produce some of the best foods you can eat in Ireland. Their Christmas turkeys, for instance, have no equal: these beauties require no effort to become the best Christmas dinner you have ever enjoyed. But their kid meat is almost as fine, their eggs are benchmark. And it is for their beautiful baskets that they are best known. They make them from their own home-grown willow and these are objects of delight and beauty. Look out for Martin at the Friday Bantry market. (Maughnasily, Kealkill, Bantry ☎ 027-66111)

Restaurant
● O'Connor's Seafood Restaurant

Peter and Anne O'Brien have reinvigorated O'Connor's
since they took over, giving this landmark Bantry address a
real sense of va-va-voom. Wisely, they have introduced new
ideas onto the menu slowly and organically, and there is a
new focus to the food. The fish and shellfish cooking is truly
enjoyable, and value, especially in the early bird menu, is
keen. (The Square, Bantry ☎ 027-50021
www.oconnorseafood.com — Open Lunch & Dinner)

Wholefood Shop
● Organico

This is one of the best wholefood shops in Ireland, a place
where you can discover superlative handmade sushi alongside hard-to-find West Cork cheeses such as the brilliant
Carrig goat's cheese as well as organic vegetables and wines
and some great handmade breads. Organico works because
it is a snapshot of the creative culinary riches of West Cork.
(2 Glengarriff Rd, Bantry ☎ 027-51391)

Café
● The Pantry

Marjorie's Pantry is a simple little room upstairs with delicious food. The cooking shows the sort of care and love of
good food that not merely sates the appetite, but also gladdens the heart. Only problem is, it's pretty darn difficult to
get a table here at lunchtime, so join the queue. (New St,
Bantry ☎ 027-52181 — Open Day-time)

Bursery
● Peppermint Farm

Doris & Achim Hoffmann propagate herbs and plants for
the kitchen garden, stocking a beautiful selection of aromatic and ornamental plants, many of which are never found in
garden centres. You can buy their produce at Bantry,
Clonakilty or Schull markets. (Toughraheen, Bantry ☎ 028-
31869 www.peppermintfarm.com)

Hotel
● Sea View House Hotel

There are fewer and fewer hotels like Sea View, Kathleen
O'Sullivan's elegant monument to true hospitality. It's a

place for folk of all ages and styles, all of whom feel comfortable and cared-for, whether they are enjoying a communion lunch, a romantic dinner, or a few days r'n'r in West Cork. Calm, gracious service is the Sea View secret: there are few places where you will feel so well looked after. (Ballylickey ☎ 027-50073 www.seaviewhousehotel.com)

Pub
● The Snug

Maurice and Colette O'Donovan's bar food is traditional in style – bacon and cabbage, good steaks, beef and onion pies; prawn cocktail – but the care and consideration shown in the cooking elevates this food out of the ordinary, giving it a true sense of goodness. (The Quay, Bantry ☎ 027-50057)

Butlerstown

Restaurant
● Otto's Creative Catering

In the newest edition of our book *How to Run a Restaurant*, we describe a particular meal at Otto's at the end of which the chef was given a standing ovation by all the assembled food lovers. It was an experience from which, quoting the Aussie cook and writer Michael Symons, everyone there got up "from a meal ... publicly in awe". That's the sort of thing Otto and Hilda Kunze can achieve in the unique OCC. They take the concept of dining and place it at the end of the food chain, and they control that food chain from beginning to end. This is no small matter, for it begins with rearing animals and plants, with collecting wild foods, and then involves bringing masterly culinary skills to bear on these foods to give them expression. The menus read like simplicity itself – nettle soup; St Tola goats cheese on a yeast base; celeriac fritters with Cashel Blue cheese cream; organic chicken with red pepper cream – but what the language disguises is the entire culinary and cultural hinterland that comes with these foods. To eat at OCC is a powerful, unforgettable experience, something to fill us with awe. (Dunworley, Butlerstown, Bandon ☎ 023-40461 www.ottoscreativecatering.com — Open Dinner & Sun Lunch)

Guesthouse
● Sea Court

David Elder's beautiful house is an architectural jewel, a building on which the owner has bestowed much love and attention. Mr Elder hopes to be able to open the house to guests for increasingly longer periods of time over the coming years, so hopefully there will be more opportunity for visitors to discover and enjoy this peach of a place. (Butlerstown, Bandon ☎ 023 40151)

The West Cork
Craft Guild

· The feasting in West Cork is not confined to artisan purveyors of food, for the region boasts many craftspeople whose work is just as much a highlight of the region as its food products.

· Indeed, an exhibition of the work of the Guild, held in mid-2004, was entitled "Feast", and featured outstanding examples of tableware, pottery, woodwork for kitchens and dining rooms and much else, and the show was curated with great sympathy and imagination by Michelle Mitton, whose Clonakilty store is home to the craft work of many members of the Guild.

· The members of the Guild work at West Cork addresses ranging from Kinsale – the porcelain work of Sarah Flynn – to Macroom – the copper, steel and alloy work of Len Clatworthy – right down to Goleen – the silverwork of Baerbel Schulz-Voss – and you can visit many of their workshops.

· What the "Feast" exhibition showed was that despite the enormous variety and disparity of their work, the members of the Guild share a vivid creativity and imagination that serves to produce gorgeous, tactile, original work. In short, they work, and think, like cheesemakers.

· www.westcorkcraft.org

Castletownbere

Bar
● MacCarthy's Bar

You've read the book, now turn up in person and see and marvel at the unique McCarthy's bar in lovely Castletown. (The Square, Castletownbere ☎ 027-70014 adrimac22@yahoo.com — Open Lunch & Dinner)

Shop
● Taste

Ciannait Walker's ethos for her lovely little shop on the square is to sell produce that is local, handmade, Slow and organic. The wines from small producers, and the foods that she sources all support this authentic and artisan philosophy. (The Square, Castletownbere ☎ 027-71842)

Castletownshend

B&B
● Bow Hall

Bow is one of the peachiest West Cork B&B's, in one of the peachiest villages. Dick and Barbara Vickery have just three rooms in their gorgeous house, and they also have some of the most memorable hospitality you have ever encountered. (Main St, Castletownshend ☎ 028-36114)

Gastropub
● Mary Ann's

"It embodies what people dream of when they think of an Irish pub: a clientèle that has turned enjoyment into an art form, great banter with the barman (and everybody else for that matter), and a lived-in, authentic interior." That's a typically accurate thumb-nail sketch of Mary Ann's, from Diana Henry's great *Gastropub Cookbook*. Ms Henry understands exactly why we all go back to MA's again and again: it fills part of our dreamscape.

The cooking is straight-ahead and well understood and simple: the right sort of gastropub food in exactly the right sort of pub. (Castletownshend ☎ 028-36146 maryanns@eircom.net — Open Lunch & Dinner)

Smokery
● Woodcock Smokery

"Using just time, woodsmoke and salt, we create a traditional artisanal product", says Sally Barnes, of
Woodcock Smokery. It is typical of this
inspiring fish smoker that she should have
such a simple and clear vision of her job,
and also that she should be so modest. For
what is missing from the equation of fish,
time, woodsmoke and salt is: magic. That artisanal
magic is what makes Woodcock smoked fish so special,
whether you are enjoying the benchmark smoked wild
salmon, the sprats, the superb haddock, the mackerel or the
tuna. And just what is artisanal magic? Believe us, you will
know it when you eat it. (Gortbrack, Castletownsend,
☎ 028 36232 sallybarnes@iolfree.ie)

Cult Choice
Les Mères of Cork

**Kay and Marog. Jacqueline and Eithne. Mags.
Mercy. Susan. Carmel. Mairead. Hazel. Martina.
Marie. Siobhan...**

We all know Myrtle and Darina, but there are many
more mighty women directing and concocting the
culinary culture of Cork, proving that making a
great food culture is women's work.

In Cork it is women who have been instrumental
in creating the country's best food culture. Then
add in the artisans – Giana, Jeffa, Mary, Sally,
Clodagh, Jane, Eve, Isabelle, Veronica – and the
front-of-houses – Aisling, Bridget, Kerrin, Jean,
Mary, Hilda, Ellmary, Marie, Gaye – and the farmers – Nora, Valerie, Avril... and you know Cork is
the women's county, the Amazonia of Ireland.

The West Cork
farmers' markets

· *Bantry* Martin and Yvonne Flynn's
Maughnasily Organic Farm sells some of the best meat
you can eat, and their fab willow basketry is superb;
Christine Hildred, a grower, and Doris Hoffmann of
Peppermint Farm — both stalwarts of the old Country
Market – produce shrubs, herbs and cut flowers; Sheila's
Middle Eastern pastries sells some of the best chocolate
brownies you can find (gluten-free brownies indeed), as
well as falafel, burekas, sambusak and kubeh. There are
always spanking fresh organic vegetables from Caitriona,
who also sells Derryvilla Blueberry farm tonics; Fiona
Burke is there with a great selection of farmhouse
cheeses (look out for the Folláin tomato chutney she
serves from the bowl. Excellent stuff.) Wally will be selling
the huge range of Gubbeen meat and smoked foods;
Sean from Macroom will be manning the Real Olive Co.
stall; Mark Hosford will be selling Clodagh's pâté,
Arbutus bread and RGI cakes and sweet baking.
The Bantry market really comes into its own on the first
Friday, when, amongst many others, Olivier Beaujouan's
On the Wild Side stall will be manned by Niall Kenny, and
if Mr Kenny has his fantastic country sausages and his
unbelievable black and white boudin, then snap them up,
along with the brilliant sea vegetable tapenade which has
no equivalent and is one of the best artisan condiments
you can buy. Local producers will have vegetables and
plants, Knockatee Dairy will be there with the best Jersey
milk butter you can buy, and some truly splendiferous
buttermilk.

· *Carriganass Castle* A new Sunday monthly community
market has just begun at the lovely Carriganass Castle,
near to Kealkill, and one of the treats here, after you have
done the shopping, is to buy some of the fine grilled

sausages from Steve and to take them down to the river-
side to enjoy a picturesque and poetic lunch, as the kids
clamber about the rocks, and fall into the water. Splash!

· *Castletownbere* A small market takes place in the centre of town on the first Thursday of each month.

· *Clonakilty* Clon has a very pretty market that winds and
wends its way through a series of buildings, and there is
a truly lovely atmosphere, especially in the autumn.
Swoop on the Rosscarbery pork, Gubbeen products,
Richard's fantastic sweet things, Clodagh's pâtés, Marc
with Cork cheeses, Frank's salamis, Glenillen butter and
yogurts, Fairtrade coffee, Shorescape smoked fish, and
lots of organic veg.

· *Dunmanway* A small market takes place just behind the
square on Fridays, with local organic vegetables, good
baking, fine fresh eggs and some crafts, and there is
usually good coffee brewing.

· *Schull* The Sunday market began as more of a crafts
market, but the food content is growing as fast as the
audience. Get West Cork Natural Cheeses straight from
the maker, along with the local Gubbeen produce and
Sonia's amazing pickles.

· *Skibbereen* The Saturday market in the car park is only
great, and you will find rarities such as the gorgeous
Glebe flowers and Ardagh Castle goat's cheese.

Clonakilty

Gastro Pub
● An Súgán

In An Súgán always order the fish and shellfish. Good
scampi, excellent crab meat, and fresh fish treated with confidence and consideration. Brash young staff, however, sometimes confuse the confident with the cocky. (41 Wolfe Tone
St, Clonakilty ☎ 023-33498 sineadcrowley@hotmail.com —
Open Day-time & early Evening)

Restaurant
● Gleeson's

Robert and Alex Gleeson's eponymous restaurant is a small and comfortable room just off the main strip of Clon. Mr Gleeson's cooking is professional and cheffy, it reads promisingly — char-grilled tuna Niçoise with basil pesto; tian of lobster and Ummera organic smoked salmon with salsa; baked cod with herb and Gruyère crust with onion boulangère; Skeaghanore duck breast with braised red cabbage – and looks stunning. But both the cooking and the room would benefit from a stronger sense of signature, and more simplicity would bring a more relaxed vibe to a promising venture. (3-4 Connolly St, Clonakilty ☎ 023-21834 gleesonrestaurant@eircom.net)

Coffee Shop
● Hart's Coffee Shop

Aileen Hart's little room in the centre of town is a good spot, and very much a local favourite. There is a wholesomeness to Ms Hart's cooking that shows a team who do things from scratch, and the care taken in sourcing ingredients is repaid in rich, bumper flavours, especially in their excellent soups. (Ashe St, Clonakilty ☎ 023-35583)

Shop & Bakery
● Lettercollum Kitchen Project Shop

Con McLoughlin and Karen Austin of Lettercullum fame, have bought the renowned Old Market House Food Store, and added a bakery and a kitchen. Here they sell their fabulous pizzas, alongside the produce of their walled garden. Unmissable when in West Cork. (22 Connolly St, Clonakilty ☎ 023-36938)

Cult Choice Clonakilty Pudding and Bacon

Clonakilty's most famous foodstuff is Edward Twomey's world-renowned Clonakilty Black Pudding. But make sure to look out for the new, and very fine, Clonakilty Dry Cured Bacon.

Craft Shop
● Mitton & Hickey

Michelle Mitton and Etain Hickey's beautiful craft store is a
stylish, handsome and irresistible home for beautiful craft
objects, many of them made by members of the West Cork
Craft & Design Guild. Don't miss this peach of a place when
in Clon, and surrender any sense of self-control: resistance
is futile. (40 Ashe St, Clonakilty ☎ 023-35412)

Bar & Bistro
● Richy's Bar & Bistro

Richy Virahsawmy's popular and well designed bar and
bistro, in the centre of Clon, has lots of accessible, enjoyable
cooking on offer. (4 Wolfe Tone St, Clonakilty ☎ 023-21852
— Open Lunch seasonally, & Dinner)

Courtmacsherry

Restaurant with Rooms
● Travara Lodge

Travara Lodge rocks. Brendan Murphy and Richard May's
restaurant with rooms is just about the most fun you can
have. The cooking is great — the signature Thai-style crab
cakes, a fine twice-baked cheese soufflé, chicken wrapped in
prosciutto with colcannon cake; sole on the bone with
lemon and chive butter; great puddings — and the room
can get positively raucous after everyone has had a few
glasses of wine and a roar of laughter at Brendan's outra-
geous sense of humour.
Travara is one of the quintessential West Cork experiences
created, as you might have expected, by two guys from
Dublin. It must be something in the air. (Courtmacsherry ☎
023-46493 travaralodge@eircom.net — Open Dinner)

Crookhaven

Pub
● O'Sullivan's Bar

You are likely to find all the McKennas in O'Sullivan's, after a
beach adventure on the sand at Barleycove. Dermot
O'Sullivan takes care of business out front in this character-

ful, changeless pub, whilst his mum, Angela, cooks the ever-simple food that we all love: seafood chowder (a good one); shrimp with mayo; crab salad and then most likely some of their nice crumble. Another drink, dear? (Crookhaven ☎ 028-35319 o'sullivans@crookhaven.ie — Open Lunch)

Drimoleague

Dairy
● Glenilen Dairy

Alan and Valerie Kingston's dairy products — country but-ter; rich clotted cream; fromage frais and yogurt, excellent cheesecakes — are distinctive, pure and delicious, and their fruit cheese-cakes and mousses are one of the very best ways to get goodness into your kids at dessert time rather than junky sugar. The country butter, in particular, is a superbly pure and good thing. Find them at the West Cork markets and in good stores, and careful searching in some of Dublin's best delis will also unearth these lovely things. (☎ 028-31179 www.glenilenfarm.com)

Dunmanway

Bakery
● The Baking Emporium

Andreas Haubold's specialist bakery is signposted just as you come into Dunmanway, heading west. Their range of cakes, breads, seed breads and gateaux are widely appreciat-ed, and you will find them in local shops and supermarkets. Look out in particular for their seed breads. (☎ 023-45260 www.bakingemporiumltd.com)

Farmhouse Cheese
● Coturnix Quail

Look out for the lovely Coturnix quail eggs in good shops. As well as fresh eggs, Brendan Ross produces cooked and peeled quail's eggs which are sold in jars, and which are super-handy for salad plates or mini Scotch eggs. (Droumdrastil, Dunmanway ☎ 087-206 5067)

Patisserie
● Richard Graham-Leigh

You will find Richard's brilliant patisserie at West Cork markets and in great stores such as URRU, and it's not to be
missed: this is high-class patisserie, executed with great skill
and attention to detail. The brioche, alone, is worth a pilgrimage. (☎ 086-0868 183 jandrgrahamleigh@eircom.net)

Durrus

Wine Importer
● Albatross Enterprise

Harro Feddersen's little wine shop is signalled by a sign on
the Durrus-Ahakista road, alerting you to the fact that
there is a shop, and a pretty cottage for rent. Mr Feddersen
imports a small range of wines from Germany, along with a
selection from other European countries, and value and
quality are high. (Ahakista, Durrus ☎ 027 67248)

Farmhouse Cheese
● Durrus Farmhouse Cheese

Jeffa Gill's raw milk washed-rind cheese is one of
the purest and most potent statements of
raw milk artisan cheesemaking in Ireland.
Indeed, Ms Gill's cheesemaking brings to
mind the words of Kevin Sheridan and
Fiona Corbett, of Sheridan's

On top of their game

Cheesemongers, quoted at the start of this book:
"and in that moment the story of the land melts in our
mouths".
So it is with Durrus: the cheese tells us two stories. The
first is the story of the cheesemaker, who has explored and
developed her cheese through two decades with a patience
that is reminiscent, for us, of the endless tweaking, refining
and rescoring of his simple compositions that has characterised the music of Arvo Part, assimilating character, assimilating potential, arranging the essence.
The second is the story of the potency, and the sense of
place, which raw milk cheeses encapsulate. As Sheridan and
Corbett point out, the raw milk "delivered today is full of
subtle differences from that in the next county, or the next
season". And the genius of the cheesemaker is to under-

stand, acknowledge, respect and work with those differences, and that is what Jeffa Gill and her team have managed
for 20 years. (Coomkeen, Durrus ☎ 027-61100)

Restaurant
● Good Things Café

Carmel Somer's intimate and simple café
opened with a bang in 2003, and became the
critical darling of the year. After only a year
of business, the confidence of this crew has
grown exponentially, and the cooking in Good
Things has acquired more of a signature simplicity
and sense of exploration: where else would you find the
Sugar Club's celebrated beef pesto on a menu – cooked to
perfection – alongside a cracking Bill Granger-influenced
dish like marinated coriander chicken with a sharp, Asiatic
cucumber relish? This is cooking for the intellect and the
culinary culture, just as much as it is cooking for the senses.
The signature GT dishes, such as Durrus cheese, spinach
and nutmeg pizza, or new season lamb with roasted
aubergine béchamel, and the great West Cork fish soup, are
better than ever. A singular destination. (Durrus ☎ 027-
61426 – Open Day-time. Evening Dinner weekends only
high season. No credit cards www.goodthingscafe.net)

Cult Choice Cooking with West Cork Cheeses

The famous West Cork Cheeses may taste great
on a cheeseboard, but don't overlook their culinary possibilities. Durrus is great on a pizza *vis.*
Good Things' can't-take-it-off-the-menu Durrus
Cheese Pizza with Spinach and Nutmeg. A mature
Ardrahan can be substituted for the cult cooking
cheese of choice – Taleggio. So, if you're cooking
Bill Granger's Roast Mushrooms with Thyme and
Taleggio, make that Roast Mushrooms with
Thyme and Ardrahan (tastes great even without
the alliteration). Long ago, Paul Rankin, whilst on
holiday in Ballylickey, made a great Desmond and
celery risotto – and, of course, the West Cork
Natural Cheeses are just made to put in a fondue.

Enniskeane

Farmhouse Cheese
● Round Tower Cheese

You will find Nan O'Donovan's cheese for sale throughout County Cork, and it's well worth hunting down, for it's an appealing, mild Gouda-style cheese with plenty of character. (Enniskeane ☎ 023-47105)

Glandore

Gastro Pub
● Hayes' Bar

Declan and Ada Hayes' bar is a legendary address, a meticulous pub that is classy without being pretentious, and where good cooking and good drinks are served with well-cultured cheer. (Glandore ☎ 028-33214 — Open Lunch. No credit cards)

Restaurant
● Café Sativa

Bevan Fleming's tiny little restaurant room in the centre of Glandore village is an unpretentious, relaxing place, and Mr Fleming is a young man beginning to make his way in the culinary world. It's a very popular room at weekends for relaxed, modern cooking where the chef aims to bring global flavours to local foods. (Glandore ☎ 028-34746 www.cafesativa.com — Open Lunch & seasonal Dinner)

Goleen

B&B
● Fortview House

Travellers to West Cork who discover Violet and Richard Connell's exemplary B&B tend to overlook every other address in West Cork: Fortview is their destination, and all others are strictly in second place. It's an outstanding address: great cooking, comforting design, terrific hospitality, and a model working farm managed with great skill. (Gurtyowen, Toormore, Goleen ☎ 028-35324 fortviewhousegoleen@eircom.net)

Country House
● Rock Cottage

Barbara Klotzer's elegant country house presents only one problem to the visitor to West Cork: it can be difficult to get a room here, at almost any time of the year, unless you have the foresight to book well in advance. So, book well in advance and then: no problems. (Barnatonicane, Schull ☎ 028-35538 rockcottage@eircom.net www.rockcottage.ie)

Kilbrittan

Restaurant
● Casino House

Kerrin and Michael Relja's restaurant is one of the West Cork stars. A beautiful room with a wacky, comfortable aesthetic, and some red-hot cooking from Mr Relja, are a potent and distinctive concoction. The lobster risotto is one of the great modern signature dishes, but you could choose anything Mr Relja cooks and it will be marked by creativity and a scintillating, controlled technique (Coolmain Bay, Kilbrittain ☎ 023-49944 chouse@eircom.net — Open Lunch & Dinner in high season)

Kinsale

B&B
● Blindgate House

Maeve Coakley's beautiful B&B is one of the most stylish houses we know, and the breakfast cooking has just as much élan as the subtle, influential modern design. A great base for getting the best out of Kinsale. (Blindgate, Kinsale ☎ 021-477 7858 www.blindgatehouse.com)

Restaurant
● Crackpots

Carole Norman's café is one of the great Kinsale stalwarts with both good, simple and well-understood cooking, and some very appealing pottery for sale. (Cork St, Kinsale ☎ 021-477 2847 — Open Dinner and Sun Lunch)

Restaurant & Fishmonger

● Fishy Fishy Café

Martin and Marie Shanahan's iconoclastic fish restaurant defines the meaning of the term "signature" when it comes to cooking and running a restaurant. Everything this couple do is done the way they want to do it, so they have sidelined any of the standard concepts of the restaurant experience, in favour of giving what they know they are best at.

On top of their game

What they are best at is cooking the freshest fish and shellfish you can find, serving it in a simple room, and making the experience unforgettable. Other folk can do the fish and the room, but no one else can make an experience so simple seem so utterly defining. You eat here, and you say to yourself: this is what cooking and eating is all about, or at least, this is what cooking and eating should be about, but so rarely is. Fishy Fishy is a concept of pure genius. So, order the daily specials from the board, buy some wet fish to take home, and ponder how simplicity can be so profound. (The Guardwell, Kinsale ☎ 021-477 4453 — Open Day-time. No credit cards)

Brewery

● Kinsale Brewing Company

The Kiely brothers brewery produces four craft beers: Kinsale Irish lager, an ale, a red ale, and the popular, very creamy stout, which is a smooth, easy-going brew that is extremely enjoyable. It's a stylish bar, excellent for taking a pint on the verandah in some good summer weather. (The Glen, Kinsale ☎ 021-470 2124 www.kinsalebrewing.com)

Guesthouse

● The Old Bank House

Michael and Marie Reise are amongst the most experienced and sympathetic hospitality providers in Kinsale, and their patient, assured professionalism — the couple were enormously successful restaurateurs in the town before opening the Bank House — is a delight for the traveller. In a town with numerous places to lay your head, The Bank House makes for a great, reliable, comfortable and comforting destination in Kinsale. (11 Pearse St, Kinsale ☎ 021-477 4075 www.oldbankhousekinsale.com)

Restaurant

● Man Friday

Philip Horgan's restaurant is one of the great veterans of the Kinsale scene, a solid-sender of good times and generous, comforting cooking that you would need a heart of stone not to be enchanted and delighted by. (Scilly, Kinsale ☎ 021-477 2260 — Open Dinner)

Wine Bar

● Mange Tout

Guillaume Lequin's traiteur shop is in a corner of the famous Boland's craft shop, and is home to good food-to-go: chicken chasseur, Thai green curries, good pâtés and some expert sweet baking, all of which will make your life easier and better. (Pearse St, Kinsale ☎ 021-477 2161)

Delicatessen

● Quay Food Co

The QFC is the star deli in Kinsale, a great little shop that manages to have the things you want, the things you need, and the things you feel like. Great service makes for an excellent all-round experience. (Market Quay, Kinsale ☎ 021-477 4000)

Restaurant

● Toddies

Pearse and Mary O'Sullivan have made a great success in Toddies, a success based on red-hot cooking and great service. They are a young pair, but they have assurance and ability far beyond their years, and that assurance and ability shines through in what is some of the finest cooking in County Cork. (Sleaveen House, Eastern Road, Kinsale ☎ 021-477 7769 http://toddies.kinsale.tv — Open Dinner)

Leap

Delicatessen & Café

● All Things Nice

Kathleen Wouman's sweet ATN is a most useful stop-over, either to put together a good sandwich and to have a cup of coffee, or to buy some choice West Cork cheeses and meats. It's a pretty shop right in the centre of the village, and it's not to be missed. (Main St, Leap ☎ 028-34772)

Rosscarbery

Free-range Pork & Sausages
● Caherbeg Free-Range Pork

Time is the secret of the sheer excellence of Avril and Willie Allshire's Caherbeg pork. Most pigs in Ireland are reared in about 20 weeks. The Allshire pigs take 30 weeks, living outside, fed a healthy diet of boiled barley, greens, some commercial feed, and bread. No gunk. No drugs. Just a big bunch of happy pigs hanging out together in a big field with some shelters for when it rains. And that is why Caherbeg sausages and rashers taste so good, with a pure sweet porky taste and a true texture that is always a treat. Care and quality give the Caherbeg foods a taste and texture that is quite distinctive, and that is why they are worthy of your table, and worthy of your precious time. (Caherbeg, Rosscarbery ☎ 023-48474 www.caherbegfreerangepork.ie)

Restaurant
● O'Callaghan-Walshe

We know of a culinary competition which is fortunate, each year, to receive a submitted entry from O'Callaghan-Walshe in Rosscarbery. What is interesting about the entry from O'C-W is that it provokes the equivalent of a (polite) fight amongst the judges as to just who is to get lucky, and pay the visit to O'C-W. "But you did it last year, and besides, I haven't eaten their mashed potatoes for two years now!" is the sort of calm, considered, critical coolness with which the judges argue the toss. And then, just to show how seriously all involved take it, the disappointed parties tend to go to O'C-W and spend their own money. Critics spending their own money! Unprecedented. That's the sort of restaurant Sean and Martina's O'Callaghan-Walshe is. You don't like it: you love it. Critical regard is irrelevant. It's just a simple room where they cook the most perfect wild fish and fresh shellfish, and it may well be the perfect restaurant, the restaurant of your dreams, the sort of magnificent, maverick, sport-of-nature that could only exist in West Cork. (The Square, Rosscarbery ☎ 023-48125 funfish@indigo — Open Dinner)

Restaurant
● Steven's Bistro

Steven's is a new venture in the square at Rosscarbery, a pleasant, bright room with simple and carefully prepared modern cooking. They open for breakfast, serving Rosscarbery's best amongst other things, and from noon the lunchtime menus and daily specials kick in: buffalo wings; Cajun chicken; salmon Creole (they definitely have a deep-South thing in here); catch of the day from Union Hall; sirloin with Cashel Blue sauce. Friendly service, and good value. (10,11 South Square, Rosscarbery ☎ 023-31950 — Open Dinner & Sun Lunch)

Cult Choice Knockatee Butter

The most vivid buttercup yellow Jersey butter, and the sweetest, most thirst-quenching buttermilk you ever did taste: Olga and Peter Ireson's unique Knockatee Dairy foods are a must-have choice to be discovered in the West Cork farmers' markets.

Schull

Bakery with Rooms
● Adele's

Adele Conner's bakery-with-rooms – there are four simple rooms up on the top floor – is home to some lovely sweet baking – that's the classic lemon cake – and some lovely savoury baking – that's the sausage rolls – and it's always a great spot for a calm mid-morning coffee and a scone or a stylish lunch. The breads are consistently excellent, especially the distinctive sourdough and the top-class ciabatta. (Main St, Schull ☎ 028-28459 www.adelesrestaurant.com — Open Day-time)

Farmhouse Cheese
● Grove House

Billy and Mary O'Shea are seriously cool people who run a seriously cool B&B where lots of seriously cool people stay when they are holidaying in Schull. (Colla Road, Schull ☎ 028-28067)

Farmhouse Cheese, Charcouterie and Plants

● **Gubbeen Farmhouse Foods**

The Ferguson family think, and work, laterally, and creatively. Milk from Tom Ferguson's prized herd of cows is made into Gubbeen cheese by Giana and Rosie Ferguson. Some of the cheese is then smoked by Fingal Ferguson. And, if you are smoking cheese, then why not some bacon? And if you are smoking bacon, why not rear pigs? And if you have pigs, then why not make salamis and a wide range of sausages and pork products, and sell them via farmer's markets and good shops? And why not grow vegetables and herbs which can be sold to local restaurants, as Clovisse Ferguson does?

In other words, why not extract all the potential from every raw product you have to work with? Farmers used to think like that, and work like that, before they became mesmerised and intellectually defeated by the boredom of monocultural farming.

The Fergusons demonstrate how the artisan imagination is actually the opposite of the modern farming mentality. Artisanship works logically, creatively and exponentially, exploiting potential, exploring a culinary and agricultural culture.

Monocultural agriculture reduces farmers to the position of mechanical misfits, unable to think sideways, unable to extrapolate value, unable to appreciate the very culture of the land and its potential that lies at their feet.

So, our proposal is this. Gubbeen farm is taken over by the State, and established as an artisan agricultural university. The Ferguson family are appointed to Professorships, and they pass on their wild, original, ageless way of thinking and working to eager students by their experience and their example. And, thus, we build the agriculture and the artisan practices that Ireland needs. Simple. (Gubbeen, Schull ☎ 028-28231 www.gubbeen.com)

Farmhouse Cheese

● **Hackett's Bar**

Trudy Etchell's Hackett's Bar is a great destination for well-made soups and good sandwiches, not to mention some cool jazz sounds. Very hip, and very good fun indeed. (Main St, Schull ☎ 028-28625 trudyetchells@eircom.net)

Charcuterie
● Krawczyk's West Cork Salamis

Frank Krawczyk's Bolg Doire – a cross between speck and pancetta, using belly of free-range pork that is rolled, then dry-cured then smoked with beech or oak before lengthy air-drying – is one of the supreme Irish artisan foods. Distinctive, different, idiosyncratic and addictive, it is the sort of speciality artisan food that everyone needs to have in their larder, and their culinary armour. Cooking with the Bolg Doire gives a richness and umami-like complexity to every dish, whilst sliced see-through thin and nibbled, it is glorious.

On top of their game

But if the Bolg Doire is outstanding, it is quickly followed by a range of salamis and sausages that are no less distinctive and addictive. The Dereenatra Dry, the Schull Salami, the Dunmanus Castle beef salami and the Three Castle Pastrami are all superb, meticulously wrought artisan foods that explore and exploit Irish and European culinary history. You simply have to try these special foods, and the best way to utilise them is to have a selection served as a starter plate. (The Barn, Dereenatra, Schull ☎ 028-28579 frankk@oceanfree.net)

Farmhouse Cheese
● West Cork Natural Cheese Company

Bill Hogan and Sean Ferry's pair of thermophilic cheeses – Gabriel and Desmond – are amongst the towering achievements of artisan cheesemaking in Ireland.

Mr Hogan and Mr Ferry use only summer raw milk from local herds who graze on the sea-salty pastures looking out over Schull

Authentic

harbour, then produce the cheeses in the Swiss style, taking the curd to a high temperature, then utilising a very long maturation period after brining. The resulting piquancy of flavour in Desmond is quite arresting, whilst Gabriel is distinguished by being more aromatic. To use a vinous comparison, Desmond is like a Chenin Blanc whilst Gabriel is like a Gewurztraminer, and we would suggest that those wines are the perfect companions for these cheeses. Sheer heaven is a fondue of Desmond cheese with a great Chenin Blanc from the Loire Valley – such bliss! (Dereenatra, Schull ☎ 028-28593)

Skibbereen

Supermarket
● Field's

John Field's shop is the finest supermarket in Ireland, a place that manages to combine the artisanally-produced with the industrially-produced, and to thereby serve and suit everyone. Just as significant as the brilliant day-to-day running of his business is the fact that Mr Field has been friend, supporter and ally to artisans for decades now. If people ask: how come West Cork has such a strong food culture? then it is partly thanks to people like John Field and his crew; people who welcome the curious, the novel, and the unlikely in food, and who continue to do so. Field's is one of the great cultural – and culinary – outposts of West Cork. (26 Main St, Skibbereen ☎ 028-21400)

Restaurant
● Island Cottage

Like the very best cooks, John Desmond cooks the same things over and over again – the roast duck; the brill with mashed potato; the lemon soufflé dessert, the simple green salad – but he never cooks a dish the same way twice. This ability to improvise with ingredients is the secret of this inspired restaurant, as maverick and out-of-the-box as you can get. Island Cottage is a single room on tiny Heir Island. To get here you must take the boat, then walk a mile along the boreen. Once you have arrived, there is no choice for dinner, and the selection of wines is limited, and there is a staff of two: John in the kitchen; Ellmary looking after you. And what you are in for, then, is one of the greatest adventures in Irish cooking, a magical mystery tour, without menus, without precedent, a chance to improvise with the very business of being in a restaurant. It's a narcotic experience, an unforgettable slice of the avant garde. (Heir Island, Skibbereen ☎ 028-38102 www.islandcottage.com — Open Dinner. No credit cards)

Restaurant
● Kalbo's Bistro

Siobhan and Anthony's excellent bistro makes it all seem so

easy. Lovely cooking, fine room, polite service, good value, see you soon. The place is always thronged with regulars, the atmosphere is always as delectable as the cooking, and the cooking has a real signature style, with fresh, open flavours right across the board. Best of all, you get the sense of a young crew who get a huge kick out of their work, and their enthusiasm is infectious. A great West Cork address. (48 North St, Skibbereen ☎ 028-21515 — Open Lunch & Dinner)

Organic Meat
● Liam O'Driscoll

Liam O'Driscoll's meat comes from his own lands, and his shop is a tiny little cabin right beside his bungalow. Buying some good beef or some nice hairy pork is, therefore, enjoyably surreal. Be patient, however: it can take a few minutes after you press the bell for the man himself to arrive. (Abbystrewry, Skibbereen ☎ 028-22355)

Restaurant
● Ty Ar Mor Seafood Restaurant

Ty ar Mor mixes Breton seafood specialities that form its basic culinary template with a new Thai theme – Thai @ Ty ar Mor is a new noodle and wine bar upstairs with Thai staff, and those of the loose-limbed amongst us can take their dinner Khantok style, sitting on cushions at low tables. The fish cookery downstairs in the original reataurant is accurate, polished and professional. (46 Bridge St, Skibbereen ☎ 028-22100 www.tyarmor.com — Open Lunch & Dinner)

Herb Preserves
● West Cork Herb Farm

Rosarie O'Byrne is a qualified medical herbalist, and the optimisation of herbs in her products gives her preserves a special quality that goes beyond taste — though taste is something they're not short of. Rosarie will consider a product and earmark each herb for a particular purpose. So a tea for colds will include a herb that acts as a diathoretic, another that boosts the circulatory system, and a third will have an anti-viral purpose. Her after-dinner teas are chosen from herbs that soothe the gut and aid digestion. Herbs that act as stimulants are banned from Rosarie's palette of ingredients, instead using soothing herbs that aid digestion. It may sound rather worthy, but her flavoured oils, teas and jellies are all strikingly delicious. Her basil oil, garden relish, and geranium jelly should always be in your cupboard. (Church Cross, Skibbereen ☎ 028-38428)

Timoleague

Café Bar
● Dillon's

Dillon's is one of the classic café bars. One of the first in Ireland, and still worth a stop over. (Mill St, Timoleague ☎ 023-46390 — Open Day-time)

Cookery Classes
● Lettercollum Kitchen Project

This is the HQ of the Lettercollum Kitchen Project, the garden that provides for the shop in Clonakilty, and the location of various classes, in cooking holidays.(Timoleague ☎ 023-46251 www.lettercollum.ie)

Wine Importer
● Anthony Staunton Wines

Anthony Staunton imports a small range of wines from the Riverina company in Australia, and they are good value, honestly-made wines with some, such as the Warburn semillon, showing classy polish and style. (Chapel Hill, Timoleague ☎ 023-46455 www.stauntonwines.com)

Smokehouse
● Ummera Smokehouse

Anthony Creswell's smoked wild salmon is one of the four members of the Slow Food presidium dedicated to the wild smoked fish. Mr Cresswell's USP is a pre-smoking brining of the fish, then smoking by the Torrey kiln method. The result gives a creamy, moist texture, with eggy, buttery scents and flavours along with a mellow oakyness, with a long aftertaste of sea salty, almost kippery smoke grace notes. It's a sublime fish. Just as good is Mr Creswell's smoked eel, and there is also a smoked chicken. The Ummera mail order service is swift and fleet. (Inchybridge, Timoleague ☎ 023-46644 www.ummera.com)

On top of their game

County Donegal

Lough Swilly Salmon, Malin Lamb, Donegal Bay Oysters, Glen Bay Lobster and Crab...

Ardara

Bar
● Nancy's Bar

This celebrated local boozer, which has been in the family of the original 'Nancy' for seven generations, is a great place for a pint and a session. Smoked salmon platters and chowders on offer for lunch. (Main St. Ardara ☎ 074-954 1187 — Open Lunch)

Café
● The West End Café

The West End is a great chipper, where you will get splendidly fresh fillets of fish fried in the best batter you have had in yonks, and great crispy, salty chips, and a good cup of tea. There are, of course, other things to eat in Charlie and Philomena Whyte's café – wild salmon cutlets; chip butties; panini; tortillas; ham or chicken salads; poached egg on toast – but what you will ask the gloriously maternal Eileen for is the fish supper, please, two times, and maybe a side order of mushy peas. You will eat it with delight, you will likely remark that the batter puts many a pretentious cheffy tempura to shame, and you will be back next time you are heading through Ardara. (Main St, Ardara ☎ 074-954 1656 — Open Lunch & Dinner)

Cult Choice

Filligan's Hot Yellow Mustard

If you want to make a mustard mash the equal of Peter Gordon's famous Sugar Club concoction, then you simply have to have Filligan's sweet, spicy, fiery, hot-and-sour HY mustard.

This beauty whips welcomingly into a mash, elevates a ham sandwich to greatness, and puts manners and attitude on your bangers.

Ballyliffin

Guesthouse
● Rossaor House

Brian and Anne Harkin's house is a soporifically comfy B&B,
the sort of place that encourages you to stay put, swaddled
up in a big sofa looking out at the dunes, rather than
encouraging you to get up and get out there. Golfers love it
for its proximity to the links, and it makes a great destination base for exploring the northern peninsulas. Do note
that the Harkins also offer some excellent self-catering
accommodation which is very suitable for families. (Ballyliffin
☎ 074-937 6498 www.ballyliffin.com/rossaor.htm)

Burtonport

Restaurant
● The Lobster Pot

Gerard and Frances O'Donnell's bar and restaurant specialises in Glen Bay Lobster, whilst hungry customers go for
the voluminous Titanic Seafood Platter, which lives up to its
name in terms of size and proportions. (Burtonport ☎ 074-
954 2012 frances21266@hotmail.com — Open Lunch &
Dinner)

Carndonagh

Restaurant
● The Corncrake

The Corncrake is one of those restaurants where the
cooking can stop you dead in your tracks. You
sit there sipping the wine, settling in, admiring the room and its wonderful artworks
and subdued but meticulous style, and then
Noreen brings your starter of twice-baked
crab soufflé and: bang! "How is it?" you ask your
companion. "Implausibly delicious!" she replies. Implausibly
delicious. Now, that is some sort of delicious.
Brid cooks and gets as much fun out of her work as
Noreen does looking after the diners. They do beautiful
food: Roquefort and celeriac tart; a sublime coq au vin; per-

fect Donegal lamb with red-currant jelly, and some of the most stonkingly delicious puddings to be found anywhere in Ireland. They cook all of these dishes as if they are freshly minted; each one made with energy and precision, with a sense not just of the style of the dish but of the culture of the dish, that is inspiring. A lemon and almond tart to finish dinner is pitch perfect, thanks to detail such as a gin syrup and so-so-fine lemon zest. Implausibly delicious. (Millbrae, Carndonagh ☎ 074-937 4534 — Open Dinner)

Culdaff

Restaurant and Bar
● **McGrory's**

There is a real sense of energy and chutzpah to be discovered in Anne, John and Neil McGrory's famous bar, restaurant and rooms. Possibly it's the confidence that comes from a successful family business that has prospered for more than 75 years. More likely, it's just the family's easy confident way with hospitality that brings music lovers, nature lovers and food lovers up to Inishowen. To hear Anne talk about the quality of the Donegal lamb they source from Ronald Bogg's butcher's of Malin, for instance, lets you know about an operation where care and concern about basic details are never taken for granted, and you will see the same sort of care shown in the wine list. Music sessions are only one element of McGrory's, albeit a very famous one, but anyone who wishes to explore this bracingly beautiful peninsula couldn't do better than to use McGrory's as their base for eating and staying and, ah, go on then, drinking. (Culdaff ☎ 074 937 9104 www.mcgrorys.ie — Open Dinner & Sun Lunch)

Donegal

Coffee Shop
● **Aroma Coffee Shop**

Head out of Donegal town to Tom Dooley's destination coffee shop, in the centre of the craft village, and you will discover a simple, pleasant place in which to enjoy good coffee and fine day-time cooking and baking. (The Craft Village, Donegal Town ☎ 073-23222 — Open Lunch)

Wholefood Shop
● Simple Simon Natural Foods

Andrew Cape's excellent wholefood shop is a great place to discover any new or special Donegal foods, as well as organic vegetables, good breads and other select and essential things. (The Diamond, Donegal ☎ 074-972 2687. Andrew Cape has another shop, Simple Simon Living Food at Oliver Plunkett Road, Letterkenny ☎ 074-912 2382)

Dunfanaghy

Restaurant and Accommodation
● The Mill Restaurant

The Mill is on a roll. Great cooking from Derek Alcorn, great service and hospitality from Susan Alcorn and her team of local girls, an idyllic location and: kazaaam! The Mill has the lot, and is one of the hottest places to eat and stay in the country.

Mr Alcorn's food has always been impressive, but the sheer confidence and accomplishment you find now in dishes such as oyster carbonara with homemade linguini and pancetta, or chicken livers with black pudding on a rosemary porridge fritter fairly knocks one sideways. He grills Horn Head mackerel and pairs it with a seafood saffron broth that is just right, whilst his improvisation on a Gordon Ramsay dish, confit shoulder and roast rump of lamb with boulangere potatoes and vegetable nicoise is outstanding. Baked Alaska is spot on, crème brulée is benchmark. Service by locals girls is superb: Mrs Alcorn should be teaching how you do it right. (Figart, Dunfanaghy ☎ 074-913 6985 www.themillrestaurant.com —
Open dinner)

Dunkineely

Restaurant with Rooms
● Castle Murray House

Castle Murray was one of the pioneers of the concept of the restaurant with rooms in Ireland, and today, under the direction of Marguerite Howley, it powers on, attracting people with good cooking, good value and – who can forget this – some of the most mystically magnificent views to be enjoyed in Ireland. Indeed, even before you have begun to enjoy Remy Dupas' cooking, just gazing out across the waters of the bay is intoxicating.

But that cooking is, and always has been, very fine indeed, and very fine value for money, the cost of dinner being determined by the choice of main course. Tomato and broad bean soup to begin, then salmon fondue with three sauces (hooray for fondue!) and a brandy mousse for pudding: solid, unpretentious and solid-sender cooking, served by charming locals, food that makes for enjoyment and a quite unique sense of away-from-it-all relaxation. (Dunkineely ☎ 074-973 7022 www.castlemurray.com — Open Dinner & Sun Lunch)

Glenties

Biodynamic Grower
● **Thomas Becht**

Thomas Becht is a pioneering farmer and cheesemaker, whose organic and bio-dynamic vegetables are sold both from a farm shop at the farm, near to Glenties, and via his Friday box delivery system, which sees Thomas scooting all over the county. There are currently three holiday flats being developed at the farm, and Thomas is part of a committee seeking to establish a farmers' market in Letterkenny, so there are lots of positive developments emanating from this dynamic farmer-producer. (Glenties ☎ 074-955 1286)

Preserves
● **Filligan's Preserves**

Philip and Sarah Moss exhibit the classic characteristics of artisan producers; as they get more experience, they get more creative, and they get better and better. It's worth stressing this point, as it is, of course, the antithesis of the commercialised food industry, which is unprogressive, repetitive and based on marketing rather than creativity. And, in many other ways, what Philip and Sarah do is the very archetype of the artisan: they live in a remote zone, where they provide employment for local people thanks to their successful micro-industry. They utilize their artistic attitudes – Mr Moss continues to paint and exhibit – as an integral part of their work with food. Best of all, their fab range of preserves, jams, mustards and chutneys tell us as much about the producers as any autobiography: quirky, idiosyncratic, left-field, determined. The Filligan's range – as beautifully packaged and presented as you would expect from this couple – are essential daily foods. (Glenties ☎ 074-955 1628)

Cult Choice Bio-Dyn in Ireland

Some people like to cock a snook at bio-dynamic farming. They like to have a laugh at the sort of techniques used by farmers such as Thomas Becht and a few other bio-dyn farmers in Ireland. Moon calendars! they chortle. Rudolf Steiner! they giggle. Well, here is how to make them laugh on the other side of their face. Just show them a vegetable, fruit or herb which has been produced according to bio-dyn practices. And show them two elements of the produce: the colour, and the scent. A more powerful true colour? For sure. And a more arresting scent? No doubt about it. Who's laughing now? Bio-dyn is the future.

Greencastle

Restaurant
● Kealy's Seafood Bar

A bright, spruce dining room that always wears a well-loved air of attentiveness, James and Tricia Kealy's smart, pier-side restaurant always has a crowd of seafood lovers in attendance, locals, tourists, day-trippers, all drawn to this remote but vital Donegal address. Lunchtime food is simple and comes from a short menu – seafood platter; battered haddock and chips; a proper chowder – and gets more interesting with the dinner menu, where there may be John Dory with anchovy butter; hake with braised fennel, and a range of meat options, such as a classic steak chasseur, or cornfed chicken and chorizo casserole. Value, as with so many Donegal addresses, is very keen, service is charming. (Greencastle ☎ 074-938 1010 — Open Lunch & Dinner)

Killybegs

Restaurant
● **Vineyard Restaurant @ The Fleet Inn**

The Vineyard has always been a most welcoming room, and nothing has changed in that regard since Karen Boyle took up the kitchen reins in this bar, restaurant and B&B, down a side street off the main strip of Killybegs. The local fish and shellfish is the best choice here: crab claws in garlic butter; stuffed garlic mussels; steamed lemon sole with white crab meat and a saffron sauce. They make a good chowder; the vegetable cookery is spot on, and when the room is busy it's an enchanting spot. (Bridge St, Killybegs ☎ 074-973 2848 — Open Dinner)

Laghey

Restaurant and Accommodation
● **Coxtown Manor**

Late evening, and a friend calls on his mobile: "I'm in Donegal. Where should I go?" Try Coxtown Manor, we say.
Next morning, the friend calls on his mobile: "I'm just leaving Coxtown. What a place! That was the best meal I have had in Ireland in the last decade. Thanks!"
This is the sort of quiet culinary and hospitality magic that Ed Dewael has been weaving at Coxtown in recent years. He has assembled a great crew who palpably enjoy their work, and who look after you supremely well. The kitchen prepares delicious food – grilled oysters with spinach and Pernod; roast wild duck with duck confit; lots of beautifully executed fish and shellfish dishes with pristine seafood; desserts with Belgian chocolate utilized everywhichway – and the quiet, peaceable nature and charm of this late-Georgian house makes for a retreat that is nothing short of enchanting. Coxtown is one of the jewels of the county. (Laghey ☎ 074-973 4574 www.coxtownmanor.com)

Letterkenny

Butcher
● **McGee's Butcher's**

Joe McGee has made a terrific name for himself as a skilful
butcher, working from his base in Emyvale, County
Monaghan. The opening of this second shop at the shopping
centre in Letterkenny will bring his carefully selected and
expertly presented modern style of butchery to a develop-
ing town. Like the growing band of young, creative charcutiers – Pat Whelan, Hugh Maguire, James McGeough,
Michael O'Crulaoi, to name but four – Joe McGee marries
butchery skills with a great dedication to service. Here is a
shop that has what you want, the way you want it, and if
they don't have it, then they will get it for you. (Unit 29
Letterkenny SC, Port Rd, L'kenny ☎ 074-917 6567)

Malin

Restaurant and Hotel
● **The Malin Hotel**

Since it was taken over in late 2002, The Malin has exhibited
lots of ambition, both in terms of the spec of the hotel –
they have been refurbishing consistently – and in terms of
the cooking in their restaurant. Pasta with squid ink; monkfish with a duo of sauces; fresh ceps in olive oil; duck breast
with kumquat, this is cooking exhibiting intense and brightly
expressed flavours. The hotel itself offers all thing to all men
– small conferences, weddings, traditional music nights, and
there are also lots of good value offers with the restaurant
food. (Malin Town, Inishowen ☎ 074-937 0702
www.malinhotel.ie — Open Lunch & Dinner)

Mountcharles

Bar and Restaurant
● **The Village Tavern**

Kim Kelly and Graham Flannery's bar and restaurant
appears at first glance to offer the standard food found in
so many places – prawn cocktail, nachos, sirloin baguette,
penne – but there is a lot more going on here than first

meets the eye. With a simple dish of bacon and cabbage, for instance, Mr Flannery shows the sort of care and discernment that is his trademark: a mellow, yellow mash, a perfect light parsley sauce, and thick slices of tender meat make for a dish that is enlivened and enlivening. A delicious pear and almond tart with crisp pastry and a sugary, nutty filling reinforces the picture of a cook who takes pains to get things right. Kelly and Flannery have been getting things right for some time now – "consistently excellent food and service at reasonable prices" was how a local described the VT shortly after they were up-and-running, and they have plenty of gas in their tank. (Mountcharles ☎ 074-973 5622 www.villagetavern.ie — Open Day-time and early Evening)

Portsalon

B&B
● Croaghross

John and Kay Deane's hillside B&B has glorious views out over Portsalon's sumptuous white strand, and to complement the views, the cooking and hospitality in this comfortable destination are simply first rate. Croaghross is one of the great places to escape to, and a great place in which to chill out, enjoying expert domestic cooking, lovely wines, and good craic with like-minded escapees from the daily grind. The Deane's alternate their roles between managing the kitchen and managing front-of-house, and they have proven that they are both as good at doing either or both tasks. Breakfasts are just as polished and enjoyable, and the air of successful creativity is mightily attractive. (Portsalon, Letterkenny ☎ 074 915 9548 www.croaghross.com)

Rathmullan

Country House
● Rathmullan House

The Wheeler family's noble country house and restaurant, with its enviable position overlooking Lough Swilly, is a firm favourite with many visitors from Northern Ireland. The cooking is country house confident, and breakfasts are justly celebrated and magnificent. (Lough Swilly, Rathmullan, ☎ 074-915 8188 www.rathmullanhouse.com)

DUBLIN
CONTENTS

County Dublin

capital cooking, ethnic capital, capital markets,
capital shopping . . .

Dublin Central —
North of the River

Wine Merchant
● Cabot & Co

Liam and Sinead Cabot's splendiferous wine shop
has defined a new optimum for Dublin, no
mean feat in a city where the choice of wines
and the quality of wine service is superb.
But the Cabots have a refined, rarified
aesthetic to their choice of wines that sets
them apart. They seek out not simply the best, but
also the most quixotic wines, the wines that have both a
voice and a soul in their make up. You don't just drink these
wines; you have a relationship with them. Our favourite way
to approach the Cabot list is to say: select us a case of the
wines with greatest signature, the greatest style. And what
you will get will be a dozen delights, that will bring you back
for a further dozen delights. A radical destination. (Unit 1a,
Valentia Hse, Custom Hse Plaza, IFSC, D1 ☎ 01-636 0616)

Restaurant
● Chapter One

Innovate and Improve. That could be the motto
of Ross Lewis and Martin Corbett's mighty
Chapter One restaurant. This crew are fastidi-
ously open to new ideas – the most recent
has been the brilliant introduction of the
salami trolley, with a mouth-watering array of
artisan smoked and cured meats on offer – and they combine this openness with a relentless polishing of both the
cooking and the service. The result is one of the great
modern Irish restaurants, with one of the most singular
offerings of modern Irish cooking: jellied ham with organic
egg and parsley puree; woodcock with swede and savoy
cabbage; baked Ardrahan with strawberry confiture. Mr
Lewis's cooking spins the seasons with understanding and
respect, and innovations are endlessly improved upon, polished, refined. Chapter One defines what it is to be on top
of your game. (18-19 Parnell Square, D1 ☎ 01-873 2266
www.chapteronerestaurant.com)

Restaurant
● China House

Chinese restaurants tend to get posh, eventually – look at Belfast's Sun Kee, now a big, slick panjandrum of great food where once it was Grotsville Incarnate. But, China House has some way to go to get there, so what you get here is fabulously authentic Chinese cooking, and an aesthetic somewhere short of Cristina Ong. It's up the stairs, the beer is warm, the food soulful and pungent: tofu soup; sweet and chilli aubergine; collarfish with orange – and it costs half nothing. (15 North Moore St, no telephone number. No credit cards)

Craft Brewery
● The Dublin Brewing Company

A series of four brews, and some wickedly wild cider, are the portfolio of the DBC. We think Maeve's Crystal Wheat is one of the great contemporary Irish beers, a light, complex, satisfying plosion of flavours, and a beer that matches superbly with food. But Beckett's Gold, 1798 Revolution Ale and d'Arcy's Dublin Stout are all drinks with excellent typicity, balance and character, a true definition of craft brewing. You will find them in bottle form in good wine shops, and there is also a small bar at the DBC itself. (141-146 North King St, Smithfield, D7 ☎ 01-872 8622 www.dublinbrewing.com)

Restaurant
● Enoteca delle Langhe

Mick Wallace's audacious slice of Italian-inspired architecture, hard by the quays, is a thrill. The Enoteca is where you can have simple Italian food and a selection of wines from northern Italy that Wallace imports himself. There is also an Italian-style café, Caffé Cagliostro, a shop called Wallace's with a range of Italian foods, a branch of Bar Italia, and there are also various funky retailers. The Enoteca has already been discovered by a bunch of admirers who like its easy sangfroid and the interesting wines, and who like to turn up here for an informal supper, or a mid-afternoon chill-out with a good bottle. Sit at the bar, order up a platter of cheese and salamis – don't miss the pecorino and honey – and some good glasses of wine, and enjoy the new Italia HQ in Dublin. (Blooms Lane, opp. Millennium Bridge, D1 ☎ 01-888 0834)

DUBLIN

Dim Sum Dublin...

Dubliners will argue the toss about whether the best dim sum is that of the ageless Imperial, or its near neighbour on South Great George's Street, the Good World, and it's easy fun to start a fight over who has the best char siu cheung fun or the slipperiest fish balls or crispiest won tons. Of course, you can outpace this argument by stressing that you are a devotee of the New Millennium, near to the Gaiety, whose chicken feet in spicy sauce are truly ace, and whose staff are amongst the most charming in the entire city – no conventional brusqueness here.

And, hidden way out in the 'burbs, is the Ming Court, in breezy Blanchardstown. The fun quoi is worth the trip all on its own, but do make sure to try the Vietnamese spring rolls, the crispy won tons, and the deep-fried bean curd.

•**Imperial Chinese Restaurant, 12a Wicklow St, D2 ☎ 01-677 2580**

•**Good World Chinese Restaurant, 18 Sth Gt George's St, D2 ☎ 01-577 5373**

•**Ming Court Chinese Restaurant, unit 453, Blanchardstown Ctr, D15 ☎ 01-824 3388**

•**New Millennium Chinese Restaurant, 51 Sth King St, D2 ☎ 01-635 1525**

Farmers' Market
● **IFSC Farmers' Market**

The Financial Services crew descend on the Mayor Square market to satisfy lunchtime hunger and the demands of the evening's dinner. So everything happens very quickly here, in the city centre outpost of Sean McArdle's Farmers' Markets Empire. (Mayor Square, IFSC. Wed 10.30-4pm)

Restaurant
● Halo

Jean-Michel Poulot's cooking in the gorgeous Halo restaurant is amongst the most distinguished in the city. His work is a triumphant assertion of the value of fusion cooking, and it succeeds largely because Poulot has a Japanese-style simplicity as his aim. The food can read complicated – boneless quail with truffled Brussels sprouts and a foie gras veal jus; or seared salmon fillet with blue crabmeat risotto, corn meal blinis, salmon tartare and a ginger and lime vinaigrette, to take two typical examples – but Poulot will find all the affinities of flavour that these ingredients share, which means that the dishes actually eat very directly, pleasingly and profoundly. This is great cooking, at very decent prices. (The Morrison Hotel, Ormond Quay, D1 ☎ 01-887 2421 www.morrisonhotel.ie)

Restaurant
● The Harbourmaster

It's the Greenhouse restaurant on the first floor that is of interest in this big, rather banal pub, in the IFSC. Last time here we had superb ravioli of lobster and langoustine with a spot-on sauce vierge, then pristine halibut with clam and white truffle risotto. Lovely cooking, and as the population in the IFSC increases, we can expect even more from the Greenhouse. (Customs House Dock, IFSC, D1 ☎ 01-670 1688 www.harbourmaster.ie)

Restaurant
● Itsabagel & the Epicurean Food Hall

Domini and Peaches Kemp's pioneering bagel bar has sprouted a pair of siblings – not to mention a raft of imitators – but like many devotees we still love joining the lunchtime queue in the Epicurean, and the expectant waiting in line as you try to make up your mind what bagel it is going to be today: the Club Bagel? The Deluxe? The Itsareuben? The Gourmet Veggie? The Epicurean Mall itself has a busy clientèle for its many food stops: you can get everything from Burdock's fish and chips to wines from Leyden's Fine Wines to patisserie to Bar Italia coffees to Turkish specialities. (Epicurean Food Hall, Lwr Liffey St, D1 ☎ 01-874 0486 www.itsabagel.com)

Pub
● O'Neill's

This Pearse Street pub has simple rooms alongside the bar and they are useful to know about, thanks to being inexpensive and smack bang in the city. The owners have a pretty much take-it-or-leave-it attitude to hospitality, unlike the charming Asian staff who make breakfast and clear up. (36-37 Pearse St, D2 ☎ 01-671 4074 www.oneillsdublin.com)

Restaurant
● 101 Talbot

Pascal and Margaret's iconic city-centre restaurant was here long before this zone of Dublin ever got smart and self-conscious, and if the city has changed, this pair of brilliant restaurateurs haven't. Their aim is today, as it has always been, to provide interesting food in a fun room at good prices. Good Caesar salad; good terrines; nice barbecued pork with caramelized onions, and the vegetarian choices are always delectable. Mighty fun. (101 Talbot Street, D1 ☎ 01-874 5011 — Open Dinner)

Café & Bakery
● Panem

Ann Murphy's ever-popular café and bakery is a great destination for interesting daytime eating, and the care lavished on everything cooked here is charming. (21 Lwr Ormond Quay, D1 ☎ 01-872 8510)

Restaurant
● Soup Dragon

A shoe-box of a room at the river end of Capel St, but the imagination brought to bear on the SD's trademark soups is big, working a whole series of variations on standard themes. So, chicken soup comes with a Thai accent, chowder is made with good smoked haddock, and the breads are doorsteppy chunky. The only problem is getting a seat at lunchtime. (168 Capel Street, D1 ☎ 01-872 3277 — Open Lunch)

Restaurant
● The Vaults

A super-hip space created out of ten 150-year-old stone

DUBLIN

vaults, Michael Martin's ambitious The Vaults somehow manages to please everyone. The cooking is good – paillard of chicken with spring onion mash; classic Caesar salad; sirloin with béarnaise, and the pizzas are more than okay – and you can do most everything here from cocktail-making classes to a boozy big-screen football bash with your mates. (The Vaults, Harbourmaster Pl, IFSC, D1 ☎ 01-605 4700 www.thevaults.ie — Open Lunch & Dinner)

Restaurant
● Winding Stair Bookshop & Café

Kevin Connolly's classic bookshop and café harkens back to a time when Dublin was bookish and less time-worn, and today it remains a series of rooms that feel great for browsing, taking coffee, having a simple lunch whilst peering out at the magnificent, muddy River Liffey. (40 Lwr Ormond Quay, D1 ☎ 01-873 3292 — Open Lunch)

Dublin Central —
South of the River

Restaurant & Shop
● Avoca

Style. Signature. Success. The Pratt family's unique cafés and shops have the lot. They are places where beautiful things are made to be eaten, and beautiful things are sourced and created to be sold. You could take what they do, tomorrow, and turn it into a global brand, for there is no one alive who, having sampled a taste of the Avoca action, wouldn't want it again and again. But that won't happen, because what is at the core of the Avoca enterprise is real content, and no global brand can empathise with those ideas. Sticking to their beliefs has allowed Simon Pratt and his company to become one of the glories of Irish food, Irish design, Irish hospitality. This is café cooking, and metropolitan shopping, at its zenith. (Suffolk St, D2 ☎ 01-672 6019 www.avoca.ie — Open Lunch)

Restaurant
● AYA

Yoichi Hoashi's groovy sushi bar is not just a winning

concept – a conveyor-belt sushi bar integrated into a slick Japanese restaurant – it's a winning reality, with great staff and a great zeitgeist. Kids adore the whole hi-tech marvel of it all, whilst everyone loves the food: sticky teriyaki; cold noodle salads; pork gyozu, and there is even chocolate mousse for the traditionalists. The crew are sparky young Aussies, the merchandise is cool, and this is some of the best food fun you can have in Dublin city. (49-52 Clarendon St, D2 ☎ 01-677 1544 www.aya.ie — Open Lunch & Dinner)

Restaurant
● Il Baccaro

This splendidly cavern-like Italian eating and drinking den is a gem, situated right at the corner of Meeting House Square where the Temple Bar market takes place each Saturday morning. Raucous good fun with lots of Italian wine and some pretty decent Italian-cliché food is the order of the day, so go with a posse and cancel the following morning. (Meeting House Sq, Temple Bar, D2 ☎ 01-671 4597 — Open Dinner)

Restaurant
● Bang Café

We think Lorcan Gribbin has made Bang into one of the best destinations in Dublin. And yet this fine cook remains known only to a very serious, chef-focused audience, whilst most folk who eat in this tiny but chic room associate Bang with its owners, the Stokes brothers.
Mr Gribbin will have his day in the sun. For now, it is sufficient to say that he is cooking some of the best food in the city, food that reads clichéd – chicken chasseur; beef with shallots; bangers and mash – but which is cooked with such loving, freshly-minted care that it animates the intellect to reappreciate why these dishes became celebrated in the first place. Excellent. (11 Merrion Row, D2 ☎ 01-676 0898 www.bangrestaurant.com — Open Lunch & Dinner)

Restaurant
● Bar Italia

Bar Italia is the sister project of the ace Dunne & Crescenzi, places where classic pastas and coffee are shown respect. (Temple Bar, D2 ☎ 01-633 4477; Epicurean Mall ☎ 01-873 4200; 26 Lwr Ormond Quay, D1 ☎ 01-874 1000)

DUBLIN

Wine Merchant
● Berry Bros & Rudd

You could confine your wine drinking to BB&R's own label series, and be a happy tippler, such is the strength of quality evident in this venerable firm's portfolio of wines. But, if your boat comes in, BB&R is also a destination from which to source the great trophy wines of the world, all of them stored downstairs at controlled temperature. The shop itself is one of the loveliest and most handsome in the city, service is professional, discreet and well-informed. (4 Harry St, D2 ☎ 01-677 3444 www.bbr.com)

Restaurant
● Blazing Salads

Joe Fitzmaurice's BS is a vegetarian take-away, offering soups, salads, sarnies and specials everyday. Of particular interest is their in-house bakery, producing natural sour-dough breads with organic ingredients along with a range of breads and cakes which are sugar-, wheat-, and dairy-free. (42 Drury St, D2 ☎ 01-671 9552 — Open Lunch)

Restaurant
● Bleu Bistro Moderne

Bleu is Eamonn O'Reilly's second venture, after One Pico, and if OP is the experimental side of his culinary brain, then BBM is the conventional side, and many like it all the better for being a little bit repressed, and more disciplined. The food is bistro's greatest hits – navarin of lamb with cocotte potatoes; honey roast parsnips with duck; roast chicken with girolles and tarragon; pear and chestnut strudel. (Joshua House, Dawson St, D2 ☎ 01-676 7015 — Open Lunch & Dinner)

Townhouse
● Browne's

Browne's is both townhouse – in which regard its destination in central Dublin is only brilliant – and handsome brasserie. Now part of the Stein boutique hotel group, it is run with efficient élan, which makes for a reliable, convenient and comforting address right in the city centre. (22 St Stephen's Green, D2 ☎ 01-683 3939 www.brownesdublin.com)

Restaurant
● The Cellar Restaurant

This handsome room in the basement of the posh Merrion Hotel has quickly become one of the favoured rooms of smart Dubliners and smart visitors to the city. With Ed Cooney managing the pans and Damian Corr managing the punters, the Cellar makes the business of delivering high-quality, creative food at decent prices with great service seem second nature. These guys are professionals, they have no pretentions getting in their way, and the result is a rockin' success, which also offers some of the best value in the city. Ham hock terrine; crispy squid; grilled black sole; chump of lamb; calves' liver with onion gravy, all lovely things. Sunday brunch sees the room in overdrive. (Merrion Hotel, Upper Merrion St, D2 ☎ 01-603 0600 www.merrionhotel.com — Open Breakfast, Lunch & Dinner)

Whiskey Shop
● The Celtic Whiskey Shop

Ally Alpine's shop doesn't just sell whiskeys – there are some really choice wines for sale, as you would expect from a former Oddbins manager – but it is with a stunning range of the precious uisce beatha that The Celtic excels. If you seek the rare and the special in the form of Irish or Scottish firewater, then this is your only destination. (27-28 Dawson St, D2 ☎ 01-675 9744)

Restaurant
● Chameleon

Carol Walsh's Indonesian-style restaurant was one of the Temple Bar pioneers, and today it retains the idiosyncratic, personable spirit that has fled from most addresses in this part of town. (1 Fownes Street, Temple Bar, D2 ☎ 01-671 0362 — Open Dinner)

Wine Merchant
● Corkscrew Wine Merchants

Peter Foley was one of the originators of Berry Bros & Rudd's Dublin branch, before opening Corkscrew, and the new shop is a good fit into a street that has the popular pizzeria Steps of Rome, as well as The Clarendon Bar and the Chatham Brasserie. (4 Chatham St, D2 ☎ 01-674 5731)

Restaurant
● **Dunne & Crescenzi**

"Dunne & Crescenzi could be an enoteca in Venice" is how the cookery writer Hugo Arnold summed up Eileen and Stefano's knock-'em-dead room on South Frederick Street. They do antipasti, panini, pasta and desserts, and thanks to careful sourcing the food is effortlessly delicious and successful. It's all about combining and assembling more than cooking, and D&C do it to perfection: great bean salads; buffalo mozzarella drizzled with extra virgin olive oil; good Parma ham and mortadella, and wickedly interesting wines to match all these dizzy flavours. If you can leave the room without spending a further small fortune on the foods, wines and coffee for sale, you are made of sterner stuff than us. A great address. (14 South Frederick St, D2 ☎ 01-677 3815 — Open Day-time & early Dinner)

Wine Bar
● **Ely**

Eric and Michelle Robson's wine bar is one of the city's great cult faves. Their wines are outstanding, with a stonking assortment available by the glass, and the latest move into the adjoining basement will allow them to expand the range of dishes offered by the kitchen. And whilst Ely is primarily thought of as a wine bar, don't for a second think that the cooking is an afterthought: it isn't. Organic foods from the family farm in County Clare are cooked and served in Ely with great imagination and creativity: Irish stew with Burren lamb; duck salad with toasted cashews; Kilkee oysters; great cheese plates. (22 Ely Place, D2 ☎ 01-676 8986 — Open Lunch & Dinner)

Restaurant
● **Les Freres Jacques**

Long may LFJ remain as changeless as it has been over the last two decades. All the while that Temple Bar was transmogrifying, this serene slice of French cuisine stayed straight on course, its cooking loyal to the flag of traditional haute cuisine. Grilled oysters. Lobster from the tank. Confit de canard. Crème brûlée. Sure, how could you tire of it? (74 Dame St, D2 ☎ 01-679 4555 www.lesfreresjacques.com — Open Lunch & Dinner)

Patisserie
● The Gallic Kitchen

Sarah Webb has developed a successful second string to her
Gallic Kitchen bow, and now works many of the best
farmers' markets. Her baking is stylish, classy, soulfully delicious, and in the 15 years since she began, the quality of
production from this essential bakery has never faltered.
Her secret is an understanding of pastry that is second to
none: crumbly, flaky, buttery, irresistible. (49 Francis St, D8
☎ 01-454 4912 — Open Day-time)

Arcade
● The George's Street Arcade Complex

How nice to see that the beatniks haven't all become
besuited conformists. The whiff of ascetic alternativism
arises happily from the grove of traders on the George's
Street arcade: the splendid **Green Olive Co** with their
choice foods and great range of pulses; fine soups and
snacks and lunches from **Lara Lu** foods at the Drury Street
entrance, right beside the snappy **Claudio's Wine Shop**, and
if you head on past the second-hand clothes and long
playing record racks you will find **Place de Simon** at the
George's Street end, one of the great retreats for forty-
somethings who wish to recall their salad days. It's all wonderfully soulful. When they have had their coffee, the beatniks pick up some ethnic foods in the eternal **Asia Market**,
their aesthetic pallor beautifully offset by the lurid lighting
of this great Asiatic emporium.

Just around the corner is what happens when the beatniks
grow up: **The Market Yard** is hip, stylish, clever, busy and
very much Dublin modern, by which we mean the cooking
has a Spanish accent. It's a great room. (George's St Arcade,
George's St, D2)

Restaurant
● Gruel

Who could resist a short-order restaurant named Gruel?
Not us. Little sibling to the mighty Mermaid, next door,
Gruel does smashing grub: Cajun corn soup that has just
the right amount of chilli spiking it; fluffy French toast with
real maple syrup; a tomato frittata with goat's cheese and
baby spinach that is just right. You eat this food, and the
instant it is gone, you want some more. (67 Dame St, D2
☎ 01-670 7119 — Open Lunch & Dinner)

Restaurant
● Restaurant Patrick Guilbaud

The team of owner Patrick Guilbaud and chef Guillaume Lebrun has been working together for over two decades, whilst manager Stephane Robin brings up the third arm of this supremely professional crew. Their restaurant is lauded, applauded, and vociferously defended by its many champions, whose support has made the restaurant an enormous success over 22 years. (21 Upper Merrion St, D2 ☎ 01-676 4192 www.merrionhotel.ie/guilbaud.asp)

Restaurant
● Jacob's Ladder

Adrian Roche is one of the city's best cooks, an imaginative, almost boffin-like chef whose culinary ideas are frequently far ahead of many of his contemporaries. He makes a cep risotto, but then cooks it like a rösti to be served with lamb. He makes a tomato tart, but pairs it with olive ice cream. He makes fried leek tortellini and serves it with roast loin of veal. This is thrilling cooking, and the room and the ambience share the same sense of purpose and intensity as the cooking. "The most experimental chef in Dublin", was how Paul Levy described Mr Roche in *The Wall Street Journal*. And so he is. (4-5 Nassau Street, D2 ☎ 01-670 3865 www.jacobsladder.ie — Open Lunch & Dinner)

Kitchen Equipment
● Kitchen Complements

A tiny kitchenware shop that is packed with all the great and good names of the kitchenware world. If you have a serious fetish for the best devices for the kitchen, it is difficult to maintain control in Ann McNamee's vital shop. (Chatham Street, D2, ☎ 01-677 0734)

Delicatessen
● Liston's

Karen Liston's shop has tripled in size, and the ambition of this cracking deli seems to have likewise tripled. They now sell great dinners-to-go; the wine selection is only brilliant, the space has allowed them to streamline their mad-busy lunchtime service, and everything here is the work of a crew who are getting everything just right and getting a real kick out of their work. The sandwiches are witty and smart

DUBLIN

– The Italian Job; The New Yorker; The Moroccan Bites – the food to go is unpretentious and real – butternut squash soup; meatballs and rice – and the selection of deli and artisan foods is brilliant, with rarities such as Caherbeg sausages or smoked fish from the Burren Smokehouse in Lisdoonvarna. "The source of good food" they say. Too right. (25 Camden St, D2 ☎ 01-405 4779, listonsfood@eircom.net)

Shop and Café
● La Maison des Gourmets

Penny Plunket's house of gourmets is a classy shop and dining room, tiny but chic, almost a little touch of Fauchon in Dublin. Excellent breads and patisserie are amongst the main attractions downstairs, whilst upstairs in the dining room, elegant tarts, elegant tartines and good soups and salads make for a winningly professional organisation. (15 Castle Market, D2 ☎ 01-672 7258 — Open Day-time)

Restaurant
● The Market Bar

This clever room – part of the Jay Bourke and Eoin Foyle empire – was clearly done on a tight budget, but skill and imagination have triumphed over resources to concoct a very sociable, metropolitan space that gets mighty crowded with sociable metropolitans. The food is Spanish in style, which is to say it presents a holidaymaker's view of Spanish cooking, but it is enjoyably naïve, with lots of anchovies, chick peas, chorizos and potato bravas everywhichway. The same team operate the nearby Café-Bar-Deli and The Globe, as well as the stylish Eden in Temple Bar. (Fade Street, D2 ☎ 01-613 9094 — Open Day-time and early Evening)

Restaurant
● The Mermaid Café

"You'll leave wishing you had a Mermaid Café within walking distance of your own home", was how Los Angeles' *Bon Appetit* magazine wistfully signed off on another critically acclaimed dinner at The Mermaid. Temple Garner's food has been wowing the critics for sometime now, and as scribblers we have

On top of their game

been successfully wowed! in here time and again. The transition between Garner's cooking and owner Ben Gorman's food was as smooth as could be, and the Mermaid's only problem these days is coping with the demand for tables, especially at weekends. The cooking is singular, eclectic, and beautifully realised – squid salad with roast peppers; hand-rolled macaroni with Stilton, cauliflower and walnut pesto; osso bucco with jerusalem artichokes – making for one of the most vital Dublin destinations. (69/70 Dame Street, Temple Bar, D2 ☎ 01-670 8236 www.mermaid.ie — Open Lunch & Dinner)

Wine Merchant
● Mitchell & Sons

There are so many young guns and arrivistes in the world of wine these days that venerable firms such as Mitchell's tend to be overlooked by the media. Don't make that mistake; this firm remains as skilful, knowledgeable and efficient as ever, their range packed with special wines, from the glorious Alsatian wines of Sipp Mack – do ask about their Catholic and Protestant Rieslings – to the brilliant wines of Domaine d'Arjolle to the quirky tokaji and other odds and sods that Mitchell's have always discovered. Their own Green Spot whiskey is one of the cult choices for any fan of sublime hootch. (Kildare St, D2 ☎ 01-676 0766. Also at Glasthule, Co. Dublin ☎ 01-230 2301 www.mitchellandson.com)

Restaurant
● Monty's of Kathmandu

You can argue the toss about whether or not Monty's is the best ethnic restaurant in Dublin, but what is unarguable is the fact that it is the best-loved ethnic restaurant in Dublin. Shiva Gautam and his crew run the most personable and pleasing room here in Temple Bar, with sublime Nepalese food that is creatively and imaginatively rendered: kachela, the raw lamb served with a shot of whiskey; the fantastic Momo dumplings (you order 'em 24 hours in advance, and you pop 'em in one at a time with a little hit of chutney); the great tandoori butter chicken; the superb monkfish with garam masala and peppers. Indeed, the chef's expertise with the tandoor means this is one address where you can order tandoor dishes with confidence. Most everyone who eats here is a regular and, you will be too. (28 Eustace St, Temple Bar, D2 ☎ 01-670 4911 www.montys.ie — Open Lunch & Dinner)

Café
● Nude

Norman Hewson's pioneering Nude does something profound. It gives people good food, and it gives it to them fast, and it has managed to make that good, healthy, natural food seem all sexy. Not virtuous, not good-for-you, not you-need-this. Just sexy, fun, tasty stuff to grab at lunchtime, or indeed anytime during the day. Wraps, juices, funky sandwiches, wheatgrass shots, bagels packed full of good, moreish ingredients, true up-and-at-'em foods.
There is a takeaway branch on Lower Leeson Street and, very importantly, there is a branch at Dublin airport which will rescue many a traveller stranded waiting for a plane. (21 Suffolk St, D2 ☎ 01-672 5577 — Open Day-time and early-Evening)

Restaurant
● Oil & Vinegar

Joop Seebu's corner shop is part of a European chain which specialises in extra virgin olive oils, and various flavoured vinegars, along with handsome paraphernalia and some speciality foods. Oils such as Bonsecco from Tuscany or Castelo Zacro from Greece are amongst their portfolio, and there are lots of funky sauces and quirky pastas. (16 South Gt George's St ☎ 01-677 6445 www.oilvinegar.com)

Restaurant
● One Pico

Eamonn O'Reilly's restaurant has one of the most gorgeous Dublin dining rooms to play with, a spot so handsome he could serve prawn bisque and shepherd's pie and pack it out. But, O'Reilly continues to get his kicks by pushing the culinary envelope, so there is a rhubarb tatin with duck confit, a foie gras foam with chicken breast; Roquefort crushed potatoes with mignon of Angus beef. When it works, it pleases both the brains and the body, but sometimes it doesn't work, and then the experimentalism seems gratuitous, shock value for the sake of shock. O'Reilly also operates the popular Bleu Bistro. (5-6 Molesworth Pl, D2 ☎ 01-676 0300 www.onepico.com — Open Lunch & Dinner)

Restaurant
● Pearl Brasserie

Sebastian Masi and Kirsten Batt's basement brasserie is surrounded by powerful competition, but gamely survives thanks to some nice cooking, good value for money, and a cool professionalism. Classics such as foie gras with brioche, or Toulouse sausage cassoulet style mix easily with many other core dishes from the brasserie repertoire – crispy prawns with mango and black pepper; baked cod with gratinated courgette; chicken supreme with tarragon velouté; salmon brochette. (20 Merrion St Upr, D2 ☎ 01-661 3572 www.pearl-brasserie.com — Open Lunch & Dinner)

Real Food At Home...

You can never tell where the great chefs of today will wind up working. Take Neil McFadden, who came to national attention several years back when he achieved a top ranking status at the gruelling Bocuse d'Or competition in Lyon. After such an achievement, Mr McFadden could have taken his choice of positions, most likely well-remunerated executive chef in some fancy hotel. Instead, today, Mr McFadden is one of the three directors – along with Ray O'Haire and founder Fabrizio Memon, of realfoodathome, a company which prepares and delivers quality food to CCTT's (can't cook, too tired), CRTP's (cash-rich, time-poor) and CCNT's (can't cook, never tried) folk throughout the city of Dublin. And a recent link up with the O'Brien's chain of wine stores sees their ambit extending further, beyond the delivery service into shops where you might stop to pick up a bottle. All you need, they say, is 20 minutes, and you will have real food, so no more gunky, feel-bad take-aways. Just let Neil make your dinner.
•www.realfoodathome.com

Restaurant
● Peploe's

Barry Canny's new venture on St Stephen's Green has met with immediate acclaim. What you will often hear people saying is that it is "an Ivy for Dublin", which is to say: simple food done accurately, good wines, great service, a stylish room, all in the manner of London's legendary Ivy restaurant. And Peploe's has all of these things, in spades. The room is great, but understated and classy. The wine list is terrific, and offers 25 wines by the glass. The food is simple – French onion soup; croque monsieur; lamb pie with root vegetables; linguini with clams; organic salmon with red wine butter; lobster in the shell with sauce choron, and, yes, there is a shepherd's pie – and delivered with a precision and confidence that is disarming. "Not just a nice place to eat when you go shopping in Dublin. It is the reason to go to Dublin", wrote our editor. Dublin just got a brand new Destination, with a capital-D. (16 St Stephen's Green, D2 ☎ 01-676 3144 www.peploes.com — Open Lunch & Dinner)

Brewery
● Porterhouse Brewing Co.

This Temple Bar veteran isn't the most stylish of bars, but anyone can overlook the dated style when you start sampling their craft beers. There are eight brews produced, and some – especially the oyster stout and the Wrasslers 4X stout – are sublime: complex, sophisticated, a million miles away from the standard commercial beers, those sad drinks which real brewers describe as "wet air". There are also Porterhouses in Drumcondra, and in Wicklow. (Parliament St, D2 ☎ 01-679 8847 www.tasteofireland.com)

Café
● Powerscourt Townhouse

Mary Farrell's *Cafe Fresh* is amongst the smart choices in the cavernous Powerscourt Centre. A member of Slow Food, Mary offers vegetarian and vegan dishes each day: Thai green vegetable curry; spinach, pumpkin and tofu with chilli oil, butterbean, leek and pumpkin stew, and there are good desserts. Cafe Fresh also operates a catering service. (Unit 21 C, Powerscourt Townhouse Centre, D2 ☎ 01-671 9669) On the second floor, Stefano Crescenzi's *La Corte* is one of the spin offs from the wonderful Dunne & Crescenzi.

DUBLIN

Good simple pastas, good panini, nice daily specials and excellent coffee is the secret of this mini-empire of Italian eating emporia, all delivered with winning charm and chutzpah. (25b Powerscourt, D2 ☎ 01-633 4477)

Restaurant
● Queen of Tarts

Regina & Yvonne Fallon make superb tarts, as well as sandwiches and delicious desserts in one of the best-loved cafés in the city. Anything and everything sweet and scrumtious is waiting here with your name written on it. (Cork Hill, D2 ☎ 01-670 7499 — Open Day-time)

Restaurant
● Shanahan's

The Shanahan's experience is the archetype of the Big Night Out and they deliver this event better than most places in Dublin. What you get is a superbly choreographed event, with perfectly executed, rather conservative, cooking. Whether the Angus steaks they cook are the best in Ireland is moot: they will be superb, you will have a ball, and your plastic will ache for months afterwards. (119 St Stephen's Green, D2 ☎ 01-407 0939 www.shanahans.ie)

Restaurant
● Sheridan's Cheesemongers

This book is dedicated to the dynamic trio who front Sheridan's – Fiona Corbett and the brothers Kevin and Seamus Sheridan. Their achievement in creating superb stalls and shops for retailing cheeses and fine foods is, however, only one part of their work. For this trio has also done two other things; they have been part of the intellectual avant garde

On top of their game

that has changed the perception of artisan foods and how they are sold, and they have also collected the most rockin' bunch of people to work with them. Whether in Dublin or Galway or at the farmers' markets, the Sheridan's crew are the coolest, the hippest, the most right-on bunch of food retailers we have ever come across. They don't just capture the zeitgeist: they are the zeitgeist, they define the zeitgeist, and they belong with the most creative and important people in Irish food. Awesome. (11 Sth Anne St, D2 ☎ 01-679 3143)

DUBLIN

Temple Bar Market

On top of their game

Critical approval has ebbed and flowed regarding the ambitious Temple Bar project, but no one doubts that the greatest success of this civic enterprise has been the Temple Bar Market. A band of hard-working stalwarts – Denis Healy, Gus and Theresa Hernandez, Ed Hick, Silke Cropp, The Gallic Kitchen, Miriam Griffith, Darko Marjanovic, Sheridan's, David Llewellyn, to pick just a handful – have kept the market tightly focused on high-quality artisan and organic produce, and in so doing they have created one of the key Dublin destinations for food lovers, curious tourists, weekenders, and anyone else who fancies a warm smoked haddock quiche with a smoothie whilst browsing and buying. The market has recently extended out into Curved Street, where you can buy grilled oriental meat dishes, fudge, sauces and marinades, coffees from Michael Kelly, shellfish from Stephen Kavanagh and eggs from one of Wicklow's great marketeers, Liz Keegan.

· *Margaret Scully* Sushi. (Spade, Nth King Street, D7 ☎ 01-617 4820 mscully@iolfree.ie)

· *J Hick & Sons* Fab sausages and pork. (15A, George's St Upr, Dun Laoghaire ☎ 01-284 2700 www.thepinkpig.com)

· *Drumeel Farm* Venison and lamb. (Clonbroney Cross, Ballinalee, Co Longford ☎ 086-3402824 pat@cremin.com)

· *The Gallic Kitchen* Patisserie. (49 Francis St, D8 ☎ 01-454 4912 galkit.iol.ie)

· *Gopa Gana* Juices, Vegetarian Food and Chutney. (11 Hollybank, Lisnaskea, Co. Fermanagh ☎ 048-677 22802)

· *John Beades* Organic Meat. (Cam, Brideswell, Co. Roscommon ☎ 086-967 1697 johnandvalerie@eircom.net)

· *J. McInerney* Shellfish. (Knocknagarhoon, Kilkee, Co. Clare ☎ 065-905 8165)

· *Chez Emily* Homemade Chocolates. (Cool Quay, The Ward, Co Dublin ☎ 01-835 2252 Helena@chezemily.com)

DUBLIN

· *Noirin Kearney* Bread & Cakes. (Ballinrahin, Rathangan, Co. Kildare ☎ 045-524078 noirin.k@oceanfree.net)

· *Olvi Oils* Oils and pastes. (Terenure Enterprise Centre, D6W ☎ 01-831 0244)

· *Sheridans Cheesemongers* (Athboy Creamery, Athboy, Co Meath ☎ 046-30373 cheese@eircom.net)

· *Brian Begley & Elena Ayuso Garcia* Tapas. (57 Parnell Rd, D12 ☎ 086-36 38211 brianbegley@caterspan.ie)

· *Denis Healy* Organic Veg. (Talbotstown, Kiltegan, Co. Wicklow ☎ 0508-73193 organicdenishealy@hotmail.com)

· *Tine Cropp & Oisin Healy* Crepes. (38 Northumberlands, Love Lane, Lwr Mount Street, Dublin ☎ 086-8047889 telgere55@hotmail.com)

· *Corleggy Cheese* Farmhouse Cheese. (Belturbet, Co.Cavan ☎ 049-952 2930 corleggy@eircom.net)

· *Brendan O Mahony* Olives. (Toons Bridge, Macroom, Co Cork ☎ 026-41471 o_mahonybrendan@hotmail.com)

· *Jenny McNally* Yogurts & Preserves. (Balrickard, Ring Commons, Naul, Co. Dublin ☎ 01-841 3023)

· *Florence and Damien Cusack* Bread. (12 Thornleigh Green, Applewood Village, Swords, Co. Dublin ☎ 086-102 2786 florencecusack@hotmail.com)

· *Lawrence Parnis* Waffles. (1 Ashwood Avenue, Clondalkin, D22 ☎ 01-457 0701)

· *Giovanni Pezzillo* Coffee. (5 Watkins Square, The Coombe, D8 ☎ 01-462 6115 serio@eircom.net)

· *Sabores de Mexico* Mexican foods. (56 Manor Street, Stoneybatter, D7 ☎ 01-272 2022 meromerocafe@hotmail.com)

· *Piece of Cake* Cakes and Bread. (Unit 53, Glenwood Bus. Centre, Springbank Ind Est, Poleglass, Belfast, BT17 OQL ☎ 04890-627956 darkopoc@yahoo.co.uk)

· *Medina McNamara* Cakes and buns. (23 Earlsfort Meadows, Lucan, Co.Dublin ☎ 01-621 6087 medinamk@tcd.ie)

· *Quickpenny Orchard* Apple Juice (Quickpenny Road, Lusk, Co. Dublin ☎ 087-284 3879 pureapple@eircom.net)

· *Paul Hederman* Fish. (67 Ardmore Wood, Herbert Road Bray, Co. Wicklow ☎ 086-2786 349 pahederman@eircom.net)

· *Gee's Jams* Jams. (Abbeyleix, Co. Laois ☎ 0502-310 58)

· *Abbey Organic Cheeses* Cheese. (Cuffsboro, Clough, Ballacolle, Port Laoise, Co.Laois ☎ 0502-38599 abbey-cheese@eircom.net)

· *John Brennan* Seasonal berries. (16 Ashlawn, Balinteer Road, D16 ☎ 01-296 0006 nobilis@indigo.ie)

· *The Berry Farm* Seasonal berries. (Ballycoras Road, Kilternan, Co.Dublin ☎ 087-2563032 nobilis@indigo.ie)

· *Earthfruit Strawberries* (Badger Hill, Kilteel, Naas, Co. Kildare ☎ 086-831 4791)

· *Judith's Wild Flowers* (47 Glenomena Park, Booterstown, Co. Dublin)

· *Joice Tang* Grilled Oriental Meat Dishes. (Beechfield Meadows, Beechfield, Clonee, D15 ☎ 01–640 3114 joice65@hotmail.com)

· *Tomas Poil* Fudge. (Station House, Ballivor, Co. Meath. ☎ 086-256 6542 neue@indigo.ie)

· *Twine Incorporated* Sauces and Marinades. (The Wicklow Enterprise Park, The Murrough, Wicklow Town ☎ 0404-66433 twineinc@eircom.net)

· *Ariosa Coffee* Coffee. (The Brook, Racehill, Ashbourne, Co. Meath ☎ 01-835 3078 info@ariosacoffee.com)

· *Stephen Kavanagh* Shellfish. (BeechGrove, Ferrybank, Arklow, Co. Wicklow ☎ 0402-29315 info@fishoutofwater.ie)

· *Liz Keegan* Eggs. (Ballinagee House, Enniskerry, Co Wicklow ☎ 01-286 9154 elisk@gofree.indigo.ie

DUBLIN

Kitchenware

● Sweeney O'Rourke

This catering supply specialist store doesn't just sell to the trade, so if you have decided that your kitchen needs a heavy duty deep-fat fryer or an extensive bain-marie, you will find it here first. Every imaginable kitchen item is here. (34 Pearse St, D2 ☎ 01-677 7212 www.sweeneyorourke.com)

Restaurant

● The Tea Room

The Tea Room, part of the stylish, U2-owned Clarence Hotel, is the most gorgeous dining room in the city and, with chef Antony Ely at the stoves, it is also home to some of Dublin's best cooking. Mr Ely's secret is to take gutsy ingredients – turnip and potato soup with black pudding straws; partridge with green beans and lentil vinaigrette; monkfish with Savoy cabbage and white beans; lamb neck with potato, carrot and onions – and then to concentrate on giving them a lush, sensual texture. No one can match him in this complex business of making a culinary silk purse out of a sow's ears, and it makes for thrilling eating, in what is the city's great date restaurant. (The Clarence Hotel, 6-8 Wellington Quay, D2 ☎ 01-407 0800 www.theclarence.ie — Open Breakfast, Lunch & Dinner)

Restaurant

● Thornton's

People may quibble about the atmosphere and the ambience, and they may get alarmed about the size of the bill it is possible to acquire in Thornton's without pushing the boat out. But no one disagrees about the passion for cre-ative cooking that drives chef-patron Kevin Thornton. The most garlanded chef in Ireland, his work has the pure pur-pose and focus of all great art and, like great artists, he can be deeply misunderstood by people who can't quite accept his uncompromising artistic vision.

The cooking is sui generis: the classic bacon and cabbage terrine with morel vinaigrette; sautéed foie gras with scallops; loin and ballotine of rabbit with fava beans and a pea-green sauce; Spanish black pig with celeriac mousse and fondant potatoes; cherry clafoutis with griotte ice cream. Flavours are razor sharp, presentation is transcendent, service is assured. (Fitzwilliam Hotel, St. Stephen's Green, D2, ☎ 01-478 7008 www.thorntonsrestaurant.com — Open Lunch & Dinner)

North Dublin

Clontarf, D3

Restaurant
● Kinara

Kinara is another example of the new breed of more sophisticated and refined Indian restaurants emerging in Dublin, notwithstanding its rather embarrassing costumed and turbaned front doorman. The food really rocks: splendid tandoori quail; mildly-spiced organic chicken wins out in murghi piaz; excellent biryani and terrific rotis. And don't miss the stellar dessert that is their own vanilla ice cream nuggeted with pistachios and caramel, a real star. (318 Clontarf Road, D3 ☎ 01-833 6759 www.kinara.ie — Open Lunch & Dinner)

Shop
● Nolan's
Nolan's is a superb, independent supermarket, offering the Northside the same quirky and choice sensibility that southsiders find in Morton's of Ranelagh. Vital. (49 Vernon Ave, Clontarf, D3 ☎ 01-833 8361)

Finglas, D11

Restaurant
● Dunn's of Dublin

Peter Dunn's family firm is one of the longest-established fish traders in the country, but they are of particular interest to food lovers on account of their smoked wild Irish salmon, which is one of the four members of the Slow Food Presidia. The fish is dry salted, then smoked using oak and the Torrey kiln method. The resulting flavours are buttery and eggy, with hints of hazelnuts and lemons. You will find the wild smoked salmon in good shops and supermarkets (Jamestown Business Park, Finglas, D11 ☎ 01-864 3100 www.dunns.ie)

Glasnevin, D9

Restaurant
● Anderson's

Continental cosmopolitan culinary culture comes to D9, and about time too. Anderson's is a beaut: a beautiful room that was converted from an old butcher's shop, filled with beautiful things to eat and drink, and boasting a serene and relaxing ambience, great staff, great sounds, great coffee. Noel Delaney and Patricia van der Velde's achievement, in bringing a little slice of San Sebastian, or Lugano, or Trieste, to this neck of the woods is considerable.
Anderson's works because it doesn't simply feel like a collection of design and food ideas pulled together. It feels organically created from a very sharp vision of just how you should serve food and wine: farmhouse cheeses; superb coffee; charcuterie plates; a good kid's menu, real focaccia and ciabatta sandwiches. Only brilliant. (3 The Rise, Glasnevin, D9 ☎ 01-837 8394 www.andersons.ie — Open Day-time and early-Evening)

Wine Merchant
● French Wine Unlimited

Alain Delhomme's company has a quirky list of French wines, and some Alsatian superstars from outstanding producers like Bruno Zorge, Domaine Josmeyer and the controversial and brilliant Jean-Michel Deiss. The wines are really sparky – Domaine de l'Espigouette is a punchy red Rhone, its style matched by the lovely Domaine Saint Amant La Borry, another lean Rhone Ranger with great typicity. The Sancerre Moulin des Vrillieres is flighty and fun, and the list has many more such wines which makes FWU a company well worth exploring. (Glasnevin Business Centre, Ballyboggan Rd, D9 ☎ 01-882 7656)

Killester, D5

Wine Merchant
● **RM Wines**

Mary Egan's wine company imports their portfolio direct
from Germany – RM stands for Rhein-Main – and they have
some real winners: just try an aged Auslese such as the
1993 Zur Schwane Riesling and the fabulous viscosity, the
deep gold colour and the youthful crispness of the wine will
blow you away. Another Auslese, from Hans Wirsching, again
shows that lush viscosity, and throughout the range there is
character, quirkiness and difference. Log on for their
newsletter, and order up a mixed case of idiosyncratic and
impressive modern German winemaking. (119 St. Brigid's
Grove, Killester, D5 ☎ 01-633 5923 www.rm-wines.com)

North County Dublin

Howth

Restaurant
● **Aqua**

Aqua is nothing more than a good, grown-up restaurant,
and Northsiders thank their lucky stars for that. It offers
service, value, consistency and creative cooking, along with
some of the best aquatic views you can find. Classy cooking
from Brian Daly brings people back time and again: salmon
with asparagus and chive beurre blanc; turbot with sauce
vierge; duck confit with figs and sherry dressing, lobster
with lemon and chilli, rock-steady food. (1 West Pier,
Howth, Co Dublin ☎ 01-832 0690 www.aqua.ie — Open
Lunch & Dinner)

Traiteur
● **Cibo**

Deborah Hughes and Brian Hearne offer glorious ready-to-
go food that is pre-packed and chilled for home reheating,
so Cibo has quickly become a favourite for pit-stop dinners
and pit-stop diners. An Italian influence is paramount,
making for good bruschetta, and there is blue cheese

gnocchi, a fine spinach and salmon florentine, and even can-tuccini biscuits and vin santo to take care of dessert. (1a Harbour Road, Howth ☎ 01-839 6271 cibofoodco@hotmail.com)

Restaurant
● Ella Wine Bar

Good cooking, good service, great wines – no wonder the good folk of Howth have taken Ella to their hearts and minds. Seared tiger prawns with white wine and a parsley butter sauce; steamed John Dory on mash with crab hollandaise; fillet of beef with mushroom and port jus – this is logical, hip cooking and its popularity is deserved. (7 Main Street, Howth ☎ 01-839 6264 — Open Lunch & Dinner)

Fish Shop
● Nicky's Plaice

One of the finest places to buy fish in the city and county, Nicky McLoughlin's little wooden shed on Howth pier attracts the piscine cognoscenti, who will make the trip all the way to the end of the pier to get the freshest fish possible, and who cherish the fact that the fish is sold with skill and understanding. Nicky's little improvised smokehouse also makes for some fine smoked salmon. (West Pier, Howth ☎ 01-832 3557)

Malahide

Restaurant
● Bon Appetit

Old school is good school for Patsy McGuirk. There is nothing remotely cutting-edge about Bon Appetit, either in its name, its design, or its cooking. But you will have to book well in advance to get a table here at weekends, and the rest of the time BA is busy with food-loving Northsiders for whom this is a well-loved and well-respected destination. Prawn bisque; sole on the bone; duckling with Grand Marnier, these dishes are so proudly old hat that they are, today, chapeau chic. (9 St James Terrace, Malahide ☎ 01-845 0314 www.bonappetit.ie — Open Lunch & Dinner)

Delicatessen
● Foodware Store

Every neighbourhood needs a Foodware Store. Aisling Boyle's shop has a selection of foods that boasts quality and flavour – home-cooked breads; cheeses from Sheridan's; a fantastic salad bar where you make your choice and then Aisling dresses the salad for you – and their ready-to-go meals are splendid tasty dishes such as lamb korma with sweet potatoes. Savoury snacks such as pâtés and sausage rolls are ace, their roast hams are fab, and they even have the wines you need to make every bite a delight. Smart cooks who wish to conserve precious energy should note the great party service, which can even come up with extra crockery and whatever else you might need. (Old Street, Malahide ☎ 01-845 1830 www.thefoodwarestore.ie)

Restaurant
● Hush

Jason McCabe's cooking in the re-christened Hush is big and generous in portions and in flavours — warm salad of tiger prawns and scallops with sweet chilli jam; an excellent beef burger and fries; lobster fettucini, beef fajitas. The room is now bright and airy, the casual tone feels right, and value is very good. (12a New Street, Malahide ☎ 01-806 1928 — Open Lunch & Dinner)

Farmer's Market
● Malahide Farmers' Market

This new market has already established itself as a fantastic northside venue for serious food discoveries: free-range meats; fresh breads; farmhouse cheeses; organic fruit and vegetables; a whole range of artisan foods from chocolates to wild game; and there are also fresh flowers and crafts. (Saturday 10am-4pm, Church Street, side of St Sylvester's GAA hall, Malahide)

Portmarnock

Wine Shop
● Jus de Vine

Tommy Cullen's wine shop has got it all: a massive range of wines from superstars through to modest quaffers, with

DUBLIN

particularly fine selections from Bordeaux, Burgundy and the owner's favourite Rhone Valley. And then there is all the stuff you need to make drinking these fine wines extra-special: superb glasses, decanters, coasters, openers, you name it, and there are cheeses, chocolates, pâtés and other delectables to challenge your resolve. Tommy also offers a gift service and features an en primeur list.
(7 Portmarnock Town Centre, ☎ 01-846 1192)

Restaurant
● The Osborne Restaurant

Mark Roe's cooking in the Osborne Restaurant has continued the recipe for acclaim created here by his predecessor, Stefan Matz. His cuisine is ambitious, stylish, award-winning stuff – like Matz, Roe has won the Moreau Chablis Fish Cookery Award – and that success, with a dish of seared sea bass with jerusalem artichoke and beetroot tortellini, served with an oyster, saffron and chablis cappuccino, lets you know the sort of intricate, cheffy – and pricey – work that Roe and his crew are producing. The restaurant is firmly bourgeois in style and service, part of the large Portmarnock Hotel. (Portmarnock Hotel and Golf Links, Portmarnock ☎ 01-846-0611
www.portmarnock.com/restaurants/osborne.asp — Open Dinner)

Raheny

Restaurant
● Il Fornaio

Good pizzas, nice bruschetta, some fine pastas, that's the simple, modest and pleasingly authentic repertoire of Il Fornaio. Late Sunday morning is the locals' favourite time to chill out with the family. (55 Kilbarrack Rd, Raheny ☎ 01-832 0277 — Open Lunch & Dinner)

Skerries

Restaurant
● The Red Bank

Terry McCoy is one of that much-respected tribe of elder culinary statesmen of North Dublin. Along with chefs such

as Aidan McManus and Patsy McGuirk, people like Mr
McCoy seem ageless, always inventive, always quirky. The
Red Bank cooks and serves fish in the traditional style, has
a smashing dessert trolley, an excellent wine list, and there
are 18 comfortable rooms in The Red Bank Lodge, for
those who want to make a night of it and escape up-county
to Skerries. (5-7 Church Street, Skerries ☎ 01-849 1005
www.redbank.ie — Open Dinner & Sun Lunch)

Swords

Café
● The Chuck Wagon

It hasn't gone away, you know. Martin Crosby's legendary
Chuck Wagon, with its heroic bacon and sausage soda
bread sandwiches – and a few other fatty, sweet, artery-
surging other savouries – is still in business, despite having
been by-passed by the new Dublin-Belfast motorway. If you
wonder why so many truckers divert off the main
motorway, it's because they are heading to the Chuck
wagon. The grub – especially those legendary sausage and
bacon soda bread sarnies – and the service remain as joyfully salubrious as ever. Worth a detour? Too right. (N1 Dual
Carriageway, Swords — Open Day-time)

DUBLIN

Wine Merchant
● The Lord Mayor's

This is a good wine shop and off licence, smack in the
centre of the town, and a slow browse will reveal lots of
interesting bottles. (Dublin Rd, Swords
☎ 01-840 9662)

Restaurant
● The Old Schoolhouse

Chef Paul Lewis and owner Brian Sinclair are a rock-steady
team of professionals, and their cooking and service has
kept TOS at the centre of eating and drinking in Swords, as
the village has become a town and gone on to become a
supertown. Professionalism is the byword here and it's a
quality and an attribute one can never tire of.
(Coolbanagher, Swords, ☎ 01-840 2846
www.oldschoolhouse.ie — Open Lunch & Dinner)

South Dublin

Ballsbridge

Café
● Bianconi

This is a bright, calm, and very popular room in which to enjoy a breakfast of good coffee and fresh juices, or a bowl of ice cream at any time of the day. (232 Merrion Rd, D4 ☎ 01-219 6033 — Open Day-time)

Restaurant
● The French Paradox

No one can resist the FP. A tiny space with a big heart, they do simple food, gorgeous wines, and they do it with style. Downstairs, behind the wine shop, they have created a new eating space with a few tables and stools, whilst the upstairs restaurant remains cramped and jam-packed. The food is simple and precise – composed salads of foie gras in various ways; nice fresh salads; cured meats; smoked fish; camembert fondue – and the wines, two dozen of which are available by the glass, are only magic: don't miss the Domaine de Jonquieres or the fine Menetou Salon from Fouassier. (53 Shelbourne Rd, Ballsbridge, D4 ☎ 01-660 4068 www.thefrenchparadox.com)

Restaurant
● The Lobster Pot

Like a favourite book, or a favourite piece of music, the Lobster Pot is eternally inviting, eternally unchanging, always delighting. Tommy Crean and his crew offer goujonnettes of sole; prawn bisque; sole on the bone; lobster à la maison; coquille St. Jacque, and if you are tired of these classic dishes, you are tired of life. Timeless. (9 Ballsbridge Tce, Ballsbridge, D4 ☎ 01-668 0025 www.thelobsterpot.ie — Open Lunch & Dinner)

Restaurant
● O'Connell's

Here's how good Tom O'Connell's restaurant is: last time we visited this bustling and busy basement the ages of our party ranged from 5

On top of their game

DUBLIN

to 75. And everyone – but everyone – had a fantastic time, enjoyed fantastic food, and would have happily gone back the following day and done it all again. Can there really be a restaurant that caters successfully for everyone from five to 75? There can be, and there is: O'Connell's. For the record, we ate everything from Ashe's Annascaul black pudding with apple compote to Pistachio Bavarian cream, with special mention for the chicken with carrot puree, the Irish pork with buttered cabbage, and a very fine sirloin steak. (Merrion Road, Ballsbridge, D4 ☎ 01-647 3304 www.oconnellsballsbridge.com — Open B'fast, Lunch & Dinner)

Restaurant
● Roly's

Dublin's most boisterous bistro is really a brasserie, and a great brasserie at that. Its secret is a room that always feels special, and that makes you feel special, and Paul Cartwright's well-crafted classical cooking just piles on the pleasure – breast of duck with grilled polenta; fillet of beef with black pepper potato cake; roast monkfish with roasted peppers; summer pudding with fresh berries. Owner Colin O'Daly would be given the freedom of the city by a decent administration: take that as a hint. (7 Ballsbridge Tce, Ballsbridge, D4 ☎ 01-668 2611 www.rolysbistro.ie — Open Lunch & Dinner)

Canalside

Restaurant
● Frank's Bar & Restaurant

Liz Mee and John Hayes are amongst the most important people in Irish food. When they established the Elephant & Castle in Temple Bar – it's still trading with great success – they created the idea of Temple Bar, they showed that you could serve creative food seven days a week, all day long, and they helped to make the restaurant experience in Dublin a democratic, living experience, rather than a stuffed-shirt bourgeois blow-out.

With the handsome Frank's Bar and Restaurant, they have made a new agenda for the new century. Frank's is pretty much about First Principles: potted shrimps with Poilane toast; steak tartare with green salad; lemon and thyme chicken with spinach and mash; rice pudding with prunes; petit pot au chocolat. Food as simple as this needs pristine ingredients and pristine execution, and in Frank's the food gets both, and the punters get one of the great new Dublin destinations. The E&C was the heart of Temple Bar; Frank's will be heart of the new Southside Dockside. (The Malting Tower, Grand Canal Quay, D2 ☎ 01-662 5870 www.franksbarandrestaurant.com — Open Lunch & Dinner)

Delicatessen
● Haddington Delicatessen

Rachel Keane's deli is a wee beauty. Smartly sourcing key ingredients for the shelves from veterans such as Sheridan's and Country Choice gives the deli section a head start – and shows Ms Keane's savvy – and then Rachel and Shelley lay on the content with good scones, their own baked hams, great sandwiches and crisp, fresh salads and soups. Splendid. (53 Haddington Road, D4 ☎ 01-667 6685 www.haddingtondeli.ie)

Restaurant & Wine Merchant
● Ciao Café & Vaughan Johnson

This second Dublin branch of the VJ chain of wine shops – the first is in Temple Bar – is tucked in at the back of Ciao, a humungously busy café-restaurant that packs in the office workers of Baggot Street. The wine shop is small, and the last time we were in the service was so charmingly helpful we wound up buying a mixed case of South African specials. The wines are also served in Ciao, an efficient, airy space, also owned by Emmet Memery, where the core offer is antipasti plates, risotto and some tasty pies. (Baggot Street Bridge, D4 ☎ 01-799 6326 — Open Day-time)

Restaurant
● Oddbins

The Baggot Street branch is the tiniest of the Oddbins' Dublin troupe, and is dwarfed by both Blackrock and the cavernous Blanchardstown shops. Changes in ownership have robbed the chain of the extraordinary dynamic it enjoyed back in the 1980's, but there are still great wines to be discovered, and a sympathetic parent could see them recovering old glories. (17 Baggot Street Upr, D4 ☎ 01-667 3033 www.oddbins.com/storefinder/Ireland.asp)

DUBLIN

Clonskeagh

Restaurant
● The Olive Tree

The Olive Tree might seem like a surreal destination in sub-urban Clonskeagh – it's part of the Islamic Cultural Centre – but there is nothing surreal about the superb Lebanese-Syrian-Iraqi food that the kitchens prepare. The cold buffet is mouthwatering, their couscous dishes delectable and the long-braised meat dishes are simply top notch. Amazing value, and amazing food. (19 Roebuck Rd, D14 ☎ 01-208 0006 Open day-time. No credit cards)

Donnybrook

Shop
● Donnybrook Fair

The southsider's Harvey Nick's is a swish, cool retailing space that sells everything a time-poor executive could need to conjure up a decent dinner at 9pm. DF doesn't have the character or personal charm of Morton's of Ranelagh, but it does manage to offer a level of service miles higher than any supermarket, and their cool bags are definitely a bourgeois badge of choice. (91 Morehampton Rd, Donnybrook, D4 ☎ 01-668 3556)

Traiteur
● Douglas Food Co

The DFC is the quintessential traiteur, as stylish as Fauchon, with truly accomplished cooking prepared by Grainne Murphy's team every day – pork terrine with prunes and apricots; vegetable terrine with basil; Thai chicken with coriander; lamb and apricot tagine; gratin dauphinois; Normandy apple tart. The sandwiches at lunchtime are just as stylish and as fine as everything else. (53 Main St, Donnybrook, D4 ☎ 01-269 4066)

Restaurant
● Ernie's

Every city needs old reliables like Ernie's, a restaurant which, like The Lobster Pot in Ballsbridge, operates outside of the fashion element that drives so many restaurant destinations. Good value and good service and a good, recently made-over, room form the background for reliable, classical cooking: poached Connemara salmon; grilled rib-eye; Wicklow lamb shank; treacle tart. (Mulberry Gardens, Donnybrook, D4 ☎ 01-269 3300 — Open Lunch & Dinner)

Restaurant
● Roy Fox Gourmet Foods

Des Donnelly's emporium is one of the city's great destinations for fruit and veg, not to mention most everything else a keen cook could ever need. And it's also a place where the art of good, helpful, charming service is seen at its pinnacle. (49a Main St, Donnybrook, D4 ☎ 01-269 2892)

Restaurant
● Furama

Great cooking and a great room make Furama one of the ultimate date restaurants, and the discreet, sophisticated staff strike just the right note of unintrusive formality. Flavours are energetic and fresh in classic dishes such as salt and pepper squid or prawns with black bean sauce, and whilst some may find the tastes a little Westernised, Furama is always reliably enjoyable, albeit expensive. (Ground Floor, Eirpage House, Donnybrook Main Road, D4 ☎ 01-283 0522 www.furama.ie)

Wine Merchant
● O'Brien's Wines

Brendan O'Brien's chain of wine shops has been in explosively energetic form in recent years, opening store after store throughout Leinster. You blink, and there is a brand new shop in Navan. Blink again, and that cute store in Drogheda is up and running, and meantime Rathmines is smartened up and Dun Laoghaire is packed with good things. There are currently nearly 20 stores, and the range of wines offered is staggering, running from the big brands through to – the best bit – their own imports and discoveries. The energy is with this company right now, and you can sense it in the tangible engagement and energy of the staff, who provide a great service, no matter which store you choose. (30 Donnybrook Road, D4 ☎ 01-269 3310 www.obrienswine.ie)

Wine Merchant
● Terroirs

Terroirs has been ten years in the ageing and maturing, but Sean and Francoise Gilley's bespoke wine shop remains as meticulous and as focused as ever, with just a few nuances of experience to mellow and polish the service and the style.

That style is important: Terroirs is really a boutique wine shop, and in a city with many great places to buy wine, that style has meant that Terroirs has always remained distinct, different and, as such, always delightful. Neither fashion nor age can alter it, thank heavens.

Meanwhile the foods, goods and chocolates imported from France are all impeccably delicious. (103 Morehampton Rd, Donnybrook, D4 ☎ 01-667 1311 www.terroirs.ie)

Portobello

Bakery
● Bretzel Bakery

Even with a change in ownership, nothing has changed in the Bretzel in decades, and the onion breads, bagels and rye breads, not to mention the sweet and sticky treats, are always welcome, and nostalgically enjoyable. (1a Lennox Street, Sth Circular Rd, D8 ☎ 01-475 2742)

Delicatessen
● East

Abrahim and Aoife Ali's neat little deli and store has lots of good eastern specialities, from baklava to couscous to hummus to stuffed vine leaves to Moroccan anchovies. Their sister store, Spiceland, just around the corner, is a great stop for ethnic specialities. (22a Sth Richmond St, D2 ☎ 01-475 7066)

Shop
● El Sinbad

We love the delicate little pastries you find in Sameh Goumaa's shop, and the feta he sells is amongst the finest you will find. A real treasure trove of an emporium. (Sth Richmond St, D2 ☎ 01-478 5358)

DUBLIN

Restaurant
● Locks

A canalside stalwart for many years, Locks is super-profes-
sional, a special room run with great skill by the team out
front. Alan Kinsella has modernised the cooking, but Locks
remains an elegant, classically bourgeois destination. (1
Windsor Tce, Portobello, D8 ☎ 01-453 8352 — Open
Lunch & Dinner)

Shop
● Spiceland

Portobello is rich in ethnic shops, and this is the busiest of
them all, combining a halal butcher, with a freezer of warm
water fish, and wonderful pastries, plus a wealth of other
gear. Get out those cookery books! (4 Sth Richmond St, D2
☎ 01-475 0422)

Ranelagh

Restaurant
● The Best of Italy

Everything you need Italian-wise, is piled-high and higgledy-
piggledy in The Best of Italy, indeed the contents of the
shop spill out onto the street where they are housed under
some trellising. (37 Dunville Ave, Ranelagh, D6 ☎ 01-497 3411)

Wine Merchant
● Brechin Watchorn

BW looks more like a couture salon than a wine shop and,
as such, it is a perfect fit with all the other stylish addresses
on Dunville Ave. There is plenty to suit the pockets of the
local tribunal barristers, but look out for their quirky stuff
from Roussillon and the pays Catalan – Chateau la
Casenove, Dominis M – or Chateau d'Exindre from the
Languedoc, wines with the same stylish attitude as owners
Stuart Brechin and Gavin Watchorn. (9 Dunville Ave,
Ranelagh, D6 ☎ 01-491 1763 www.brechinwatchornwine.com)

Restaurant
● Mint

Oliver Dunne's cooking has made Mint the critical darling of the moment, and it's easy to see how his snazzy, avant-garde cuisine burst with a bang into sedate Ranelagh. Saddle of venison has a turnip and prune gratin. Sea bream has a pied de mouton foam. Panna cotta here is made with goat's cheese. Scallops have a fish jus to counterpoint their Clonakilty black pudding partner. This is provocative, purposeful stuff and, thanks to assured execution, it has been met with a welcoming big WOW! This cooking is grown up, and wonderful, and whilst prices are high, it's worth every cent. Mr Dunne has all it takes to be a major player. (47 Ranelagh Village, D6 ☎ 01-497 8655 — Open Lunch & Dinner)

Shop
● Morton's

A second branch of Morton's has opened under Eric Morton's control in Salthill in Galway, whilst the old lady of Dunville Avenue sails ever on, gracious, choice, serene, choosy, superlative. It's not fair to describe Morton's as a supermarket, for where supermarkets are trashy, Morton's is classy. It's a boutique emporium of fine foods, fine wines, superb service, a place that respects the great traditions of sourcing carefully, selling what you know and trust, and serving customers with patience and respect. Priceless. (15-17 Dunville Ave, D6 ☎ 01-497 1913 www.mortons.ie)

Off Licence
● Redmond's of Ranelagh

Jim and Aidan Redmond's shop is one of those singular addresses that is truly a sport of nature: nowhere else is quite like it. And, like a true sport, it keeps morphing, mutating, evolving, or, to put it simply, it just keeps on getting better. The commonplace of the wine world is here along with the arcane, the obscure, the rare, the special occasion bottle that has your name on it. It has always been a great neighbourhood shop – some folk buy nothing but beer in here – but it's much more than that: Redmond's is a great shop, full stop. (25 Ranelagh Village, D6 ☎ 01-496 0552)

Restaurant
● Tribeca

Ger Foote and Trevor Browne's Tribeca has opened a

second branch in Stillorgan, and this little chain is responding to the zeitgeist whereby people want relaxed food at decent prices in modern, unpretentious rooms. The cooking draws down all the current global failsafes – buffalo wings, nachos, Thai chicken salad; shrimp BLT, ricotta hotcakes; char-grilled burger, noodle salads – and it's very popular with a young crowd. (146 Upr Leeson St, D2 ☎ 01-664 2135 www.tribeca.ie — Open Lunch & Dinner)

Rathgar

Restaurant
● Poppadom

As with so many Indian restaurants, Poppadom has begun to create a small chain of branches, with a take-away branch at Newland's Cross and a sister restaurant in Limerick and Sligo, addresses which aim to match the high standard of the original.. (91a Rathgar Rd, D6 ☎ 01-490 2383 — Open Dinner)

Wine Merchant
● The Vintry

Think of all the things a good wine shop should do – sell good wine knowledgeably, organise wine courses, have a good delivery service, have all the requisite wine accessories – and, happily, Evelyn Jones's shop does all of these things, which is why it is one of the capital's best places to buy wine, learn about wine, and learn about the culture and enjoyment of wine. Great wines, ports and sherries, and splendid beers, and truly great service. (102 Rathgar Rd, D6 ☎ 01-490 5477 www.vintry.com)

Rathmines

Restaurant
● Crema

"If I try to take something off the menu, people say to me 'That's ridiculous!" says Terry Fitzgerald. So, Crema's menu never changes and Terry and the crew have been cooking the same things: great burritos, hash, soups, fine cakes, for nine years. (312 Lower Rathmines Rd, D6 ☎ 01-496 5555)

Patisserie
● Fothergills

Tom O'Connor and the ever-effervescent Carmel – who after 17 years of devoted good service and good humour behind the counter has earned the title of "Mrs Fothergill"– continue to power this vital emporium with good taste and good cooking. Celebrated for decades for excellent sweet baking, this is the place to find great gateaux such as the lovely Opera, classic Gateau Diane, their signature lemon mousse cake, or a fine mixed berry tiramisu. (141 Rathmines Rd Upr, D6 ☎ 01-496 2511)

Shop
● Hennessy's Food Store

John and Pauline's special little store, in the gormet belt of Upper Rathmines, is home to shelfloads of well-chosen, esential goods, sold with a sincere smile and good grace. (151 Rathmines Rd Upr, D6 ☎ 01-496 2636)

Ringsend

Shop
● The Good Food Store

Vanessa Clarke's GFS boasts the confident grasp of an owner who knows just what good food is: carefully sourced, carefully chosen, carefully presented, all the better to be good food that is good for you and makes you feel good. (16 Gordon St, Ringsend, D6 ☎ 01-668 4514 goodfood@eircom.net)

Terenure

Butcher
● J Downey & Son

John and Mark Downey's butcher's shop has 50 years of service to the good people of Dublin under its belt, more than half of that in their shop in Terenure. They have long been famous for a particularly outstanding spiced beef and very fine corned beef, and the move towards selling organic meats has given them a further quality edge.

Downeys is also a brilliant destination for those seeking something unusual, from suckling pig to bison, and the shop always has an energised, lively feel. (27 Terenure Rd East, D6W ☎ 01-490 9239 www.organicfoodsireland.com)

Butcher
● Danny O'Toole

Danny O'Toole sells organic meat, and marries the quality of his raw product with enviable charcuterie skills. It would be fair to say that his shops – the second is in Glasthule – take an holistic approach to buying and selling meat and poultry, and it's an approach that people crave and need, as is evidenced by the huge amount of money that people spend in the shops. Service, attitude and the sheer quality of the meat all make you feel special. (138 Terenure Rd, Nth, D6W ☎ 01-490 5457)

South County Dublin

Blackrock

Traiteur
● Butler's Pantry

Eileen Bergin's Butler's Pantry was the original Dublin trai-teur, nearly 20 years ago, and since they first opened, the company has never stood still. Today, there are four shops – two in Blackrock, one in Donnybrook and one in Bray where their production is based – and their foods-to-go can be found in supermarkets and many more deli and wine shop outlets. Head chef Niall Hill sees that the range is con-sistently updated and changes with the seasons, and this sort of bespoke approach is exactly what has made BP such a success. They innovate – most recently the range of pantry basics – they cook creatively, they source carefully, they are the CCTT's dream. (53 Mt Merrion Ave, Blackrock ☎ 01-288 5505; 1 Montpelier Pl, D'Laoghaire ☎ 01-284 3933)

Wine Importer
● Burgundy Direct

Conor Richardson's bespoke wine company is a real gem.

They don't sell only Burgundies, despite their name, having branched out in recent years to trade in Italian wines, in particular, along with some Spanish varietals. But, those Burgundies are really special – we would walk a country mile for the Domaine Joblot Givry, with its luxurious, sensual colour and magical flavours, not to mention the Domaine Corison Saint Veran with its quintessential Burgundy qualities of butter and honey. The Italian wines show Mr Richardson's discrimination is just as keen when he moves away from Burgundy, and the wines from S.W. France are just as perspicacious and just as special. (8 Monaloe Way, Blackrock ☎ 01-289 6615 www.burgundydirect.ie)

Patisserie
● Cakes & Co

Joannie Langbroek and Rosanna Mulligan's supremely artful cake shop is one of the cult choices of Dublin food lovers when it comes to creating masterfully imagined cakes for a special private or corporate event. Their skill with sugarcraft is intense, allowing them to create any and every manner of pictorial representation to celebrate and commemorate any special occasion. But, it's not only pictures; these cakes are edible, and deliciously so at that. (Jane Cottage, Newtownpark Ave, Blackrock ☎ 01-283 6544 www.cakesandco.com)

Restaurant
● Farmers' Market, Blackrock

The farmers' market at Blackrock Park is just the newest arrival amongst the wave of east coast markets. Old favourites are here, but also new arrivals, such as Colin Fitzpatrick with his apple juices, coffee-roaster Michael Kelly with his brews, amongst others. Friday from 10am is when you need to be there with your shopping basket.

Wine Merchant
● McCabe's

Jim and John McCabe's great wine shop on Mount Merrion Avenue has been joined by new ventures in the city, on Harcourt Street, and in Foxrock, where the shop is paired with The Gables restaurant. The original remains the best, however, a sleek and stylish emporium that wears its years well, and which houses a stupendous selection of wines. McCabes are strong though every wine country and through every wine region, but it's not just the jaw-dropping selection that is impressive here. Like the best people in the world of wine, McCabe's understand that it's not just about selling bottles of plonk, so what you will get here also is the culture of the wine world, all the fun business of their wine club, tastings both small-scale and large-scale, and all the help and advice you need. (51-55 Mount Merrion Ave, ☎ 01-288 2037 www.mccabeswines.ie)

Cookery School
● Valentia Cookery

Lynda Booth's cookery school feature guest chefs in addition to the demonstration classes given by the boss herself. Neven Maguire, of Cavan's MacNean Bistro, is a regular performer, Antony Ely of The Tea Room is another, whilst Edinburgh's acclaimed Martin Wishart has also wowed! the regulars.

Lynda's classes take place on Friday evenings and Saturday mornings, covering topics such as Mediterranean cooking, a taste of Italy, barbecues and entertaining, with the longer classes occupying six sessions. (25 Avoca Pk, Blackrock ☎ 01-278 2365)

Dalkey

Wine Merchant
● On the Grapevine

Pamela Cooney's shop, just off Dalkey's main strip, is part of the Cabot & Co empire, which includes not just the Cabot wine shops in Dublin and Westport, but also a wine importing business, Wineknows. As one would expect from the Cabot organisation, the entire culture of the wine world is here: the most idiosyncratic wines, every manner of wine accessory and, best of all, that deep knowledge and background that solve anyone's problems when it comes to buying the right bottle. (21 St Patrick's Rd, Dalkey ☎ 01-235 3054 www.onthegrapevine.ie)

Café
● Idle Wilde Cafe

Snappy, polite, helpful service is the Idle Wilde USP, and it ensures this room is always bright and busy with locals

enjoying good coffee and some tasty savoury foods. There is
a real sense of team spirit exuded by the staff, so whether
you are grabbing some quick caffeine or lingering with the
girls longtime, Idle Wilde works either way. (20 St. Patrick's
Rd, Dalkey ☎ 01-235 4501)

Pub
● IN

Smack on the corner at the end of the village, IN has
carved out a reputation for good quality pub food that
belongs more to the gastro-pub generation than to the
toasted ham 'n' cheese brigade. It can be over-ambitious at
times, but when in the groove, IN makes for an excellent
Dalkey destination. (Coliemore Rd, Dalkey ☎ 01-275 0007
www.indalkey.ie — Open Lunch & Dinner)

Restaurant
● Nosh

Nosh is such a gorgeous room that even before you have
sat down in the Farrell sisters' café your spirit is uplifted:
this is one of the sexiest rooms to eat anywhere in the
county.
The cooking has the same sense of uncluttered logic and
rigorous style as the room, good timeless fare that you
simply can't tire of: grilled mussels with lemon, garlic and
parsley; goat's cheese tartlet; roast cornfed chicken; sea bass
with Parmesan and sage; sticky date pudding, and weekend
brunches perhaps see the room at its very best. Nosh is the
local hero. (111 Coliemore Rd, Dalkey ☎ 01-284 0666 —
Open Lunch & Dinner www.nosh.ie)

Restaurant
● PD's Woodhouse

Peter White and Helen Argyle's restaurant has been pleasing
the people of Dalkey for a decade now, their ever-reliable
format of oak wood-grilled dishes and an intimate room an
alluring proposition on any occasion. (1 Coliemore Rd,
Dalkey ☎ 01-284 9399 — Open Dinner)

Restaurant
● Ragazzi

Ah! The 1960's all over again! In Ragazzi, the waiters will
flirt with your female date, and pay short shrift to you, as if
they are acting in some sort of pre-feminist, pre-equal

opportunities, macho B-movie. What a blast! And where is Dean Martin? There is food, of course, mainly a pretty standard take on Italian cooking, but most folk go to Ragazzi for the good pizzas and the flirting. That's amoré. (109 Coliemore Rd, Dalkey ☎ 01-274 7280 — Open Dinner)

Restaurant
● Thai House

Tony Ecock has steered the cosy, clubby Thai House with unflustered calm and assurance over the years, the food an always-welcome and always-well-understood Thai cuisine: lots of good, fresh curries; Thai salads such as spicy meat or spicy seafood; noodles and excellent vegetarian choices. This is a solid, service-driven restaurant, always looking to innovate and improve, and do note that value for money, especially for their early bird menus, is terrific. (21 Railway Rd, Dalkey ☎ 01-284 7304)

Delicatessen
● Thyme Out

Berna and David William's tiny deli is a vital Dalkey address, for here is a pair with the real zest and passion for good food. There are fine foods on the shelves, including that rather good bread from La Boulangerie des Gourmets, but it is with the foods coming out of the kitchen that one sees the measure of this pair: choose things as diverse as their excellent chicken liver pâté, or their signature poached chicken in basil and lime juice or their signature, fantastic Tunisian cake, and you see not just great quality, but real flair and care and imagination. Glenillen butter, Rosscarbery rashers and loads of other great artisan foods, and heck they have most everything your heart could desire. Vital. (2a Castle Street, Dalkey ☎ 01-285 1999)

Dun Laoghaire

Farmers' Market
● Dun Laoghaire Farmers' Markets

There are two FM's in Dun Laoghaire: Thursday sees the market taking place down near the ferry terminal, whilst Sunday sees a second market taking place, appropriately enough, in the People's Park. Expect many of the usual

DUBLIN

artisan suspects plus the core of new arrivals who have gal-
vanised the markets in south Dublin. (Ferry Terminal from
10.30am Thursday; People's Park, Sunday, Dun Laoghaire)

Fishmonger
● The Ice Plant

Fresh fish are brought daily from Howth and sold in this
little shed at the very end of the pier. Open Tues-Fri 10am-
5pm and Sat am. (Dun Laoghaire Pier ☎ 01-280 5936)

Shop
● Passion

Hermione Winter's lovely little shop, just up the hill from
the centre of Dun Laoghaire, has all the good stuff: Tea
Merchant teas; Hederman smoked fish; Gubbeen bacon; G's
jams; and the cheese counter is one of the best on the
southside. Helpful, sparky and right-into-it, Hermione and
her crew put the passion in Passion. (104 Patrick St, Dun
Laoghaire ☎ 01-284 6300 www.passion.ie)

Restaurant
● Roly @ The Pavilion

Roly Saul's restaurant is part of the large Pavilion complex,
just across from the yacht club. It's a stylish modern room
and has a devoted local clientèle who appreciate the excellent value for both food and wines. Other addresses in The
Pavilion include a branch of Itsabagel, a branch of Mao and
the chic The Forty Foot. (The Pavilion, Dun Laoghaire ☎ 01-
236 0286 www.rolyatthepav.com — Open Lunch & Dinner)

Foxrock

Restaurant
● Bistro One

There is nice cooking in Bistro One – linguini with organic
mushrooms; east Cork smoked haddock fish cakes with
béarnaise; roast duck with mashed turnips and poached
pear – and it's a welcoming and cosy room. And whilst the
cashmere-and-suits Foxrock set who eat here don't appear
to be troubled by the fact that prices are really rather high,
even a simple mid-week dinner can add up to an alarmingly
high final bill. If you have the largesse, however, then apart

from the fact that service can be a little disorganised, this is a fine neighbourhood restaurant. (3 Brighton Road, Foxrock Village, D18 ☎ 01-289 7711)

Restaurant
● The Gables

The craic and the buzz and the conviviality of a stylish room is what attracts folk to the Gables, a restaurant and wine shop venture that matches the wine expertise of Jim McCabe with Ann-Marie Nohl's Espresso Cafe culinary background. Wine buffs like the fact that there is a flat fee for corkage after you have chosen a bottle from the wine shop, but whilst the restaurant has won a dedicated following, the cooking needs to find a focus and simplicity that will see it match the fantastic array of wines more suitably. (2 Brighton Rd, Foxrock ☎ 01-289 2689 (wine shop), ☎ 01-289 2174 (restaurant) www.thegables.ie)

Delicatessen
● Thomas's Delicatessen

Thomas's is a very fine deli, a splendid greengrocer, and a very good wine shop, all under the one roof. (4 Brighton Rd, Foxrock ☎ 01-289 4101)

Glasthule

Restaurant
● Caviston's Deli & Seafood Restaurant

Caviston's is the people's darling and the critic's darling. When visiting restaurant writers come to Dublin, they tend to stay city-centre, save for taking the Dart out to Glasthule to marvel at this extraordinary restaurant. Three lunchtime sittings a day, serving the freshest, most delicious fish you can eat, is their formula, and they haven't had to tweak it a jot ever since they opened up back in '97. "It's likely to become your benchmark for good fish cookery in the future", said America's Bon Appetit magazine. Well, hang that above the door. But, Caviston's is not just a restaurant. It is also a splendid fish shop, and a great deli which has all you need and more. Why haven't the Caviston brothers been given the Freedom of Dublin? They deserve it. (59 Glasthule Rd ☎ 01-280 9245 www.cavistons.com — Open Lunch)

GLASTHULE - Co. DUBLIN (SOUTH)

Wine Merchant
● Mitchell's

The southside branch of the benchmark Dublin city wine shop is just as distinguished as its parent branch. Great wines, lovely room, and helpful service make for a vital neighborhood address. (Glasthule Rd ☎ 01-230 2301 www.mitchellandson.com)

Restaurant
● Danny O'Toole

Tom O'Connor heads up this branch of Danny O'Toole's organic meat enterprise, with just as much energy and charisma as the boss himself brings to the Terenure branch. The quality of everything sold here is superb, and we have never seen another butcher's shop where people spend such huge amounts of money on meat. Mr O'Toole's decision to sell only organically-reared meat was brave and visionary, and just what people needed and wanted. (1 Glasthule Rd ☎ 01-284 1125)

Restaurant
● Rasam

Nisheeth Tak's restaurant has one of the most gorgeous interiors, a fabulous agglomeration of furniture and colour that is spiffingly luxurious, and which makes you feel good from the moment you walk up the stairs and leave quotidian Glasthule behind. Prepare to be delighted.
Delight is what you can also expect from the cooking. The menu is not so much "Indian fusion" as a wide representation of dishes from all over the country: Goan fish cakes stuffed with pickled shrimps, served with mango chutney; beef tossed with pathar ke phool (a specially imported Indian herb), garam masala, and a pomegranate reduction, from Kerala. Presentation and execution is excellent, and so is value for money. A major new player. (18/19 Glasthule Rd, ☎ 01-230 0600 www.rasam.ie)

Glenageary

Indian Takeaway
● The Bombay Pantry

The Bombay is one of the best-loved take-aways on the

THE BRIDGESTONE IRISH FOOD GUIDE   **169**

southside. They take their cooking seriously here, so there is no question of getting fast-food quickly: if you turn up, you will have to wait. The quality of the Indian dishes is matched by their consistency: we haven't had a bad dish in years of ordering take-aways from here. (Glenageary Shopping Centre, Glenageary☎ 01-285 6683)

Goatstown

Wine Shop
● Bin No 9

Andy Kinsella's hip wine store is a cult address on the southside, an uber-bling destination tucked away in Goatstown's residential Farmhill Road. To this gorgeous store, Mr Kinsella, who hatched the idea of the shop when working in the world of marketing for Guinness, has brought 500 choice wines from all over the world. Interestingly, much of the focus is not on slick New World wines, but on rarer beasts from Italy, southern France and the ever-more-popular South Africa, proof that it is to these favourite old haunts that wine lovers are turning as the New World wines become more samey. Finding the good stuff is then the work of wine merchants such as Mr Kinsella, and No.9 gives ample proof that he can do just that. (9 Farmhill Rd, Goatstown ☎ 01-2964844)

Leopardstown

Restaurant
● Leopardstown Farmer's Market

Leopardstown gets all funky and cosmopolitan on Fridays when the Farmer's Market rolls into the racecourse. There is Sean Moran, the Tea Merchant, with his oolongs and his orange pekoes, like No 104 Pettiagalla Garden. And there is the Haruko sushi stall. And fresh goat's milk cheeses from Tullynascreena. And Manish breads from Palestine, who are selling baba ghanoush and dagga and hummus as well. There are Wicklow soft fruits and French bread and Mediterranean olives and Irish farmhouse cheeses and Cork sausages and Temple Bar patisserie and real eggs and real yogurts, and doesn't it make you feel good, so good? (Friday 11am-7pm)

DUBLIN

Monkstown

Restaurant
● Caviston's

Stephen Caviston's Monkstown restaurant has an arresting interior, sort of cool-meets-Dada, and the short, fishy menu is an echo of the Glasthule parent which has enjoyed such success. Dishes have provocative pairings – seared haddock with grapefruit and vodka salad; marinated hake in banana leaf; cod with artichoke and caper salsa – but as yet the signature style of the restaurant has yet to emerge. They just need to relax, and to write the menus correctly. (17a Monkstown Cres, Monkstown ☎ 01-284 6012 www.cavistonmonkstown.ie)

Restaurant
● The Purty Kitchen

Locals tend to keep the fine cooking by Sheenagh Toal in the venerable Purty Kitchen a local secret, but this chef deserves a wider audience for cooking that has real élan, and we reckon this local secret won't stay local for too much longer. Ms Toal will match grilled seatrout with seafood sausages and a horseradish mash, for instance, just the sort of hip gastropub cooking that the capital and its suburbs could sure use a whole lot more of. (Old D'Laoghaire Rd ☎ 01-284 3576 www.purtykitchen.com)

Wine Merchant
● Searson's

Glossier, more glamorous wine shops have emerged in Dublin in recent years, splendid emporia which make Charles and Frank Searson's little room seem modest and yesteryear. But, for us, Searson's remains one of the very best wine shops. Service is more than personable, always well-informed and modest and wise, and there isn't a casually-chosen bottle of wine on these shelves: don't miss the 2003 Huia pinot gris, the newly-arrived Stickleback range, the lovely Poggerino chianti, and the Domaine Saint Gayan is a smashing value Côtes-du-Rhône. Value; service; information and a very genuine signature style are all here. And can we use this book to salute the work of Frank Searson, who has retired after half a century sourcing and selling great wines. (6a The Crescent, Monkstown ☎ 01-284 0405)

DUBLIN

Mount Merrion

Shop
● Michael's Food & Wine

This is a great shop, one of those rare addresses that turns the conventional business of retailing on its head. For instance: 70% of the wines Michael Lowe sells are Italian, many of them imported directly by himself. 70% of his customers are female, another curious stat for a wine shop. Except it's not just a wine shop, so don't miss the excellent Italian cheese and salamis and hams, and don't miss the specially blended coffees – Michael hails from the foothills of Mount Kilimanjaro, so coffee is as much a passion as wine. There are plans to open a coffee and wine shop adjacent to the shop, which will make Michael's even more a don't-miss! (57 Deerpark Rd, Mount Merrion ☎ 01-278 0377)

Stillorgan

Restaurant
● China-Sichuan

David Hui's ever-consistent Chinese restaurant has been a safe haven of true ethnic cookery in Dublin for the best part of two decades. Twenty years on, it still packs in the Stillorgan and southside punters, especially at weekends when getting a table can be difficult. It's the sort of place where you can – and should – let them do the ordering for you, and thereby get a taste of the real thing. (4 Lr Kilmacud Rd, Stillorgan ☎ 01-288 4817 — Open Lunch & Dinner)

Restaurant
● Tribeca

The second outpost of Trevor Browne and Ger Foote's Tribeca chain is above the Millhouse pub in Stillorgan, a long way from Tribeca. It's another bright, indeterminate room, with the food that Browne and Foote understand and deliver well: goat's cheese salad; fish cakes Thai-style; designer burgers; buffalo wings; slick pizzas. Browne and Foote are unlikely to stop at two Tribecas, and with the Northside crying out for smart, all-day food stops, expect a slice of N Y soon in your suburb. (1 Lwr Kilmacud Rd ☎ 01-278 6024 www.tribeca.ie — Open Lunch and Dinner)

Tallaght

Coffee & Tea

● Java Republic

David McKiernan's Java Republic coffees are to be seen most everywhere nowadays, a testament to the sheer hard work this passionate guy has invested in building up his business. The coffees have recently been joined by a range of bespoke teas, which have all the distinctiveness and quality of the coffees. McKiernan understands coffee, understands the need for freshness and balance in order to make the best brew, and we have never had a bag of JR that was anything less than perfect. (Citylink Business Park, Old Naas Rd, Tallaght ☎ 01-456 5506 www.javarepublic.com)

Dublin Artisans...

Artisans used to be as rare in Dublin as the city's signature dish – Dublin coddle – is scarce today. But farmers' markets have allowed artisans to go forth, and multiply.

David Llewellyns' apple juices, ciders, and cider vinegars, from Quickpenny Orchard, for instance, exhibit the most precious quality of the artisan producer: they keep getting better and better. The packaging gets better, the varieties get more numerous and creative, and the juices, ciders and cider vinegar show an artisan working craftily, patiently away. The markets have made Mr Llewellyn and his bottles familiar to food loving Dubliners, a situation where producer and consumer both win.

But you will find the same qualities with other Dublin artisan producers. Ed Hick may no longer maintain his butcher's shop in South Dublin, but his ferocious creativity just gets better. Miriam Griffith's Olvi Oils have become a staple of Dublin life, thanks to the farmers Markets. Sabores de Mexico is a staple of funky, exotic, genuine Mexican produce, thanks to Gus and Theresa Hernandez's hard work. From Helene Hemeryck's Chez Emily Chocs to the McNally family's yogurts, the flow of artisans in Dublin is on a roll, and it is the markets from Temple Bar to Marlay Park that have made it happen.

DUBLIN

Dublin A-Z

Cafés, Restaurants & Gastro Bars

Food

Markets

Shops

DUBLIN

Wine & Beer

Cookery School

County Galway

Galway Bay oysters, smoked salmon, Connemara lamb,
woodcock, organic vegetables and fruits, cured duck...

Connemara

Ballinafad

Hotel and Restaurant
● **Ballynahinch Castle**

One hesitates to say that chef Robert Webster and manager Patrick O'Flaherty are at the zenith of their
powers in Ballynahinch. The pair have fast-
forwarded this magnificent, other-worldly
destination into one of the best-loved places
to eat and stay in Ireland so quickly and deci-
sively that one doesn't doubt that they are at
some sort of zenith. But it would be a brave gambler who
would bet that these guys won't get even better.
The service, the cooking, the place: in Ballynahinch, all is of a
one, concordant, comfortable, gracious and grand, but without a jot of pretension. O'Flaherty and Webster have created one of the outstanding addresses, but don't make a mistake and only stay one night: once is not enough. (Ballinafad,
Recess, Connemara ☎ 095-31006
www.ballynahinch-castle.com)

Ballyconneely

Smokehouse
● **The Connemara Smokehouse**

Graham Roberts started working in the family smokehouse
aged 6, and today that wealth of experience
shows in some very accomplished smoked
fish and, most especially, in innovative new
products such as their superb honey roast
smoked tuna. It's a great treat to visit the
smokehouse, which sits at the edge of the
Atlantic ocean, with infinite space all around it, and to
depart, then, with a bag of salmon and honey roast smoked
tuna. (Bunowen Pier, Ballyconneely, Connemara
☎ 095-23739 www.smokehouse.ie)

Clifden

Shop
● The Connemara Hamper

Eileen and Leo Halliday's shop is a beacon in busy Clifden, a place where the good things to eat are collected so that you can come and shop with pleasure. They have a good eye and a sound palate, this pair, and what they collate is always choice, appropriate, delicious. "We happen to like food," says Mr Halliday, and it shows, it sure does. (Market St, Clifden ☎ 095-21054)

B&B
● Dolphin Beach

It's as simple as this: Billy and Barbara Foyle's gorgeous house is one of the most popular addresses in the Bridgestone guides. Great style, great food, astonishing views out over the ocean and, best of all, a feeling of being far, far away from it all, cast adrift out here on the mercurial Sky Road. Dolphin Beach works because it has the space and elegance of a small hotel, with the intimacy of a country house, but its style is sui generis. It's a place that makes you feel a million dollars. (Lower Sky Rd, Clifden Connemara ☎ 095-21204 www.connemara.net/dolphinbeachhouse)

Cooked Food To Go
● High Moors Foods

Many holidaymakers in Clifden probably wondered what on earth they would do when Hugh and Eileen Griffin decided to close their seminal restaurant, High Moors. They need not have worried. You can still enjoy Eileen's cooking, but now you order it 30 hours in advance, collect it from the house between 5pm and 6pm, and then, hey presto!: red onion and Parmesan bread; spinach soup with nutmeg; fresh crab with chilli mayonnaise; lamb cooked in cider and cream with gremolata; new potatoes from the garden; and those mighty puddings – summer berries and currants in brandy syrup; whiskey and walnut tart; raspberry and lemon roulade. There are excellent wines at very good prices, and summer holidays suddenly have a High Moors smile once again. (Dooneen, Clifden ☎ 095-21342)

Guesthouse
● Quay House

Paddy and Julia Foyle understand style better than just
about anyone else in Irish hospitality. They live
and breathe the stuff, and you can see and
enjoy how they work with it in their glorious house: where to put a table, how to
match colours, when to be ironic with fur-
nishings, how to make bricolage seem destined
to be together, how to create comfort and style out of
what seem to be random things. They make it look easy, just
as they make the business of hospitality seem easy, but of
course, they conceal the hard work and the patient consideration that lies behind everything they create. Best of all,
there is no sense of self-consciousness about what they do:
it's simply what they do, and the rest of us can only admire
and envy their sense of style, and how it has made their
beautiful house, down by the harbour in Clifden, into one of
the greatest Irish addresses. (Beach Rd, Clifden, Connemara
☎ 095-21369 www.thequayhouse.com)

B&B
● Sea Mist House

Sheila Griffin's town-centre house is a bohemian, happy
place, somewhere that seems to sum up the holiday zeitgeist of Clifden. Ms Griffin congratulates the artistic ambience with a splendid, low-key and subtle design aesthetic,
and with fine breakfasts, using the best local foods such as
Des Moran's fantastic pork sausages, and produce from
other shopkeepers in the town such as George Mannion
and John Malone. The breakfast room in Seamist is so exuberant, packed with happy travellers having the time of their
lives, that it's like a morningtime happy hour, with everyone
high on having a good time. (Clifden, Connemara ☎ 095-
21441 www.connemara.net/seamist)

Coffee Shop
● Steam

Claire Griffin's coffee shop in the Station House complex
has some really nifty food: Ardrahan cheese and red onion
marmalade wrap; bruschetta with Parma ham and tapenade;
open crab sandwich with tarragon mayo; potato and chorizo frittata, along with lots of coffees and fine sweet things.
(Station House, Clifden — Open Day-time)

Internet Café
● Two Dog Café

Jane Hackett and Jon Lemon's café and internet lounge is a
cult address in Clifden. Good food comes in the form of
daytime sandwiches and wraps, the coffee is the peerless
Illy, the vibe is good, the room is slinky and hip. The most
left-field location in the most westerly location. (Church
Hill, Clifden ☎ 095-22186 www.twodogcafe.ie — Open
Lunch)

Leenane

Country House & Spa
● Delphi Mountain Resort & Spa

Peter Mantle's elegant lodge has a jaw-dropping location,
excellent cooking from Cliodhna Prendergast, and the sort
of country house-weekend atmosphere that is almost
impossible to drag yourself away from. It's a curl-up-and-
sup-claret delight, whether you might ever catch a fish or
not. Hell, who cares about the fish. (Leenane ☎ 095-42987
www.delphiescape.com)

Letterfrack

Restaurant and Cookery School
● Pangur Ban

John Walsh's popular stone-cottage restaurant in the centre
of Letterfrack combines an accessible, friendly restaurant
with a cookery school, and Mr Walsh's culinary explorations
in the school leap over onto the menus, where Thai and
Taiwanese dishes co-exist happily and easily with Irish country classics such as venison cooked with Guinness.
(Letterfrack, Connemara ☎ 095-41243
www.pangurban.com — Open Lunch & Dinner)

Country House
● Renvyle House Hotel

With chef Tim O'Sullivan heading an adroit, creative kitchen
and manager Ronnie Counihan heading up a personable
front-of-house crew, the lovely Renvyle has been getting
better and better in recent years, with the palpable sense of

a team that has glimpsed success and like what they are seeing. Renvyle has always been a grand, comfortable house, with a delectable Arts & Crafts style that is quite unique, and its moniker as a stress-free zone is no exaggeration: once you drive through the gates, the so-called civilised world disappears. The collaboration between cooking, hospitality and cosiness in Renvyle is altogether intoxicating. (Letterfrack, Connemara ☎ 095-43511 www.renvyle.com)

Country House
● Rosleague Manor

Mark Foyle is beginning to make waves in the beautiful Rosleague, continuing the distinguished tradition of the Foyle family into another generation. It's a most gorgeous house, with a heart-stopping location, and the cooking is right on the money: beef with Bordelaise sauce; scallops with a spaghetti of courgette and a saffron butter sauce. Best of all, kindly local ladies make sure you have all you need, and more. Rosleague is well on its way to being one of the great westerly destinations. (Letterfrack, Connemara ☎ 095-41101 www.rosleague.com)

Moyard

Guesthouse
● Garraunbaun House

Delia Finnegan's house is a classic Victorian mansion, an architectural jewel that is so well designed it manages to seem completely contemporary. It's a great destination for chilling out, and for spending lazy days in the garden, looking out at the Twelve Bens whilst anticipating a fine dinner. (Moyard, Connemara ☎ 095-41648 garrraunbaun.house@ireland.com)

Oughterard

Restaurant
● Le Blason

A commodious, comfortable room overlooking the river is a great backdrop for some nice, simple French cooking at the atmospheric Le Blason. (Bridge St, Oughterard ☎ 091-557111 http://homepage.eircom.net/~leblason)

Butcher
● McGeough's Butchers

James McGeough's creativity is a wonder to behold. Like many second-generation artisans, he has come to the business keen to further the rock-solid foundations established by his dad, Eamonn. This he has done by thinking laterally: Connemara lamb is smoked and air-dried and then sliced thin as Parma ham, one of the new cult artisan foods. The same lamb is also used to make Connemara sausages, to be used as part of a cassoulet-type concoction. Great traditions such as corned beef, or kassler, are endlessly worked on and improved. Every time you visit there is a new invention, some intriguing new concoction from a butcher whose creative skills place him in the vanguard of contemporary Irish charcuterie. McGeough's is an operation driven by critical regard and by creativity, and one senses we are only at the beginning of a creative ferment. (Barrack St, Oughterard ☎ 091-552351)

Wine Merchant
● Probus Wines

Paul Fogarty's fine wine shop, on the road out to Clifden, has already spawned a sister shop in Moycullen's Wine Cluster, where Ivan Edwards mans the store. The shop in Oughterard is small, but the range is choice and select, right throughout the wine world, and Mr Fogarty's direct connections with French winemakers – his mother-in-law has a vineyard in Cadillac – sees excellent Burgundies, great bubblies and some cracking value from regional France, such as the Montmarin range and the Defaix Chablis, with its clean, crisp, fair winemaking. (Camp St, Oughterard ☎ 091-552084)

Bakery
● The Yew Tree

Elizabeth Folgen says, "I always wanted to have a village bakery". Well, she's got one, and praise the stars for that, for The Yew Tree is a wee beauty in little Oughterard. With Teresa Tierney baking alongside, this duo asserts that "We want to do it right, or we won't do it", and the excellent quality of their ingredients shines through in their baking, and the excellent lunchtime treats made with their lovely breads. Look out for the Swiss country bread, the Norwegian Rye and the very fine focaccia. Galwegians should note that you can get the Yew Tree breads in McSwiggan's and Mortons of Salthill. (Main St, Oughterard ☎ 091-866886)

Recess

Country House
● **Lough Inagh Lodge**

Maire O'Connor's pretty country hotel is a fisherman's favourite, but its stunning location and nice, simple food make it a good space in which to chill-out Connemara-style. (Recess, Connemara ☎ 095-34706 inagh@iol.ie)

Roundstone

B&B
● **The Angler's Return**

Lynn Hill's 18th century sporting lodge is a valuable address, a peaceful and stylish getaway that has just the right Connemara spirit. (Toombeola, Roundstone, Connemara ☎ 095-31091)

Bar & Restaurant
● **O'Dowd's Seafood Bar & Restaurant**

Finger-lickin' seafood cookery is the theme in both the bar and restaurant of this ageless Connemara institution. (Roundstone ☎ 095-35923 www.odowdsbar.com)

Cult Choice
Air Dried Connemara Lamb

James McGeough's pioneering charcuterie has created Ireland's very own Parma Ham. His air-dried, smoked Connemara Lamb, sliced see-through thin is the most exciting new meat product to have been created in Ireland in yonks.

The Aran Islands

The Aran Islands are different, and their difference demands a different strategy when visiting. So, take your time, allow a few days at least to explore the island of your choice, and don't make the mistake of believing that an afternoon whistle-stop will let you know what these ancient, mysterious islands are all about. The more time you take, the more you will know, the more you will enjoy.

Inis Meain

· An Dun is a pretty B&B and restaurant owned by Teresa and Padraic O Fatharta. There are five rooms in the house, along with a small spa, and aromatherapy sessions can be arranged, for those exhausted from walking this gorgeous little island. Nice simple cooking in the restaurant, and make sure to order a bottle of the Concannon from the wine list. (Inis Meain, Aran Islands ☎ 099-73047 anduninismeain@eircom.net)

· And speaking of Concannons, Mairin Concannon's B&B in Moore Village is another lovely base for exploring this magical place. (Moore Village, Inis Meain, Aran Islands ☎ 099-73019)

· Also in Moore Village, Tig Conghaile offers an all day menu, with clever use of local seafood and organic produce and some fine baking. (Moore Village, Inis Meain, Aran Islands ☎ 099-73085)

Inis Mór

· Treasa and Bertie Joyce's Kilmurvey House is a legendary address on Inis Mór, famous for meticulous housekeeping and great cooking, and it's also close to one of our favourite beaches, at Kilmurvey Bay.

(Kilronan, Inis Mór, Aran Islands ☎ 099-61218 www.kilmurveyhouse.com)

· Joe and Maura Wolfe's historic Man of Aran Cottage at Kilmurvey offers accommodation in three small rooms, whilst the cottage is also home to a sweet little restaurant that features Joe's garden produce for lunch and dinner. (Kilmurvey, Inis Mór, Aran Islands ☎ 099-61301 www.manofarancottage.com)

· Our readers are divided about Joel d'Anjou's Mainistir House Hostel and its famous vaguely vegetarian buffet, which Joel cooks each evening. Some love the ruck and the mixing and the enthusiastic internationalism of the buffet event, and can overlook the bohemian nature of the surroundings. Others can't warm to the bedsit chic that is evident everywhere, however much they admire the creative and tasty food. (Kilrnonan, Inis Mór, Aran Islands ☎ 099-61351 www.mainistirhousearan.com)

Inis Oirr

· Brid Poil's B&B, Radharc an Chlair, is one of the best-loved B&B's anywhere in Ireland, and it's so popular that you will not get a room here unless you book well in advance – and well in advance means at least a month ahead, and probably two! Mrs Poil is a keen cook, and produces lovely domestic baking and charming, comfort food dinners for guests. (Inis Oirr, Aran Islands ☎ 099-75019)

· Another member of the Poil clan, Anita Poil, serves home grown food at the Mermaid's Garden in Castle Village. Ms Poil is a highly regarded cook, with funky, imaginative cooking on offer during the day and also for dinner. There is also accommodation, and they can conjure up seaweed baths for a sybaritic delight. (Castle Village, Inis Oirr, Aran Islands ☎ 099-75062)

Galway City

Restaurant
● Ard Bia

The little room above Ti Neatain's legendary pub in the centre of town has given a start to several Galway restaurateurs, and Ard Bia's interesting food bodes well for the future: chorizo, apricot, pecan and Parmesan risotto; frittata of lovage and Knockalara sheep's cheese; braised beef cheeks with red wine and ceps; sea trout with lemon butter; bread and butter pudding with brandied sultanas. There is a short and simple list of wines and a lovely selection of drinks including Lebanese cardamom coffee and Moroccan mint tea, and Ard Bia is a cult choice with local food lovers. (2 Quay St, Galway ☎ 087-236 8648 — Open Day-time)

Café
● The Cobblestone

Kate Wright's vegetarian café has eight daily options, from roasted vegetable lasagne to spinach and cheese tarts to felafels to nut roasts, and do enquire about Kate's cookery classes. (Kirwan's Lane, Galway ☎ 091-567227 — Open Day-time)

Restaurant
● Da Roberta

No one believes that you can get real, simple and true Italian cooking in Salthill, but thanks to Sandro and Roberta, you can. Head out to Salthill and you will discover real pastas, good bruschetta and, good heavens, even the tiramisu is good, and the charm and energy of the room is just darling. (169 Upper Salthill, Galway ☎ 091-585808)

Restaurant
● Da Tang Noodle House

Catherine O'Brien and Du-Han Tuo's lovely noodle house in the centre of town is unique in Ireland, offering real Chinese cooking from north of the Yangtze. Whilst dumplings and other fried dishes are offered, it's the noodles that are the prize catch, offering pure, vivid energy food with sparklingly fresh and chilli-hot flavours. (2 Middle St, Galway ☎ 091-561443 — Open Lunch & Dinner)

The Galway Saturday Market

"New York brownies made with Belgian chocolate", the sign proudly announces.

On top of their game

Sure, where else could you be but the Saturday Galway Market, where Gearoid Browne's Aran smoked salmon scented with truffle rubs shoulders with Govinda's Pure Vegetarian Food, and where New York brownies are ennobled with best Belgian chocolate to be sold on the street in Galway city?

In a city where everyone is a character, there is no bigger, better and more vivid a bunch of characters than the stalwarts and stallholders of the cosmopolitan Saturday market. The major players in Galway have been joined over the years by idiosyncratic crafts-people, local bakers, vegetable growers, hat sellers, wood carvers, crêpe bakers, an endless kaleidoscope of the curious, the strange, the gifted, the leftfield.

Together, this crew has made the Galway market into a major tourist attraction, not to mention the most invaluable resource of great food for Galwegians themselves. Over the years, battles have been fought with the local authorities, but today the market is celebrated by the city, and plans to extend the opening of the market into Sunday have focused on maintaining the high standards insisted upon by the traders. This setting and maintaining of standards is an important characteristic of the market, and the reason why it has become such an iconic success story. Left to their own, the traders have created the delicate network of diversity that gives the market its colour, its charm, and its capacity to bring great food to the city centre. Food lovers should note that smart Galwegians actually shop at the market very early in the morning, in order to secure the very best of everything.

In total, there are almost 90 pitches arranged round and about the St Nicholas market, many of them craftspeople, some of them fairly sophisticated producers of vegetables, flowers and other necessities. The following are a sample of food producers to look out for:

· *Aran Smoked Salmon* Gearoid & Michael Browne's smoked salmon comes over on the ferry from Aran to the market, and along with the classic smoked fish there is also gravad salmon, flavoured with mustard and dill, wild garlic-flavoured salmon and a peat-smoked salmon.

· *BoyChik Donuts* Doughnuts and all manner of specialist organic breads and cakes: wheat free, yeast free, sugar free and dairy free. Contact Paul. (☎ 087-295 4596)

· *The Bread Stall* The BS's olive bread is their standard bearer, but Dave Holland's company has lots of other tasty types. (☎ 087-245 4100)

· *Breckish Dairies* Huge Zyderlaan has been selling the splendid Breckish dairy cows and goat's milk cheeses in the market since 1979. Look out for their particularly fine yogurts.

· *Cait Curran's Organic Vegetable Stall* Cait Curran is one of Ireland's pioneering organic gurus – she edits the magazine *Organic Matters* (www.organicmattersmag.com) – and she grows a wide range of organic fruit and vegetables that are sold at her stall. Look out for great purple sprouting broccoli, lovely fresh cos lettuce; celeriac, spring cabbage, and Cait also has a small selection of organic standard imported fruit. (☎ 091-844973 ccurran@ireland.com)

· *Da Kappa-ya Sushi Stall* Fantastic echt Japanese sushi from Sheridan's stalwarts Yoshimi and Junichi – Smoked Salmon Roll Teriyaki, Chicken Roll, Japanese Roll,

Vegetarian Roll. This is some of the very best sushi you can find.

· *Dirk Flake* Dirk's organic vegetables, grown out further west at Aughinish, are one of the stars of the market, and Mr Flake has matched them with a range of imported organic wines in recent times, so that Sunday morning brunch omelette can now be poured with a glass of prosecco from the Pizzolate azienda in Northern Italy. (☎ 065-707 8140)

· *Joachim Hess* Joachim's organic vegetables and excellent fresh breads are not to be missed.

· *The Madras Curry Stall* Nice home-cooked Indian vegetarian curries, with chapattis, pickles and stuffed breads.

· *Real Olive Company* The familiar, and familiarly amazing, range of olives and other gourmet foods, sold with honest chutzpah.

· *The Hummus Stall* Great hummus, plus fine oat date cake and real chocolate biscuits.

· *Sheridan's Cheesemongers* This is where it all began for the most dynamic food team in Ireland: with a tiny stall, Saturday morning, selling cheeses. The Sheridan crew have never forgotten their market roots, and today Sarah Bates and her Sheridan's van are a fixture of the east coast markets every weekend, whilst the Galway crew take turns manning the table each Saturday.

· *Yummy Crêpes* Established almost a decade ago in Cork in 1995, YC offer a selection of savoury and sweet crêpes, made with organic flours and free-range eggs. Just the thing for that Saturday morning hangover that refuses to budge. (Woodquay, Weir Road, Tuam ☎ 093-24955 or 086-898 4996)

Café
● Delight Gourmet Food Bar

This tiny food bar is a cult address, thanks to some very imaginative cooking. Sandwiches include a corn bread base with duck confit and Mediterranean vegetables, or ciabatta with turkey, bacon and stuffing, which is just what your body needs after a heavy Galway night. Good breakfast choices, good salads, and a smattering of daily concoctions on the blackboard all make for interesting, funky eating. (29 Upr Abbeygate St, Galway ☎ 091-567823 delightgfb@eircom.net — Open Day-time)

Bakery
● The Galway Tart Co

Michelle and Fintan Hyland's bakery produces the best pies you can find, made with a skill and artfulness that is simply brilliant. Tarts such as raspberry and custard or creamy lemon are dreamy perfection, the almond croissants are noble and brilliant, the seed breads and meringues are state-of-the-art. You will find the Tart Co's produce at week-end markets along the west coast as well as their outlets in Galway, which range from Salthill to a fab wee caravan in Eyre Square. (65 Henry St, Galway ☎ 091-588384)

Patisserie & Coffee Shop
● Goya's

Emer Murray's elegant room serves the most elegant baking you will find. Everything this meticulous, gifted baker and cook touches has a modest, accomplished magic about it, everything is destined to be as good as it can possibly be. Whether you are having the chicken, leek and mushroom pie, or the smoked bacon and avocado salad for lunch or grabbing a slice of chocolate torte and a cup of coffee, this food will simply delight the senses. Brilliant. (2/3 Kirwans Lane, Galway ☎ 091-567010 www.goyas.ie)

Bakery
● Griffin's Bakery

This humungously busy bakery in the centre of Galway looks pretty conventional at first – the breads and cakes look pretty much the same as those that are sold in every other bakery in Ireland — but look further and you will see that they also sell interesting sourdough and pain au levian breads and other artisan quality baking. (21 Shop St, Galway ☎ 091-563683

Catering
● The International Food Circus

They may be media darlings, but Enrico Fantasia and Dave Gumbleton are also – and more importantly – two of the most gifted cooks currently working in Ireland. Food Circus is what they do when they aren't producing beautiful food and selling gorgeous wines in Sheridan's, and if you are having a major cook-fest, you need these men there to sort out your catering, whatever the occasion. Quite frankly, they could cook old hats and shoes and make them fab. (Enrico ☎ 087-1314338; Dave 087-9185836 foodcircus@hotmail.com)

Shop
● McCambridge's

McCambridge's have made serious improvements to their wine shop offer in recent times, with Eoin McCambridge and Og Cunningham sourcing lots of new beauties at very decent prices. The deli section of the shop is a timeless beauty where you will find lots of rare Galway foods and most everything your food-loving heart desires.
(38/39 Shop St, Galway ☎ 091-562259 retail@mccambridges.com)

Restaurant
● McDonagh's Seafood House

This city-centre fish restaurant and take-away is one of the most enduring Galway institutions, and an ever-reliable destination for simple, traditional fish cookery. (22 Quay St ☎ 091-565001).

Wine Bar
● Martine's Quay Street Wine Bar

Martine McDonagh's cosy wine bar is a spot-on destination for good wine drinking, along with some smart, simple seafood cookery. Martine's is a real cult in Galway city, so make sure to have a reservation. (21 Quay St, Galway ☎ 091-565662)

Shop
● Morton's of Galway

There is no need to build and stock the supermarket of your dreams. Eric Morton has done it for you, and it's in Salthill, and it's one of the most exciting new openings in Ireland in yonks. Think of all the good things you need in your life – David Llewellyn's apple juice; Laragh Stuart foods; the fine new Magnetti fresh pastas which are made in Clarinbridge; Ortiz anchovies; Olivier's olive oils, and let the list spin out as long as you want, and you will find all these fantastic foods here, chosen by a truly epicurean eye, a truly epicurean palate. Morton's is, quite simply, a Super Market. (Lower Salthill, Galway ☎ 091-522237)

Bakery
● Nimmo's

No other restaurant in Ireland has an aesthetic quite like Nimmo's. All of the positive, quirky things we enjoy about French culture – the bricolage style; the simple but pro-foundly understood food; the insouciant welcome; the fin de siecle ambience – are rendered here in the most winning way. And it makes one think that, in fact, only Galway people would have the style and chutzpah to pull off something like Nimmo's. The secret of Nimmo's is not just the style: it's the staff, a bunch of people, who come from all over the world, but who all behave as if they are Galway-born. They synchronise the food and wine here with elegance and skill. (Spanish Arch, Galway ☎ 091-561114 — Open Dinner & Weekend Lunch)

Wine Shop
● The Noble Vine

Noel O'Loughlen's company has some really excellent wines sourced direct from France – Château Les Pins from Roussillon; Bergeracs from Château Grinou; the very fine Domaine Camp Galhan range including the unusual Liquerol – and if the range is small, it is nevertheless very choice. Mr O'Loughlen also organises wine tours in France and via the company Galway Wine Producers, they manage and produce bespoke wines for Irish clients. (Terryland Retail Pk, Headford Rd, Galway ☎ 091-565749 www.theNobleVine.com)

Restaurant
● Oscar's

Michael O'Meara's funky restaurant has a nightclubby style interior, and the food has a similarly eclectic and abstract style, ranging from wild Irish salmon served with mung beans to baby back ribs cooked on the barbecue and basted with their own barbecue sauce, which they also bottle so you can take some home. This sort of eclectic, international style of cooking could only be found in Galway. (Upper Dominick St, Galway ☎ 091-582180 www.oscarsgalway.com — Open Dinner)

Restaurant
● Royal Villa

Charlie Chan's excellent Chinese restaurant has spawned a second branch, at a small shopping centre near the junction at Claregalway on the road out to Tuam, whilst the city centre branch sails serenely on, offering echt Chinese cooking – crispy duck with thin pancakes, hot Sichuan dishes, black bean sauce, delicate garnishes – that is always a pleasure. (13 Shop St, Galway ☎ 091-563450, Hughes Supermarket, Claregalway ☎ 091-739876)

Cheesemonger & Delicatessen
● Sheridan's Cheesemongers

What is the secret of Sheridan's? Quite simply, it is that they attract the coolest staff on the planet, people who are so hip, so capable, so damned good at what they do, that to engage with them in the simple business of buying cheeses, vegetables, cured meats and wines is a pure thrill – these guys and girls bring the culture and the spirit of great food to the business of selling great food to you.

The shop on Churchyard St is a glory, and on Saturdays they set out their stall for the market, a reminder of where it all began. In the Wine Shop Upstairs, Enrico Fantasia sources and selects a brilliant range of wines, many of them brought directly from Italy, and they are wines which – like the foods Sheridan's source and sell – define the optimum: Borgo Scopetto is quintessential Chianti; the Domini Veneti Valpolicella will make you reconsider this over-looked wine; and the Vignai da Duline Viburnum and Morus Alba are sublime, sensual wines, star quality, world class. Sheridan's is the epicentre of good food and great wines on the west coast, and wherever else they lay their hat. (16 Church Yard St, Galway ☎ 091-564829, wine shop 091-564832 www.sheridanscheesemongers.com)

Butcher
● C.R. Tormey & Sons

The Galway branch of the legendary Midlands family of butchers occupies an unremarkable space in an unremarkable shopping centre, but the quality of meat that has made Tormey's shops in Mullingar and Tullamore so famous is happily in plentiful evidence here. (Unit 17 Headford Shopping Centre, Headford Rd, Galway ☎ 091-564067)

Restaurant
● Tulsi

As with virtually every other Indian restaurant in Ireland, Tulsi has blossomed out into a chain of restaurants dotted around the country. They cook nice things here – good chicken shaslik kebab; nice sag ghost, some very fine breads – and this friendly, good-value food is deservedly popular. (3 Buttermilk Walk, Middle St, Galway ☎ 091-56483)

Restaurant
● Vina Mara

Padraig Kielty has built a dedicated audience for his imaginative modern cooking in the cosy Vina Mara. Unusually, Mr Kielty seems most at home with clever fish and vegetarian cookery – he will match roast cod with a ravioli of smoked trout, and pair them up with fennel and a chive mash, or he will fill a spring roll with wild mushrooms and feta cheese and scent the dish with orange. Mr Kielty is still a young man, and one senses that we can expect a lot more from him over the coming years. (19 Middle St, Galway ☎ 091-561610 vinamara@hotmail.com)

Wine Shop
● The Vineyard

If you seek a bottle of Marilyn Merlot 1999, with the sumptuous shape of the late Ms Monroe languishing languorously across the label (we're not making this up), then you will find this Californian rarity in The Vineyard, amidst a stupendous selection of wines that embraces all categories, all countries, all price points, all creeds. Everything you could possibly quaff, consume and imbibe is here, along with cocky staff. (14 Mainguard St, Galway ☎ 091-561816)

Wine Shop
● Woodberry's

This is a splendid wine shop, which is saying something in a town as well served with wine as Galway. More than 500 wines on two floors and courteous service, along with a nice old-style ambience, makes for great wine shopping. (Middle St Mews, Middle St, Galway ☎ 091-533706)

Galway County

Clarinbridge

Restaurant
● The Old Schoolhouse

Clarinbridge has been famous for its oysters for decades, but if Kenneth Connolly and his whip-smart crew keep on doing what they are doing, then the Old Schoolhouse will soon eclipse the Clarinbridge oysters as the reason to head to this Galway hamlet.

Mr Connolly's restaurant is a model of modern professionalism, the sort of place that is completely focused on the customer and making sure that the customer gets what the customer wants. It's no surprise, then, to see happy families in here, all enjoying delicious cooking, having a great, convivial time whether they are four or 64 years young. It's that sort of space: democratic, generous, and with excellent cooking. (Clarinbridge ☎ 091-796898 — Open Lunch & Dinner)

Kilcolgan

Pub & Restaurant
● Moran's Oyster Cottage

Willie Moran's legendary Oyster Cottage has a simple secret when it comes to cooking: they really don't do very much of it. What they do is to open oysters, source great cooked crab and smoked salmon, then assemble them elegantly and sympathetically. They do grill some oysters, and then cook up some mussels, but for the most part the secret here is sourcing and assembling, rather than cooking. And, it works beautifully, especially with a pint or two of stout. If only more pubs had the confidence to keep things so simple, and to make them so elegant. (The Weir, Kilcolgan ☎ 091-796113 www.moransoystercottage.com — Open Lunch & Dinner)

Kinvara

Pub
● Keogh's Bar

Michael Keogh's bar is a busy pub in Kinvara where the simpler dishes tend to be the best bet on a menu that is rather ambitious – order some of the Kinvara smoked salmon with brown bread and you can't go wrong. Excellent service is prompt and polite. (The Square, Kinvara ☎ 091-637145, keoghsbar@eircom.net)

Smokehouse
● Kinvara Smoked Salmon

Declan Droney's organic smoked salmon has won every conceivable culinary accolade in recent years, and it's a product that deserves every ounce of praise. Sourced with care from Clare Island off the west coast, the organic fish is of superb quality, and is then smoked with care and finally, packed and sold with great skill. The salmon is delectable, a subtle, sexy food that is always a special treat. Just as fine are the Kinvara roast smoked salmon, and a particularly good gravad lax. (Kinvara ☎ 091-637489 www.kinvarasmokedsalmon.com)

Bar & Restaurant
● Pier Head Bar & Restaurant

Michael Burke's popular bar and restaurant, down by the sea, is a good destination for seafood and drinks in the bar and restaurant. (The Quay, Kinvara ☎ 091-638188 www.kinvara.com/eatpierhead.html

Moycullen

Butcher
● Martin Divilly

This is the second outpost of Martin and Audrey Divilly's dynamic butcher's operation, with the original shop based in the Westside Shopping centre, just on the outskirts of Galway city.

In common with the best of the new generation of artisan butchers, Divilly's has style and content: their own cured bacon; beef from Loughrea, a true dedication to service, and a hunger to win culinary and retail prizes, which they have been hauling in over recent years. Both shops have been extensively renovated in recent times, so the new, hip style of beef boutique is what you can expect from Divilly's. (Main Street, Moycullen ☎ 091-523947)

Country House and Restaurant
● Moycullen House

Richard and Louise Casburn's country house and restaurant showcases Mr Casburn's work as chef, and Mrs Casburn's confident work out front, and together they are a good team. Moycullen is a beautiful old Arts & Crafts house set amidst acres of rhododendrons just up the hill from the centre of Moycullen, so it's a particularly good place to stay even before you have dinner. Mr Casburn's cooking is confident, modern and individual, just as you would expect of someone who worked with local culinary hero Gerry Galvin. (Spiddal Road, Moycullen ☎ 091-555621 www.moycullen.com — Open Accommodation & Dinner)

Wine Merchant
● The Wine Cluster

The second branch of Paul Fogarty's wine empire is set on the main road in ever-expanding Moycullen. Ivan Edwards – an alumnus of Gerry Galvin's seminal Drimcong House, as is Mr Fogarty himself – knows his wines back-to-front, so if you can't decide whether you want a bottle of Paul Zinck from Alsace or some Chablis by Bernard Defaix or some Omaka Springs from New Zealand, then Mr Whelan will guide you gently through the more than 500 different bottles on the shelves. (Main St, Moycullen ☎ 091-868882 probuswines@eircom.net)

Cult Choice The International Food Circus *Street Food*

If you hear that the Food Circus is coming to your town, book early and book often. FC is Enrico and Dave from Sheridan's, and their street food is a high wire culinary act. Expect the unexpected. Alongside the freshest mackerel on the grill there will be melt-in-the-mouth lamb's tongues, and the smoothest buttercup-yellow polenta doused with a slurp of extra virgin olive oil. This is street food as art. Markets, festivals and Slow Food events are where the Circus pitches its tent.

Restaurant
● White Gables

Good service and accurately cooked and presented traditional food explains how and why Kevin and Ann Dunne have been packing them into White Gables for almost 15 years now. (Moycullen Village ☎ 091-555744 www.whitegables.com — Open Dinner & Sun Lunch)

Loughrea

Restaurant
● Slatefort House

Rosario Africano and Maura Winter's Italian restaurant is a real curio. Firstly, its location is remote. Secondly, it serves authentic Italian food, the sort of thing Mr Africano understands perfectly: subtle, unshowy, delicate in flavour, real regional Italian cooking. Put these two things together in the hills of Tuscany and it might work. But near to Loughrea? Well, it works like a dream near to Loughrea, and how. This is a lovely destination, and a real local secret, and who could blame the locals for not wanting to let on about a place where you can enjoy stuffed baby squid, or Italian sausage with borlotti beans, or skewered chicken, sausage and beef cooked on the griddle, or sea bass cooked under a bed of salt. The real thing, right down to the strangely echoey rooms and the obscure and delightful Italian wines. (Slatefort, Bullaun, Loughrea ☎ 091-870667 — Open Dinner & Sun Lunch)

Spiddal

B&B
● Iverna Cottage

Patricia and William Farrell's B&B is animated by great hospitality, and a winning, tactile, engaging style of décor and design. Breakfasts are a true treat, and are amongst the best served anywhere, which further adds to the sense of tactile luxury in this rather special place. (Salahoona, Spiddal ☎ 091-553762 www.ivernacottage.8m.com)

Tuam

Wine Shop
● Nectar Wines

John McGrath and Carl Byrne's wine shop, just off the main square, is a real treat, with the choicest pickings to be found amongst the wines the guys import themselves: great Côtes-du-Rhône from Mas Libian; fantastic cava from Masia Sagué; sublime Beaujolais from Daminae Métrat et fils; and a lovely Châteauneuf from Domaine de Fontavain. There is great enthusiasm and energy in this young company, and somehow it makes the wines all the more enjoyable. (☎ 01-623 3846 www.nectarwines.com)

Country House
● Waterslade House

Adrian and Vicky Brennan have streamlined operations at their gloriously slinky Waterslade House, just down at the river bridge in Tuam. With local man Anthony Carney in the kitchen, menus are direct and popular, and have already attracted a local audience to this beautiful house.
The rooms, meantime, are superb, vital little cocoons of tactile, sensual comfort that revel in smart use of colour and furniture, which makes Waterslade a fantastic Tuam destination that should be on everyone's itinerary. (Tuam, Co Galway ☎ 093-60888 www.waterslade.ie)

10 GREAT
HARBOUR DESTINATIONS

1

BALLYCOTTON, Co CORK
GRAPEFRUIT MOON

2

BALTIMORE, Co CORK
THE CUSTOMS HOUSE

3

DINGLE, Co KERRY
OUT OF THE BLUE

4

DUNGARVAN, Co WATERFORD
THE TANNERY

5

DUNMORE EAST, Co WEXFORD
THE SHIP

6

GREENCASTLE, Co DONEGAL
KEALY'S SEAFOOD BAR

7

HOWTH, Co DUBLIN
AQUA

8

KINSALE, Co CORK
FISHY FISHY CAFÉ

9

ROSSLARE, Co WEXFORD
LA MARINE

10

WARRENPOINT, Co DOWN
THE DUKE

County Kerry

the Kerry cow, handmade chocolates, Dingle bay crab,
black pudding, Atlantic sea vegetables, artisan ice cream,
Jersey milk, Kenmare prawns, Valentia scallops,
wild salmon, Kerry mountain lamb...

Annascaul

Black Pudding
● **Ashe's Black Pudding**

When you detour into little Annascaul to have
a pint in Antarctic hero Tom Crean's pub, The
South Pole, take yourself up the street to
Ashe's little supermarket and buy some of
the best, Kerry-style black pudding you will
find. Cinnamony and spicy, dense and quite delicious, this is a relic of past tastes and textures and one of
the signature foods of the peninsula. Then head on down to
Dingle, and make sure to order it as a starter in The Chart
House. These Kerry-style puddings – you will find another
example made by P. J. Burns in Sneem – are valuable foods,
as they exemplify local culinary characteristics and individu-
alities, and it is vital that they should be respected and pro-
tected, and enjoyed. (Annascaul ☎ 066-915 7127
www.annascaulblackpudding.sitestogo.biz)

Ballinskelligs

Chocolate
● **Skelligs Chocolate Company**

There is nothing nicer than to drive all the way down the
ring of Kerry with a child or two in the car, with your destination firmly fixed as Michael and Amanda McGabhann's little Skelligs Chocolate factory. It's an unforgettable trip: gorgeous scenery, ever-mounting excitement as you get closer
to Ballinskelligs, then the arrival at the cute little factory
itself, a look around watching the chocolate being tempered
and perfected, and then a brace of beautifully packaged
choccies to take back home. If you can't get to the Ring, the
chocs are available in smart shops: you will know them by
their exquisite, artistic packaging, a thing of beauty and a joy
forever all by itself. (The Glen, Ballinskelligs ☎ 066-947 9119
www.skelligschocolate.com)

Caherdaniel

Farmers' Market
● Caherdaniel Country Market

The best of the local markets is held each week in pretty Caherdaniel: this is the one not to miss if you are holidaying in a rented cottage on the Ring. And do look out also for the small street market that takes place in Cahirciveen where you will find rarities such as Dereenaclaurig farm-house cheese. (Friday 10am-noon June-September)

Guesthouse
● Iskeroon

A gorgeous house with a – truly – unbelievable location, Geraldine and David Hare's dream of a house is a cult address, if ever there was one. You even have to drive over a beach to get to Iskeroon, and this after you almost abseiled down the hill from the Ring of Kerry, taking all the bends, twists and turns as you wind down, and there you find a house that had previously only ever existed in your dreams. Iskeroon is seriously, seriously cool, and seriously unforgettable. (Iskeroon, Caherdaniel ☎ 066-947 5119 www.iskeroon.com)

Cahirciveen

Bar & Restaurant
● QC's

Kate and Andrew Cooke's bar and restaurant is the destination for food lovers in Cahirciveen, and certainly the Spanish-accented dishes – crab claws and crab meat baked in a Zarzuela, for instance – are funky and a lot of fun, if a little less red-blooded than true Spanish cooking.
Fish and shellfish are always a good bet in QC's, as the Cookes are related to Quinlan's fish shop, which is just a few doors down the street.
We find the bar a little gloomy during the day, so the restaurant at eveningtime – especially during the holiday season when it will be heaving with holidaymakers – is the more atmospheric choice. (3 Main Street, Cahirciveen ☎ 066-947 2244 www.qcbar.com — Open Lunch & Dinner)

An Artisan Union...

Maya Binder and Olivier Beaujouan are a formidable duo of artisans. They live and work together in Castlegregory, but each run separate artisan food businesses.

Ms Binder's excellent farmhouse cheeses, including a unique cheese flavoured with seaweed, are the pride of the peninsula: individualistic, quirky and painstaking. Hunt these down at good shops and at the markets where they are sold in Kerry and West Cork.

M. Beaujouan, meantime, is the leading sea vegetable expert of the country and one of his products in particular – his tapenade of sea vegetables – is utterly superlative. This is one of the vital foods to have in your armoury, and in our opinion one of the outstanding artisan foods of Ireland. The enigmatic M. Beaujouan can be found selling his sea vegetables and many other fish and artisan products – he also makes a mighty pork sausage, not to mention a superb boudin noir – at farmers' markets throughout the region.

· *Dingle Peninsula Cheese*
www.dinglepeninsulacheese.com
· *On The Wild Side*
seatoland@hotmail.com
(Kilcummin, Castlegregory
☎ 066-713 9028)

Dingle

B&B

● The Captain's House

Everyone loves The Captain's House. Everyone loves the true greeting and hospitality from Jim and Mary Milhench, the fantastic home-baking which is Mary's trademark, and the cosy, spick-and-span style of this cracking B&B. To be honest, it can be a bit of an effort to drag yourself away from the breakfast table to get out and about in Dingle, so comfy and welcoming is the Captain's style. Sure, what's your hurry, and another scone with jam and cream never did anyone any harm. (The Mall, Dingle ☎ 066-915 1531 homepage.eircom.net/~captigh/)

Smokehouse
● The Chart House

We could watch Jim and Carmel McCarthy working front of house in the cosy, sweet Chart House all night, and never cease to be amazed at just how masterful this couple are at running a great, signature destination restaurant. That adjective, "cosy" is important: this is a cosy room with cosy cooking, with a real feel-good vibe that you can't get enough of. The McCarthys run a restaurant that mirrors their own styles: open, amusing and amused, fun, inquisitive, hard-working and astute. The menu is all classics: crab and cod cakes with coriander and lime tartare sauce; Kerry lamb with red onion and feta tarte tatin; skate with balsamic butter sauce. The fantastic South African wines Jim brings in direct from the Cape are only brilliant. The only potential downside is that you really must book in advance to be sure you will get in during the season, so just make sure you book. (The Mall, Dingle ☎ 066-915 2255 www.charthousedingle.com — Open Dinner)

Chocolate Shop
● Chocolate Dreams

In Dingle town, as you walk up Green Street, look out for the little Chocolate Dreams shop, which specialises in funky artisan chocolates. (Green St, Dingle ☎ 066-915 0779)

Bakery
● Courtney's Bakery

Set back in a small courtyard just off Green Street, there is some cute, domestic-style baking to be enjoyed at Courtney's Bakery. (Green St, Dingle ☎ 066-915 1583)

Seafood
● Dingle Bay Shellfish

Ted Browne understands shellfish and fish in a way that only a real gourmet can. Where other processors are looking for ways in which they can pump their product full of water, Mr Browne is looking for ways in which he can utilise every last glorious, tasty morsel of the fish and shellfish he uses in order to make the very best products you can buy. Dig a bag of his crabmeat or his crab claws or his shelled prawns out of the freezer in Garvey's Supervalu, take them back to your cottage, prepare them that evening, and you will be blown away by the sheer quality this dynamic guy achieves. The cooked crab meat, in particular, is as good as it gets, something smart restaurateurs know only too well.

As if that wasn't enough, Mr Browne then uses the shells to make compost, a fine, darkly black crop of delight for your garden. Synergistic, and environmental, and not to be missed. (Ballinaboula, Dingle ☎ 066-915 1933)

Guesthouse
● Emlagh House

Marion and Grainne Kavanagh's lovely house is grand, beguiling, expensive, and worth the money. There is a real touch of class to the way in which mother and daughter run this fine house, and not just class, but generosity, too. It's a place that makes you feel special, thanks to their hard work, and their good taste, and the excellent cooking at breakfast-time, which means that the luxuriousness of Emlagh is never overstated or overdone. This is disciplined luxury, not indulgent luxury. You will enjoy Dingle a whole lot more if you stay in Emlagh. (Emlagh, Dingle ☎ 066-915 2345 www.emlaghhouse.com)

B&B
● Greenmount House

John and Mary Curran's guesthouse is well respected, and being a five minute walk from town, it's also a peaceful address. (Upper John St, Dingle ☎ 066-915 1414 greenmounthouse@eircom.net)

Shop
● An Grianan

Elaine Avery's wholefood shop is one of the best in the county, and to call it a wholefood shop is really a misnomer: this is a stylish wholefood supermarket, with great organic vegetables and a brilliant cheese counter and excellent locally baked breads. If you are renting a house in Dingle, An Grianan is a don't-miss! to find all the best local foods. Service by Elaine and her crew is spot on, and this is a sparkling address. The small farmers' market which used to be held out front of the shop has now moved down the town to the quays, where the best Kerry artisans can be found selling their goods every Friday during the season. (Green St, Dingle ☎ 066-9151910)

B&B
● Milltown House

Mark and Tara Carey's waterside B&B, Milltown House, just
out of town across the bridge heading to Ventry, is a good
choice if you want to be away from the ravening crowds
during the season in Dingle. (Dingle ☎ 066 915 1372).

Ice Cream
● Murphy's Ice Cream

The Murphy brothers are a dynamic duo, and they are
steadily creating one of the best new brands you can buy in
Ireland. They have done it slowly. Their lovely
ice cream shop in the centre of Dingle has
been trading happily for some years now,
letting them experiment on their range
and getting feedback direct from customers. Now, they have begun to move out,
and their delicious range of full cream ice creams can be
found in the best delis and supermarkets. But, we still like
to haul ourselves in here of an afternoon, and to take the
most extreme sensual delight in slowly demolishing a
Murphy's ice cream. One of those foods that makes life
altogether better. (Milseoga Uí Mhurchú Teo, Sráid na Trá, An
Daingean ☎ 066-915 2644 www.murphysicecream.com)

Restaurant
● Out of the Blue

We were slightly disturbed to see workmen taking apart
Tim Mason's pierside restaurant during the
spring of 2004, as we worked on this book.
Please God, don't let them be tarting up or
making posh this minimalist, pauvre eaterie,
one of the best places in Ireland to eat fresh
fish and shellfish in bohemian simplicity.
No worries: they were just doing some work on the
kitchen. Out of the Blue will continue to be as simple and
stark as it gets, and the cooking will continue to be simple
and delicious and just what Dingle needs: fresh fish off the
boats, no messing about, major good times for all concerned. Sole on the bone with almond cream for me, John
Dory with garlic aubergines for my dearest, haddock with
tomato tagliatelle for the kids, and a bottle of our fave
Chateau Court-les-Muts Bergerac sec. (Waterside, Dingle
☎ 066-915 0811 — Open Lunch & Dinner)

Smokehouse
● Port Yarrock Smokery

If you are promenading near the pier, make sure to stop at
Mo Crawley's smoked foods stall, near to Out of the Blue,
to get some smoked nuts, smoked garlic and smoked tomatoes and smoked sea salt, all from the Port Yarrock
Smokery. (Cloghane ☎ 066-713 9046)

Restaurant
● Wild Banks

Laura Walker first made a name for her good cooking when
working in The Chart House, and her Main Street restaurant, Wild Banks, has confident, classic cooking and good
value for money. (Main St, Dingle ☎ 066-915 2888
www.thewildbanks.com — Open Dinner)

Guesthouse with Restaurant
● Gorman's Clifftop House

Situated just outside the town, Gorman's combines guesthouse and restaurant and has a high standing amongst
locals. (Glaise Bheag Ballydavid, Dingle ☎ 066-915 5162)

Kenmare

Restaurant
● d'Arcy's

Pat Gath never stops working to improve the clubby and
companionable space of d'Arcy's, and his self-critical nature
pays off to deliver a very professional, enjoyable experience.
Brendan O'Brien's cooking gets better year-on-year, finding
more confidence and style: here is a chef whose food has
an instinct for flavour, whether with some splendid roast
Kerry lamb, or fresh John Dory with salsa, or local mussels
in a coconut broth. The redesign of the room and bar has
further made d'Arcy's one of the hot spots in a hot town.
(Main Street, Kenmare ☎ 064-41589 www.neidin.net/darcys
— Open Dinner)

Restaurant
● An Leath Phingin

Sincerity and skill are evident in Con Guerin's ever-popular
restaurant, which has been pleasing the punters of Kenmare

for the best part of two decades now. Their Italian-accented cooking is a surprise – it's not the cliché-riddled rubbish that so many so-called Italian places offer – and as such it's a real treat. (35 Main St, Kenmare ☎ 064-41559)

Restaurant
● The Club

Martin McCormack's new restaurant has a charming modern room – situated in the original market house of the town – and more of the stylish modern food that has characterised Martin's work at The Cooperage in Killarney. (Market St, Kenmare ☎ 064-42958)

Traiteur
● Gaths Foodstore

Pat Gath's new traiteur sells cooked-food-to-go along with good quality breads, wines and other culinary necessities of life. (12 Main Street, Kenmare ☎ 064-40717)

Café
● Jam

James Mulchrone's lovely café has spawned a sister branch in Killarney, but the original remains the best version of this smart deli and cafe. Lovely breads and sweet things, good salads and savouries, and excellent service from a keen crew make the Jam equation add up to a winner. (6 Henry St, Kenmare ☎ 064-41591 www.jam.ie — Open Day-time)

Restaurant
● The Lime Tree

Tony Daly's popular restaurant is a real crowd pleaser, a cosy and convivial series of rooms where chef Conal Brehony's cooking is light and delicious. Dishes such as roast monkfish on Asian noodles in a ginger broth, or their splendid vegetarian dishes – Mr Brehony is a graduate of Cork's Café Paradiso – are delivered with confidence and assurance. The sort of care that they take in The Lime Tree is evidenced in the excellent herbal teas the kitchen creates, delicious, subtle infusions of real leaves made by hand. (Shelburne St, Kenmare ☎ 064-41225 — Open Dinner)

Bar & Restaurant
● Mickey Ned's

This fine old bar is now managed by Chris Farrell, who was

formerly the head chef across town at the Sheen Falls Lodge. Mr Farrell has adopted a steady-as-she-goes approach to the pub and the cooking, with chef Kelly Oliver still manning the kitchens whilst Mr Farrell takes on a new venture at front-of-house. It's a stylish pub, with low tables and modish decor to suit the modish food, though the coal fire is kept burning and ancient photographs adorn the walls as a monument to the old style. Good sandwiches and snacks and, in particular, bowls of excellent, crisp and salty chips are just the thing to feed the younger brigade. (The Square, Kenmare ☎ 064-40200)

Pub
● Modo

Slickly designed modern pubs are becoming so numerous they threaten to morph into one endless burgundy-and-cream-and-stainless-steel and beechwood vision, all with a plasma screen that never gets switched off. If that is your bag, then Modo – sister to The Club – is for you. The food is as restlessly nervy and modern as the style – breaded chicken sandwich with salad and fries is the sort of snappy, salty thing that shows their style – and service is polished. (Main St, Kenmare ☎ 064-40722)

Restaurant
● Mulcahy's

Bruce Mulcahy is on a roll these days, a position best illustrated by the fact that you could be sitting in here enjoying the superb Sunday lunch, and if you cast an eye around the room, chances are you will see a troupe of Kenmare restaurateurs and hoteliers doing likewise. The locals always know where the real talent is at. Attention to detail, not to mention stonking value for money, brings in locals and visitors, and classic Sunday dishes like stuffed rolled pork with apricots and pistachios and a roast garlic mash are delivered with superb assurance. The evening menus are less experimental than before, but the style of the food remains utterly personal: Kerry lamb with cep and pistachio crust; paupiettes of sole with seafood colcannon; confit of duck leg with red wine and prune essence; seared salmon with coriander and ginger broth. Mr Mulcahy is set to be one of the stars of the decade. (Henry St, Kenmare ☎ 064-42383 — Open Dinner & Sun Lunch).

Restaurant
● Packie's

Martin Hallissey's assumption of the kitchen reins in the legendary Packie's has been smooth and sweet. Great modern Irish cooking is the chef's signature: crubeens (pig's trotters) with mustard and apple relish; a gracious and subtle Irish lamb stew; seared Castletownbere scallops; buttery champ and beautiful chips; lovely ice creams; great sticky toffee pudding. This is comfort food and comforting cooking, and the service is as maternal and motherly as the cooking. All told, Packie's is simply one of the most enjoyable restaurants you will find in Ireland. (Henry Street, Kenmare ☎ 064-41508 — Dinner)

Shop
● The Pantry

This is a splendid wholefood shop which always has a good selection of locally grown organic vegetables as well as the necessities of life. Visitors to Kenmare should also note that Wednesday is the day when the farmers' market winds its way around the square of the town, with a great selection of stalls and fine producers. (Henry St, Kenmare ☎ 064-42233)

Hotel
● The Park Hotel

Francis and John Brennan's grand hotel remains a by-word for the very best Irish hospitality and service. They have received a great deal of attention for their luxurious new Samas spa – check out former Roxy Music sax player Andy McKay's groovy soundtrack commissioned specially for the spa – but for us it is the meticulous attention to detail paid to every facet of this meticulous hotel that is the real pleasure principle. (Kenmare ☎ 064-41200 www.parkkenmare.com)

Wine Importer
● Mary Pawle Wines

Mary Pawle sources and sells organic wines, and she has both a good eye and a good nose for some vinous stars. Her basic wines, such as the excellent Spanish Can Vendrell white, or the peachy Osotri Rioja, are beauties and offer fab value for money. More recent arrivals on the list, such as the lovely Barbera d'Asti wines from Rovero Vigneto Gustin, show Ms Pawle putting a toe into Italian wine waters with the same confident assurance and style that has marked out her Spanish and French wines. Further new wines from Chile, Australia and New Zealand are all just as fine, and this is a dynamic, funky wine company. (Gortamullen, Kenmare ☎ 064-41443 www.marypawlewines.com)

Gastro Bar
● The Purple Heather

Grainne O'Connell's bar has some of the very best bar food to be found anywhere. In fact, it's wrong to call it bar food: it's simply excellent, modest, reliable food that happens to be served in a bar, and a very clubbable and calm bar at that. Good sandwiches, good seafood, nice soups and omelettes, all done with consummate TLC. (Henry St, Kenmare ☎ 064 41016 — Open Day-time & early Evening)

Country House
● Sallyport House

Sallyport House, just outside the town, is a very comfortable, quietly luxurious small country house. (Kenmare ☎ 064-42066 www.sallyporthouse.com)

Hotel
● Sheen Falls Lodge

Aidan McGrath, formerly of Muses restaurant in Bunratty, has taken over in the kitchens at the magisterial Sheen Falls, whilst manager Adriaan Bartels and his crack crew continue to demonstrate the art of running a 5-star hotel to the very highest standards of service and hospitality. The SFL succeeds because this team is so capable, and so charismatic, a splendid combination that is the hotel's signature. (Kenmare ☎ 064-41600 www.sheenfallslodge.ie)

Guesthouse
● Shelburne Lodge

Maura Foley, the grand dame of Kenmare cookery, is every bit as distinguished a designer as she has been a restaurateur, and Shelburne is the gorgeous proof of her skills with design. She has an artist's eye for using colour, and an architect's schema for placing furniture. Ally this with some of the best breakfasts you can eat in Ireland and you have a jewel of a destination, a genuinely unforgettable address. (Killowen, Kenmare ☎ 064-41013)

Café
● The Store Café

Bruce Mulcahy's original restaurant has morphed stylishly into a casual eating destination, but the high culinary standards evident in Mr Mulcahy's restaurant – just across the street – are just as evident here. The excellent quality of the coffee shows people with a determination to get things right, and the daytime salads – duck salad, Thai beef salad – or lovely classic concoctions like asparagus with poached eggs and hollandaise, are right on the money. If you want to get the day off to a good start, then some pancakes with maple syrup and a brew of coffee in The Store will set you up for whatever will be. (Henry St, Kenmare ☎ 064-41110 — Open Day-time)

Wine Shop
● Taberna

This cute little wine shop across the road from Mulcahy's has a bespoke air about both its style and its concise list. Mike Webster has worked with Joe Karwig and sommelier Alain Bras to bring together a nice bunch of vinous odds and sods: some of our favourites include the minerally, spicy Moulin de Gassac sauvignon, the tarry, aromatic Casale Vecchio Montepulciano d'Abruzzo, and the Cora Loxarel Muscat from Spain, with its dry, short aftertaste. Some nice olive oils and good drinking paraphernalia, as well as good service from Joanne Hannagen, make for a quirky, distinct wine shop. (22 Henry St, Kenmare ☎ 064-40805 www.tabernawines.com)

Killarney

Restaurant
● Bricin

The restaurant over the ground-floor craft shop in Bricin is a busy spot with locals who enjoy the carefully prepared food, and the genuine and solicitous welcome. (26 High St, Killarney ☎ 064-34902 bricin@eircom.net)

Butcher
● The German Butcher

Armin Weise's shop is a mile or so out of Killarney and it's a detour worth anyone's time to buy the splendid charcuterie of this dedicated artisan. The frankfurters, bratwurst and Polish salami are subtle and satisfying, the rare items such as smoked pork belly are worth the trip all on their own. Do note that Mr Weise operates a very efficient and speedy service through the mail. Email or phone to sign up for their regular newsletter/order form. (Fossa, Killarney ☎ 064-33069 germanbutcher@esatbiz.com)

Restaurant
● The Cooperage

Mo Stafford's busy town-centre restaurant has been a fixture of Killarney for more than half a decade now. With partner Martin McCormack now heading up new ventures in Kenmare, Simon Deegan now has control of the kitchen, and Mo's confident management of the room makes for a reliable, friendly spot for eclectic modern cooking. (Old Market Lane, Killarney ☎ 064-37716 — Open Lunch & Dinner)

Restaurant
● Gaby's

Geert and Marie Maes's enduring fish restaurant is one of the best-loved Killarney destinations, a place of high standards in both food and service. Mr Maes is a veteran of the kitchen, but he cooks like a young blood, with a huge sense of creative ambition brought to every plate. Great dishes such as pan-seared scallops with a ravioli of foie gras, an apple and parsnip purée and some baby leeks show the careful architectural imagining that is evident in all the fish cookery here, yet the work is never fussy. As a wine lover, Mr Maes is always concerned to have flavours and textures that work serenely and sublimely with wine, and the wine list is another work of thoughtful consideration. (27 High St, Killarney ☎ 064-32519)

Hotel
● Killarney Park Hotel

Padraig and Janet Treacy's hotel is the glory of Killarney: there are droves of places to stay in this town, but none the equal of this

On top of their game

monument to good service, hospitality, good housekeeping, and stellar standards. The seriously stylish spa treatment rooms have upped the ante once again, making the hotel even more desirable as a destination, but everything is of a piece here: service, cooking, style, all delivered with an understatement and a graciousness that is inspiring. In The Park Restaurant, Odran Lucey's cooking is serene and mature: crabmeat with ginger and apple; pithivier of wild mushrooms and quail; duck breast with cider braised red cabbage; Dover sole with lemon and caper butter, and there is great fun to be had with imaginatively worked desserts such as rhubarb and custard. Do note that a complete, serious vegetarian menu is available every evening. (Kenmare Place, Killarney ☎ 064-35555 www.killarneyparkhotel.ie — Open Dinner)

Café
● Panis Angelicus

PA is a neat little café just off the main street of Killarney, and the modern cooking and the coffee both show care and aptitude. It's a great place for a quick lunchtime stopover. (15 New St, Killarney ☎ 064-39648 — Open Day-time)

Killorglin

Bar & Accommodation
● The Bianconi

Just at the lower end of Killorglin, at the river bridge, this big bar and accommodation is a popular spot for bar food. (Killorglin ☎ 066-976 1146)

Country House
● Carrig House

Frank and Mary Slattery run a sparkling country house and restaurant in this beautiful lakeside address, a real dream destination on the Ring, just a few miles west of Killorglin. The comfort is irresistible, but it's the fine cooking from an excellent kitchen crew that will have you dreaming of dinnertime: confit of duck with roasted chestnuts; smoked eel and potato with mustard vinaigrette; seafood sausage with fennel and caviar vinaigrette; turbot with oyster, fennel and tomato sauce; pork ribsteak with sauce poivrade. There is a smartly selected list of wines that includes some serious heavy hitters, and Carrig is emerging as one of the best of the new generation of country houses, an address with both ambition and execution aligned together. (Caragh Lake, Killorglin ☎ 066-976 9100 www.carrighouse.com)

Restaurant
● Nick's Restaurant

Nick's is a happy spot for bumper servings of good cooking, served with a smile. This is also a child-friendly space, and a great party space during race weeks in Listowel. (Lwr Bridge St, Killorglin ☎ 066-976 1219)

Farmhouse Cheese
● Wilma's Killorglin Farmhouse Cheese

Wilma O'Connor is a most talented cheesemaker: just take a slice of her mature, Gouda-style Killorglin and your taste buds will be assailed by sweet, fudgy flavours, with notes of apricot and honey; this is a beauty of a cheese, and shows great cheesemaking skills. There is also a cumin-flavoured cheese, and you can buy the cheeses and others from the shop at the farm: follow the Caragh Lake road out of Killorglin and look for the signs to the farm. (Killorglin ☎ 066-976 1402)

Listowel

Bistro & Accommodation
● Allo's

Helen Mullane's beautiful bar and bistro boasts a seriously talented chef in the form of Theo Lynch, which means the food here in both bar and bistro is top notch. Mr Lynch cooks up big flavours: whole Dover sole with caper and herb butter; Kerry lamb rack with garlic and rosemary gravy; fried hake with tartare and fries; grilled Castletown oysters with bistro butter.

What you find in Allo's is lovely, logical, soulful food that will put a smile on your face, and there are three cosy, comfy rooms upstairs, just in case you find it impossible to prise yourself away from the beautiful bar, one of the most atmospheric and attractive traditional pubs to be found any-where in the country. (41 Church St, Listowel ☎ 068-22880 www.alloslistowel.com — Open Day-time)

Farmhouse Cheese
● Kerry Farmhouse Cheese

Eilish Broderick has taken over the production of the Kerry cheeses, originally made by her late mother, Sheila. The waxed rind cheeses are available either plain, or flavoured with garlic or nettle. (Coolnaleen, Listowel ☎ 068-40245 kerrycheese@netscape.net)

Farmers' Market
● Listowel Farmers' Market

Look out for the very distinguished produce of local organic grower Carl Knapp at the Listowel market, along with lots of other delicious local specialities. (Thursday 11am www.listowelfoodfair.com)

Milltown

Shop & Market
● Milltown Natural Centre

Do not miss the brilliant adventure that is Mary O'Riordan's Milltown Natural Centre. Housed in a gothic, draughty old church surrounded by gravestones, just up from the centre of the village, this is the most surreal place in which to find excellent foods, great natural products and a lively Saturday morning market. They sell gardening tools of fine provenance, rustic hand-made chairs and other furniture, clothes, lots of good wholefoods, books and lots of farm implements. Look out for local specialities such as Callinfercy Organics who have organic meat products, and vegetarian food from The Phoenix. Pure brilliant! (Old Church, Milltown ☎ 066-976 7869 www.milltownorganicmarket.com, Open Tue-Sat. Farmers' Market takes place Sat 10am-1pm)

Portmagee

Bar, Restaurant & Guesthouse
● The Moorings @ The Bridge Bar

Gerard and Patricia Kennedy's bar, restaurant and guest-house in pretty Portmagee is an excellent choice for good seafood, served in a true, unpretentious setting. There is food in both the bar – seafood potato skins; seafood basket of the day – and in the restaurant, where classics such as grilled black sole on the bone or seafood medley with garlic butter share menu space with honey roast duck and medallions of sirloin steak with madeira and grape sauce. The Kennedys show a real commitment, determination and ambition in The Moorings, and the comfortable – and inexpensive – rooms are more than enough to persuade one to make a serious night of it. (Portmagee ☎ 066-947 7108 www.moorings.ie)

Sneem

Farmhouse Cheese
● Dereenaclaurig Farmhouse Cheese

Harry van der Zanden's cheese is one of the most difficult to find, but it's worth hunting down the cheesemaker at local markets in Caherdaniel, Cahirciveen and elsewhere to get your hands on an expert Gouda-style cheese made with milk from his own herd. We like to buy some, take it home and then mature it for an extra couple of months, at which time this raw milk cheese begins to express a dense, dry lacticity which is most appealing. Look for the sign as you drive around the Ring, for you can also buy from the farm, where if you are lucky you will also find some whey butter for sale. (Derreenaclaurig, Sneem ☎ 064-45330)

Butcher
● PJ Burns

Make sure to stop at this little butcher's shop in pretty Sneem to buy some of Mr Burn's justly celebrated black pudding. Made in a cake-style shape, in the Kerry fashion, it's a delight for the morning's fried breakfast, or fry some slices to serve with a casserole of pulses for a tingly, salty charge. Only excellent. (Sneem ☎ 064-45139)

Tralee

Bakery
● Kiely's Cameo Bakery

This small bakery produces some extremely interesting seed breads, made for the Lifefibre Company, which are well worth searching for. The fruit and fibre bread, for instance, has linseeds, sunflower seeds and sesame seeds alongside sultanas and soyabeans. Cameo stress the obvious healthful benefits of their range, of course, but the assortment of breads are first and foremost good and tasty. (Tralee Road Industrial Estate, Castleisland ☎ 066-714 2944)

Shop
● Kingdom Food & Wine

Maeve Duff and Pat Fitzgibbon's food and wine shop is the destination Tralee has needed for yonks. This pair are experienced and choosy, and their selection of deli goods, ready meals and wines is excellent. (Tralee ☎ 066-711 8562)

Restaurant
● Restaurant David Norris

David Norris is the outstanding cook of Tralee, and he has a handsome, up-the-stairs room in which to reveal his delicious work. In a conservative town, Mr Norris has always offered food cooked with imagination and passion – loin of venison with a ravioli of chicken livers; scallops with crisp Serrano ham and a coral sauce; Kerry beef with brandy cream and French-fried onions. Flavours are elegant, subtle and pleasing, and service is only excellent. (Ivy House, Ivy Terrace, Tralee ☎ 066-718 5654 — Open Dinner)

Tuosist

Dairy
● Knockatee Dairy

Olga & Peter Ireson have a tiny herd of adorable Jersey cows, whose milk is used to produce organic buttermilk, cheeses and country butter. Their Jersey butter, with its powerful flavour and rich yellow colour, and in particular their outstanding real buttermilk, are incredible foods. Here is a true buttermilk, sweet and savoury enough to slake any thirst on a hot day, and using it to bake soda bread makes for a dreamily perfect loaf. Peter likes to flavour his cheeses with all manner of unusual flavourings, but we like the fudgy, open flavours of the plain cheese, as they best express the superlative qualities of the milk. You will find their foods in local shops and markets such as Carriganass Castle. (Tuosist ☎ 064-8436)

County Kildare

gourmet pizza, Ballysax organic broilers,
markets, farm potatoes, pickled herring...

Ballymore Eustace

Restaurant
● **The Ballymore Inn**

Georgina and Barry O'Sullivan's Ballymore Inn is one of the
glories of Irish cooking. Writing in *The
Gastropub Cookbook*, Diana Henry says that
"Georgina takes inspiration from everywhere – there's Moroccan lamb couscous,
Thai fish broth with coconut milk, and beef
and wild mushrooms in Guinness – and she
is true to the roots of all these dishes".
And that is the secret of the Ballymore. Mrs O'Sullivan is an
authentic cook: her culinary search is the search for authenticity. Having hunted it down and worked it out to her satis-
faction, she cooks it in the restaurant: chicken with Fran
Frazer's wild mushroom pasta and truffle oil; Wexford king
scallops with saffron sauce; Wicklow lamb with organic
leaves; Sheridan's farmhouse cheese. Her search for the real
in her cooking is helped by using vegetables from Penny
Lange's bio-dynamic farm, and Thomas Doyle's potatoes, and
lots of other local suppliers. "Home cooking" is what Mrs
O'Sullivan calls it. Home cooking never tasted so fine.
(Ballymore Eustace ☎ 045-864585)

Ballysax

Organic Chicken
● **Margaret McDonnell**

Margaret McDonnell's organic chickens are available
through specialist outlets such as Danny O'Toole of
Terenure, the Leopardstown Market and the wonderful
Saturday market in Kiltiernan, but anyone seeking a top-
quality organic bird can also buy direct from the farm. The
Ballysax bids are the real thing: reared for up to three
months, minded meticulously and then processed on the
farm, they are a vital alternative to the tragic and insupport-
able condition that is the fate of the modern battery chick-
en. Ballysax is just a couple of miles from Kilcullen.
(Martinstown Rd, Ballysax, The Curragh ☎ 087-210 8895
magmcdonnell@eircom.net)

Carbury

Farm Shop
● **Deirdre & Norman O'Sullivan**

Deirdre and Norman are amongst the great stalwarts of
the Dublin Food Co-Op, but have recently
expanded into importing some organic produce to sell alongside their own excellent
organic vegetables and eggs, and they have
created a farm shop which opens on Friday
afternoons from 2pm-7pm. Their system is
ingenious: on Wednesdays an e-mail is sent to their customer list, stating what will be available. Customers reply,
but the beauty of the system is that you can collect your
order from the farm at any time over the weekend.
Deirdre's sister Rose also sells their produce in Trim, on
Fridays at the Tourist Office and Heritage Centre in the
town. (Carbury ☎ 046-955 3337 organicveg@eircom.net)

Castledermot

Restaurant and B&B
● **ffrench's The Schoolhouse**

The Schoolhouse has long been one of the central features
of Castledermot, but with new owners and a new livery, it
has been attracting attention for some smart cooking –
their own pork sausages; salmon fishcake; mushroom risotto, good desserts – as well as some good breads, which are
also sold in the Naas farmers' market. The Schoolhouse also
has half a dozen comfortable rooms, so it's an ideal spot for
staying over if navigating the N9. (Main St, Castledermot
☎ 059-914 4099 www.theschoolhouse.ie — Open Dinner)

Clane

Café
● **Zest Café**

Mark Condron's busy café touches all culinary bases, from
homemade burgers, wraps and sandwiches to pastas, funky
pizzas and a broad selection of main courses at dinnertime.
(Clane Shopping Centre, Clane ☎ 045-893 223
zestcafeclane@eircom.net — Open Lunch and Dinner)

Kilcullen

Sausages
● Jane Russell's Original Irish Sausages

Jane Russell has a strong claim to the use of the term
"Original" for her sausages, as her family has
been involved in the pork sausage business
for 150 years. Mrs Russell has simply gone
back to the old ways of the old days with
her sausages: no fillers, no rubbish, just
pork and natural fillings. The result, with her
standard pork sausage, is clean, fresh flavours of pork meat
and a sausage that is drier in texture than one is used to
these days – those familiar with Olivia Goodwillie's
Lavistown sausages will know what to expect. The plain
pork bangers are lovely for breakfast, but would be equally
fine poached with lentils. There are also beef and Guinness
sausages, lamb and mint, and an already-popular Toulouse
sausage amongst the range.
(Link Business Park, Kilcullen☎ 045-480100
straightsausages@eircom.net)

Herring
● Scan Foods

Catherine Noren will be remembered by many food lovers
for the superb Swedish cooking she produced
at Dunworley Cottage, in Butlerstown,
West Cork. Well, if you have been hanker
ing after that magisterial pickled and pre
served herring, with some sweet
Scandinavian mustard sauce, and want an
excuse to break open that bottle of aquavit, then
look out for the little jars of Scan Foods herring that Mrs
Noren produces in Kilcullen. The pickled herring is seasoned with Jamaican allspice; the mustard preserved fish has
both French and Scandinavian mustards, there are herrings
flavoured with juniper and others, and these are little jars of
sheer delight, and unique amongst Irish artisan foods. So, go
on: crack open that bottle of Aalborg Jubilaeums Akvavit,
and look out for the herring in Cavistons of Glasthule,
Mange Tout in Kinsale, at Frank Hederman's market stalls, in
Field's of Skibbereen in West Cork, and at the
Leopardstown Friday market, where it is sold by Catherine
herself. (Kilcullen ☎ 045-482953)

Kildare

Bistro
● Kristianna's Bistro

Peter and Bernie Hoffmann's engagingly simple bistro in Kildare town has heartfelt, comforting cooking in the northern European style, and friendly, personal service. (Market Square, Kildare ☎ 045-522985 — Open Dinner)

Leixlip

Country House Hotel & Restaurant
● Leixlip House Hotel

Sean Hicks' cooking in the Bradaun restaurant is the main attraction in this popular hotel. Mr Hicks is a competitive, creative talent and his food has lots of style. (Leixlip ☎ 01-624 2268 www.leixliphouse.com — Open Lunch & Dinner)

Maynooth

Wine Merchant
● Mill Wine Cellar

This splendid wine shop is a mainstay of the town, both for beer-guzzling students and choosy, wine-loving locals, both of which groups are well served by a shop with a splendid selection of drinks. The Mill is a splendidly atmospheric shop, handsome inside and out, and it's packed with all manner of drinks, accessories and whatnots. Locals should lookout for their annual wine fair, and at Christmas they offer an excellent hamper service, with prices to suit all pockets. (Maynooth ☎ 01-629 1022 www.millwinecellar.ie)

Moyvalley

Wine Merchant
● Furey's of Moyvalley

Furey's is probably everyone's favourite pull-over stop on the Dublin-Galway road for reliable, energy-giving cooking; food that will either console you as you draw breath having finally slipped away from the Dublin gridlock, or else it will gird your loins as you head east, giving you strength and fortitude to face that gridlock. (Moyvalley, Broadford ☎ 046-955 1185)

Naas

Farmers' Market
● Farmers' Market, Naas

Siobhan Popplewell has organised a dynamic farmers' market in Naas, bringing together such great marketeers as Ardsallagh Goat's Cheese, Sheridans, Carrowholly Farmhouse Cheese, Dan Aherne's Organic Chickens from Cork, J&V Organic Meat from Leitrim, Shorescape Smoked Fish from Bandon, Castleuddery Organic Fruit & Vegetables from Wicklow, Twineinc. organic herbs and oils, also from Wicklow, G's Jams from County Laois, The Gallic Kitchen pastries and baking from Dublin 8, as well as a new local arrival, ffrench's Schoolhouse Restaurant breads from Castledermot. A change of location has now brought the market next door to the Storehouse restaurant. (Friary Lane, beside Storehouse, Sat 10am-3pm)

Craft Bakery
● The Gourmet Bakery

Michelle and Laurence Kiely's craft bakery produces an excellent range of breads, an ever-expanding range that is limited only by the amount of time Laurence has to concoct new varieties. Their large loaves of Italian-style bread are particularly fine, but the range is unified by artisan levels of creativity. (33 North Main St, Naas ☎ 045-899112)

Deli, Foods-to-go, Café
● Harvest Kitchen

Susan Rouine and Valerie O'Hanlon's sparkling deli, café and wine shop is one of the key addresses in the county. Long treasured for their take-home dishes, good breads and other practical and vital foods for time-starved folk, they now have created seating for 20 people inside The Kitchen, where they offer wraps, panini, pitta pockets and salads. At Christmastime they specialise in gourmet Harvest Hampers. (1 Sallins Rd, Naas ☎ 045-881793)

10 GREAT
SAUSAGES

1

CAHERBEG
FREE RANGE PORK SAUSAGE

2

THE GERMAN BUTCHER
FRANKFURTER

3

GUBBEEN SMOKEHOUSE
SUN-DRIED TOMATO & FETA SAUSAGE

4

HICKS
WINE & GARLIC SAUSAGE

5

LAVISTOWN
CUMIN & GARLIC PORK SAUSAGE

6

McGEOUGH'S
CONNEMARA LAMB SAUSAGE

7

MOSSBROOK FARM
SPICY BUT NICEY SAUSAGE

8

MOYALLON
WILD BOAR SAUSAGE

9

ON THE WILD SIDE
FREE-RANGE PORK SAUSAGE

10

JANE RUSSELL
BEEF & GUINNESS SAUSAGE

County Kilkenny

artisan apple juice, farmhouse sausages, organic wines,
crafts, boutique hotels . . .

Bennettsbridge

Pottery & Café
● **Nicky Mosse Pottery**

This gorgeous showcase for the beautiful pottery and furniture of the Mosse family is one of those stores where maintaining self-control is all but impossible. The artful arrangement of so much beautiful craft work means you just chuck
self-denial out the window and get down to some serious
retail luxury. And, after the credit card has been punished,
there is a charming café in which to take lunch, and the
cooking shows the same artful consideration as everything
else that is for sale. (Bennettsbridge ☎ 056-772 7105
www.nicholasmosse.com)

Graiguenamanagh

Restaurant and B&B
● **Waterside**

The rooms are fairly basic in this attractive old mill just
down from the bridge in Graiguenamanagh, but Brigid
Roberts' cooking has a pleasingly simple style – blini with
crispy bacon, cabbage and sour cream; trout with toasted
almond hollandaise; confit duck leg with spiced lentils and
caramelized onion sauce. In the town itself, do drop into
Doyle's Bar & Grocery for a pint, or a packet of fig rolls.
(Graiguenamanagh ☎ 059-972 4246 — Open Dinner)

Kilkenny

Wine Merchant
● **Le Caveau**

Pascal Rossignol is – if you will pardon the
pun – steeped in wine. He hails from
Gevrey-Chambertin, in the heart of
Burgundy's Cote d'Or, his brother
works with the superstar Burgundy
winemaker Vincent Girardin, his cousin is

On top of their game

married to Joseph Roty, and the net result of all this wine culture is one of the very best shops to buy wine in Ireland. Mr Rossignol and his wife, Geraldine, work with some 30 different producers, are constantly and patiently adding more to their list, and the wines they select are beauties: Tour des Gendres from Bergerac is a super rustic wine at great value; Meyer-Fonné pinot blanc from Alsace is a superb example of fruit extraction from truly superb wine makers; a Regnie from Domaine des Forchets is a lovely, tart Beaujolais. Wherever your gaze lands, there are great bottles to be enjoyed, with the Burgundy wines of Joseph Roty, Vincent Girardin, Philippe Rossignol, Jacky Truchot-Martin and Louis Michel a particular treasure trove of great winemaking, and some of them are pretty affordable. Delivery service is fleet, the web site efficient, and there are frequent special offers. A model wine company.
(Market Yard, Kilkenny ☎ 056-775 2166 www.lecaveau.ie)

Café
● Chez Pierre

Try to overlook the furniture, which is spindly and uncomfortable, and concentrate instead on CP's nice line of tartines – a thick slice of good white bread, with different toppings (leek and prosciutto; goat's cheese; duck and red onion marmalade) and lots of olive oil. In the evenings there is a short dinner menu, including a most memorable boeuf bourguignonne. (17 Parliament St, Kilkenny ☎ 056-776 4655 — Open Lunch & Dinner)

Crêperie
● La Crêperie

La Crêperie offers a big range of crêpes – gorgonzola and walnuts is a particular local favourite – and toasted panini – grilled aubergine and mozzarella – and some salads, accompanied by bottles of flavoured olive oils on all the tables. Value is a premium: you can have a stonking lunch for under a fiver and good hot chocolate and Illy coffee are good attractions. (John St, Kilkenny)

Restaurant
● Fleva

Michael Mee's skill pulls the diverse dishes of Fleva's menus together – Cajun spiced chicken; Shanghai noodles; monkfish wrapped in Parma ham; Asian duck – and he makes them work successfully, and with aplomb. A particular strength is some fine game cooking: Canadian goose with sliced potatoes is delicious; warm slices of pigeon breast with mango is very fine, which makes Fleva a good choice for wholesome winter dining. It's a comfortable room, demurely lit, and value for money is very keen. (84 High St, Kilkenny ☎ 056-777 0021)

Delicatessen
● The Gourmet Store

An excellent destination for vital cooking necessities and some nice food-to-go. (Main St, Kilkenny ☎ 056-777 1727)

Hotel
● Hibernian Hotel

The Hib is a local secret, a place where insiders come to enjoy the good bar food in Jacobs Cottage, in particular the wonderfully comforting bread and butter pudding, and some pleasant service. (1 Ormonde St, Kilkenny ☎ 056-777 1888 www.kilkennyhibernianhotel.com)

Design Shop and Café
● Kilkenny Design Centre

The beautiful Kilkenny Design centre has always had a fine café in its original location. Fans of their modern, Avoca-accented cooking should know that the chain has opened a new branch out west, in the centre of Galway.
(Castle Yard, Kilkenny ☎ 056-772 2118
www.kilkennydesign.com)

Hotel
● Kilkenny Ormonde Hotel

This recently-expanded hotel is home to a talented chef, Mark Gaffney, a cook whose work is characterised by vivid colours and intelligent combinations, and also by excellent value for money, whether you eat in the bistro or in the restaurant, Fredricks. Mr Gaffney is a talent to watch.
(Ormonde St, Kilkenny ☎ 056-772 3900
www.kilkennyormonde.com)

Gastro Bar
● Marble City Bar

The groovy MCB is one of Kilkenny's best destinations for a sit-down-but-not-expensive lunch. There is an extensive

choice of dishes which prove to be consistently good –
mussels in Thai soup; bangers and mash, beer battered cod,
fishcakes, all served with salad and/or chips. The lighting in
the David Collins-designed room is quite dim and you sit at
the bar or at small tables, so the MCB definitely feels like a
pub. There are nice innovative touches on the menu like
being able to have half-size portions of the main courses for
lunch. It's packed to the rafters between 1pm and 2pm and
stays full into the early afternoon, so get there early. (66
High St, Kilkenny ☎ 056-776 1143 — Open Day-time)

Restaurant
● Rinuccini

Antonio Cavaliere's restaurant is set just down off the
street across from the castle, and it's long been a very popular destination for locals and visitors who enjoy the fresh
flavours of classic Italian cooking and the good value for
money. Antipasti, good fresh pastas and some rich meat and
fish cookery may not be the Italian cooking that is in vogue
today, but it's always deeply enjoyable food. Seven rooms
upstairs allow visitors to stay right in the heart of the city
in comfortable rooms. (1 The Parade, Kilkenny ☎ 056-
776 1575 www.rinuccini.com — Open Lunch & Dinner)

Café
● The Room Café

Unpretentious and honest, the way all good food should be,
this little room with its ten tables has some of the freshest,
most colourful and uncomplicated food you can find in the
city. If they do an open sandwich with Cashel Blue cheese
on stromboli bread, the cheese will be in perfect condition,
the bread just ace. A vegetable quiche will have delicate,
buttery pastry; soups are heartwarming, and other mains
such as chicken with roast red pepper sauce, or a good Thai
chicken curry, are direct and enjoyable. Desserts are excellent, and it's a treat to enjoy them with a cup of tea in mid-
afternoon. Splendid. (Friary St, Kilkenny ☎ 056-778 6996 —
Open Day-time)

Asian Delicatessen
● Shortis Wong

Shortis Wong is where Sheridan's meets The
Asia Market: stratospheric standards, great
foods, fantastic service, and the funkiest Asian

street food you will find anywhere. Chris Wong's spring rolls are the best, his curried samosas are the best, heck, the man can even make a quotidian sausage roll into something eminently scoffable. Aside from the food-to-go, the shop is simple and exciting, crammed with things to cook with and eat with. Peachy. (John St, Kilkenny ☎ 056-776 1305)

Wine Merchant

● Vendemia Wines

Helen and Urs Tobler's wine company specialise in directly-imported organic and bio-dynamic wines, from Spain, France, Italy and Switzerland. Some of the wines contain delightful surprises – an intense scent of tinned mandarin oranges from the Zusslin Pinot Auxerrois, for instance, whilst the same winemaker's Riesling is muted on the nose but lush and full in the mouth. Nice wines, and very fast, efficient delivery service. (Hebron Rd Industrial Estate, ☎ 056-777 0225 www.vendemiawines.com)

Wine Merchant

● The Wine Centre

The astonishing selection of drinks in Edmund O'Keeffe's Wine Centre really has to be seen to be believed. Whatever your heart desires is here, from modest wines to plastic crunching superstar bottles and ancient vintages, along with an incredible selection of spirits distilled from every source imaginable and, finally, an incredible array of beers from all over the world. If you seek something rare, the chances are you will find it here. (John St, Kilkenny ☎ 056-772 2907)

Hotel and Restaurant

● Zuni

Sleek, hip, successful: the Zuni formula has been a wow! from the day this restaurant, bar and rooms first opened its doors, and the only problem they face today is coping with the fact that le tout Kilkenny always wants to eat here. The cooking is smart and hip, modern and quite fashionable, but Maria Raftery takes standard dishes that you see everywhere else these days – risottos, fresh pasta dishes, braised lamb shank; the ubiquitous Caesar salad, modish desserts – and gives all the food her own signature. Flavours are light, polished and pleasing, and the cooking is always exceptionally well-balanced.

The dining room is one of the most delightful anywhere in Ireland, a great hub of energy that is the equal of any room in the capital. The rooms upstairs in the boutique hotel are not as successful as the dining room or the bar, and may well be due a revamp, but they are good value, and the combination of bar, restaurant and rooms together makes for Kilkenny's don't-miss! destination. (26 Patrick St, Kilkenny ☎ 056-772 3999 www.zuni.ie — Open Lunch & Dinner)

Lavistown

Farmhouse Cheese & Sausages
● **Lavistown Farmhouse**

One of our favourite crackpot theories insists that farmhouse cheeses are a mirror image of their cheesemakers. So, how does Olivia Goodwillie's Lavistown farmhouse cheese measure up? Let's say that, like the cheesemaker, this is an intellectual, modest, inquisitive cheese, with a subtlety that you could almost miss. It's in the style of a Caerphilly, but truthfully it's a Lavistown, pure and simple, for the template of a territorial style has long been erased by the cheese's own character. It's beautiful with wine and, sacrilegious as it may seem, it is also one of the best cooking cheeses, melting to a lush richness that is damn well irresistible.

Being a great cheesemaker would be enough for most people, but Mrs Goodwillie also makes some of our favourite pork sausages, subtly flavoured with garlic or cumin – and also runs the exhilarating Lavistown study centre, which is host to a fine range of craft and culinary-based courses run throughout the year. (Lavistown ☎ 056-776 5145 www.lavistownhouse.ie)

Piltown

Apple Juice
● **The Little Irish Apple Co.**

Philip and Oren Little keep 60 acres of apple orchards just by the edge of the River Suir, near to Piltown, and using their own fruit they make an organic apple juice, with jonagold apples used exclusively for the cuvée, whilst their standard juice uses a mixture of their apples, including bramleys and seasonal dessert apples. Both are refreshingly delicious and very well-crafted, and juices of this artisan quality are always particularly fine with a good simple lunch of bread and cheese. And, for kids, they are a pure and trustworthy treat. (Clonmore House, Piltown ☎ 051-387109)

Honey
● Mileeven

Eilis Gough's sparkling range of honeys, organic jams, pre-serves and fruit cakes are all distinguished by exceptionally high standards, in particular the Mileeven organic jams which are mighty wollops of pure fruit that are a sure treat. Ms Gough started off as a bee keeper, and has steadily expanded her range from pure honeys through flavoured honeys, and logically on into marmalades and preserves and then into fine baking of traditional fruit cakes. Beautiful packaging means that the Mileeven foods also make superb gifts for food lovers, especially their Christmas range. You will find them in good shops and delis throughout the coun-try. (Owning Hill, Piltown ☎ 051-643368 www.mileevenfinefoods.com)

Thomastown

Restaurant
● Hudson's

Richard and Kyra Hudson's restaurant is the star of the dis-trict. A pair of well-appointed and comfortable rooms makes an apt venue for splendidly professional service and cracking food: crab spring rolls with a soya butter sauce are a 10-out-of-10 dish, a carefully composed Caesar salad is respectful and restrained, whilst Barbary duck with figs and a balsamic dressing is truly delicious, and sea bass with pea and chorizo risotto is precise, smart cooking.
Desserts are almost as strong an asset – plum crumble with flaked almonds and clotted cream, a deep, wide dish of crème brûlée – and Hudson's manages with ease to make dinner into a special event. The wine list could do with some notes, but everything else about this hip destination is truly shipshape. (Station Rd, Thomastown ☎ 056-779 3900 — Open Dinner)

County Laois

country fruit jams, smoked farmhouse cheeses, craft baking,
cosy B&B's, country houses...

Abbeyleix

Jam maker
● **G's Jams**

Helen Gee's jam operation has gone from
zero to hero in double-quick time, thanks
to brilliant fresh fruit flavours in the jams,
and the sheer charm of the jam maker
herself, busy and chatty selling her foods via
various farmers' markets. It's a smashing
combination. (Abbeyleix, ☎ 0502-31058)

Ballacolla

Farmhouse Cheese
● **Abo Cheese Co.**

Pat Hyland is a tireless cheesemaker and cheeseseller, a man
you will meet at numerous markets selling the extensive
range of Abo cheeses. There are smoked cheeses, organic
cheeses, cheeses preserved in oil, along with the brie-style
Abbey cheeses – the Abbey Blue brie and the plain Abbey
brie – with which Mr Hyland first made his reputation.
(Cuffsborough, Ballacolla ☎ 0502-38559)

Mountrath

Country House
● **Roundwood House**

In Frank and Rosemary Kennan's lovely old country house:
"Recreation mainly consists of good food, good wine and
conversation", they write. And that, indeed, is Roundwood
House in a nutshell, and that's why people adore this elegantly crumpled old Palladian house. There is nothing lavish
about Roundwood, nothing pretentious, nothing stagey or
fake. What Frank and Rosemary offer is simply the joys of
the country house experience, enjoyed amongst friends, in
the heart of the beautiful and unspoilt Slieve Bloom mountains in the heart of the country. (Mountrath ☎ 0502-32120
roundwood@eircom.net)

Portlaoise

B&B
● Ivyleigh House

Dinah and Jerry Campion's super-smart B&B is a treasure of a destination. Mrs Campion is a meticulous housekeeper, a meticulous hostess and a meticulous cook, so everything she does has a sheen of sheer class and quality about it. (Bank Place, Portlaoise ☎ 0502 22081 www.ivyleigh.com)

Restaurant
● The Kingfisher

Khurshid Googee's Indian restaurant is a stylishly made-over bank that has carved out a fine reputation in Portlaoise. It's manned by a well-motivated crew, and whilst it was Punjabi cuisine that initially comprised most of the food offer, the kitchen has begun to incorporate more dishes from other regional Indian cuisines, though old favourites continue to feature on extensive menus. (Main St, Portlaoise ☎ 0502-62500 www.kingfisherrestaurant.com — Open Lunch & Dinner)

Restaurant & Food Store
● The Kitchen & Food Hall

Jim Tynan's brilliant bistro and delicatessen is home to great food, great cooking, and caring service that starts with the boss himself. This crew love food, they love to cook and bake, and it shows in the lush, true flavours of everything prepared and sold in both the lovely shop and the fine restaurant. Mr Tynan has been an ambasssador for good food for years, and is a major player in our food culture. (Hynds Sq, Portlaoise ☎ 0502-62061 — Open Lunch)

Restaurant
● The Lemon Tree

Kevin Hennessy's restaurant has created quite a buzz, with Mr Hennessy proving himself to be a magisterial host, and the kitchen firing out some fine cooking: hot smoked salmon with beetroot and coriander salsa; Angus sirloin with basil mash; goat cheese, pine nut and tomato charlotte. Food and drinks are priced with great keenness, so value is at a premium and one can have a fine time without breaking the bank. (Main St, Portlaoise ☎ 0502-62200 — Open Dinner)

10 GREAT
IRISH BACONS

1

**BALLYBRADO
ORGANIC BACON**

2

**DAVID BURNS
THICK CUT BACON**

3

**CAHERBEG
FREE RANGE PORK BACON**

4

**CLONAKILTY
DRY CURED BACON**

5

**GUBBEEN SMOKEHOUSE
MAPLE CURED BACON**

6

**MOYALLON FOODS
DRY-CURED SADDLEBACK BACON**

7

**O'DOHERTY'S
BLACK BACON**

8

**O'FLYNN'S
DRY-CURED SMOKED BACON**

9

**JOHN DAVID POWER
DRY CURED BACON**

10

**UMMERA
SMOKED BACON**

County Leitrim

gourmet sauces, rare breed cattle, artisan patés, fresh goat's milk cheeses, organic growers galore...

Arigna

Sauces and Preserves
● Gleann Gourmet Sauces

Maimie Lambert's artisan sauces are a must-have for busy families, because their ease of use gives you convenience whilst their excellence gives you pleasure and peace of mind. The sauces are excellent with pasta dishes, and the jams and chutneys are a mainstay of any smart larder. (Glenkillamy, Arigna ☎ 071-964 6303)

Ballinamore

Cakes
● Cannaboe Confectionery

Sharon Sweeney's company creates the most exquisite cakes for specialist occasions, everything from weddings to anniversaries to corporate celebrations to Barbie doll cakes for that little imp in your life. Ms Sweeney's work is characterised by a strong sense of modern style, especially in her imaginative, and yet restrained, decoration of the cakes. (Willowfield Road, Ballinamore ☎ 071-964 4778 www.cacamilis.com)

Carrick-on-Shannon

Country House
● Hollywell

Tom and Rosaleen Maher have hospitality in their blood, and it shows. Their sons, Ronan and Conor, run the super Oarsman restaurant in town, whilst Mum'n'Dad run a glorious, cosy, comfy country house just on the other side of the river. The Mahers' confidence and expertise in the hospitality business is never clinical or slickly professional. Instead their deep professionalism translates as affability, and the skill to make guests relax and enjoy this lovely house. A great destination. (Liberty Hill, Carrick-on-Shannon ☎ 078-962 1124 hollywell@esatbiz.com)

Restaurant & Bar
● The Oarsman

Conor and Ronan Maher's smashing pub and restaurant in
the centre of town offers organic pasta dishes, smart sandwiches and wraps as well as particularly great puddings
from chef Sheila Sharpe, which ensure the Oarsman is
always jammed at lunchtimes. Dinner upstairs lets the menu
open out and let's the kitchen crew flex their muscles, with
ravioli of salmon with sautéed scallops, loin of venison
stuffed with morels and served with baby vegetables, and
cannon of lamb with ratatouille and sweet potato. Lovely
cooking, lovely place. (Bridge Street, Carrick-on-Shannon
☎ 078-962 1733 www.theoarsman.com)

Wine Shop
● The Wine Experience

This stylish wine store in the atmospheric and beautifully
restored Market Yard centre has a fine range of wines, and
they offer a delivery service, a gift service, a party service
and regular tastings. (Market Yard Centre, Carrick on
Shannon ☎ 078-50535 info@the-wine-experience.net)

Dromahair

Artisan Pâtés
● The Irish Bay Tree Company

Jean and Andrew Campbell Gaffney's model artisan company makes a splendid range of gourmet pâtés, based on the
belief that "the best foods can only come from the best
products". The pâtés, therefore, are made in small batches
and then blast frozen to maintain quality. Allied to this quali-
ty-driven directive is a vivid creative imagination. So, their
chicken liver pâté also has poitin and cranberries. A little
chilli is added in with the smoked salmon pate, and classic
blue cheese and pear are allied together for an intriguing
texture. Look out for the Irish Bay Tree pâtés in good shops
and delis, and at farmers' markets. (The Old Rectory,
Dromahair ☎ 071-916 4579 irishbaytree@eircom.net)

Farmhouse Cheese
● Tullynascreena Goat's Farm

Michael & Marika Tolksdorf's fresh goat's milk cheeses are
of organic standard, and are flavoured with fresh herbs, gar-

lic, and various spices. The cheeses are sold very fresh
and have a piquant pleasantness, and an agrestic richness.
You will find them in Sligo's Tir na nOg and at
Leopardstown Market. Michael also makes a cheese preserved in oil, and there are plans to create a hard goat's
cheese. (Dromahair ☎ 071-916 4590)

Keshcarrigan

Restaurant
● **Anthia's Restaurant**

Smart local knowledge has identified Maureen & Ricky
Irawan's canalside restaurant, with its fusion of Indonesian
and European cooking, as one of the best waterway venues.
(Ceiscarrigan Lawn, Keshcarrigan ☎ 071-964 2555)

Kinlough

Restaurant with Rooms
● **The Courthouse**

Piero Melis's sweet and simple restaurant with rooms in
lovely Kinlough is a charming address. Mr Melis is from
Sardinia, and whilst his cooking has something of a
Mediterranean accent, what impresses most about the food
is the strong individual signature of the cooking. Ravioli with
spinach and ricotta is a classic Italian dish, but Mr Melis' version has its own textures and idiosyncrasies, whilst veal
chop with rosemary and white wine is likewise no mere
reiteration of a classic combination. The wine list offers several wines that Mr Melis brings in from Sardinia – the
Argiolas red and white wines are fab, whilst the 1998 Turiga
I.G.T. is an awesome blockbuster of a wine that is well
worth its high price. (Kinlough ☎ 072-42391 — Open Dinner)

Lecarrow

Rare Breeds
● **Galloways of Lecarrow**

Barbara & Joachim Schaefer breed
Galloway cattle, and in a world where our
respect for the diversity of breeds is often

little more than lip service, the Schaefers are doing a valuable job of asserting the value of these shaggy, resilient cattle. What also asserts the value of the Galloways is their superb eating quality: sweet, with a deep umami saltiness, rich and dense in texture, the Galloway beef is a real treat. The Galloways are a hardy breed, so they need little in the way of supplements to their diet of pasture, which means the meat is very healthful. (Lecarrow House, Drumkeeran ☎ 071-964 8271 www.iolfree.ie/~galloways)

Manorhamilton

Shop
● The Co-Op Shop

Leitrim has many organic growers, and they all tend to make their way to the pioneering Co-Op shop with their fine produce. The shop is modest and unpretentious, the produce they sell always uniformly excellent.
(Manorhamilton ☎ 071-985 5609)

Rossinver

Herbs
● Eden Herbs

Rod Alston is the man who created the rich organic food culture that animates so many Leitrim farms and farmers. You can find and buy his superb Eden Herbs vegetables and salad leaves and herb plants in Tir na Nog in Sligo, the Co-Op Shop in Manorhamilton, as well as from the farm itself. (Rossinver ☎ 071-985 4122)

Organic Centre
● The Organic Centre

John O'Neill is manager of this pioneering and visionary concept, where education about organic practices meets with practical demonstrations, and where the produce of the centre itself can also be bought. The range of courses are always imaginatively conceived and delivered, and the centre and its gardens have a great, practical, utilitarian feel that is perfectly charming. (Rossinver ☎ 072-985 4338 www.theorganiccentre.ie)

County Limerick

the Milk Market, organic college, sassy salsas, creative chocolates, craft butchers...

Adare

Restaurant
● The Wild Geese

There isn't a better himself-and-herself team in Irish Food than David Foley and Julie Randles (who actually are, but don't say we told you, Mr & Mrs Foley). Their match of talents is magisterial: she commands front of house with a skill that is a joy to witness, whilst Mr Foley's intricate and beautifully measured modern Irish cooking is a thrill. The fact that their stage is also one of the most beautiful rooms in the country means that the Wild Geese is as top-of-their-game as it gets.

Mr Foley's food reads complicated on the menu – pan-fried fillets of john dory with a potato and rosemary crust, fennel, dill and tomato compote, with a basil hollandaise is a fairly typical example of his tri-partite arrangement of elements – but it always eats true and clean, for this is a quietly intellectual cook who makes sure everything is perfectly resolved. Indeed, this food is fun to eat for all the senses, for the compositions of foods engage your intellect whilst the flavours ping-pong about the senses with delight. The Wild Geese is a veritable archetype of the contemporary Irish restaurant in every way, a destination where you can take the heartbeat of Irish country cooking. (Rose Cottage, Main St, Adare ☎ 061-396451 wildgeese@indigo.ie)

Ballingarry

Restaurant
● The Mustard Seed

Dan Mullane is one of the most significant figures in Irish hospitality, a man whose sense of welcome, whose eye for design, and whose craving for comfort – whether in his food, his rooms or his restaurants – has always been totally unique. We can perhaps explain his gifts best by reference to his sense of humour: others who have been in the business as long as Mr Mullane might take themselves rather seriously, but Dan has a glint in his eye that takes away any sense of preciousness, and this humour makes him one of the truly great hosts. Comfort is his quest: comforting cooking in the beautiful Mustard Seed restaurant – sea bass with Swiss chard and a lemongrass, chilli and coconut cream is the sort of straight-forward-but-with-a-twist cooking that Mullane allows the kitchen team to get their head around – and whilst you can marvel at the acuity of the design and its contemporary knowingness, it is always the profound feeling of homeliness that you remember about Echo Lodge and its gorgeous rooms, a homeliness that will have you returning for more. (Ballingarry ☎ 069-68508 www.mustardseed.ie)

Drumcollogher

Organic College & Market
● **Organic College Market**

Jim McNamara's inspirational and educational organic college features a small market, in addition to an excellent range of
courses on horticulture, farming, sustainable
development and organic enterprise.
(Drumcollogher, ☎ 063-83604 www.organiccollege.com)

Glen-O-Sheen

Farmhouse Cheese
● **Oisin Farmhouse Cheese**

The Oisin farmhouse cheeses are superbly crafted artisan
cheeses. Whether they are making plain or
flavoured goat's cheeses, hard cheese or soft
feta cheeses, Rochus and Rose van der
Roche demonstrate a truly extraordinary
ability to maximise the flavours of the milk,
and to maximise the varying textures of the
cheeses. What impresses above all is the purity of the
cheeses: they are as fine as a Brancusi sculpture, impeccably
crafted and expressed, genuine works of culinary art. And
what they deliver in texture and appearance is more than
matched by delicate, crystalline flavours. Superb.
(Kilmallock ☎ 063-91528)

Limerick Market

Corkonians pride themselves on their famous English Market in the centre of Cork city, but they aren't the only ones to have a rather special space dedicated to a food market. Limerick's beautifully restored Milk Market is also a wonderfully atmospheric destination to shop for good things, and its development over the last decade, from down-at-heel venue to swish, uber-bling location, is a precise echo of the fate of the city itself during the last ten years. The smarter it has become, the better it has become, and for west coast artisans, the Milk Market is a key destination from which to start a business.

· *The Bavarian Butcher* Shoppers need sustenance, so if you have completed your tour of the Milk Market and are only famished, then the BB is the man for you: get a good frankfurter and restore your blood sugar level. If it's a hangover you are nursing, then a double-barrelled bratwurst roll with lots of mustard will soon perk your up. Look out also for the excellent meat loaf. (Michael Kolbe, Lackamore, Newport LK, Co Tipperary michaelkolbe@t-online.de)

· *Buddha's Belly* Who could resist a food company with a name like Buddha's Belly? We can't, and nor can we resist any of the chilli-based concoctions that Mr Buddha makes and sells: this is cracking stuff. Currently, we are addicted to the Caribbean papaya and chilli, and the chipotle and ancho salsa. And, as you know, we are not easily addicted. Demon stuff, and make sure to get a cute Buddha candle so you can get way, way into the groove. (Emoh-Ruo, O'Shea's Cross, Ballysimon, pmcollins@oceanfree.net)

· *Cocoa Bean Chocolate Co* Emily and Sarah and their Cocoa Bean Chocolates have come from nowhere to be on top of their game. They only began experimenting in

2002, have only had a factory space since the end of 2003, but by 2004 these superlative dark chocolate confections were knocking anyone who nibbled these choccy narcotics for six. The fact that they have no training in the demanding business of chocolate making makes their success even more extraordinary. "We just like it, we have a passion for it, and we only do dark chocolate," explains Sarah. These girls create wild, radical work: chocolate blocks blended with various nuts such as pistachio, almond, hazelnut, walnut and brazil nut; chocolate discs with flavours from Earl Grey tea to juniper, and superb fresh truffles with an aftertaste of pure chocolate that goes on forever. Inspired artisanship. (3b Limerick Food Kitchens, Crossagalla Ind Est, Ballysimon Rd, Limerick 061-446615 www.cocoabeanchocolates.com)

· *Forbidden Soups* Connie Devlin makes her delicious soups 100% vegetarian, and she also sells spicy samosas. (6 Reidy Park, Clancy Strand ☎ 086-104 4443)

· *Gourmet Tart Company* The Galway wizards of all things sweet and savoury in tart form have one of the busiest stalls in the market. This is great baking, both sweet and savoury. (65 Henry St, Galway ☎ 091-588384)

· *Greenacres Cheese Store* Marie Murphy's favourite cheeses are a reflection of the lady herself: powerful, expressive, mighty fun, up-for-it and into-it. Over the years, Greenacres has become the lynchpin of the Milk Market, and it's where you go for strong coffee, fresh juices, and refulgent, delicious cheeses. On Saturdays, the shop migrates out onto the square: don't miss it. (Limerick Milk Market ☎ 061-400334)

· *Kilshanny Cheese* Peter Nibbering sells the excellent raw-milk Gouda-style Kilshanny, one of the lesser-known stars of the west coast. Sweet and delicate when young, with gentle notes of allium, the older cheese then thunders through with notes of fudge and toffee. The only problem is getting a mature Kilshanny, for the cheeses are often sold out when young! There are various flavoured cheeses – garlic, herbs, cumin – but we love the subtle raw-milk, savoury-sweet pleasure of the plain cheese. (Derry House, Lahinch, Co Clare ☎ 065-707 1228)

· *Real Olive Co* Where would we be without them? We don't have to ask, for wherever there is a market, we aren't without them. (Cork Market Office ☎ 021-427 0842)

· *Sunflower Bakery* Vi is the baker, Kelly – formerly a pharmacist and wildlife biologist – assists, and the Sunflower breads are fine things: we love smoked cheese with the cinnamon and walnut bread, and our kids go a bundle on their cute gingerbread men. You will also find them at the Saturday Ennis market, where regulars snap up the brown bread, the chocolate truffle cake and the excellent scones, and at Tuamgraney on Sunday, and the breads are also sold by the Grainery in Scariff. (Capala Heen, Kilkeshen, Co Clare ☎ 061-367924)

· *Theresa Storey* Theresa's homemade preserves include a lemon and dill mustard that goes stunningly well with fish. You'll never again want to eat a hot dog without her garlic and chilli mustard, and her spicy tomato chutney packs a real punch. Don't leave the market without one of these in your bag. (Glenwilliam, Ballingarry ☎ 069-68524. Also at the Dromcolloher Market)

· *On the Wild Side* Niall Kenny tends to man the brilliant Wild Side stall at the market, and he's a great professional artisan, utterly know-ledgeable about all the Wild Side foods. Whilst the company has a great repu-

Authentic

tation for its smoked fish and sea vegetable products, do not miss their fabulous sausages and the brilliant black pudding, which is styled like a boudin noir. Wild Side foods are amongst the most exciting foods you can find in Ireland. (37 John's St, Dingle ☎ 087-9957694)

Limerick City

Restaurant
● Brulées

Donal and Theresa Cooper's on-the-corner restaurant has created a loyal following in the city for some elegant cooking: barbary duck with honey-glazed peaches; rack of lamb with pinenut and apricot stuffing; sea bass with fennel and white wine. It's a compact, pretty room. (Henry St, Limerick ☎ 061-319931)

Restaurant
● Cheong Heng Hong Oriental Supermarket

This oriental supermarket is a big, anodyne, slightly surreal and rather cold space, but it has everything your ethnic cookbooks tell you that you need to make that Asian speciality just perfect. (95-96 Henry St, Limerick)

Hotel, Bar & Restaurant
● Clarion Hotel

The most elegant and graceful new building in Limerick houses a hotel that seems to have found its métier. Under Sean Lally's management, the crew in the Clarion seem to have upped a gear, and they are more focused and efficient than when the hotel first opened its doors. The Kudos bar is a gorgeous space to hang out in, and the Asian-style food here is well achieved: to be honest, this is probably the best bet in town to meet someone for lunch, for standards in Limerick are variable at best, and pretentious and over-priced at worst. The cooking is Asian-accented – there are grilled dishes that include satays and spring rolls, but which also find room for chicken wings – and a variety of wok dishes with noodles, chop suey and fried rice are joined by some groovy Asian sandwiches that don't aim to offer anything other than punchy flavours.

But it's in the Synergie restaurant – another gorgeous space – that things seem to have come together most successfully. Whilst we wouldn't say the restaurant has a signature style just yet – the menu is still too extensive to allow the proper focus that a signature demands – they are certainly getting there. Dishes such as haddock and salmon potato cakes, or stuffed roast pork with mash, or very fine teriyaki salmon with bok choi, are spot on, and value for money is

good. It's easy to see why the hotel has become popular, but we reckon they still have gas in the tank, and will begin to show their true status soon. (Steamboat Quay, Limerick ☎ 061-469555
www.clarionhotellimerick.com — Open B'fast, Lunch & Dinner)

Restaurant
● Copper & Spice

Brian and Seema Conroy's restaurant has been the toast of the town since it opened in 2003, and its success has quickly spawned a sister restaurant in Annacrotty. The room is great, the service is great, and the food is real, both the Indian specialities and the Thai dishes they also offer. Where other Indian restaurants offer a rather dull and non-specific formula, C&S feels like a creative, dynamic restaurant, even though the food reads straightforward at first: prawn jalfrezi; keema maatar; karahi chicken; alu gobi, alongside Thai red and green curries and various satays. But, there is animus and energy and a search for perfection here, a determination to avoid the clichés, and it lifts C&S way, way above the norm. (2 Cornmarket Row, Limerick ☎ 061-313620 www.copperandspice.com)

Fishmonger
● René Cusack

This dock-side, long established fish shop, just across the road from Steamboat Quay as you head out of town, is an excellent and always reliable source for good wet fish. (Dock Rd, Limerick ☎ 061-317566)

Wine Shop
● Fine Wines

Ralph Parkes' company has half a dozen branches scattered throughout the city, with a packed-to-the-roof shop in the city centre at Roches Street. Playing loud pop radio probably attracts those in search of beer, but it doesn't make for much mood as you peruse the shelves in search of some good bottles. And there are good bottles here, in amidst the standard stuff found in many shops and supermarkets, so do look carefully. The other branches are at: Parnell Street, Limerick; Dublin Road, Castletroy; Ambassador Centre, Dooradoyle; Thomondgate; Corbally. (Vintage House, 48 Roches St, Limerick ☎ 061-417784 www.finewines.ie)

Butcher
● Jim Flavin

When you get to Flavin's butcher's shop at Castletroy, ignore the petrol station location and the standard appearance of Mr Flavin's shop, and focus instead on the skilfulness evident in the preparation and presentation of the meat: there are choice cuts to be found here, and helpful, knowledgeable staff to make sure that you get just what you want. (Dublin Rd, Castletroy, Limerick ☎ 061-331977)

Café
● Ducarts at the Hunt Museum

Ducarts is a stylish café and a calm, useful destination for meeting up to enjoy pleasant, simple foods at lunchtime. The elegant terrace, overlooking the River Shannon and the Curragour Falls, is a charming spot for al fresco eating in the summertime, enjoying the balmy Limerick weather. (Hunt Museum, Rutland St, Limerick ☎ 061-312662 — Open lunch — www.huntmuseum.com)

Restaurant
● Ivan's of Caherdavin

Just on the outskirts of the city, Ivan's is a handsome, swish store – the Morton's of Limerick, if you like. They do a huge trade in good sweet cakes and big, generous helpings of cooked-food-to-go throughout the day, and the charming and polite staff give the shop a bustling, occupied air, so shopping is always really enjoyable. (Caherdavin, Limerick ☎ 061-455766)

Restaurant
● Jasmine Palace

This is a big, busy and well-regarded Chinese restaurant that draws in diners from many miles around to its city centre location. (O'Connell Mall, O'Connell St, Limerick ☎ 061-412484 www.jasminepalacerestaurant.com — Open Lunch & Dinner)

Butcher's Shop
● Brendan Loughnane

Loughnane's is an ambitious, creative butcher's shop: look out for the award-winning spiced beef, the traditional pork sausages, and some good black and white puddings. (Upper William St, Limerick ☎ 061-414213)

LIMERICK CITY - Co. LIMERICK

Restaurant
● Poppadom

The Limerick branch of Amjad Hussain's excellent Indian restaurants, whose original branch in Rathgar in Dublin has now been joined by three other branches, offers the same enjoyable contemporary Indian cooking that has created such a loyal following. (2c Robert St, Limerick ☎ 061-446644)

Fish & Game
● John Sadlier

It's just great to see a small, specialist fish and game shop of the style of Sadlier's continuing to survive right in the centre of Limerick. Lovely fresh wet fish, good poultry and game, great service. (Roches St, Limerick ☎ 061-414232)

Wine Shop
● Terrys' Wine Shop

Just a step or two off the main strip of Limerick, Terry's is a clubbable, petite wine shop, but there are a lot of bottles packed in here, and the choice is both expansive yet interestingly personal. (Denmark St, Limerick ☎ 061-412445)

Café
● The Wild Onion

Trying to get a table in Bob and Ruth's terrific Wild Onion on a Saturday morning, when the Milk Market is in full flow, is akin to Mission: Impossible. Crazy busy. It's a great spot for American-style foods: Texas-size muffin; Eggs McOnion with hash browns; hot sandwich of Chicago burger; chicken with barbecue sauce and nice big baking specialities like Southport slices or real American carrot cake. Major, major fun. (High St, Cornmarket, Limerick ☎ 061-440055 www.wildonioncafe.com — Open Lunch)

Restaurant
● The Wine Buff

The Limerick outpost of Paddy O'Flynn's smart wine franchise is manned by Michael McDonnell, and you can expect to find and enjoy the same smart collation of lesser-known French appellations, along with other good value wines from Spain and Italy, that feature throughout their stores. (17 Mallow St, Limerick ☎ 061-313392 www.thewinebuff.com)

THE BRIDGESTONE IRISH FOOD GUIDE   247

County Longford

artisan chocolate factory, craft baking, organic vegetables,
quail eggs, local herbs . . .

Longford

Restaurant
● **Aubergine Gallery Café**

Stephen and Linda Devlin's Aubergine Gallery has moved
down the street to a smart new upstairs dining room over
the White House pub, a stylish room that offers well-considered modern cooking from late morning through to early
evening. The Aubergine is a vital address in Longford, and Mr
Devlin and his crew have worked hard for their deserved
success and popularity over the last five years. (17
Ballymahon St, ☎ 043-48633 Open — Lunch & Dinner)

Market
● **Longford Community Market**

This exciting new venture in Longford has brought together
local growers of vegetables, salad leaves and herbs along
with domestic bakers, chocolate makers, crafts people and
others in Longford's first attempt at a farmers' market.
There are almost twenty stalls, from smoked fish to quail
eggs to redcurrants to root vegetables to freshly dug cab-
bages and marrows. Don't miss it. (Temperance Hall, beside
the Cathedral, Saturday 10am)

Chocolate Truffles
● **Torc Truffles**

Ruth McGarry-Quinn's splendid little chocolate factory has
been the energised and creative home to Torc
Truffles for years now, whilst her fine shop in
the centre of Longford town offers excellent foods and coffees during the day, along
with great deli foods and some rather nice
cooked foods-to-go for those who are starving
and starved of time. The quality of Ruth's chocolate concoctions is always reliable, and they remain a special treat. You
will also find Ruth, the most significant player in Longford's
emerging culinary culture, with her produce at the Saturday
community market at the Temperance Hall.
(Athlone Rd, Longford ☎ 043-47353
www.torctruffles.com)

County Louth

Cooley l`amb, Cooley beef, Carlingford oysters and mussels,
Ballagan lobster, Annagassan salmon,
Farmhouse Blue Cheese...

Castlebellingham

Farmhouse Cheese
● **Bellingham Blue**

Peter Thomas' excellent raw milk blue cheese is the star of
the county. The cheesemaker's milk comes from
a closed herd of Friesian cows, the blue
veining then being created with penicillium
roqueforti, and the cheeses are hand-
turned each day during the six-week maturation period. Bellingham Blue has a texture
reminiscent of a good Stilton, being firmer than
a Cashel Blue and quite unlike the new Wicklow Blue. We
like the agrestic pungency the cheese enjoys thanks to raw
milk and careful maturation. Look out for the cheesemaker
himself, selling the cheese at the Castlebellingham Farmers'
Market. (Mansfieldtown, Castlebellingham ☎ 042-937 2343)

Farmers' Market
● **Castlebellingham Farmers' Market**

The Bellingham market has been a great success story –
4,000 people turned up here on one autumn Sunday to
meet and greet and buy – so get there early and look out
for the local Bellingham Blue cheese, George's brilliant
patisserie and breads from Slane, relishes and preserves
from Virginia in County Cavan, and lots of other producers
and craftspeople. (1st Sunday in the month, 11am-5pm)

Carlingford Peninsula

Guesthouse
● **Beaufort House**

A superbly professional B&B, Michael and Glynis Caine also
have links to a yacht charter and sailing school for those
who want to mess about on the water. For those who
don't, Beaufort is a great, quiet base to get the most out of
lovely Carlingford. (Ghan Road, Carlingford ☎ 042-937 3879
www.beauforthouse.net)

Shop
● Food For Thought

T.J. Hayes' beautiful shop is a peachy place to buy great
foods – some of them very hard to find, such as Suzanne
and Terry Smith's Drumgooland Smokehouse products from
just over the border – and it's also a smashing place to grab
a bite to eat. Mr Hayes has the happy, hospitable nature of a
guy who relishes his work, and it shows here in a great
selection of foods and some nice, simple cooking: beef
lasagne, chicken and bacon pie, a small range of pizzas and
tortillas. (Trinity Mews, Dundalk St, Carlingford
☎ 042-938 3838

Tearooms
● Georgina's Tearooms

This little room is simply magic. Georgina's may be small –
okay, it's basically a large box – but it is perfectly formed,
and always buzzy with people enjoying taking tea, and having
a slice of something sweet with their tea: lemon and orange
cake; carrot cake, and a gingerbread man for the kids.
People are so relaxed in here, because the whole vibe is
simply so relaxing, the pleasure of taking tea, and taking
time out. Mind you, there are fine sandwiches and tarts and
soups, so it's not only a place for a cuppa. Just brilliant.
(Castle Hill, Carlingford ☎ 042-937 3346 tedf@eircom.net)

Guesthouse with Restaurant
● Ghan House

Paul Carroll's fine house, with chef Jeremy
O'Connor established in the kitchen and
turning out soulful food, is one of the beacons of hospitality in the borderlands, and
it's the star turn of pretty Carlingford.
Mr Carroll is a thoughtful proprietor, both host and guide,
and he orchestrates a happy team here, a crew driven by a
desire to do their very best.
The new bar is a great addition to the place, and then it's
time for dinner upstairs in the big Georgian dining room:
Carlingford mussel broth with glass noodles; pheasant and
wild mushroom casserole with celeriac mash; stuffed fillet of
pork with a Stilton and apricot butter; rib-eye steak with
mash and onion rings; cherry pannacotta with poached
cherries. Everything fits here: the food matches the house,
the service and hospitality chime resonantly, and Ghan

House is a destination that is consummately logical and consummately enjoyable. Look out especially for their occasional cookery courses. (Carlingford ☎ 042-937 3682 www.ghanhouse.com — Open Dinner)

Bistro
● Kingfisher Bistro

Mark Wood's tiny bistro could be another of those simple café rooms that have become so important to Irish cooking in recent years – Fishy Fishy, Café Hans, Idaho, Grangecon. There is obvious culinary talent here, however, and the ability to conjure exciting flavours and textures. However, sometimes the service can lose its rhythm on a busy night, and the cooking, though excellent in itself, needs to find more of a thought-through groove. The obvious dedication, goodwill and hard work of the Kingfisher team just makes little hiccups, such as the music and the awkward loos, an annoyance. But, with just a little tweaking, our money is on Mr Woods to emerge as a real player in the next few years. (Darcy McGee Grainstore, Dundalk St, Carlingford ☎ 042-937 3716 kevinwoods@eircom.net — Open Dinner)

Bistro
● The Oystercatcher

Linda and John Brennan are now responsible for the cooking in Brian and Denise McKevitt's bistro, whilst the McKevitts continue to look after the simple but comfortable rooms upstairs and to cook breakfast for residents. The food is local and logical: smoked salmon with herb blinis and mustard and caper dressing; seafood chowder; oysters served natural, grilled or baked, then herb roast chicken with wild mushroom velouté, or tempura of cod with crushed peas, or maybe lamb shank with champ, just what you will want to eat if you have been messing about on boats or walking the Tain Way. (Market Sq, Carlingford, Accommodation ☎ 042-937 3922 Dining ☎ 042-937 3989 www.theoystercatcher.com — Open Dinner & Sun Lunch)

Pub
● Lily Finnegan's

Lily Finnegan's pub, down near Whitestown, is worth an hour or two of anyone's time, for it's a delightful, unspoilt country pub, in a particularly delightful, unspoilt neck of the woods. (Whitestown, Carlingford ☎ 042-937 3730)

Dundalk

Wine Shop
● Callan's Wine Shop

Mary and Kevin Callan's Wine Shop on Park Street has a super range of wines, and a particularly fine selection of beers in the shop. (Park St, Dundalk ☎ 042-933 4382, www.callanswines.com)

Restaurant
● Cube

Cube is impressive, but it's a little uptight. The place feels a little too thought-through and by-the-book, a little too conceptualised, albeit that the restaurant handbook that chef Aidan Stewart and his crew have used to create their space and their food offer is very thorough.

But changes to the menu style introduced in 2004 have helped to simplify the concept, and Cube now feels more focused, and more relaxed: it's now more about the customers than the concept, and feels all the better for it. You can order fine old stagers such as smoked haddock chowder, or wild boar and apple sausages with mash, and the cooking is respectful and precise, in the tradition and in the groove. The room is lovely, albeit narrow, which makes the other diners seem proximate. The wine list is splendidly well-chosen and packed with treats. One feels Cube will continue to become simpler, and thereby continue to get better and better – this a restaurant with ambition and ability. (5 Roden Place, Dundalk ☎ 042-932 9898 www.cuberestaurants.ie — Open Lunch & Dinner)

Coffee
● Food Solutions

Paddy Sands imports and distributes the brilliant Italian Illy coffee, which improves the daily lives of so many people throughout the country. (Unit 1, Coes Rd, Dundalk ☎ 042-933 4862/1850 33 33 22)

Restaurant
● The Jade Garden

The Jade Garden is a favourite Chinese restaurant in Dundalk town. (24 Park St, Dundalk ☎ 042-933 0378 — Open Dinner & Sun Lunch)

Fishmonger
● Johnny Morgan

Johnny Morgan's fish shop may be diminutive, but it is packed with sparklingly fresh fish, all beautifully arranged on ice and begging you to walk in the door and snap it up. This is a great shop, the sort of place that has just what you need and just what you feel like, and no more. Essential. (7 Eimer Court, Market Square, Dundalk ☎ 042-932 7977)

Restaurant
● No. 32

Susan Heraghty has long been central to Dundalk's culinary scene, having masterminded The Hazel Tree before opening the comfy, end-of-street room that is No. 32. Her restaurant is commendably mature, unfussy and disciplined, and her international style of food – Provencal lamb shank; Creole salmon; tempura of aubergine – is handled with deftness and instinctive care. Ms Heraghty has always aimed to create places that are accessible in terms of price, service and food, so No. 32 is like an old friend you are always pleased to see and spend some time with. Value for money – especially for the early evening (5.30pm-7pm) express menus – is just fantastic. (32 Chapel St, Dundalk ☎ 042-933 1113 www.no32.ie)

Beer Importer
● Noreast Beers

David McIlheron's company specialises in three premium beers – Budvar from Czechoslovakia, Erdinger and Krombacher from Germany – all of which are particularly fine with food, so keep an eye out for these in good restaurants and wine shops. (Coes Road Industrial Estate, Dundalk ☎ 042-933 9858)

Restaurant
● Quaglino's at the Century

Pat Kerley has moved his long-established restaurant, Quaglino's, across town to the Century Bar, opposite the cathedral, where the restaurant is now upstairs over the bar. Good, generous cooking from an extremely experienced and inquisitive chef, and, in particular, some very tasty bar food at lunchtime, makes Quaglino's a key address in Dundalk town. (19 Roden Pl, Dundalk ☎ 042-933 4147/ 933 8567 quaglinos@unison.ie — Open Dinner & Bar Lunch).

Drogheda

Fishmonger
● Kirwan's Fish Merchants Ltd

Patrick Kirwan's shop is a good destination for fresh wet fish and shellfish. (55 Lawrence St, Drogheda ☎ 041-983 0622)

Off Licence
● O'Brien's Wine Off Licence

Turn a corner in an Irish town – pick a town, any town – and another O'Brien's wine shop has opened. This super-smart new store is a great addition to Drogheda for wine lovers, for O'Brien's is always distinguished by excellent staff, an ever-expanding range, and good value for money. (Unit 5, The Haymarket, Drogheda ☎ 041-987 6362 www.obrienswine.ie)

Termonfeckin

Farm Shop
● Forge Valley Farm Shop

Owen and Geraldine Kirwan's smart new shop, signposted at the roadside just south of Termonfeckin village, is a great place to find local potatoes, fresh eggs, and lots of good fruit and vegetables. Charming. (Termonfeckin, ☎ 041-988 3939)

Butcher's Shop and Deli
● McEvoy's Farm Shop

Down a lane in the centre of the village, David McEvoy's shop proves to be an Aladdin's cave when you push back the door of what seems a very unpromising little building. Inside, there is a butcher's counter at one end, and a deli section straight ahead, and David McEvoy's shop is such a success that new branches are planned in both Blackrock and Slane.

They make their own sausages, cure their own bacon, have their own turkeys at Christmas and are rearing Wessex sad-dlebacks. The beef currently used is Belgian Blue, and we would love to see their skills used with Angus and Hereford beef. Angela takes care of the deli, where you will find their own scones and their own cooked meats. This is a great wee place. (Nunneryland, Termonfeckin ☎ 041-988 1242)

Restaurant
● Triple House Restaurant

Pat Fox has been cooking good food in the characterful Triple House since long before Termonfeckin became the growing, frisky commuter-belt town it is today, and the new arrivals to the village are lucky to have this thoughtful and hospitable cook as their local destination, and to have a restaurant with superb service. Both foods and wines are carefully and idiosyncratically chosen: Clogherhead prawns; Duff's farm mushrooms; local beef, lamb and fish and shell-fish, and the cooking is quirky and generous and pleasingly devoid of any sense of fashion-following. (Termonfeckin, Drogheda ☎ 041-9822616 — Open Dinner)

Cult Choice Irish Charcuterie

Air-dried smoked Connemara lamb, sliced see-through thin and served like a classic Parma or Serrano ham. Bolg Doire – Irish pancetta from West Cork, using belly of pork that is dry-cured, then rolled and smoked to produce the tenderest, deepest flavour imaginable. Pastrami from County Monaghan. Stout-cured Irish beef. Beef and feta salami. Smoked fresh salami.

Irish charcuterie has begun to move sideways, drawing in European traditions to broaden the range of smoked and cured meats we can buy and enjoy. From Malone's of Monaghan with their pepper salami to Frank Krawczyk's Dereenatra Dry from West Cork, a dry-cured, oak smoked, air-dried sausage, and on to James McGeough's pioneering air-dried smoked Connemara lamb, via Fingal Ferguson's Gubbeen farm salamis or Dave Gumbleton's salt-cured duck, there are now artisan charcuteries that mine the deep history of European charcuterie techniques, and bring these traditions to a new fruition with Irish beef, lamb and pork. These are the foods of the ancients, made modern in 21st century Ireland.

County Mayo

Achill pré-salé lamb, Moy salmon,
artisan sausages, designer wine shops,
Clew Bay shellfish . . .

Achill

Restaurant
● **The Beehive**

Patricia and Michael Joyce's restaurant overlooks Keel beach
in the centre of Achill, and the high-quality domestic cooking and baking that has been their signature ever since they
opened back in 1991 is as enjoyable and respectful today as
it has ever been.

Good soups and chowders, lovely breads and cakes of all
varieties, and The Beehive is the sort of place where, happily, there proves to be something deliciously suitable for
everyone in the family. There is also a craft shop in the
complex, and ask also for details of accommodation that
they offer on the island. (Keel, Achill Island ☎ 098-43018
joycesbeehive@msn.com — Open Day-time)

Guesthouse
● **Bervie**

Elizabeth and John Barrett's B&B is a cult address on Achill,
with a charming, individualistic style of design that creates a
great sense of comfort and well-being, not to mention a
sense of away-from-it-all. There is also some excellent cooking and baking enjoyed at breakfast and dinner, not to mention direct access to the beach via the garden gate. There
are 15 rooms, all told, and it's a very child-friendly location,
so roll on the summer hols. (Keel, Achill Island
☎ 098-43114 www.bervieachill.com)

Restaurant
● **Calvey's**

Maeve Calvey's pretty restaurant is a perfect little space in
which to enjoy some fine cooking of good Achill ingredients, and not just the local fish and shellfish, but in particular the pré-salé lamb of the island which really must be
tried on any trip to the west: the Achill lamb is quite different to anywhere else. The taste is earthier and more gamey
than the sweeter east coast lamb. We look forward to seeing it developed as charcuterie. (Keel, Achill Island
☎ 098-43158 — Open Lunch & Dinner)

Ballina

Fish Smokery & Delicatessen
● Clarke's Salmon Smokery

Kevin Clarke and his brothers – John, Dara, and Peter – are a quartet of dynamic fish smokers and retailers. They have consistently improved and upgraded their lovely shop, and they have pinned their success on a knowledge of, and expertise in, fish that has kept this family business ahead of the posse for decades. What was formerly a small fish shop is now a grand fish delicatessen, centred around a superb wet fish counter. But you can also buy many of their own smoked seafood products, along with wines and other artisan foods. Their smoked salmon is superb, and we have bought wild salmon from the River Moy in Clarke's, during the season, that had a red hue like none we have seen before or since. In 2005 they will celebrate 60 years in the business. Now, we reckon that will be a party. (O'Rahilly St, Ballina ☎ 096-21022 www.clarkes.ie)

Wine Shop
● Fahy's

A stranger to Ballina could be forgiven, viewing the high quality of the small retail shops here, that the locals live on fine wines and smoked salmon when they aren't buying pricey threads. Certainly, John and Deirdre Fahy's wine shop shows that the people of Ballina have a thirst for fine, well-chosen wines, not to mention baubles such as great chocolates, super glasses, fine giftware, knowledgeable service and whathaveyou. The shop has deservedly won awards for its range of wines and service, and it is one of the pioneers of fine wine retailing in the West, a position in which it is beginning to face competition. (Teeling St, Ballina ☎ 096-22143)

Wine Shop
● Gaffney's

Another excellent, stylish wine shop for Ballina, with a broad, well-chosen range right across the price spectrum and a groovy space in which to browse for a good bottle. (Garden St, Ballina ☎ 096-78959)

Ballycastle

Coffee House
● Mary's Bakery

Mary Munnelly and her girls run a darling wee coffee house and restaurant, right smack on the main street of Ballycastle. It's the sort of place where they make sure you are well looked after, so a lovely bacon and cheese quiche, the sort of thing that shows domestic baking at its very peak, will also have some potato salad, some homemade coleslaw, and a doorstep of good brown bread, just in case you have been up painting, or snagging turnips, since dawn. (Main St, Ballycastle ☎ 096-43361 — Open Day-time)

Shop and Bar
● Polke's

Brian Polke's shop and bar is famous on account of the brilliant collection of art gifted to the genial host by many of the painters who have come to Ballycastle's Ballinglen Centre over the years. Even if your speciality is Dulux, however, you will find the lounge at the back of the shop to be a darling space to take a pint and have a chat. A word about the housekeeping: meticulous. (Main St, Ballycastle ☎ 096-43016)

Country House
● Stella Maris

Terence McSweeney and Frances Kelly's lovely converted coast guard station has also seen action as a convent for the Sisters of Mercy and as a private home. But, Stella Maris is in its glory period right now; this is a sparkling North West address, with all the potential to become a major player over the next few years.

Ms Kelly is charming, and an excellent cook – we haven't forgotten a breakfast in Stella Maris that was one of the highlights of a Mayo sojourn – and her cooking has the right mix of technique, texture and taste to be wholly convincing. Best of all, nothing about Stella Maris is slick. Instead, it's real, the hard work of two people who are working very hard indeed. We found it pretty darn difficult to drag ourselves away from Stella Maris, and the extraordinary beauty of its surroundings, from sea to mountains, after a short stay; don't make the same mistake. (Ballycastle ☎ 096-43322 www.stellamarisireland.com)

Castlebar

Café
● Café Rua

It's a little tricky to find Café Rua, even though Colleen McMahon's little restaurant is brightly painted, but it is well worth the effort, for here you will find some true cooking. For locals, Café Rua is a treasure, a place where fresh local foods are used with imagination and creativity. You can choose from a well-made sandwich to any of the daily dishes chalked on the blackboard, but everything, from the panini to the salads, is signed with care and respect. (New Antrim St, Castlebar ☎ 094-26159 — Open Day-time)

Mulrany

Guesthouse & Self-catering houses
● Rosturk Woods

Louise and Alan Stoney's B&B and self-catering houses are one of those places that, quite simply, have the magic. Magical location, magical ambience, utterly otherworldly, just turn off the Newport to Achill road and disappear from the modern world. This is one of the great escape addresses, and the Stoneys' intimate knowledge of everything in their area means that whatever one needs – from reiki therapy to some soda bread – can all be catered for with aplomb. (Mulrany, Westport ☎ 098-36264 www.rosturk-woods.com)

Newport

Butcher
● Kelly's Butchers

Kelly's is one of the great west coast butcher's shops, a shop where pride in the art of charcuterie and a delight in service come together to make it special, even if you are only buying a pound of sausages.

On top of their game

Mind you, don't miss those sausages, for they are amongst the very best bangers you can buy in Ireland. Sean Kelly regularly wins awards for his pork sausages, and they are superlative. Last time he ventured away from home, Mr Kelly came back from the huge Fresh Food competition in Utrecht with four gold medals, hauling in three further awards for his black, white, and mixed black and white puddings, so don't miss those either. His beef and lamb are just as fine as everything else, and this is a jewel of a shop. (Main St, Newport ☎ 098-41149)

Restaurant
● Kelly's Kitchen

Kathleen Kelly's lovely little restaurant is sister to the family's butcher's shop, just next door, so you can have a simple savoury dish of some award-winning sausages and pudding, or push the boat out for superb local meats. (Main St, Newport ☎ 098-41647 — Open Day-time)

Country House
● Newport House

Newport is one of the great country houses. Patrician, elegant, and fronted by the remarkable Catherine, a woman who can achieve several demanding tasks simultaneously, Newport is an expression of sumptuous luxury that is cultural rather than self-conscious. John Gavan's cooking is a bourgeois haute cuisine ennobled by great country flavours, and as such it fits into the concept and reality of noble, relaxed, chivalrous pleasure that Newport embodies better than anywhere else. Why Newport? Because you're worth it. (Newport ☎ 098-41222 www.newporthouse.ie)

On top of their game

Westport

Wine Merchant
● Cabot's House of Wine

The name Cabot is synonymous with the cutting-edge of wine sourcing and selling, and just as they have conquered the east coast from their base in Dublin's IFSC, so the Cabots have moved to conquer the west coast, with Redmond Cabot leading the assault against complacent winemaking and conservative tastes. The range is as fine as you would expect from the Dublin shop, and the rules here are the same as for Dublin; ask them to make up a case of the funkiest, mid-range wines, and you will have a case of vinous delights to treasure and to appreciate slowly and with care. (1a Upper Bridge St, Westport ☎ 098-50474)

Restaurant
● The Creel

Frank and Julie Bennet's restaurant has great coffee, fantastic sweet baking – a real star attraction – and smart lunches, ranging from paninis to some nice hot dishes, good salads, and a variety of daily specials. The Bennets also have occasional theme evenings in the restaurant, where they show just how well they can master ethnic cuisines such as Indian cooking. (The Quay, Westport ☎ 098-26174)

Restaurant
● The Lemon Peel

Robbie McMenamin has been turning out happy food for happy folk for years now, and he remains the local hero even as many other addresses have opened up all around him. The food has all those jazzy signatures you find today – teriyaki, Cajun, Caesar salad with half a dozen additions, black beans, noodles, duck confit – but it's all done in a winning, breezy way, and value is good. (The Octagon, Westport ☎ 098-26929 www.lemonpeel.ie — Open Dinner)

Restaurant & Shop
● The Linenmill

"Attention to detail, the food and the service have been impressive." That's a fine encomium from some of our friends out west, but you won't hear anyone demur from this assessment of what owner Robert Coakley has been achieving in The Linenmill, part of the Linenmill shop and museum that specialises in fine bedlinens and towels. (The Demesne, Westport, ☎ 098-29500 www.linenmill.ie)

Restaurant
● Quay Cottage

Kirstin and Peter McDonagh's Quay Cottage Restaurant has been 20 years in the business, pioneers of good food out west and great survivors in booming Westport. Having a fantastic location and a beautiful, atmospheric room has helped, but the McDonaghs' consistency and professionalism over the decades has been a joy to enjoy. Happy birthday. (The Harbour, Westport ☎ 098-26412 — Open Dinner)

Restaurant
● Il Vulcano

A bustling and busy Italian restaurant with good pastas and great pizzas, with a thin, crisp base and a real stone-baked character. You can take the pizzas away and, should you be in Castlebar, find more of the same in Al Moretto. (High St, Westport ☎ 098-24888 — Open Lunch & Dinner)

Country Market
● Westport Thursday Market

The Westport Country Market, held in the Town Hall every Thursday morning of the year, has long been a standard-bearer for local foods in the county. Free-range eggs, local cheeses, home baking both sweet and savoury, hand-made jams and preserves are all here, along with locally-grown organic vegetables. As with the best country markets, there are also plants and cut flowers, and Westport also features local crafts, including homespun wool, woodcrafts, rod baskets, works in bogwood and patchwork. So, get there early, hoover up all the edibles and the crafts to brighten the house, then sit and take some tea with a nice slice of cake. Shopping, as it should be. (Town Hall, Westport, Thursday mornings)

Cult Choice Real Milk

New Irish brand milks, such as Mary Burn's smart Adrahan Lullaby and the Cleary brothers' Glenisk organic cow's and goat's milk, are just two of the indicators suggesting that the days of bulk branding, marketing and selling of milk are at an end. The failure of Irish Co-Ops to develop niche brands with their basic product has been an extraordinary failing over recent decades – mind you, they have failed to do anything imaginative with butter either – but the time is ripe for specific grades and qualities of milk to be separated from the herd and sold as premium products. We look forward to West Cork Milk, and Jersey Cattle Milk, and more Organic Milks. Above all, we look forward to Irish Raw Milk, the chance to buy the unpasteurised, unhomogenised, glorious food that Irish cows and the Irish climate can give us. The nation's health demands that Raw Milk returns.

County Meath

artisan red ale, organic bread, Duleek lamb, patisserie,
organic pork, unpasteurised black and white pudding...

Ashbourne

Organic Bakery
● The Baking House

Claire Mooney's organic bakery remains unique in Ireland in
its commitment to organic materials. The result however, is
breads that are not simply agitprop organics, but which are
simply delicious, accessible and distinguished.
(Harlockstown, Ashbourne ☎ 01-835 9010)

Athboy

Butcher
● Brogan's Butchers

Niall Brogan's butchers is an archetypal country butcher's
shop, with splendid quality meat. (Main St, Athboy
☎ 046-943 2122)

Bettystown

Restaurant
● Bacchus at the Coastguard

Kieran Greenway & Anne Hardy's seaside restaurant offers
crisply executed classical cooking. Tian of crabmeat with
gazpacho sauce; deep-fried prawns with mango; roast duck
with potato stuffing; Duleek lamb with rosemary, are the
sort of signature dishes that are a constant of the menus.
Bacchus is refreshingly free of any sort of banal fashion-following: it is a professional neighbourhood restaurant that
has served a local audience well with good food for almost
a decade. (Bayview, Bettystown ☎ 041-982 8251
bacchus@eircom.net — Open Dinner)

Dunshaughlin

Butcher
● Charlie Walshe

Charlie's butcher's shop is highly regarded by locals for par-

ticularly superb pork sausages and real blood puddings.
(Dunshaughlin ☎ 01-825 8894)

Enfield

Craft Brewery
● **The Celtic Brewing Co**

The CBC produce two fine brews at their small plant here
in Enfield. The pair are Finian's Irish Red Ale, and Finian's
Original Gold, and whilst both of the brews are pasteurised,
tey are bright with flavour. (Enfield ☎ 0405-41558)

Kells

Restaurant
● **Vanilla Pod Restaurant**

The Vanilla Pod is part of the Headfort Arms Hotel, though
it operates independently. An element of its seriousness can
be gauged by the fact that they hold bi-monthly wine dinners, when wine producers and sellers conduct tastings
over dinner. The food and the room are both modern in
style. (Kells ☎ 046-924 0084 — Open Dinner & Sun Lunch)

Navan

Fish Shop
● **Connolly's Fish Shop**

Connolly's is a smashing wee seafood shop right in the
heart of the town, and Kieran and Noleen always have a
cracking range of fish and shellfish in ace condition.
(43 Trimgate St, Navan ☎ 046 907 2233)

Delicatessen & Wine Shop
● **Cooper's Fine Food & Wine**

This funky shop is the Terroirs of the Midlands, an
aesthete's dream, packed with good things to
eat and drink. Cheryl Cooper and Franck le
Moemmer have great taste, as well as great
discrimination, and it shows in everything
they have selected to sell. From the locality

they bring in Chez Emily chocolates, made just on the border of the county, and the splendid local Spicer's Bakery bread – look out for a particularly fine sourdough bread made by this little-known bakery. The selection of wines, specialist foods and treats is only superlative, and they have a great cheese-counter with artisan cheese in excellent condition. Cooper's is yet another Navan address worth a detour into town in its own right. (Market Square, Navan ☎ 046-907 5275)

Organic Eggs and Pork
● Highdell Organic Farm

The Crowe family produce superb quality organic eggs on their farm at Haystown, as well as organic pork that can be ordered direct from the farm. (Haystown, Navan ☎ 046-902 4954)

Butcher
● Hugh Maguire

"I have a great love of natural food", is how Hugh Maguire explains his brilliant range of foods in the town centre butcher's shop he runs with his brother, William. Natural here means pure and elemental, and simple. Mr Maguire makes an artisan black pudding, with unpasteurised blood, which on its own is worth the trip to Navan by any lover of

On top of their game

great charcuterie. This is as good as it gets, a subtle mix of spice with an earthy richness that is outstanding. But you could say just the same about his amazing range of sausages, or the dry-cured bacon, and also about the excellence with which all the meat sold here is prepared. Underpinning this excellence is a countryman's respect for, and knowledge of, great meat. Mr Maguire was raised on a farm in Bellewstown, studied at Athenry agricultural college, and served time with great butchers such as Tormeys of Mullingar. This patient time-serving has created a butcher who will tell you that "I decided to stick to traditional methods – not to deviate at all, to concentrate on the sausages, the puddings and the bacon", and the result is outstanding charcuterie.

A new shop in Ashbourne shopping centre will bring this quality to an even bigger audience. (13 Trimgate St, ☎ 046-902 1697)

Wine Merchant
● The Noble Rot

Elaine Teehan's shop has an excellent selection of wines.
(48 Kennedy Rd, Navan ☎ 046-907 3489)

Wine Merchant
● O'Brien's Wine Shop

A Midlands outpost for the dynamic Dublin wine chain.
(Kennedy Rd, Navan ☎ 046-907 3206 www.obrienswine.ie)

Restaurant
● Ryan's Bar

Ryan's is a hugely popular place for bar food, and the
kitchen is distinguished by using a lot of locally bought fish
and meat, in contrast to many bars whose produce comes
deep-frozen. Interesting menus, polished cooking and a nice,
comfortable big room. (22 Trimgate St, Navan
☎ 046-902 1154)

Wine Merchant
● The Ryan Vine

Paddy Ryan's wine shop is a great storehouse of
fantastic wines, and helpful, courteous service.
The shop extends to a second storey where
fine wines are kept alongside reference
books, wine magazines and an armchair, and
the effect makes you want to plonk right
down and open up a bottle straight away. The smart, cul-
tureddesign throughout the shop has a clubby atmosphere
that is very winning, and here is a wine store that offers the
zeitgeist, the culture, of wine, in spades. (22 Trimgate St,
Navan ☎ 046-907 8333)

Oldcastle

Chocolates
● Aine's Chocolates

Ann Rudden's bespoke chocolate company, Aine, manufacture an excellent range of chocolates, distinguished not just
by their funky packaging – which is superb, and superbly
witty – but also by clean, precisely achieved flavours.
(Oliver Plunkett St, Oldcastle ☎ 041-982 4493
www.aineschocolates.com)

Slane

Patisserie
● George's Patisserie

George Heise's confectionery is amongst the finest you will
find in Ireland. This is patisserie as art: this man makes a
passion fruit mousse that can stop you in your tracks with
its potent deliciousness, whilst a pear and almond frangipane is nothing less than a statement of the art. For goodness sake, this man makes a Black Forest gâteau that could
make the foods of the 1970's fashionable all over again, so
archetypal and fine is its cherry, creamy deliciousness. There
is also a range of breads, but whilst interestingly different –
rice bread, soya bread – these don't seem to us to scale the
same heights as the sweet baking. There is nothing better, as
you pull up the car to buy a cake, than to sit at one of the
few tables in the shop, have some Green Bean coffee and a
slice of Black Forest gâteau, and to allow the shameless
indulgence of great baking to course through your veins.
The shop also has some interesting foods, including eggs
from the local Highdell Organic farm. (Chapel St, Slane
☎ 041-982 4493)

Trim

Restaurant
● Franzini O'Brien's

This big, popular, likeable restaurant, beside the magnificent
Trim castle — the largest Norman castle in Europe, and the
place where they filmed Braveheart — is sister to the adjacent Benninis, a daytime restaurant. The cooking here has all
the modern culinary strophes that are currently popular in
the county, and service is very professional and engaging.
(French's Lane, Trim ☎ 046-943 1002 — Open Dinner)

Organic Market
● Trim Visitor Centre Organic Market

The Castle is an apt backdrop to the organic market held
here each Friday. There are home-made cakes, organic
cheese, Baking House organic bread, and Rose O'Sullivan
sells her organic veg, all in the splendid medieval surroundings of the castle. (Trim Visitor Centre 3pm-6pm Fri
trimvisitorcentre@eircom.net)

County Monaghan

cured meats, organic eggs,
palatial country houses and castles...

Carrickmacross

Hotel & Restaurant
● Nuremore Hotel

Raymond McArdle's cooking is some of the most perfectly
conceived and executed food you can eat in
Ireland. A meticulous, driven chef who
attracts other young meticulous, driven
chefs to his kitchen, McArdle is a vision of
the chef as radical creator, as culinary
transformer, a Beethovenian radical force
expressing himself through food that aims for transcendence, via culinary perfection.

Other chefs have abandoned this demanding track, opting
instead for a signature style that does not aim to reach the
summit of the business, but which is simply the expression
of their personality. Ray McArdle is old school: he works
within the canon, he maintains the tradition, and aims to
improve it. The cooking can be magical, irrespective of
whether the concept is simple – a rabbit and wild mushroom pie that is to die for – or demandingly complex: can
you get a dish more arty than caramelized veal sweetbreads
with braised red cabbage, turnip fondant and red wine?
McArdle has the technique and the temperament to make
both into something transcendent. Happily, whilst you
would part with a king's ransom, to try this food, the prices
charged for such accomplishment are amazingly low.
(Carrickmacross ☎ 042-966 1438 www.nuremore.com —
Open Lunch & Dinner)

Castleblayney

Cured Meats
● Malone Foods

Des Malone's company produces some truly
splendid cured meats. There is a very fine pastrami, possibly the star of the range. There is
sweet and lovely stout-cured beef. They produce good salamis, flavoured with whiskey,
garlic and pepper, and they package and present

these cured meats in the most user-friendly, accessible way. Once you start to use the Malone meats, you quickly find that they make themselves indispensable in day-to-day living and day-to-day cooking — as high-quality sandwich box lunchtime foods for children, they are exceptional. Quality is high throughout the range, and these products have enormous potential. The range also extends to black and white puddings along with hams and spiced beef, and the company also produces a range of meats for food service companies. (Lough Egish, Castleblayney ☎ 042-974 5102 www.malonefoods.ie)

Clones

Country House
● **Hilton Park**

Cook. Gardener. Author. Journalist. Lucy Madden is quite the renaissance woman, especially when one considers that she is not simply a cook, gardener, author and journalist, but is distinguished in all of these fields. Her cooking in the gothically grand Hilton Park has always been outstanding, for she has an artist's eye for creating beautiful dishes, and a cook's instinct for extracting flavour. This means that the cooking in Hilton is amongst the very best to be found in Irish country houses; wonderfully spry and energised food that carries a unique signature style. And, if dinner is a treat then breakfast, served downstairs in a lovely room adjacent to the kitchen, is amongst the best you will enjoy anywhere. The house and the gardens have a magical air of timelessness, making it easy to feel that, in staying at Hilton, you have disappeared into some fairy tale destination. (Scotshouse, Clones ☎ 047-56007 www.hilton-park.ie)

Derryhellan

Organic Eggs
● **Connolly's Eggs**
Look out for these very fine organic symbol eggs in good shops around the country. You will recognise them by the bright photograph of happy gambolling hens on the box. (Carrickroe, Derryhellan ☎ 047-87859)

Emyvale

Butcher
● **McGee's Foods**

Joe McGee has recently opened a second shop in Letterkenny's new shopping centre, a further sign that this dynamic young butcher is a man on the move, and a man whose progress is by no means exhausted – keep watching this space to see what Mr McGee will do next.

His template for success marries the dynamism of the best Northern Ireland butchers – where he trained – with a countryman's instinct for good meat based on experience and skilled charcuterie, and with his dedicated team he unifies everything with especially good service. It is this excellent service – helpful, informed, focused on finding food solutions for busy people and hectic families – that sets McGee's apart from the herd, and which makes it such a pleasure to shop in Emyvale. (Main St, Emyvale ☎ 047-87967)

Glaslough

Country House and Restaurant
● **Castle Leslie**

You might have trouble convincing the happy diners, wedding party guests and other regular leisure and pleasure customers who pack out the preposterously enormous Castle Leslie, but we can remember a time when Sammy Leslie's place was little more than a bad joke. The food was dire, the waitresses dressed as if they were living in 1895, and nothing worked properly. The place was a mausoleum. Fast forward a few years. Let Sammy Leslie get well in charge. Bring in a great chef like Noel McMeel, and voila! Castle Leslie is suddenly an international destination for the great and the good. This transformation has been one of the most amazing acts in modern Irish hospitality, and a tribute to the dedicated hard work of Ms Leslie and Mr McMeel. They have done it by concentrating on creative cooking, and by making CL into a special destination; this is one of those addresses that people simply fall in love with, so prepare yourself for the magic. (Glaslough ☎ 047-88109 www.castleleslie.com — Open Dinner)

County Offaly

organic milk and yogurt, organic vegetables, organic shops,
blueberries, guinea fowl, ducks and geese...

Birr

Pub
● The Chestnut

This discreet pub, situated just off the main square of Birr
and opposite the garage, is run by Clodagh Fay and Conor
McGlone, who have created a hip, stylish pub that would
grace any metropolis: daringly dark wood colours and
sumptuous leather make for a state-of-the-art style statement, the sort of aesthetic that could transform many a dull
country pub. Roaring fires, good pints, and good coffees
complement serious style. (Green St, Birr ☎ 0509-22011)

Organic Store
● The Organic Store

Jonathan Haslam's shop on the main street of pretty, personable Birr is a visionary venture, a place
where everything sold is of organic standard.
Thankfully, there is much produce from local
growers in the county and nearby, such as
Maura Deegan of Limekiln Farm, Jens
Krumpe's organic eggs from Terryglass, chickens
from Paul Crotty, potatoes and vegetables from
Coolnagrower Farm and from Mossfield Farm, near to
Kinitty, as well as from local producer Philip Draper. The
shop has an ambience somewhere between an intimate
country shop and a wholesome wholefood shop, and there
is no doubting the determination and the drive for singular
quality that lies behind the Organic Store. The range and
the quality is excellent, and make sure to ask about all the
wonderful queer gear produced by these splendid growers.
Local organic foods for local people; that seems to us to be
a future worth supporting. (Main St, Birr ☎ 0509-25881)

Bar & Restaurant
● The Thatch Bar & Restaurant

Des Connole's atmospheric pub, a mile outside of Birr in
the little hamlet of Crinkle, has an enduring reputation for
good cooking and good hospitality, built up over more than
a decade of good service, catering successfully for local
tastes. (Crinkle, Birr ☎ 0509-20682 — Open Dinner)

Edenderry

Butcher
● Bergin's Butchers

Brendan Bergin's butcher's shop is a good destination in
which to find the excellent Ballysax organic chickens, produced in Kildare by Margaret McDonnell and distributed to
butchers shops throughout the Midlands. You will also find
organic lamb amongst other choice local meats. (JKL St,
Edenderry ☎ 0405-31180)

Organic Shop
● Van Buurens Organic Shop

Danielle van Buuren's shop has a superb range of organic
produce, which she imports in tandem with Deirdre
O'Sullivan, the celebrated organic grower of Carbury, in
County Kildare. But Danielle takes the organic concept to
its peak, and everything in the shop is of organic symbol,
including organic eggs and organic bread. Van Buuren's is a
pivotal local destination. (JKL St, Edenderry
☎ 087-6533742)

Killeigh

Organic Dairy
● Glenisk Organic Dairy

The Cleary brothers pioneering organic dairy is one of the
great success stories of both organics and
niche marketing in modern Irish agriculture
and food production.
Using the old Tullamore dairy plant created
by their father, the brothers have crafted a
range of organic milk products that show
sharpness, hipness and commercial savvy, and they were
doing it long before the guys at Innocent drinks got witty.
Beautiful yogurts, excellent cow's and goat's milk, great pro-
biotic drinks for kids (the McKenna children are addicted)
and a new organic cheese show a team who can think sideways, adding value to the basic organic milk, and in the
process paying farmers the highest price for the milk that
they supply to Glenisk. Every county should have a small,
quality-conscious dairy like Glenisk, and the big dairy opera-
tors, whose lack of innovation in recent decades should be

regarded as a national disgrace, could profit from looking at what these guys do, and what they do so well, and maybe profit from basing their policies and practices on principles, rather than simply profit. Vital. (Glenisk Ltd, Newtown, Killeigh ☎ 0506-44259 www.glenisk.com)

Portarlington

Blueberries
● Derryvilla Farm

John and Belinda Seager's Derryvilla blueberry tonic is one of the most refreshing drinks you can buy in Ireland, a rasping, slightly tart tonic that enlivens the body like no other, though the apple and blueberry tonic isn't far behind. The Derryvilla range of preserves, sauces and relishes, all made with blueberries, are of exceptional standard, and during the short season fresh blueberries are also available. (Derryvilla, Portalington ☎ 0502-43945 www.derryvillablueberries.com)

Riverstown

Restaurant
● The Riverbank Restaurant

Declan Leonard and Des O'Connor's restaurant, close to Birr and hard by the border with County Tipperary, has a sure professional focus and delivery, as one would expect from a team who originally worked together in Kinitty Castle before moving to the banks of the Brosna. Modern country cooking and good value for money are the signature. (Riverstown, Birr ☎ 0509-21528 — Open Lunch & Dinner)

Tullamore

Relishes
● The Scullery

Florrie Smye's impressive range of relishes includes a particularly fine sweetcorn relish, a tomato relish, and a sweet chilli sauce. Flavours are as elemental and direct as the lovely packaging, which makes these jars easy to spot in good delis in the Midlands. (Tinnycross, Tullamore ☎ 0506-22566)

County
Roscommon

Brittle Blue pigs, Irish organic vegetables, artisan cheeses, smoked Roscommon bacon...

Boyle

Delicatessen and Wine Shop
● Heran's Cheese & Wine Shop

What a splendid shop Heran's is, and what a gem to discover in sleepy Boyle, a town that appears to have nodded off to sleep back when they built the by-pass. All the best Irish artisan foods are here, some fine wines, and Heran's is the hero of the locality, a characterful, unique shop. (St Patrick St, Boyle ☎ 071-966 3352)

Roscommon

Organic Shop
● Tattie Hoaker

This pioneering organic shop grew out of the sales of a walled garden, and now sells produce from throughout the region, always organic, local where seasonally possible. Owners John Brennan, Aiden Gillan and Maureen Brosnan also operate "Organic Express," a wholesale organic operation, servicing conventional shops in the area with organic produce. (Athlone Road, Roscommon ☎ 090-663 0492 agillan@eircom.net)

Strokestown

Organic Pigs
● Ted & Kay Mole

Ted and Kay Mole breed Brittle Blue pigs, which is what you get when a cross between Saddleback and Landrace pigs are put to a Great White boar. The pork is prepared by Joe Hayes in Ballinsaloe, and can be bought from the farm. The rest of the pork meat is then smoked, cured, brined and transformed by Fingal Ferguson of Gubbeen farm, and Ted and Kay's bacons and hams have the signature of that splendid artisan. (Strokestown, Roscommon ☎ 071-963 3775)

10 USEFUL
WEBSITES

1

http://ireland.iol.ie/~organic

2

www.bordbia.ie

3

www.bridgestoneguides.com

4

www.ciwf.ie

5

www.foodstuffireland.com

6

www.irelandmarkets.com

7

www.irishcheese.ie

8

www.irishorganic.ie

9

www.sheridanscheesemongers.com

10

www.slowfoodireland.com

County Sligo

sea vegetables, seaweed baths, artisan pasta,
craft baking, organic herbs . . .

Ballymote

Country House
● **Temple House**

Roderick Perceval has now taken over the day-to-day running of the sublime Temple House, working with his mum,
Deb, whilst dad Sandy has retired to a house in the woods
from where he continues to use his healer's touch to help
folk with bad backs, migraines, frozen shoulders, all the
aches, pains and gripes of the modern world that Mr
Perceval can sort out and solve.

It is spiriting to see Temple House enter a new generation
of hospitality and management. Ever since Sandy and Deb
opened their great big country pile to guests, it has been a
beacon of great good times, of great conviviality, it has
effortlessly been one of the great country house experiences that guests could discover anywhere in Ireland. There
is no place so relaxing, bewitching, beatific or surreal, no
address where the purity of the cooking and the gothic
charm of the house intermingle so dramatically and effec-
tively. (Ballymote, Sligo ☎ 071-918 3329
www.templehouse.ie)

Castlebaldwin

Guesthouse & Restaurant
● **Cromleach Lodge**

Christy and Moira Tighe's house and restaurant on the hill,
with its glorious views over Lough Arrow and the Curlew
Mountains, is a formal, calm destination, with excellent
cooking based on using the very best ingredients Mrs Tighe
can get her hands on. As such, Cromleach has carried the
mantle for serious, committed cooking in the region for
many years now. The rooms are large and comfortable,
service is measured and impeccable, and if some find the
service rather too formal, that is surely missing the point.
Cromleach is all about rest and recreation, not raucousness.
(Ballindoon, Castlebaldwin, Boyle ☎ 071-916 5155
www.cromleach.com — Open Dinner)

Cliffoney

Restaurant
● **La Vecchia Posta**

This attractive and meticulously maintained house on the main Sligo-Donegal road is owned and run by the Dunlevy family. Local fish and shellfish is the star attraction on menus that showcase modern styles of cooking rather than any conventional concept of regional Italian food, and the views down across the sea from the dining room are magic. (Cliffoney ☎ 071-917 6777 — Open Dinner & Sun Lunch)

Curry

Organic Pasta
● **Noodle House Pasta**

Ingrid Basler's artisan pasta company has been a mainstay of the wholefood and delicatessen scene in Ireland for many years, whilst Mrs Basler's presence at farmers' markets is a smart technique of marketing her excellent quality pastas. Made with the best organic ingredients, Noodle House pastas are a true lifesaver for busy families, for you can feed the kids in five minutes, and know that they are getting organic standard food, which also happens to be utterly delicious. (Rathmagurry, Curry ☎ 071-918 5589)

Enniscrone

Victorian Seaweed bathhouse
● **Kilcullen's Hot Sea Water Health Baths**

A Victorian seaweed bathhouse in a book about food specialists and gastronomy? The connection is purely one of sybaritic pleasure – great food is a sensual delight, and so is a seaweed bath in Kilcullen's lovely, archaic old bathhouse. They wash and steam the seaweed, heat the salt water (so you float in the gorgeously tactile, enormous soup of a seaweed bath!), and then you pull the cord and get doused in a shower of freezing sea water to bring you back to your senses. That last bit is the hard bit, but there is no pleasure without a little pain. (Enniscrone ☎ 096-36238)

Mullaghmore

Seafood Restaurant
● Eithna's Seafood Restaurant

Eithna's is one of those little harbourside seafood places that you dream about discovering. A simple room, cooking fresh fish and shellfish, it is an experience that taps into our psyche of culinary desire. And we want to share it with friends, in a relaxed, informal way, probably with someone taking a goofy snap of us as we raise our glasses. I'll be having the Rick Stein Goan seafood curry again, and just a little salad of organic leaves with that, please, and another bottle. (The Harbour, Mullaghmore ☎ 071-916 6407 www.eithnaseafood.com — Open Dinner & Weekend Lunch)

Rathlee

Sea Vegetables
● Carraig Fhada Seaweed

Frank Melvin is the sea vegetable hero. For more than a decade, Mr Melvin has combed the Long Rock, near to his base at Rathlee, seeking out kombu, dilisk, carrigeen, kombu royale and spaghetti de mer, then drying and bleaching the vegetables on the stony beach. The result is the most superb assortment of sea vegetables, a natural source of sheer goodness, especially when you see the pure quality of the west coast waters from which the sea vegetables are collected. Brilliant, natural foods. (Cabra, Rathlee, Easky ☎ 096-49042)

Riverstown

Country House
● Coopershill House

Brian and Lindy O'Hara's imposing country house has long been a great favourite with individual travellers, who enjoy good cooking in one of the most meticulously maintained country houses, and also with groups of friends who like to take over the house for a big country house winter weekend party. (Riverstown ☎ 071-916 5108)

Rosses Point

Restaurant
● **The Waterfront**

Joe Grogan's restaurant and bar has had the considerable talents of Alan Fitzmaurice producing imaginative cooking to the delight of a local audience for some years now. The food served in the bar is hugely popular with locals who drive out from Sligo and quickly pack the place out, but it's in the restaurant that Mr Fitzmaurice allows his culinary scope free range, especially with fish and shellfish at which he is exceptionally imaginative. (Rosses Point
☎ 071-917 7122 — Open Dinner & Sun Lunch)

Sligo

Gallery Café
● **The Atrium Café**

The Atrium is the best thing to have happened to Sligo in yonks. In a town that has been dormant – in a culinary sense – for some time, Brid Torrades (formerly of Glebe House, Collooney) has produced a culinary cocktail in the Model Arts centre that has some real magic to it: this is rockin' food in a rockin' space. Mrs Torrades' signature is seen with piercing clarity in dishes such as roasted vegetables with soft polenta and Ardsallagh goat's cheese, a truly magical combination of subtle, symbiotic ingredients that coalesce to form a riotous plate of pleasure. And she manages this with everything, from the simplest sandwich through to some truly fine sweet things. And, whilst the Model Arts centre is one of the best galleries in the country, the newest artistic success here is the art that you will find on the plate. (The Model Arts & Niland Centre, The Mall, Sligo ☎ 071-914 1418 — Open Lunch & Sun Brunch)

Coffee Shop
● **Bar Bazaar**

Richard and Tamasin's coffee shop is one of the town's best and best-loved addresses, with excellent coffees and brews. (35 Market St, Sligo ☎ 071-914 4749)

Country Grocer
● Cosgrove's

Cosgrove's is the archetypal country town grocer's shop,
unchanged, unchanging, a timeless template of great design,
great foods, and great, polite service. Cosgrove's is one of
the most beautiful food shops we know, a store that looks
as if it has been designed and arranged by leading
Hollywood set designers for a movie directed – perhaps –
by the Coen brothers. Great things to buy, an utterly unique
ambience, and altogether a peach of a place. (Market St,
Sligo ☎ 071-914 2809)

Coffee Shop & Restaurant
● Eurobar

Adrian Kenny's funky coffee bar and eaterie, just close to
the bridge in the new part of town – known as the choice
part of town, and soon to be the rive gauche, is a great
address for hanging out and enjoying good brews and nice
simple foods. (Stephen St. car park, Sligo ☎ 071-916 1788
eurobar@eircom.net)

Food-To-Go
● The Gourmet Parlour

The GP has been a staple of Sligo for as long as we have
been writing Bridgestone Guides. Back in 1991, we praised
Annette and Catherine's ability to conjure "accessible
tastes... with the girls' own direct and accessible style".
Nothing has changed in more than a decade: the savoury
and sweet baking is domestic and delicious, the party service an invaluable resource, and goodness follows the girls
whatever they create. (Bridge St, Sligo ☎ 071-914 4617)

Pub
● Hargadon's

One of the great atmospheric pubs, not just of the west
coast, but of the entire island. That pint of porter has your
name on it. (4 O'Connell St, Sligo ☎ 071-917 0933)

Delicatessen
● Kate's Kitchen

Kate's is the shop that sells everything that is good. You
name it, and Kate Pettit and Frank Hopper's shop has it.
Helena chocolates from Mayo. Irish Bay Tree pâtés from
Leitrim. O'Doherty's sausages and bacon from Fermanagh.

Tipperary Organic ice cream. Manoucher breads. Stable Diet foods from Wexford. A fantastic range of wines that has simply gotten better and better over the years. Everything you could need for sugarcraft and cake decoration. It is all here, and more, much, much more, in a glorious store that redefines one-stop-shopping. Kate's is an index of artisanship in Ireland, a don't miss! in Sligo town. (3 Castle St, Sligo ☎ 071-914 3022 www.kateskitchensligo.com)

Wine Merchant
● Octavius Wines

Michael Gramsch has moved his wine operation from the centre of town to the outskirts, to a sparkling, groovy store down at Ballast Quay. A decade of experience, and good contacts throughout the wine world, have allowed Mr Gramsch to build an excellent list, one which is particularly strong on Germany, France and Italy. Being down at Ballast Quay has made the whole business of buying by the case much easier, but do note that you can buy via a well-designed website also. (Ballast Quay, Sligo ☎ 071-915 3555 www.octavius.ie)

Restaurant
● Poppadom

Amjad Hussain's smart Indian restaurant has been making waves in Sligo with its excellent, imaginative ethnic cooking, and it is now the fourth branch of the chain to have opened, following on from their excellent restaurant in Dublin's Rathgar village. Poppadom is a long way from the balti house or the cheap-and-cheerful school of ethnic cooking, and as such it marks an important new address for Sligo. (O'Connell St, Sligo ☎ 071-914 7171)

Wine Merchant
● Patrick Stewart

A new wine shop in the Wine Street car park, which also houses other fine stores, Patrick Stewart's wine destination pulls in a great assortment of good bottles from more than 30 different suppliers, including rarities such as the Sardinian wines brought in by Piero Melis of Leitrim. One heck of a lot of fine bottles have been packed into this small arena, and excellent helpful service from the boss makes for a most promising place. (Sligo Shopping Centre, Wine St, Sligo ☎ 071-915 1811)

Wholefood Shop

● **Tir na nOg**

Mary McDonnell is one of the guardians of good food in the North West. Her shop acts as a beacon to producers, encouraging them, supporting them, promoting them. And it acts also as a magnet for the food lovers of the town, who know that everything sold here will be selected and chosen with expert, dedicated appreciation.

On top of their game

What those food lovers also know is that shopping in Tir na nOg is great craic, for Mary has always had a mighty crew of helpers and assistants who are smack bang into their job. Last time we called in, we bought brilliant, floury Irish Colleen spuds, brought up from Kilkenny. There was fresh basil from Crimlin Farm, and vegetables from Eden Plants. The lovely Woodville House eggs were on sale, as were Limerick's Oisin gouda cheese, County Clare's Bluebell Falls cheese, and Sligo's own Knocknarea honey, and organic produce from Coolnagrower Farm near Birr. All the good stuff, all of the time. Brilliant. (Grattan St, Sligo ☎ 071-916 2752)

Cult Choice Artisan Cider

The work of artisan cider producers in Ireland, such as Dublin's David Llewellyn, or Con Traas of Tipperary's The Apple Farm – see opposite – is the antithesis of the commercial ciders which are so heavily advertised and branded throughout the country. For the artisans, vintages are important, for they signal the change in the climate and the fruit, and cuvées are there to be made with different bottlings, and with new varieties, new blendings. Every time one meets David Llewellyn at various farmer's markets, he seems to have some newly crafted cider, the most recent arrival being his quirky, florid Ellison's Orange. These ciders echo and continue the great traditions of farm cider making that distinguished Tipperary, Armagh and many other counties.

(David Llewellyn Quickpenny Road, Lusk, Co. Dublin ☎ 087-284 3879 pureapple@eircom.net)

County Tipperary

apple juices; amazing fries; blue cheeses; Tipperary beef; organic ice cream, tea rooms, cider ...

Cahir

Orchard
● **The Apple Farm**

Con Traas is a superb artisan, a man with an artist's sensibility when it comes to producing and making cutting-edge foods. The sheer quality of his fruit – from August's Discovery apples through to Delbar Esteval, then Early Windsors, then into Cox's, Elstar and his signature Karmine – is a constant treat (though it's not actually constant, as this fruit sells quickly from the barn, the good people of Tipperary knowing a good thing when it is on their doorstep). He also has fresh strawberries from May – varieties include El Santo, Florence and Eros – then raspberries and plums. All are grown with infinite care and skill.

But perhaps Mr Traas' greatest achievement is the juices he makes from his fruit. The Karmine blend includes some James Grieve and Bramley, whilst the special cuvée of Karmine uses hand-selected fruit – "These apples have more of everything; they are the apples the tree gives most to" – explains Mr Traas of his selection of fruit. Finally, there is a superb cider vinegar. 95% of this superb produce is sold direct from the farm, completing a close relationship between farm, farmer and customer. This is how all farms should be run and managed. We reckon Mr Traas would be a fine Minister for Agriculture. (Moorstown, Cahir ☎ 052-41459 www.theapplefarm.com)

Farmers' Market
● **Cahir Farmers' Market**

This is a lovely wee market, held each Saturday morning, just by the craft centre. Look out for Pat Hartley's fish and fish pies, Apple Farm juices, Baylough Cheeses, organic lamb from Michael Peters, Tipperary organic hill beef; Cashel Blue cheese, local vegetables and juice from Pat O'Brien, whose farm shop is just a few miles north on the main Dublin road (look out for the signs), and lots of fine domestic baking. (Saturday 9am-1pm)

Restaurant & Gastropub
● Gannon's above The Bell

Dermot Gannon has really gotten on a roll in his restaurant, just off the main square of Cahir. Mr Gannon describes his cooking as "Modern and Traditional Irish Food", and by exploiting the produce he has all around him – all of which is name-checked on the menu – he puts this statement of intent into action: shredded Ballybrado organic pork salad; Bluebell Falls organic goat's cheese with Mediterranean vegetables; roast cod with crispy prawns; Kashmiri-style Tipperary lamb, or that lamb braised with vegetables in an Irish stew; Whelan's 21-day aged sirloin with whiskey pepper cream. The food Mr Gannon cooks for the bar downstairs is just as successful – Irish stew; fish and chips; Ballybrado organic bangers and mash; Baylough cheese crêpe. (Pearse St, Cahir ☎ 052-45911 — Open Dinner)

Organic Meat
● Good Herdsman

Josef Finke's new organic production plant in Cahir represents a major advance for organic meat production, and for his Good Herdsman brand, in Ireland. (Cahir ☎ 052-45500)

Farm Shop
● O'Brien's Farm Shop

You will meet the O'Brien family selling their farm produce at the Saturday market in Cahir, and you can also buy from their pretty farm shop at Outrath, just a couple of miles north of Cahir. (Outrath, Cahir ☎ 052-62282)

Carrick-on-Suir

Wine Merchant
● Approach Trade

Rafael Alvarez's company wholesales Spanish wines and foods to many of the country's best restaurants and shops, but private customers can also be accommodated, so long as you buy a case of wine. Buy it you should: Mr Alvarez has an eye for the finest wine producers of Spain, and his list is magic. (Mill River Pk, Carrick-on-Suir ☎ 051-641580)

Cashel

Guesthouse & Restaurant
● Bailey's Guesthouse

Both guesthouse and basement restaurant, Bailey's has extremely spacious, well-appointed and well-maintained rooms for those who are visiting the Rock and want to make an evening of it. The restaurant offers generous, well-realised modern food, and the quality of breakfasts in the attractive dining room is excellent. (Cashel ☎ 062-61937 www.baileys-ireland.com)

Café
● Café Hans

Café Hans is a blast. Into this tiny sister room of the brilliant Chez Hans, the Matthiae brothers pack in delirious food lovers who are cock-a-hoop at managing to get a table so that they can enjoy Steffi Matthiae's sharp, smart cooking. All they do in CH is a quartet of Caesar salads, some house salads, some open sandwiches, including a coronation chicken that you would walk a country mile for, and some other mains, not to mention the very best chips you have eaten in ages. Hansi and his crew serve it sharply and smartly, the room is delightful, and CH has been a wow! from day one. Desserts come in from the main restaurant, a smart compromise, and this newcomer is as radical and accomplished as Fishy Fishy Café or Idaho Café or Grangecon Café. Irish café society is alive and well, nowhere more so than in this brilliant address. (Cashel ☎ 062-63660 — Open Lunch)

Farmers' Market
● Cashel Farmers' Market

Held every second Friday, at the small mart just a short walk down the hill from the centre of Cashel, this is another promising farmers' market for the county. (Friday 10am-1pm)

Restaurant
● Chez Hans

Jason Matthiae has taken the cooking in the legendary Chez Hans – established in baby-booming 1968 – to a new plane of perfection, placing this gorgeous room right up there with the most radical and cutting-edge cooking in Ireland. Chez Hans has always been renowned for rich, generous, luxurious cooking, but there is a finesse and level of accomplishment evident in the dishes today that suggests Jason Matthiae has truly found his own signature: this cooking is in the groove.

From their trademark risotto with duckling, chorizo and baby spinach to CH classics, such as sirloin of veal with chasseur sauce of scallops with mango and pickled vegetables, this cooking is really rockin': food with energy and brio, food that celebrates the glory of the country and the kitchen, food that is art for the eating. (Moor Lane, Cashel, ☎ 062-61177 — Open Dinner)

Sheep's Milk Cheese
● Crozier Dairy Products Ltd

Harry Clifton-Brown's herd of sheep produce the cult Crozier Blue cheeses — for details, see page 289, Cashel Blue Cheese. (Ballinamona, Cashel ☎ 062-61120 cliftonbrown@eircom.net)

Restaurant with Rooms
● Legends Restaurant

Michael and Rosemary O'Neill run one of the cult Tipperary addresses, a restaurant with rooms that has glorious cooking and the most glorious location: right smack at the foot of the Rock of Cashel. Mr O'Neill is a cook's cook, his food poised, logical and supremely delicious. The food reads simply — crab salad with marinated cucumber, garlic toasts and chive and ginger cream; gratin of prawns with light curry cream; duckling with bitter orange; rabbit with wild mushroom stuffing — so that the level of successful accomplishment comes as a delightful surprise. There is no fashion following here, no egotism, just pristine flavours presented at optimum effect. The rooms are simple, and value and service are excellent. (The Kiln, Cashel ☎ 062-61292 www.legendsguesthouse.com — Open Dinner)

Bakery and Café
● The Spearman

The Spearman is a sweet little café with nicely modest, domestic-style baking available to eat in the café, or to take away. (97 Main St, Cashel ☎ 062-61143 — Open Lunch)

Clonmel

Restaurant
● Angela's Coffee Emporium & Restaurant

A little slice of Avoca Handweavers for Clonmel, by which
we mean that the flavours in Angela Ryan's cooking are
light, crisp and clean, and very pleasureful. That explains why
this pretty room is such a success with locals — it can be a
hard act to get a table in here at lunchtimes, as the well-
heeled — the very well-heeled — population of Clonmel take
some time out to enjoy ace cooking: chicken with tomato,
basil and black olives; salmon with a chilli mango dressing;
lovely grilled bruschetta. Angela and Fulvio run everything
with a focused and relaxed style, and this is an ace destination. (14 Abbey St, Clonmel ☎ 052-26899 — Open Lunch)

Restaurant with Rooms
● Mr Bumbles

Declan Gavigan's restaurant also offers bed and breakfast.
Mr Gavigan has always worked hard to provide an accessible, popular restaurant, with food that can appeal to all
tastes and pockets. And with food served continuously
throughout the day, Mr Bumbles is an exceptionally useful
address in Clonmel. (Kickham St, Clonmel ☎ 052-29188 —
Open Lunch & Dinner)

Restaurant
● Clifford's

Michael and Deirdre Clifford's restaurant has given the
good people of Clonmel the destination this well-heeled
town has needed for years. It's a pretty room in a pretty
old CIE building, the interior crisp and bright, with a small
bar, and Clonmelites have taken to Mr Clifford's cooking
with élan. The signature dishes of this great chef, such as
quenelles of chicken with Milleens cheese, or his legendary
trademark black pudding gateau, are in as fine a fettle as
ever, and indeed Mr Clifford's cooking now enjoys a confident serenity and sense of purpose which is truly winning.
Service will grow in confidence with time and there is a fine
list of wines from Rafael Alvarez of the superb Approach
Trade wines to enjoy along with some truly animated and
accomplished cooking. (29 Thomas St, Clonmel ☎ 052-
70677 — Open Lunch & Dinner)

Wholefood Shop
● The Honeypot

Next-door neighbour to Angela's restaurant, this is a fine, busy wholefood shop with lots of good things. (The Honey Pot, 14 Abbey St, Clonmel ☎ 052-21457 — Open Day-time)

Café
● O'Tuama's Café

"If life throws lemons at you, make lemonade". That's what it says on the wall in Dorothy O'Tuama's lovely café, at the shopping centre in Clonmel, and it summarises the can-do, creative, hard-working métier and attitude of the team here. Renowned for delicious homemade desserts and cakes, which makes it a favourite spot for taking coffee at any time of the day, O'Tuama's also does snappy savoury food, so it's jammers in here from breakfast time onwards. (Market Pl, Clonmel ☎ 052-27170 — Open Day-time)

Craft Butcher
● Tipperary Organic Ice Cream

Paddy and Joyce O'Keeffe's lovely ice creams are superb icy delights, and not to be missed. (Carrigeen Business Park, Clonmel ☎ 052-81905)

Craft Butcher
● James Whelan

Pat Whelan's shop has revolutionised the retailing of meat in Ireland. This stylish shop is really a meat boutique, and when you get down to the real bespoke stuff, specifically the superb Angus and Hereford beef from Pat Whelan's farm, then this is as good as it gets: the union of breeding and feeding, fine charcuterie skills, and the experience of shopping for Irish meat that is fun. The staff have the hungry motivation of the boss, and we would like to see more of these meat superstores being rolled out across the country. (Oakville Shopping Cntr, Clonmel ☎ 052-22927 www.jameswhelanbutchers.com)

Wine Shop
● The Wine Buff

A pretty shop by the Westgate is the Tipp outpost of the WB chain. The French wines offer quality and value. (2 The Westgate, Clonmel ☎ 052-80494 www.thewinebuff.com)

Fethard

Farmhouse Cheese
● Cashel Blue Cheese

The Grubb family produce the legendary Cashel Blue farm-house cheese, and have in recent years also created one of the cult cheeses of the new generation of Irish cheeses, the superb Crozier Blue, made with sheep's milk from the farm of cousin Harry Clifton Brown. In the hands of a talented affineur, and brought to 10 weeks' maturity, Cashel Blue is a superlative cheeses. Crozier Blue has the same potential to find a mass audience, for its flinty flavours are only superb. (Beechmount, Fethard ☎ 052-31151 jlgrubb@eircom.net)

Kilgarvan Quay

Restaurant
● Brocka-on-the-Water

Ann and Anthony Gernon have an aesthete's eye for every detail, from the layout of a table, to the craft-ing of food, to the orchestration of an evening's dining. Their distinctiveness places them amongst the great individuals of Irish hospitality, and with Mum Nancy cooking beautifully controlled country cuisine in the kitchen of Brocka, an evening here is amongst the most sublime, romantic and unforgettable enchantments in Irish food. This is a restaurant like no other: you simply have to experience the grace and aesthetic of beautiful Brocka. (Kilgarvan Quay, Ballinderry ☎ 067-22038 — Open Dinner)

Nenagh

Country Shop
● Country Choice

Peter Ward is the guv'nor, a man whose intellectual respect for artisan foods is expressed in the best way: Peter Ward runs Ireland's best shop.

Like other great thinkers on food, such as Ballymaloe's Myrtle Allen, Mr Ward talks it and walks it, and in tandem with his wife, Mary, he sets the benchmark by which every other retailer is judged. His selection of foods is inspiring, the standard of cooking in his café is startlingly fine, and his shop is not merely a place to buy things: it is a place in which to enjoy the culture of great foods, of great culinary creativity, or the work of a master of the art. (25 Kenyon St, Nenagh ☎ 067-32596 www.countrychoice.ie)

Nostalgic Tea Rooms
● Gleeson's Tea Rooms

Step in the door of the lovely Gleeson's and you step back in time. It is 1956, or maybe 1963, and it is time for tea and a slice of cake. (37/38 Mitchell St, Nenagh ☎ 067-31518)

Craft Butcher
● Hackett's

Michael Hackett's magnificent, traditional butcher's shop is home to great, true-tasting Tipperary beef, minded and prepared by Mr Hackett with great skill. (94 Silver St, Nenagh ☎ 067-31340)

Craft Butcher
● Hanlon's

Gregory and Michael Hanlon's shop is a benchmark country butcher's shop. (14 Kenyon St, Nenagh ☎ 067-41299)

Organic Farm
● Terryglass Organics

Jens Krumpe's Terryglass organic eggs are some of the best eggs you can eat. Available mainly through wholefood shops and farmers' markets, which is where you will see Jens, with his splendid Breughelian appearance, piling them artfully high, and painting them in glorious colours for Easter treats. But eggs are only one part of the story for this gifted artisan, for Mr Krumpe also makes some of the best pork we have tasted. His sows are large whites and saddlebacks, the boar is a cross of saddleback and tamworth, which means "that we get lovely 101 dalmatian cartoon-like banbhs in most litters". The flavour is sublime, the texture buttery and rich, the fat sweet and delicious, and don't miss also the Angus beef, their pork sausages and vegetables, for you can get a selection of both in Jen's meat boxes, with prices starting at only 25 euro. (Lorrha, Nenagh ☎ 090-974 7341 terryglassorganics@eircom.net)

Terryglass

Gastropub
● The Derg Inn

Sunday lunch sees all the smart food-lovin' locals packing out the charming Derg Inn, an excellent Tipp gastropub. (Terryglass ☎ 067-22037 derginn@eircom.net)

Thurles

Artisan Cheesemaker
● Cooleeney Cheese

Breda and Jim Maher's cheese company is one of Ireland's biggest, with 10 full-time staff along with two part-timers, and a herd of 120 friesians to milk. In addition, goat's milk is bought in to make the excellent Gortnamona, whilst pasteurised milk is used for the popular Dunbarra cheeses.

On top of their game

However, it is the superb raw-milk Cooleeney and the rich, lush Maighean cheeses that show Mrs Maher's cheesemaking signature, cheeses that manage to be both agrestic yet subtle, fulsome yet restrained, cheeses that forge a balance and a harmony out of these conflicts, and do so with distinct grace and power, creating two of the most distinctive, original Irish artisan cheeses. (Moyne, Thurles ☎ 0504-45112 cooleeney@eircom.net)

Country House & Restaurant
● Inch House

Nora and John Egan's country house and restaurant is very much the destination address in its zone, just a few miles out of Thurles. There is good, hearty country cooking, excellent hospitality, and splendid bedrooms in this fine house for those staying the night. (Thurles ☎ 0504-51261 www.tipp.ie/inch-house.htm)

County Waterford

blas, turnovers, pan loaves, viennas, bloomers, ringpan, soda bread, currant soda, bosses, rich bracks, white bracks, brown pans, health pans...

Annestown

Country House
● Annestown House

John and Pippa Galloway's house is set on the much-over-looked Copper Coast, a splendidly undiscovered part of Waterford that invites you to discover it in a lazy and lingering way. Base yourself at Annestown, and the comfort of the house, the hospitality and the cooking will have you beating a happy retreat home from your explorations each evening. (Annestown ☎ 051-396160 www.annestown.com)

Ardmore

Restaurant
● White Horses

Sisters Christine and Geraldine run one of the county's most charming, relaxed, fun restaurants in busy, pretty little Ardmore. Christine looks after the punters, Geraldine looks after the ingredients, and together they have created a sublime seaside destination. The cooking is pleasingly moreish: chicken with a root ginger and mushroom sauce; prawns in garlic cream; beef bordelaise with maitre d' butter. The daytime cooking is simpler but no less precise – good open sandwiches, nice things for the children – and one simply must have a dessert here, for the display of cakes and bakes offers treats that are irresistible. Charming. (Main St, Ardmore ☎ 024-94040 — Open Lunch & Dinner)

Ballymacarbry

Country House & Restaurant
● Hanora's Cottage

The Wall family's restaurant with rooms is one of West Waterford's most celebrated destinations, home to superb hospitality from Mary Wall, and excellent cooking in the restaurant from Eoin and Judith Wall. For many habituées of Hanora's, the passing of Seamus Wall in 2004 will have marked the end of an era, but how splendid that a new generation should be carrying on the great tradition of exuberant hospitality which has always characterised this family, and this address. (Nire Valley, Ballymacarbry ☎ 052-36134 www.hanorascottage.com — Open Dinner)

Cappoquin

Country House
● Barron's Bakery

Joe and Esther Barron's traditional bakery is one of the great relics of Irish culinary history. Here is the sort of bakery that every town used to boast, but whereas almost all the others have disappeared, Barron's continues to bake excellent breads in the traditional method on the original stone ovens. At a time when artisan bakers are beginning to re-emerge, and as we become more conscious of the sheer uselessness of mass-produced bread – known to real bakers as "water standing upright" – it is apt to celebrate and congratulate those, like Barron's, who have continued to ply their noble, distinguished trade. (Cappoquin ☎ 058-54045)

Apple Juice
● Crinnaghtaun Apple Juice

Julie Keane's apple juice is one of the benchmark drinks in Ireland. The Crinnaghtaun juice is a cloudy, agrestic, lush concoction, with a kaleidoscope of sweet and sharp flavours that are captured in perfect balance by the juice maker. The Keane's own high-quality fruit explains why Crinnaghtaun is so successful, but the consistency of the juice can only be explained by patient, expert artisanship. (Cappoquin ☎ 058-54258 www.irishapplejuice.com)

Farmhouse Cheese
● Knockalara

Wolfgang and Agnes Schliebitz's Knockalara sheep's milk cheese has been joined in recent years by their Dromana range of fresh cheeses. Whilst the Dromana range is delicious, for many cooks and chefs it is the sheer versatility, not to mention the compact, fulsome and complex flavours, of the Knockalara that make it well nigh indispensable as a culinary kitchen tool. Today, Knockalara is probably the cheese of choice for cutting-edge Irish chefs, useful in countless dishes, brilliant in starters especially, and for vegetarian dishes it is the most pleasing of cheeses to work with, its soft, almost crumbly texture adaptable and versatile in hot and cold dishes. Once you have a block of Knockalara in the fridge, you will find it impossible to cook without it. (Knockalara, Cappoquin ☎ 024-96326)

Butcher
● Murphy's Meat Centre

Murphy's is a fine wee butcher's shop, right in the centre of Cappoquin, and apart from some excellent quality beef and lamb, the shop is distinguished by some cracking pork sausages; just the thing for breakfast. (Main St, Cappoquin ☎ 058-54539)

Country House
● Richmond House

The chefs of Waterford are great individualists – think of Ken Buggy, Michael Quinn, Jenny McNally, Paul Flynn, Arnaud Mary, to name but a quintet of them – and Paul Deevy of Richmond House is just as individualistic a culinary artist as any other in the county. His cooking in Richmond House is amongst the very best country house cooking in Ireland, in one of the very best country houses. His cuisine is inspired by a modest insistence that food be treated with maximum respect and sympathy. What he achieves is culinary harmony – paupiettes of Dover sole with asparagus risotto and a saffron cream; aubergine and potato millefeuille; tian of crab and smoked salmon with lime dressing; salad of smoked duck with hazelnuts; warm orange pudding with orange sauce; jaffa cake tart with chocolate ice cream. The house itself is lovably unselfconscious, concerned with hospitality and warmth rather than being fashionable, and it is superbly run by Claire Deevy and her team. (Cappoquin ☎ 058-54278 www.richmondhouse.net — Open Dinner)

Cheekpoint

Bistro
● McAlpin's Cottage Bistro

Aidan & Marian McAlpin's Cottage Bistro is charmingly simple, both in style and in Marian's honest country cooking. (Cheekpoint ☎ 051-380854 mcalpinscottagebistro@eircom.net — Open Dinner)

Dungarvan

B&B
● Gortnadiha House

Eileen Harty's B&B, up the hill of Ring a few miles outside of Dungarvan, is a cult address, with disarming, direct hospitality from the lady herself, and some great breakfast cooking. (Ring, Dungarvan ☎ 058-46142 ringcheese@tinet.ie)

Bar & Restaurant
● The Parrish Bar

The Parrish is a hugely popular bar, and the bright, clean flavours and imaginative combinations of the cooking explains just why it is so popular. (41/42 Mary St, Dungarvan ☎ 058-45700 — Food served at lunchtime)

Butcher
● John David Power

JD Power's butcher's shop is a quintessential country town shop, and is especially renowned for some terrific, high-quality dry-cured bacon. (57 Main St, Dungarvan ☎ 058-42339)

Country House
● Powersfield House

Eunice Power's country house, just a little bit outside the town on the Clonmel Road, is an ace address. Mrs Power has the energy of half a dozen normal folk, raising a family whilst running the house, cooking superb dinners for guests, writing cookbooks, and running a very successful small outside catering company.
The design of the house is as sparky and individual as the

cooking, and the cooking is excellent. Mrs Power has an autodidactic ability to master any culinary challenge, so classics such as Spring lamb with a herb crust will be offered alongside piadina with roasted red peppers and Ardsallagh goat's cheese. Quail will be roasted with Capagh honey and soy, whilst soups might feature roasted aubergines, or Swiss chard and rosemary, and the dessert baking is delicious. (Ballinamuck West, Dungarvan ☎ 058-45594 www.powersfield.com)

Restaurant
● **The Tannery**

Paul Flynn has been blessed with the two essential qualities of the great chefs. Firstly, his hunger is as much cultural as it is culinary, which means his cooking is a means of artistic expression, and not simply putting food on a plate. Secondly, he can improvise, which means that *On top of their game* he never cooks the same dish twice, which means that his food always has a sense of inquiry, rather than a sense of repetition.

Using these skills, Flynn and his wife, Maire, have made The Tannery into one of the contemporary glories of Irish food, and Irish culture. The cooking here has strophes of flavours and textures that no one else can manage. It is one of the most delirious versions of modern Irish cooking, and one gets to enjoy this animated food in a beautiful room that is a fine example of timeless design. (10 Quay St, Dungarvan ☎ 058-45420 www.tannery.ie — Open Lunch & Dinner)

Dungarvan Farmers' Market...

· *Ardsallagh Goat's Cheese* Jane Murphy's goat's cheese, tailored for farmers' markets. (☎ 021-488 2336)

· *Tara's Handmade Quality Foods* Cakes, cookies and brownies made from pure ingredients.

· *Glenribben Organics* Organic vegetables and fruit from Tim & Fiona York. (☎ 058-54860)

· *"Naked Lunch"* Louise Clarke's fresh coffee, barbecued

home-made sausages and lamb burgers, home-made pasta sauces, tartlets, buns and cakes.

· *Barron's Bakery* Esther Barron's long-established traditional-style bakery products. (☎ 058-54045)

· *Knockalara Cheese* Fabulous farmhouse sheep's cheeses. (☎ 024-96326)

· *O' Flynns of Cork* Declan O' Flynn brings his traditional meats, specialising in tripe, drisheen and black/white puddings. (☎ 021-427 5685)

· *Old Drumlohan Cottage Nursery* Olde world cottage garden plants and rare varieties from Miriam Matthews.

· *Joe Condon Organic Beef* from Ballymacarbry.

· *Mary Merritt* Home-made Italian breads, cakes and buns, and home-made pasta sauces.

· *Clashganny Organic Apple Juices* First large organic orchard – Jonagold red apples produce the juice.

· *Killowen Orchard* Varieties of locally grown Irish apples, farm-pressed juice, plus daffodils and tulips.

· *Organic Fruit & Veg* Siobhan La Touche. Large range of organic fruit and veg and seasonal Irish produce.

· *Ann Cotter* Plants and shrubs.

· *Deirdre Hannigan* Home-baked produce.

· *Shorescape* Richard Fitzgerald's range of smoked fish. (☎ 087-280 9368)

· *Fiona Burke* Splendid cheesemonger and charcutier. (☎ 026-43537)

· *Arbutus Breads* Declan Ryan's sublime artisan breads. (☎ 021-450 1113)

· *The Real Olive Co.* Otherwise known as Toby's Olives. (☎ 021-427 0842)

· *La Boulangerie* Claudia Lane & Arnaud Mary. Traditional artisan French food – pastries and croissants, salad dressings, and a range of flavoured oils.

Dunmore East

Organic Chickens
● Born Free Organic Chickens

Paul Crotty and JJ Ahern of Midleton collaborate in rearing
and producing organic standard chickens, real birds which
are reared to 11 weeks, and which you will find in good
stores and at farmers' markets in Cahir and Dungarvan.
Prices for such carefully-reared fowl are excellent, which
means it doesn't cost much more to avoid the horror of
battery-produced birds, so look out for the Born Free label
(Ballymabin, Dunmore East ☎ 087-279 2613)

Bakery
● Indulge

Indulge is a small specialist bakery run by Mary Merritt, who
in addition to selling from her store in pretty Dunmore
now also sells her range of breads at two of the newest
farmer's markets, Waterford Saturday Market at Jenkins
Lane, as well as the Dungarvan market. (Dunmore East
☎ 086-3895631)

Traiteur
● The Lemon Tree

Mary Boland's nifty little traiteur-style food operation,
housed in a very stylish extension to a bungalow in
Dunmore, offers home made breads and cakes, and a fine
selection of ready to eat dinners, such as escalope of pork
in mustard and cream sauce; garlic potatoes; lasagne; penne
with chicken and garlic, vital good food for time-poor folk.
(Dunmore East ☎ 051-383164)

Gastro Pub
● The Ship

With a recent change of ownership, the legendary Ship is
just settling in with a new crew in the kitchen. The menu's
focus on fish and shellfish wisely remains intact – scallops
with beetroot; crab claws in garlic butter; sole meuniere;
monkfish and mussels with linguini in a saffron sauce – and
whilst there is still some tweaking to be done before a signature style emerges, the crew already exhibit confidence
and an ability to punch out some good flavours. (Dunmore
East ☎ 051-383141 — Open Lunch & Dinner)

Ferrybank

Chocolatier
● Gallwey's

Ciara Power has taken over the much-respected chocolatier firm of Gallwey's, and moved operations to Ferrybank where the company operates out of a new chocolate factory. The award-winning range of Gallwey's chocolates and truffles has stayed the same – the sublime whiskey truffles with dark chocolate, the brilliant white chocolates with coffee and whiskey, the rich pralines – and Judy, the chocolate maker, and the original staff are all still in production. (Abbeylands Business Park, Ferrybank ☎ 051-830860 www.gallweys.com)

Glencairn

Gastro Pub with Rooms
● Buggy's Glencairn Inn

Ken and Cathleen Buggy's country inn has a unique style, unique cooking, a unique ambience. People who discover this modest little place in Glencairn often cannot believe their good luck. If it was the Tuscan hills, or San Sebastian, well then, okay, but this sort of magic, this artistry, *On top of their game* this individuality, in Glencairn? Well, why not? And that is how Mr and Mrs Buggy think. They do what they do, and they do it their way, and why not? You cannot legislate for originality. The Buggys are mavericks, radicals, modernists, artists of living. (Glencairn, Nr Lismore ☎ 058-56232 www.lismore.com — Open Dinner)

Kilmacthomas

Butcher
● Thomas Halloran

Little Kilmacthomas has been by-passed by Waterford's grand N25 road, but lovers of good meat – and especially lovers of a good pork sausage – will still find time to detour into Halloran's, an unremarkable shop, with lovely meats. (Main St, Kilmacthomas ☎ 051-294179)

Free-range Fowl
● Englishtown Farm

Look out for chickens, ducks and turkeys raised by Michael Murphy on Englishtown Farm, which are sold in many retailers throughout the south east with a label that lets you know where they hail from. (Kilmacthomas ☎ 051-291167)

Knockanore

Farmhouse Cheese
● Knockanore Cheese

Eamonn Lonergan's handmade cheeses are made with expert patience and care, and the fruits of his long career as a cheesemaker can perhaps be best seen in the mature Ballyneety cheeses (Ballyneety, Knockanore ☎ 024-97275)

Lismore

Bar & Restaurant
● barça

Whilst the style of barça draws heavily on Spanish influences, and a large part of their offer is a tapas menu served in the evening, which you can enjoy sitting at the bar with a glass of wine, they also wheel out theme evenings in the restaurant, where French-style dishes and wines might be served to celebrate Bastille Day, for instance. This gadabout style will likely settle down as the restaurant finds its signature through greater experience, and becomes more focused. (Main St, Lismore ☎ 058-53810 barcawine@eircom.net — Open Lunch & Dinner)

Café & Delicatessen
● Café Molise

Gino Lommano's café-cum-deli has made quite a splash in Lismore, winning local favour for good, direct cooking with a minimum of pretension. It's where you go for good coffee during the day, then maybe a pleasing, simple dinner dish of grilled lamb chops and lentils, or a good lasagna. There are also some choice Italian foods for sale. (Main St, Lismore ☎ 058-53778 — Open Lunch & Dinner)

Butcher
● Michael McGrath

Michael McGrath's butcher's shop in Lismore is a legend in the area, a traditional shop where meats are prepared according to time-honoured fashion. Expert understanding and great charcuterie work hand-in-hand here, and the shop itself is simply a joy to visit, a step back in time to a more patient, less frenetic Ireland. Shopping in McGrath's is a tonic. (Main St, Lismore ☎ 058-54350)

Portlaw

Organic Apple Juice
● Clashganny Apple Juice

Richard Galvin's brilliant organic apple juice is produced from Jonagored apples and these are hugely exciting drinks: crisp, clean, complex and the product of an ideal micro-climate and careful stewardship. (Portlaw ☎ 051-387041)

Country House
● Portlaw Bakery

Thank heavens that the Waterford bakeries maintain the tradition of craft bakeries producing a wide variety of loaves. At the head of this chapter, the whacky names of some of the Waterford bread styles are listed, and what rich, evocative memories they summon up, from the days before the local craft bakeries were decimated. Michael Madder's bakery is firmly in the tradition, surviving against the odds, producing more than a dozen styles of loaf, bringing colour to our daily bread (Portlaw ☎ 051-387221)

Tramore

Restaurant and Guesthouse
● Coast

"Coast - heaving with people, buzzing with summer electricity of people winding down for the weekend and having a great time in a great room run by a great host".
That's the sort of balanced, on-the-one-hand, on-the-other-hand type of thing people write to you about Coast, Turlough

On top of their game

McNamara and Jenny McNally's ground-breaking restaurant with rooms. And that is only the beginning: "A starter of crab claws and garlic butter had the rest of the table looking on enviously - they were huge and superb. My main course of Angus beef with bearnaise was really one of the finest pieces of meat I have ever tasted. It just melted in the mouth. Wonderful summer dessert of crushed meringue with raspberries was just what you want in this kind of weather." So, abandon critical objectivity, and just get into the magical mêlée McNamara and McNally have concocted. (Upr Branch Rd, Tramore ☎ 051-393646 www.coast.ie — Open Dinner & Sun Lunch)

Chipper
● Cunningham's Chipper

Cunningham's is a legend, and has been a legend for almost half a century, ever since they first fried a fine chip, way back in 1947. Always busy, with spick and span staff who are always charming, it's a don't miss! in Tramore, and worth the climb up the hill. (Main St, Tramore ☎ 051-381529)

Gastro Pub
● Rockett's of the Metal Man

Rockett's is the original gastropub, with the archetypal gastropub food: crubeens; ham and cabbage; colcannon; bacon ribs; roast chicken on Sunday; boiled spuds; sherry trifle (sherry trifle!) and apple pie. It's not, however, cooking the way your Mammy made it: your Mammy never had the reservoir of wit and attitude that the sprightly girls who run John and André O'Brien's bar have. A sport of nature. (Westown, Tramore ☎ 051-381496 — Open Lunch & Dinner)

Waterford

Restaurant
● Bodega!

You need to have a pretty special USP to attract attention in County Waterford these days, as culinary standards rocket. But Cormac and Donagh Cronin's brilliant Bodega! has USP's to throw away. It's whacky. Loud. Fun. Surreal. Has great wines at great prices. Has knockout food. And it just may be the best fun place to have dinner. Walk through the doors, and you shed a decade of years to find yourself back in your salad days, and when Arnaud Mary's smart, punchy cooking lands on your table, than the buzz gets even better. Bodega! isn't just a gastropub. It's a gastropub! If you like your good times and your good cooking to come with an exclamation! mark, then you are in the right place. (54 John St, Waterford ☎ 051-844177 www.bodegawaterford.com — Open Lunch & Dinner)

Country House
● La Boulangerie

Arnaud Mary, the celebrated chef at the funky Bodega!, has just opened this little bread shop a few doors down from the restaurant. You can also find the breads for sale - as well as salad dressings and flavoured oils, at the Jenkin's Lane market in Waterford. (John St, Waterford ☎ 051-843767)

Restaurant
● Fitzpatrick's Restaurant

Billy Fitzpatrick, formerly chef at Dunmore East's The Ship, now heads up the kitchen in the big new Fitzpatrick's restaurant, just on the outskirts of the city. The new owners have enlarged the interior, creating a brasserie-size room. (Cork Rd, Waterford ☎ 051-378851 — Open Dinner)

Café
● Gatchell's at Waterford Crystal

Local heroine Paula Prediville has made Gatchell's a destination for locals as well as visitors to the glitzy Waterford Crystal centre. Good tasty food for loads and loads of people is what they do, with an Avoca-style template and Avoca-style discipline ensuring consistency and high quality. (Waterford Crystal Visitor Centre, Kilbarry, Waterford ☎ 051-33257 — Open Lunch)

Shop
● Jay Bees

Jay Bees is run by the Mennonite Amish community, and this lovely shop, with its beatific ambience, is home to locally grown organic vegetables, super Amish-style baking, and you can also buy the handmade furniture that the community produce. (Campus Stn, Ballinakina, Woodstown ☎ 051-382305)

Country Market
● Jenkin's Lane Country Market

The Jenkin's Lane market is held every Saturday morning in
the lower level of the car park, behind Argos. Look out for
breads from Arnaud Mary's La Boulangerie and Mary
Merritt's Indulge Bakery from Dunmore East. Cheeses are
from Wolfgang and Agnes of Knockalara and from Fiona
Burke. The Amish community from Jaybees sell their own
granolas, handmade soaps, woven baskets, and some amazing artisan furniture. Sinead Cheevers has breads, hummus
and chutneys and also has one of the Waterford icons –
Chapman's coffee, roasted in Waterford city, for sale. There
are juices from Clashganny organic farm, and Michel Quinn
of Waterford Castle, one of the prime movers of the market, has pâtés and smoked fish. (Saturday 10am-4pm)

Butcher
● Kearney's

Tom Kearney's butcher's shop is regarded by food loving
locals as the surest, safest bet for great tasting beef and
lamb, sourced from the family's own farm. (27a John St,
Waterford ☎ 051-874434)

Restaurant
● La Palma Restaurant

This long-established Italian restaurant is well-loved by
many locals. The menus range through all the great classic
Italian dishes. (4 Parnell St, Waterford ☎ 051-879823
www.lapalma.ie — Open Lunch & Dinner)

Country House & Restaurant
● Waterford Castle

Michael Quinn is a great cook, with a culinary style that is
exuberant with both freshness and simplicity,
two signature culinary trademarks that are
amongst the most difficult for chefs to master. If he makes a tempura of prawns, the
batter is featherlight, a simple mango salad giving a sharp contrast. Asparagus with hollandaise is a
reminder of how and why great dishes ever became great
dishes. John dory with crushed peas and an orange beurre
blanc sings with flavour, every element utterly correct, as is
a dish of roast turbot with leeks and asparagus hollandaise.
Mr Quinn is a classical cook – his sauces are always text-

book, and he is too modest to experiment for the sake of it – and yet he can carry his signature style right through any collection of standard preparations. It all makes for great eating. The castle itself is blessed by the fact that the ferry ride over and back to the island is so achingly romantic, and whilst service in the restaurant is formal, it does strike a medium with the style of the room. Good value, and a thoroughly excellent destination.(The Island, Ballinakill, Waterford ☎ 051-878203 www.waterfordcastle.com - Open Dinner)

Restaurant
● The Wine Vault

David Dennison has celebrated a decade in The Wine Vault with a major revamp and simplification of his menus, focusing more on snappy, tasty dependable food – pumpkin and spinach quiche; baked cod with sauté potatoes and spinach; rack of lamb with herb crust; chicken kiev with herb, garlic and lemon butter – at very, very keen prices. The selection of wines is simply fantastic, chosen and imported with discrimination by Mr Dennison, and the list is a model of concise, wise wine writing. The WV is ten years old, but feels ten years younger. (High St, Waterford ☎ 051-853 444 www.waterfordwinevault.com — Open Lunch & Dinner)

Wine Shop
● World Wide Wines

Declan and Claire Brady's wine shop is a masterpiece of design, and a testament to the choicest wine selection. Step in the doors and the dramatic lighting, the ergonomic arrangement of the wines, and the knowledgeable service, all make for one of the most seductive and tactile wine buying experiences you can enjoy in Ireland. And that is before you get into their fine wine room, a tabernacle of beautiful, expensive superstar wines that has the feel of lush, lascivious luxury. The wines the Bradys stock do indeed come from the entire world of wine, but so do the assortment of craft beers, a selection which shows the same diligent, patient care and sense of choice that you see in the wine range. WWW is a marvellous kaleidoscope of the vinous world. (Cove Centre, Dunmore Rd, Waterford ☎ 051-878798 worldwidewines@eircom.net)

County Westmeath

Westmeath rib of beef on the bone, smoked eel,
Ballinagore potatoes, bespoke wines...

Athlone

Wine Shop
● The Artisans

Liam Hough's wine shop has a cracking selection of wines
sourced from the best importers – Mitchells, Febvre,
Sheridan's, Probus – and there is a handsome array of foods
as well, including farmhouse cheeses. (Unit 1, Belhavel,
Golden Island, Athlone ☎ 090-647 7522)

Restaurant
● Le Chateau

Steven & Martina Linehan's popular restaurant is a massive,
theatrical space down by the river. (The Docks, Athlone
☎ 090-649 4517 — Open Lunch & Dinner)

Restaurant
● Kin Khao

Many of the newer Thai restaurants in Ireland are franchis-
es, but Kin Khao is the real thing. Quirky and quite charming, the upstairs room is simple, and so is the cooking: hoi
jo is a fine starter of crab and chicken wrapped in chicken
then steamed, and served with a dipping sauce. A beef red
curry has galangal, chilli, red and yellow peppers and peas
and comes with steamed rice. Perky, pleasing cooking, and
service is excellent. The restaurant is just across the street
from the Tibetan Buddhist Meditation Centre, so things are
sure getting very left field on Athlone's left bank. (Abbey
Lane ☎ 090-649 8805 kinkhaothai@eircom.net — Open
Lunch & Dinner)

Restaurant
● The Left Bank Bistro

Mary McCullagh and Annie MacNamara's smart, hip and
stylish restaurant is one of the beacons of the
Midlands, with hip, smart and stylish food and
the kind of service that has you purring
with contentment. Order up some duck
confit with mash and cracked pepper, as a
typical lunch dish that they prepare, and just get
blown away by how this food is both elegant and gutsy,

modern yet ageless, soulful yet stylish. No matter what they cook, the food bursts with flavour and goodness, with flair and élan. The same can be said about the room, one of the most comfortable custodians of the art of feng shui to be found anywhere in Ireland. Annie and Mary make it all look easy, so easy, but there is metal in their method, and standards here have never dipped since they first opened their doors. They were on top form from the start: they are on top form today. Unmissable. (Fry Place, Athlone ☎ 090-649 4446 www.leftbankbistro.com — Open Lunch & Dinner)

Indian Restaurant
● Saagar

The popular chain of Indian restaurants that began in nearby Mullingar and which includes a Dublin address has a branch down near the river in Athlone. (Lloyd's Lane, Athlone ☎ 090-270011 www.saagarindianrestaurants.com — Open Lunch & Dinner)

Glasson

Bar & Restaurant
● Grogan's of Glasson

Simon Grogan's bar and restaurant is one of the most popular destinations in the region, with good quality, accessible food. There is traditional music in the bar on Wednesday and Sunday nights (Glasson ☎ 090-648 5158 — Open Lunch & Dinner)

Restaurant with Rooms
● Wineport Restaurant

Ray Byrne & Jane English's excellent restaurant with rooms has a drop-dead-gorgeous location, right by the edge of Lough Ree. The views from the rooms and the restaurant, out across the water, would inspire even the most jaded traveller, and the standard of the rooms is worthy of superlatives. Mr Byrne and Ms English are amongst the most perspicacious and professional people you can meet in the world of hospitality: efficient, reserved, discreet, endlessly capable, and they have navigated the addition of the rooms – and 10 further new rooms – to the original restaurant with astonishing skill. For locals who are not staying over

the Wineport restaurant remains one of the leading destinations in the Midlands, a beautiful room where the in-the-
groove vibe is always charming and relaxing. Chef Fergal
O'Donnell's tasty modern cooking has the right sort of
unpretentious directness to be of a piece with this excellent destination, and you really owe it to yourself to have a
night or two in this great escape. (Glasson, Athlone ☎ 090-
643 9010 www.wineport.ie — Open Lunch & Dinner)

Horseleap

Country House
● **Temple Country House**

Declan & Bernadette Fagan's country house and
spa has the sort of graceful, elusive air of
magic that few houses are blessed with.
Simple, subtle, beautifully decorated, the
house itself is a charmer, even before you
indulge in the excellent spa treatments, or
enjoy Mrs Fagan's splendidly individual cookery. The alliance
of these three elements – house, spa and cooking – is done
with such graceful intuition and correctness that it makes
Temple into an oasis for the soul. (Horseleap, Moate
☎ 0506-35118 www.templespa.ie)

Mullingar

GastroPub
● **The Belfry**

Therese Gilsenan masterminds both restaurant and cookery school at the glorious Belfry, a superbly converted
church from which the Murphy family have created a magical restaurant space. Ms Gilsenan has been one of the leading lights in gastronomy in the Midlands for years, but there
remains a youthful and adventurous spirit in her cooking,
which can range expertly from carpaccio of Mullingar beef
with roast aubergines, to Asian-marinated loin of pork with
gingered sweet potatoes, to Amaretto, praline and meringue
parfait. Her skills can also be seen in the regular cookery
classes which have become such a feature of the Belfry, with
courses for both kids and adults. (Ballynegall, Mullingar
☎ 044-42488 — Open Dinner)

Wine Shop
● Cana

Bernard Smyth and Paul Walsh have moved Cana across the
street to bigger premises, adding in spirits, beers and a nifty
selection of foods to their calling card of smartly chosen
wines. Their own USP is a specially imported range of Italian
wines, sourced mainly from the Veneto, alongside a range
that is cherry picked from larger importers, and some specialists such as Simon Tyrell, who concentrates on the
Rhone Valley. Paul and Bernard have a knowledgeable,
gentlemanly and low-key approach to their trade, so the
atmosphere in Cana is benign and helpful, making it a
delightful place to browse. But it is those Italian wines, in
particular, that demand your attention; the powerful muscu-
lar whump of Brunelli's Corte Cariano 2001 is brilliant;
Antonini Ceresa's Merlot from Veneto shows how well this
grape can perform in Italy, whilst the Astoria Prosecco di
Valdobbiadene is a smashing fizz at a great price. (6 Castle
St, Mullingar ☎ 044-42742)

Restaurant with Rooms
● Crookedwood House

Noel Kenny's country house, a few miles outside of
Mullingar near to Crookedwood village, has an intimate,
welcoming restaurant arrayed around a series of rooms on
the ground floor, as well as several comfortable rooms for
those staying over. (Crookedwood, Mullingar ☎ 044-72165
cwoodhse@iol.ie http://www.iol.ie/~cwoodhse — Open
Dinner)

Café
● Gallery 29

The Barr sisters, Ann and Emily, don't smile too much as
they cook and chase about the place in the pretty little
Gallery 29, right in the centre of town. This is something of
a pity as their cooking gives everyone a lot to smile about.
The precision and care seen in something simple – a pork,
herb and leek pie, for instance – really gladdens the heart,
and a lovely fresh salad and the very best potato wedges
you will find – real wedges, not junk bunk – makes for some
cracking lunchtime eating. The food from breakfast, through
takeaway sandwiches and some fine cakes and pastries all
shows TLC. (29 Oliver Plunkett St, Mullingar ☎ 044-49449
— Open Day-time)

Coffee Shop
● iLiA A Coffee Experience

Julie Kenny has created a rockin' success story in Ilia, and with her chef, Linda, the pair have fashioned a template of modern foods and flavours in a modern setting that is pretty irresistible, as the droves of locals who pack the place out every day will testify.

She starts the high standards with the coffee, serving excellent brews of the terrific Java Republic, and then the food is a smart, snappy mixture of wraps, bagels – very fine bagels – soup, good breads and fine pastries. The specials of the day manage to offer whatever you feel like – good club sandwiches; soup and bread for the bank employees; panini stuffed with flavourful ingredients – and from breakfast through to 6pm the place is alive with energy. (28 Oliver Plunkett St, Mullingar ☎ 044-40300 — Open Day-time)

Market
● Mullingar Farmers' Market

The Mullingar Market got off to a riotous success in early 2004, when stallholders were almost mobbed, and everything was sold in an hour. Since then, things have settled down, the market has gotten established at the rugby club on the Castepollard Road, and a core of locals and other marketers have emerged. Look out for local grower Kevin Harmon, from Fore, who brings in organic vegetables. John Rogan will have his smoked fish from Rathowen. Jill Wright will be down from Cavan with her sauces and savouries, as will Sean Moran with his splendid teas. Ann Rudden from Meath will have her Aine's Chocolates, Andrew McGuinness will have local honeys, and Bennie and Effie Gerber will have brought their Millhouse sheep's milk cheese over from County Offaly – this is one of the rarest of farmhouse cheeses, so hunt it down. Therese Gilsenan from The Belfry will have some cooked foods to sustain you, and it all happens every 3rd Sunday of the month, from 10am, so get there early. (Contact: Sheena Shanley ☎ 044-49180, or Joan Mullen ☎ 044-49222)

Restaurant
● Oscar's

Oscar's is where everyone in Mullingar goes to eat. A long, narrow room that ends in an open-plan kitchen where Tony and Noel and their team slide about the place at gimcrack speed, its virtues are simple and obvious: tasty, punchy, indeed what you might call macho food, and rock-solid consistency. In fact, if you had 10 euro for every time someone in the town tells you that 'Oscar's is sooo consistent!' you could afford to eat here every night of the week. The veal is a big favourite; the Italian chicken is another, and the steaks are generous and cooked as requested. Best of all, Oscar's is affable, lively and unpretentious, and that is a considerable trinity of USPs. (21 Oliver Plunkett St, Mullingar ☎ 044-44909 — Open Lunch & Dinner)

Restaurant
● Saagar Indian Restaurant

Sunil & Meera Kumar's Indian restaurant has long been a fixture of Mullingar, and appreciated by locals for some very true Indian ethnic cookery. (2 Dublin Bridge, Mullingar ☎ 044-40911 www.saagarindianrestaurants.com — Open Lunch & Dinner)

Butcher
● C. R. Tormey & Sons

The Tormey family are legendary in the Midlands, and have been legendary for more than 60 years, for the quality of their beef, sold not just in Mullingar, at their excellent shop in the shopping centre, but also through their branches at Tullamore – on Bridge Street – and in Galway, at the Galway Shopping Centre. James Tormey takes care of business in Mullingar, and this is a shop to gladden the eye and the heart. Beautifully prepared meats are presented in couture fashion, and when you bring that beef home and cook it, it is a revelation: sweet, with deep umami scents and tastes, there is simply nothing like the Westmeath beef. A benchmark address. (Harbour Place, Mullingar ☎ 044-45433)

Wine Importer
● Wines Direct

Like a medieval pilgrim, traversing hither and thither, Paddy Keogh doggedly continues his search for great wines made by great people throughout the vinous world. Most recently, he did the Santiago de Compostela route – backwards, mind you – hunting down new discoveries in Spain, turning up new jewels that conform to his spec: wines made with care and TLC by individual and family winemakers, wines with energy and character. Thirteen years into the business, and after seven years of full-time work, Mr Keogh and his team of 17 staff are as enthusiastic and committed as any wine merchant in the country. There is a zeal about this dynamic business that – it seems to us – transmutes into the pleasure of enjoying the wines. Drinking them, you can feel a personal connection with the winemakers, you can sense the criteria of sensual pleasure which Mr Keogh demands of the wines he sells. Two points distinguish this crew: their delivery system is second to none, both for private and restaurant clients, and their hunger to get better, to be better, never slackens. Finally, just to prove their zeal, they have just opened a retail shop for the wines at the warehouse in Irishtown. (Irishtown, Mullingar ☎ 1890-579 579 www.winesdirect.ie)

Rathowen

Fish Smoker
● **Corry Lane**

John Rogan's fish smokery is in the most remote part of Westmeath you could imagine, but this doesn't hinder this able fish smoker from producing a range of smoked fish, including mackerel, salmon, sea trout and eels. John uses beechwood shavings, and the fish is brined before smoking. You will find John at local farmers' markets, and also at markets on the east coast. (Rathowen ☎ 043-76264)

Cult Choice Westmeath Beef and Potatoes

You will have to look hard to find Ballinagore potatoes in Westmeath. We found some in the little village of Ballinagore itself, on a rack outside a petrol station, buried underneath a bag of firewood. "Quality Irish Potatoes" was all it said, as it says on a million other bags of spuds. Thanks to travelling with a local food lover, who knew they were the local speciality, we paid our 7 euro for a bag, which were identified only by a Grower's Number: 022683, and there was a little tick at the designation: Records. Otherwise, there was nothing to tell you that the potatoes from Ballinagore have a precious reputation.

But, bring them home, peel off the thick, claggy skins, boil them or steam them, sprinkle on some salt and a lather of butter and Wowee! Goodness, gracious, great balls of flour! Well done 022683! These are spuds such as one remembers from childhood, mighty floury spuds such as the best Golden Wonders from Tipperary or North Cork. So, why is there no appellation contrôlée for these great potatoes? Why is there no proudly printed grower's name? Why no recipes and serving suggestions? Why should something – of which people should be justifiably proud – be sold as if it is something of which people should be slightly ashamed? This is the old Kerrygold culture: never mind the difference, sell it as if it is all the same. Spuds are spuds, butter is butter, and beef is beef. Phooey! Just as spuds are not just spuds, beef is not just beef, and the other speciality to hunt down in Westmeath is the legendary local beef. The quality of Westmeath beef found in butchers' shops throughout the county, is superb: sweet, tender, darkly coloured. Get a rib of beef on the bone and all you need to do to make the perfect family dinner is to sprinkle it with some salt and pepper and shove it in the oven. Add some Ballinagore spuds, open some red wine, make the juices into a rich gravy, and enjoy the goodness of Westmeath.

County Wexford

strawberries, asparagus, raspberries, new potatoes,
Bannow Bay oysters, soft goat's cheese...

Blackwater

Farmhouse Cheese
● **Croghan**

Luc and Anne van Kampen are amongst the greatest of Irish
cheesemakers. They use the raw milk from
their goat herd to make the small Mine
Gabhar and the larger Croghan, both of
which are only available seasonally as
natural milking cycles are practised.
"Part-artist, part-scientist" is how some
have described Mr van Kampen, and certainly the fusion of
an artistic sensibility with a meticulous, rigorous approach
to production and maturing is what explains the stellar
nature of these cheeses. Both Croghan and Mine Gabhar
represent the pinnacle of cheesemaking – distinctive, pure,
speaking of both the region and the cheesemakers in their
complex and subtle meld of flavours. Superb. (Dunbroghan
Goat Farm, Bally Na Drishoge, Blackwater ☎ 053-27331)

Bridgestown

Apple Juice
● **Ballycross Apple Farm**

Look out for the excellent Ballycross Apple juices in local
shops and stores. There are three varieties produced –
Jonagold, Elstar and Bramley – and they are fine, cloudy, true
artisan juices. (Bridgestown ☎ 053-35160)

Campile

Farmers' Market
● **Dunbrody Abbey Market**

Pierce McAuliffe of the Dunbrody Abbey Cooking Centre
orchestrates this small but vibrant market at the visitors
centre, opposite Dunbrody Abbey, near Campile. A lovely
mixture of food stalls, local vegetables, fruit, handmade
cakes and biscuits, local preserves, ready-made sauces,

smoked foods, and it also has a coffee shop. However: be warned! You need to get here early, for there will be nothing left come the afternoon. (Dunbrody Abbey Cooking and Visitor Centre, Sunday noon-2.30pm)

Cooking Centre
● Dunbrody Cooking Centre

Pierce and Valerie McAuliffe's cookery school specialises in elaborating practical, contemporary cooking techniques, styles and methods to small groups of students on short courses. Pierce and Valerie are joined in the school by the celebrated Waterford chef Martin Dwyer. (Campile ☎ 051-388933 theneptune@eircom.net www.cookingireland.com)

Restaurant
● Shelburne Restaurant

A young French cook, Dominic Dayot, has taken on the lease of Shelburne, and this cook is making waves with some superbly disciplined cooking. A good choice of excellent breads begins a meal, then graciously light starters such as tempura of prawns and scallops in a featherlight batter, or crab claws imaginatively paired with walnut bread croutons in the accompanying salad, show a cook who likes to fire tangents on classical ideas. The fish cookery is spot on: sweet, fat, split prawns pair with perfectly cooked turbot; black sole with lemon butter gets no complication, just ace cooking to showcase some superb fish. Desserts are just as polished as everything else, value is good, and Shelburne really is a place to watch. (Main St, Campile ☎ 051-388996)

Carne

Seafood Bar
● The Lobster Pot Seafood Bar

Ciaran Hearne's popular bar and restaurant is well-regarded for fish and shellfish cookery. (Carne ☎ 053-31110)

Duncannon

Restaurant
● Sqigl

Sqigl is behind the famous Roche's bar in the middle of

Duncannon village, and chef Wayne Neville's cooking has gradually been finding its groove, and finding an audience, in recent times. Whilst Mr Neville's style is modern, he never overcomplicates matters, leaving the tongue-twisting side of things to the restaurant's name, so his fish cookery is straightforward and impressive, and consistency is maintained from starters through desserts. (Quay Rd, Duncannon ☎ 051-389700 sqigl2003@eircom.net — Open Dinner)

Enniscorthy

Farmhouse Cheeese
● Carrigbyrne Farmhouse Cheese

Paddy Berridge's excellent cheeses are easy to spot: the St. Killian is a pale white hexagonal shape, with a smooth white rind and a delicate paste with a grassy, fresh aroma. The larger, circular St Brendan brie is a somewhat midler cheese than the St. Killian, but the confident expertise of the cheesemaker still shines through in pure, analloyed flavours, and if you have the patience to keep either cheese for a few weeks, the clean, elemental flavours come through even stronger. (Adamstown, Enniscorthy ☎ 054-40560 prb@iol.ie)

Cookies
● The Great American Cookie Company

Our children love Teri Morris's American cookies, and what they love almost more than eating them is the simple business of cooking them: lift the cookie roll from the fridge, cut it into pieces, bake in a hot oven and voila!, they can believe they are master patissiers. The good news is, as Teri says, that they "don't use anything funny – only what you'd use in your own kitchen". (Templeudigan, Ballywilliam, Enniscorthy ☎ 051-424462 virginian@indigo.ie)

Country House
● Salville House

Jane and Gordon Parker's beautiful house is one of the cult addresses in Ireland, thanks to a calm ambience in the house, thanks to excellent hospitality, and thanks to some seriously fine cooking from Mr Parker. This man is a real country cook, his food nuanced with bright, alert flavours that are a delight for the appetite: cod with spinach and pretty, pert, pink fir apple potatoes; tarragon chicken with straw potatoes and a garden salad; passion fruit caramel with vanilla ice cream. The cooking is always delivered with an exactitude that transcends most country house cooking. Charming food, and a most charming, elegant house in which to enjoy it. (Enniscorthy ☎ 054-35252 www.salvillehouse.com)

Ferrycarrig Bridge

Hotel & Restaurant
● Ferrycarrig Hotel

The Ferrycarrig has always maintained a well-above-average reputation for the cooking in both its large Boathouse Bistro, and in the smaller Tides Restaurant. The location, and the views, are utterly spectacular. (Ferrycarrig Bridge, Wexford ☎ 053- 20999 www.ferrycarrighotel.ie)

Gorey

Wine Merchant
● Halpin's Fine Wines

This small, adroit wine store has an equally smart sister branch in Wicklow town. Both shops have lots of good bottles arranged elegantly, and this is a credible and worthwhile new destination for wine lovers in Gorey. (Esmonde St, Gorey ☎ 055-81704)

Butcher
● Terry Redmond Butchers

Terry Redmond's shop doesn't look like much when you step in the door, just another average butcher's store, just off the main strip of Gorey. But Alan Redmond's multi-award-winning sausages are worth making the journey to Gorey, just to sample a piece of banger bliss. This is the classic breakfast sausage: porky, peppery, perfect, the sort of sausage that kickstarts the morning. Only excellent. (John St, Gorey ☎ 055-21344)

Cult Choice Wexford Soft Fruits

At a time when we have become fixated with farmers' markets, it is apt to remember that the fruit growers of the South East, and of Wexford in particular, have long been the pioneers of selling direct to the customer from a simple roadside stall. In June and July, as the strawberries and raspberries, the plums and the redcurrants come into season, all the main roads of the South East will be necklaced with producers, selling their soft fruits, and the first early potatoes, from the back of trailers, from little trestle tables, with stripey parasols to protect the sellers from the sunshine of the sunny South East. It's a wonderful tradition, bringing grower and customer together, so pull over and pick up a few punnets and some spuds.

Kilmore Quay

Pub
● Kehoe's Pub & Parlour

James and Eleanor Kehoe's popular bar is home to a welter of marine paraphernalia, as well as some smart, well-delivered bar food – crab mornay, Slaney salmon; chicken breast stuffed with leek and potato. (Kilmore Quay ☎ 053-29830 www.kehoes.com — Open Day-time and early Evening)

New Ross

Bakery
● The Bakehouse

This a sweet little home bakery, right on the corner of North and South Streets. (18 North St, New Ross ☎ 051-422951)

Farm Shop
● Farmer Direct

Beside the river and adjacent to the garden centre, Farmer

Direct is a modest shed that is home to lots of excellent local foods, supplied by local producers. The concept is simple: the shop is supplied by a small troupe of local artisans from the region, all of whose produce is proudly labelled and displayed with care. There are lovely things from Stable Diet of Yoletown; juices from Ballycross Farm; good meats from Brendan Stafford, fresh local potatoes, handmade preserves. FD manages to sell everything you need, delivering great quality, and no air miles. (Marshmeadows, New Ross ☎ 051-420816)

Café & Wholefood Shop
● In A Nutshell

The front section of IAN is a health food shop with a sandwich counter that offers pristine salads and meats, whilst a second counter offers homemade apple tarts, fruit crumbles, carrot cake. The restaurant section is at the back of the shop in a lovely airy space filled with light by virtue of the double height ceiling with glass roof. The laminated menu of basics such as pannini, open sandwiches, soups and some imaginative fry-ups, is augmented by an attached sheet of daily specials: summer vegetable soup; tomato and red pepper soup; roast rib of feile bia beef with horseradish cream; fillet of beef curry with basmati rice, mango chutney and yoghurt, and a seafood platter, to give a few examples. Soups are clean and fresh, served with good brown bread, whilst pasta dishes such as organic penne pasta with smoked chicken, roast red pepper sauce, sundried tomatoes, spinach and pine nuts are the work of a kitchen crew who know how to taste and know what works. Lovely puds, Illy coffee, friendly staff, a great place. (18 South St, New Ross ☎ 051-422777)

Rosslare

Resort Hotel
● Kelly's Resort Hotel

Bill Kelly's legendary hotel has just created a new spa, SEASPA, at a cost of six million euro. Last year, they extensively revamped their dining roon, Beaches. The year before, they redid the bar. Before that, they added a new wing of bed-

One cup of their name

rooms. And it is only a few years ago that they created the magnificent La Marine bistro.

In fact, if you went all the way back to 1895, when Kelly's first opened as a tea room, chances are you could find a new project undertaken and completed each and every year. And that is why Kelly's is the finest hotel in Ireland: they set their own standards, and then they exceed them, year in, year out. Nobody and nothing can rest on their laurels here, and their hunger for the new challenge is as inspiring as their peerless hospitality. (Rosslare ☎ 053-32114 www.kellys.ie)

Restaurant
● La Marine

Eugene Callaghan has always been the most mature and sophisticated of cooks, a man who dares to produce food of stunning, elegant simplicity. Other chefs waste time on elaborate presentation: Mr Callaghan simply goes for flavour. When the food arrives it looks almost domestic in appearance: confit of duck; stuffed shoulder of lamb; salmon Niçoise with green beans and new potatoes; plaice with champ and chive beurre blanc. But when you eat, the amazing layers of precise, articulated flavour that assail the tastebuds make for an experience that few other chefs can match. "Faultless cooking of the highest order – the benchmark against which all others would be judged" wrote a correspondent after a particularly fine lunch. And so it is: Mr Callaghan's cooking in La Marine is unique in its simplicity. And, don't be self-conscious about having a fight with your partner about who gets to eat the last bits of the duck confit: everyone does. (Rosslare ☎ 053-32114 — Open Lunch & Dinner)

Wexford

Restaurant
● La Dolce Vita

Roberto Pons' Italian restaurant is also a vital store of quality Italian ingredients that you can buy to take away after a good Italian lunch has inspired you to have a go at making your own gnocchi with brown butter, or Italian sausages with lentils. The menus in the restaurant unambiguously assert the potent power of classic Italian domestic cooking – good antipasti selections; tagliatelle with pesto; fish with salmoriglio; panna cotta – and the experienced Mr Pons is very comfortable and exceptionally confident with this lovely food. (6-7 Trimmer's Lane, Selskar, Wexford ☎ 053-70806 — Open Day-time)

Restaurant
● Forde's Restaurant

Liam Forde's punchy, flavoursome cooking has won a great audience in Wexford and in the county. A rather fussy upstairs room that always has lots of energy is home to food that has lots of tactility and lots of flavour: lemon sole with crab claws, ginger and roast pepper; scallops in ketaifi pastry basket; pan-fried prawns with roast garlic and lovage; fillet steak with onion rings, brie fritter and a sage jus; chateaubriand with barley and sauerkraut; good tarte tatin with homemade vanilla ice cream. Value is good, service is spot on. (The Crescent, Wexford ☎ 053-23832 — Open Lunch & Dinner)

Wine Merchant & Delicatessen
● Greenacres

Greenacres is an amazing wine shop, one of the country's very best. A brilliant winestore, a great food store and with an art gallery into the bargain, it really is one of the great destination addresses for sourcing and discovering great foods, amazing wines, and perhaps a little piece of local art. James and Paula O'Connor never slow down on the continuous improvements that have marked Greenacres as a uniquely ambitious wine shop, and Greenacres is worth a detour into Wexford all on its own. (56 North Main St, Wexford ☎ 053-22975 www.greenacres.ie)

Townhouse
● McMenamin's Townhouse

Seamus and Kay McMenamin's townhouse probably provokes more letters of praise into the Bridgestone Guides annually than just about any other address. Good hospitality, big breakfasts, and whilst the rooms are small, they are very comfortable. (3 Auburn Terrace, Redmond Rd, Wexford ☎ 053-4642 www.wexford-bedandbreakfast.com)

10 GREAT
IRISH BREWS

1
BLACK BIDDY
BIDDY EARLY BREWERY

2
CURIM GOLD
CARLOW BREWING CO.

3
DARCY'S DUBLIN STOUT
DUBLIN BREWING CO.

4
FINIAN'S GOLD
CELTIC BREWING CO.

5
GUINNESS PINT BOTTLE
DIAGEO

6
HILDEN ALE
HILDEN BREWING CO.

7
KINSALE STOUT
KINSALE BREWING CO.

8
MAEVE'S CRYSTAL WHEAT
DUBLIN BREWING CO.

9
O'HARA'S STOUT
CARLOW BREWING CO.

10
PORTERHOUSE OYSTER STOUT
THE PORTERHOUSE

Supermarket
● Pettitt's Supermarket

Des Pettitt's brilliant chain of supermarkets – there are branches in Arklow, Gorey, Athy and Enniscorthy, as well as in Wexford – have always seemed to us the model for what a local supermarket should be. The staff are brilliant, there are lots of local foods, great wines, and a knowing, proud confidence in every store. These are supermarkets with character, and the chain is also a major player in many local and community affairs, so profit and philanthropy go together hand in hand. (Saint Aidans Shopping Centre, Wexford ☎ 053-24055 www.pettitts.ie)

Restaurant
● Warren Gillen's La Riva Restaurant

It is an ambitious chef who decides to put his name above the title of his restaurant, but Warren Gillen has the ambition, and his cooking has a cheffy energy and particularity that is impressive. La Riva is an upstairs room, with views out over the harbour, and staff are well focused and helpful. The cooking style is cheffy and tall, and involves layers and layers of elements and flavours: local beef is served in medallions and comes with raviolo of bacon and cabbage, and onion and mushroom confit, and a marjoram and truffle oil jus, for instance, a welter of tastes that hearkens back to the frenetic cooking of the 1990's in its elaboration. Where the cooking is complex, the room is simple, and there is a hunger and a desire to succeed evident in Warren Gillen's La Riva. (Crescent Quay, Wexford ☎ 053-24330 — Open Dinner & Sun Lunch)

Yoletown

Food Producer
● Stable Diet Foots

Whilst Catherine Carroll and Vincent Power's company is particularly well-known for a very good breakfast muesli, they also specialise in very fine and very consistent sweet baking, as well as good chutneys and salad dressings. Look out for their flapjacks. (Yoletown, Broadway ☎ 053-31287)

County Wicklow

Wicklow lamb, sourdough bread, blue-veined cheese,
bio-dynamics and organics, Wicklow venison, wild food...

Arklow

Bakery
● The Stone Oven Bakery

Egon Friedrich's lovely little bakery has been an invaluable
source of hand-made artisan, multi-grain, seed and sourdough breads long before they ever enjoyed their current
vogue. (65 Main St Lr, Arklow ☎ 0402-39418
friedrich@tinet.ie)

Cheesemaker
● Wicklow Farmhouse Cheese

John Hempenstall's unique blue-veined cheese is made with
pasteurized milk from their own herd of
friesians. The blue vein runs through the
centre of the cheese, the curd is mellow
and subtle, and the rind is smooth and edible. Whilst some describe it as a brie-style
cheese, the truth is that it's actually a charming sport of nature, and one of the most exciting of the
new generation of farmhouse cheeses being made in
Ireland. (Curranstown, Arklow ☎ 0402-39543)

Ashford

Country House & Cookery School
● Ballyknocken House

Catherine Fulvio is one of the stars of the younger generation of Irish country house keepers and cooks,
the sort of dynamic personality that attracts
media attention even outside the food and
travel pages. Part of her secret is a simple
brilliance with public relations, but above all
else the success of the splendid Ballyknocken
House is built on two foundations: sheer hard work, and
terrific country cooking.
The house is modest in size, but Mrs Fulvio has a good eye

for decoration and detail, which means this is a comfortable house. Her cooking is a splendid starburst of flavours – we would rate dinner here as being amongst the best country house cooking in Ireland, quite a feat when you consider that Mrs Fulvio has no formal background in cooking. She simply praises her mother's "good wholesome food using local ingedients, and I've carried that tradition on". As if all this – and two small children! – wasn't enough, Catherine has also opened the Ballyknocken Cookery School, in the old milking parlour of the farmhouse, with an excellent range of courses designed for small groups. (Glenealy, Ashford ☎ 0404-44627 www.ballyknocken.com)

Wine Shop
● **Caprani**

Conor Caprani's handsome wine shop is one part of the family-run Chester Beatty hotel, and it's packed with excellent, carefully sourced wines, which make it well worth taking a detour off the main road into Ashford. (Ashford ☎ 0404-40682)

Aughrim

Organic Farm
● **Gold River Farm**

Alan Pierce's farm concentrates on supplying superlative organic fruits and vegetables to restaurateurs. Gold River tailor their production to suit the demands of restaurant kitchens, which makes them a vital resource for serious creative chefs. (Aughrim ☎ 0402-36426)

Baltinglass

Food Producer
● **Wicklow Fine Foods**

Jim and Mary Healy's company produces a range of specialist chocolate products, from waffle biscuits to cinnamon sticks to handmade truffles. Our kids especially appreciate the WFF luxury chocolate spread, which they devour with relish. (Lathaleere, Baltinglass ☎ 059-648 1999 www.wicklowfinefoods.com)

Blessington

Café
● Grangecon Café

Richard and Jenny Street haven't renamed their brilliant café since they moved from their original location in little Grangecon to the mighty metropolis of Blessington. They have more space now, but what hasn't changed is the sparky, punky, superbly considered cooking which has made their reputations. These guys really know how to cook, and they do so in the most delightfully free-form, improvised way imaginable, cooking whatever takes their fancy on the day – a lasagna made with peperonata; pancakes made with spinach and ricotta; lamb roasted with chillies and tamarind; salmon baked in puff pastry; excellent desserts such as classic tarte tatin and perfect lemon tart. Everything about Grangecon is so innocent, unassuming and logical that it makes other restaurants seem bizarre and absurd: all cooking should be this pure and motivated. (The Old Schoolhouse ☎ 045-857892 — Open Day-time)

Bray

Cider
● KSD Sales

Larry Keegan's company sells some very fine quality ciders from France: look out especially for the artisan Le Terroir, from Brittany. You will find them for sale at farmers' markets and in wine shops and delis. (2 Duncairn Mews, Bray ☎ 01-276 0919)

Delgany

Country Market
● Delgany Country Market

A small country market takes place on Friday mornings in the schoolhouse of pretty little Delgany. The traditional Wicklow markets are amongst the best country markets to be found anywhere in Ireland, offering good domestic baking and local vegetables. (Old Schoolhouse, Friday 10am-noon)

Butcher
● Farrelly's Butchers

The brothers Padraig and Anthony Farrelly source their beef and lamb from Wicklow farmers, they have the great good fortune to have their own abattoir at the back of their little butcher's shop, and these men know their animals and they know how to hang and prepare meat, and the result is a gem of a butcher's shop, with charming, helpful service the final element to an already stellar equation. Having a chat about meat in here is akin to a masterclass in the art of great, expert charcuterie.

Mr Farrelly senior took over a pre-existing butcher's shop in Delgany in 1958, so there is nearly a half century of patient expertise at work here, and it's an expertise that is evident in the confidence and vast depth of knowledge exhibited by Padraig and Anthony. Knowing their farmers means that the brothers can be sourcing young lamb from the Wicklow hills late into the summer, when most other lamb is finished. Their beef is dense with complex flavours They can specify that their pork should have crackling, and if you are one of those epicureans driven demented by the inability to get lamb's sweetbreads, then call in here, where at certain times of the year they will be available. The shop also sells excellent organic beef and lamb from Philip Emmett's Altidore Farm in the county. Only brilliant. (Main St, Delgany ☎ 01-287 4211)

Hotel & Restaurant
● Glenview Hotel

Whilst the style of the Glenview is somewhat dated, the cooking by the kitchen crew under executive chef Derek Dunne is hugely ambitious, and a zillion miles away from what one frequently expects of food in a country hotel. This crew is hungry for success and recognition, and it shows in expressive, mature food: a warm tart of leek, wild mushroom and Gubbeen cheese; steamed seabass on a herb risotto; supreme and confit leg of pheasant with shi-itake mushroom and cashew nut ragoût; pear and almond frangipane with vanilla ice cream. A little updating of the décor could see the Glenview become a major player. Service is extremely good. (Glen O The Downs, Delgany ☎ 01-287 3399)

Enniskerry

Shop
● Murtagh's

Denise Murtagh's pretty shop in pretty Enniskerry is a great source of excellent, choice wines and good foods such as La Maison de Boulangerie breads and many other vital things. The shop has a particularly lovely aesthetic which gives it a special ambience. (Enniskerry ☎ 01-276 0404)

Café
● Powerscourt Terrace Café

This is the second outpost of the inspiring Avoca Handweavers operation in Wicklow, and it's a particularly beautiful location for lunch. The cooking has exactly the same imaginative modern satisfying signature as the Avoca branches in Kilmacanogue and Dublin. (Powerscourt House, Enniskerry ☎ 01-204 6070 www.avoca.ie)

Farmers' Market
● Waterfall Farmers' Market

Liz Keegan decided to start a market by opening up an out-house on her farm near to Enniskerry, a subsidiary enter-prise to her main business, which is producing fine quality hen's eggs from her 1,500 hens. Great local vegetables, great Wicklow lamb from Gary Crocker, farmhouse cheeses, home baking, local dairy produce, exotic plants, and lots of nice things to eat and drink as you shop. This is a charming market, in a county blessed with many great places to buy its splendiferous produce. (Enniskerry ☎ 01-286 9154)

Glendalough

Farmer's Market
● Glendalough Farmers' Market

Glendalough is one of the many east coast farmers' markets organised by Sean McArdle, and features many of the pro-ducers who will be well-known from Sean's other markets. It takes place every second Sunday, and the beautiful loca-tion of picturesque Glendalough means a trip here makes for a great day out for all the family. (Brockagh Resource Centre, 11am, Sunday)

Greystones

Café
● Baker J and Co

Richard and Judy's pert little café has some lovely food – tomato and lentil soup; good ciabatta stuffed with pastrami and Swiss cheese with rocket – and the Greystones girls with the bling bling Blahniks know a good thing when they eat it. (Gweedore Church Rd, Greystones ☎ 01-287 5477)

Wine Shop
● Cheers Take Home

Dennis Byrne's newly refurbished Burnaby now has a smart wine shop run by Tom Monaghan, whom many will recall as the courteous and hugely knowledgeable sommelier of Bray's legendary Tree of Idleness. Mr Monaghan has a great list of wines to offer, from superstars such as Penfolds Grange to some excellent quaffers at keen prices. (The Burnaby, Main St, Greystones ☎ 01-287 4015)

Restaurant
● The Hungry Monk

Pat Keown's hugely successful restaurant is the Greystones destination for good food, great camaraderie, and for great wines, all offered at very keen prices. Mr Keown has a rich sense of humour – check out that funky, roller-skating monk on the menus – and that bonhomie and lack of pre-tension shines through everything, especially the rock-solid cooking: tian of crab; lamb's kidneys dijonnaise; rack of Wicklow lamb; boeuf bourguignonne; crispy duck with kumquats. The wine list is an astonishment of choice, and one of the very best anywhere in Ireland. (Church Rd, Greystones ☎ 01-287 5759 hungrymonk@eircom.net)

Food To Go
● Indian Spice Co.

Ronan Fleming made a terrific reputation for his ethnic cooking in Glenageary's Bombay Pantry, and in Greystones his food-to-go shop – one of the most imaginative buildings made from nothing we have ever seen – has his signature élan: punk rock chicken – vindaloo to you – railway lamb, spice co. c.t.m.; jungle bandits choice, and there are organic vegetables from Marc Michel – courgettes cooked with

tomatoes, ginger and garlic – and good breads. Excellent
funky ethnic music soothes the short wait for dinner, and in
conjunction with the local branch of O'Brien's wines you
can also score a discount on wines when you present your
receipt. (Church Rd, ☎ 01-201 0868)

Wholefood Shop
● Nature's Gold

Brod Kieron's very fine wholefood shop is one of the great
and enduring food features of Greystones, and it is an
invaluable resource of good things. (Killincarrig Rd,
Greystones ☎ 01-287 6301 natgold@iol.ie)

Restaurant
● Le Paysan

Thierry Peurois's modest little restaurant offers the bistro
dishes that made French cooking famous – lamb navarin;
pork with prunes; coquilles St Jacques; sole meuniere. For
DART travellers returning to Greystone late in the evening
from the big smoke just up the coast, solace awaits as you
can order the dishes to take home with you. (Church Rd,
Greystones ☎ 01-287 2167)

Kilmacanogue

Café
● Avoca

The original branch of the Wicklow Wonder has increased
in size whilst slowly and surely improving
each and every year. Along the way, a second Wicklow outlet has been created at
Powerscourt, serving more of the same
snappy, accessible food, and doing it in
beautiful surroundings.

On top of their game

It would seem to be one of the facts of life about the
Wicklow food community that so many of them – from the
Brook Lodge Inn to Penny and Udo Lange to Marc Michel –
can marry so perfectly all the disparate aesthetics of their
work, and so thereby achieve an offering that is total, complete, underscored with the strong signature of these strong
people. Simon Pratt and his team are masters of all they
offer, and working in Avoca should be a right-of-passage for
anyone in Irish food and Irish retailing who wants to under-

stand how to create and control a distinct Irish aesthetic. The cooking is rock-solid reliable, and suits every age group and every pocket, a truly democratic achievement, as is evident from the enormous numbers of people who join the queue here almost every day of the year. In France, the entire family would already have been awarded the Legion d'Honneur. Couldn't we at least start with a few honorary doctorates? (Kilmacanogue ☎ 01-286 7466 www.avoca.ie — Open Day-time)

Chutneys & Relishes
● Janet's Country Fayre

Janet Drew's sweet pepper relish is probably the most-copied artisan food product ever produced in Ireland. Where Ms Drew pioneered, many others have come and copied, but the original remains the best, and Ms Drew's sharp culinary aptitude is seen right throughout her range of chutneys and relishes. These are cherishable foods, and you will find them in good delis, and you will recognise them by their joyfully exuberant scripted labels. (Copsewood Farm, KIlmacanogue ☎ 01-204 1957)

Kilpedder

Organic Shop & Café
● Marc Michel Organic Life Shop & Café

Marc Michel has always had the ability to think sideways. He went into organics before it was fashionable, and he made it fashionable. Then, he opened up a farm shop just off the N11 motorway, to take advantage of the vogue for farm shops. Now, he has taken the next step, and created a tiny café right beside the shop – not much more than a coffee machine, a counter and tables and chairs under brollies – to offer the food of the farm cooked for lunch. It's all logical, synergistic, organic, and delicious – marinated fillet steak from Farrelly's of Delgany; a fine beef burger with onion marmalade; Caesar salad with the freshest cos lettuce imaginable; good salads with farm beans and vegetables. Others please note. (Kilpedder ☎ 01-201 1882 — Open Tue-Sat Day-time)

Kiltegan

Byo-Dynamic Produce
● Penny & Udo Lange

Wicklow has some of the finest farmers working today in
Ireland, and the inimitable Penny and Udo
Lange of Kiltegan, whose bio-dynamic
produce is some of the most brilliant
food one can eat, are amongst the very
best. These farmers are significant. They
have a name, a reputation, and their produce
has a signature. As such, they are the opposite of the anony-
mous, and uniform practices of Irish farming. Mr and Mrs
Lange grow beautiful fruits and vegetables on a beautiful
bio-dynamic farm, and their skill imparts all the goodness of
their care directly into their foods. Then, they take their
produce directly to their customers, and we have happy
customers, and happy farmers, farmers whose skills are
world class. It is simple, and logical, and it will be the new
template for Irish farming when the Government wakes up.
In the meantime, you should get the Lange Farm produce
into your life. (Ballinroan House, Kiltegan ☎ 059-647 3278)

Kilternan

Country Market
● Kilternan Country Market

Believe it or not, but the Kilternan Country Market is now
40 years young. One of the great institutions of Wicklow
country life, it offers superb quality local foods, all sold in
the most frenetic whirlwind of a mêlée every Saturday
morning. Until you have stood in the queue with number in
hand at Kilternan, you have not experienced Wicklow life.
(Golden Ball, Kilternan, Saturday 10am)

Macreddin

Country Hotel
● The Brook Lodge Inn

The Sunday afternoon market and barbecue at the Brook Lodge, with the sun

shining, painters and potters exhibiting, dogs gambolling, teenagers courting, artisans selling, parents sipping cocktails and pints, food grilling and toasting, is one of the great events of Irish food and hospitality. It is proof, also, of the extraordinary vision of Evan Doyle and his brothers, Bernard and Eoin, a trio who have created an institution in less than the blink of an eye, simply by being original, smart and generous. The Brook Lodge offer encompasses everything that makes us feel good, from their fine spa – The Wells – straight through to assimilating those archetypes that we seek in our lives – the goodness of wild and organic food to eat; the luxury of superb wines to drink; the glamour of stylish rooms in which to mingle; the comfort of brilliant staff to assist us. The Brook Lodge is an extraordinary achievement. (Brook Lodge Inn, Macreddin ☎ 0402-36444 www.brooklodge.com — Open Dinner)

Newcastle

Country Market
● Country Market, Newcastle

The excellent North Wicklow Country Market has had a change of venue, and now takes place every Saturday morning from 11am in the Newcastle Community Centre. Lots of good local foods, and a lovely, community atmosphere.

Farm Shop
● Sweetbank Farm

The fourth generation of the Johnston family have stewardship of Sweetbank Farm today, and from their farm shop, just outside Newcastle on the road to Rathnew – look out for the sign – they sell their own soft fruit, along with freshly pressed apple juices and Wicklow lamb. (Newcastle ☎ 01-281 9286 sweetbankfarm@iolfree.ie)

Rathdrum

Butcher
● Synnott's

This tiny butcher's shop, just off the main street of Rathdrum, sells some of the very best beef we have eaten in recent times. The

Synnott brothers know their produce, and when they get to know you, you can expect some of the highest quality beef and lamb imaginable, sold with sagacious Wicklow wit. The striploin steaks alone are worth the trip to Rathdrum, so start grating the horseradish. (Rathdrum ☎ 0404-46132)

Roundwood

Country Inn
● **The Roundwood Inn**

Jurgen Schwalm's popular country inn is a favourite with walkers and hikers, but you don't need to be a sporty sort to enjoy some unpretentious and well-realised country cooking, much of it with a German accent on flavour and style, in a pleasant, comfortable country bar. (Roundwood ☎ 01-281 8107)

Wicklow

Wine Shop
● **Wicklow Wine Co**

Ben Mason and Michael Anderson cram more than 600 groovy wines into their shop on the main street of Wicklow town, including an unmatched selection of Portuguese wines, a fantastic Italian selection, and an idiosyncratic, alluring range of beauties from the French regions.

As with the best wine merchants, the best way to sure-fire success is to take Ben and Michael's advice, and to ask them to recommend what you should drink: a sweet Bergerac from Court-les-Muts for dessert; their fine house wine, Cuvée Oreille for a good value party white; a bottle of Pierre Paillard bubbly for a celebration that won't break the bank; good Burgundies from Domaine Arlaud, and once you discover those Portuguese, then there will be no looking back – Niepoort from Douro; Quinta da Cabriz; Casa da Lago and many others. Proving that an instinct for food and wine is a family affair, Ben's brother, Tim, runs Dingle's superb Out of the Blue fish restaurant. (Main St, Wicklow ☎ 0404-66767)

NORTHERN IRELAND

Belfast City

authentic Chinese cooking, pub grub, tapas,
sliders, nut brittle, griddle bread, the Belfast bap . . .

Cathedral Quarter

Bagel Café
● **Bagel Bagel**

Paul and Joan Barr's BB import their bagels from England
and dish 'em up in a myriad of flavours, with tasty fillings:
Nova lox; classic club; BLT; Chicken Caesar. Melts, soups,
coffee and cakes are all available, and they will deliver to
your door. (60 Donegall St ☎ 028-9024 2545
barrbagelbagel@aol.com — Open Day-time)

Wine Merchants
● **Direct Wine Shipments**

DWS is one of the key wine buff's destinations, with a fantastic range of bottles arrayed around their atmospheric
salesroom, and with all the wine courses and specialist
knowledge and wine paraphernalia to make this a one-stop
shop. The Spanish selection, in particular, is ace.
(5-7 Corporation Sq ☎ 028-9050 8000)

Gastro Pub
● **The John Hewitt**

Friendly staff and some decent, if occasionally wayward, Irish
pub grub — leek and mushroom tart with roast spuds; chick-
en and smoky bacon with champ; banana crème brulée —
are the JH signature. (Donegall St ☎ 028-9023 3786 —
Open Day-time)

Restaurant & Wine Bar
● **Nick's Warehouse**

For more than 13 years, Nick's - upstairs restaurant, wine
bar and their stylish, punky and popular Anix — has offered
modern comfort cooking, from a kitchen team whose sense
of inquiry never dims. Above all, there is no preciousness
about this restaurant: they cook the food they like to cook
and eat — grilled salmon with parsnip purée and basil; calf's
liver with shallot and red wine sauce; bumper comfort food
like rare breed meats and artisan sausages with mash — they
discover new foods and ideas and pass them on with enthusiasm, and above all they serve the wines they like to drink.

This complete lack of pretension means Nick's is always a fun warehouse to find yourself in, and one of the great Belfast city addresses. (35-39 Hill St ☎ 028-9043 9690 www.nickswarehouse.co.uk — Open Lunch & Dinner)

Wine Bar
● Quarter

A sharp wine bar with restaurant service, Quarter has ambition in its kitchen. Crisp belly pork with celeriac rösti; Roquefort and spinach tart; battered haddock with petits pois and a good homemade tartare make this a worthwhile new destination. (Waring St ☎ 028-9031 1414 — Open Day-time)

Pub
● White's 1630

The oldest tavern in Belfast is home to a smoky turf fire and some good simple food such as shepherd's pie, Irish stew, and nicely un-chilled Guinness, (2-4 Winecellar Entry ☎ 028-9024 3080 — Open Day-time)

City Centre

Café
● Café Renoir

This is the city centre address of the respected Café Renoir whose university zone restaurant is the beacon of Botanic. Queen's Street is a well-organised self-service restaurant and it delivers on good daytime eating and fine value. (5-7 Queen's St ☎ 028-9032 5592 — Open Day-time)

Restaurant
● Cayenne

Cayenne has doubled in size in the last year, and now has a slinky bar along with a bling-bling private dining room. Paul and Jeanne Rankin's flagship remain's Belfast's hottest address, no mean feat when you consider that they opened the year we wrote our first ever Guide book. Since 1989, the innovation has been continuous, the desire to deliver an

On top of their game

out-of-this-world experience has rarely faltered. Being a great teacher has enabled Rankin to keep a hungry crew of wanna-be-great chefs in the kitchen, and the food has true verve: pumpkin and coconut soup has a Malay twist; seared foie gras is brilliantly paired with grilled gingerbread; roast squab with onion soubise is a dream dish; pecan tart with banana rum ice cream is dreamy deliciousness. Still cutting-edge after all these years. As we go to press, there are plans to re-open the original Roscoff, in the city centre. (7 Ascot House, Shaftesbury Sq ☎ 028-9033 1532 — Open Lunch & Dinner)

Shop
● Chef's Shop

Vincent McKenna's shop, just off Great Victoria St, is a little haven of professional tools and must-haves for the food lover. It's a choicely stocked shop and it is a much better destination for serious cooking gear than the department stores. (2 Little Victoria St ☎ 028-9032 9200, thechefshop.net)

Coffee Shops
● Clements

The Clements coffee shops are classy, and probably the most consistent address for good coffee in the city. There is a most excellent squidgyness in both their cakes and the leather sofas, and cool sounds are a big bonus. Also at: 127-131 Royal Ave, 66-68 Botanic Ave, 4 Donegall Sq West, and 139 Stranmillis where the café has a nice local feel and staff recognise regulars. (37-39 Rosemary St ☎ 028-9032 2293 — Open Day-time)

Restaurant
● Restaurant Michael Deane

Michael Deane has opened a casual, Asian restaurant, Chok Dee, alongside the on-going demands of his ambitious first-floor restaurant and the ground-floor brasserie here on Howard Street. Mr Deane's food is lavish, singular and luxu-rious, a series of intellectually challenging forays into grand dining, with an Asian influence that is beautifully realised and which is his distinctive signature. As chef, he is imperious, capable of producing food that is genuinely unforgettable. As restaurateur, his strengths are not so manifest. (38-40 Howard St ☎ 028-9033 1134 www.deanesbelfast.com Open Dinner Wed-Sat & Lunch Fri)

Shop & Café
● Equinox

The seriously chic Equinox, home to covetable and choice artefacts for home and kitchen and yourself, has a small café at the rear where you will find nice pasta dishes, some imaginative salads, all powered with a light, modern-Mediterranean ethos. (32 Howard St ☎ 028-9023 0089 — Open Day-time)

Fishmonger
● Walter Ewing

Walter Ewing's modest shop belies its importance to the city; this is the first stop for all serious cooks and chefs who want seriously fresh fish, so whilst you are in for a wee fillet of haddock, the 'phone will be hopping with orders from the city's best restaurants. Mr Ewing also smokes some seriously good salmon, the smoking giving a gentle caress of volatile liveliness. Brilliant. (124 Shankill Rd ☎ 028-9038 1120)

Delicatessen
● Feasts

Craig and Penny Nash's Feasts has been amazingly consistent over the years; its tried-tested-and-true template of superb pastas, great cheeses and ace charcuterie combining to make a fab daytime offer that Belfast food lovers never tire of. Rigid adherence to quality means that they deliver what it says on the menu with accuracy and style, and even the take-away sandwiches are tops. (39 Dublin Rd ☎ 028-9033 2787 www.feasts.co.uk)

Café
● Flour

A shoe-box-sized room that offers porridge with honey for breakfast and crêpes and coffee the rest of the day, along with lots of house music. Flour piles mature cheddar with caramelised onions and thyme, or Parma, Parmesan, rocket and olive oil, or lemon chicken and tarragon mayo into good crêpes. But do leave room for something sweet: Belgian chocolate with almonds and coconut or – if you are from Glasgow – Mars bar and Bailey's ice cream. (46 Upper Queen St ☎ 028-9033 9966 — Open Day-time)

Restaurant
● Ginger Café

Simon McCance, who wowed! Belfast with his punky cooking in Ginger, on the Ormeau Road, is opening a new café here in the Parks store on Great Victoria Street, and one awaits the re-emergence of this singular chef with impatience. A bistro, on Hope Street, will join the café soon. (68-72 Gt Victoria St ☎ 028-902 99496 — Open Day-time)

Restaurant
● The Grill

Prawn cocktail. Grilled fillet of beef. Deep-fried onions. Crisp chips. Lemon meringue pie. I'm sorry; have we died and gone to 1970's heaven? Where are Starsky & Hutch? Where is Marc Bolan? Great ideas never die, they just need to be re-invented every now and then. The Grill in the fab Ten Square has simply re-invented the grill bar concept: simple classic food from Caesar salad to ribs to chocolate Diane, sharp service, cool room, are we all happy? Yes we are. The grill concept is one of the fundamentals of good restaurant eating, and when it is done as well as it is here, it's a cracker. (10 Donegall Sq Sth ☎ 028-9024 1001 — Open Day-time)

Restaurant
● Istana

A clean, lean, convivial canteen, Istana's pan-Asian mix of Chinese, Thai and Indian cooking works surprisingly well, but it's the Malay specials that have the most oomph!. Penang laksa is spot on, the golden grilled skate with its turban of soft-fried onions is a beaut, and the ABC dessert is ace. (127 Gt Victoria St ☎ 028-9023 2311 — Open Lunch & Dinner)

Restaurant
● James Street South

Vincent McKenna's converted warehouse attracts a well-heeled crew to a handsome room, where the chef offers dishes that reflect his fondness for the sweet comfort of the Mediterranean, but which also have a sharply focussed modern attitude. He takes a traditional cassoulet apart to serve it as crisped belly pork, duck confit, black beans and a sweet-spiced liquor. Pork fillet has sweet potato purée, crackling and an apple jus, whilst salmon has creamed fennel

and artichokes, and sea bass has seared scallops with tomato compote and watercress salad. Service is as polished as
the cooking, which is to say very polished. (21 James St Sth
☎ 028-9043 4310 — Open Lunch & Dinner)

Bakery
● Millar's Bakery

Marty Millar's bakery has two shops in town, at Chapel
Lane and Holywood Road, and both demonstrate the atten-
tion to detail and commitment to quality of this bakery. (18
Chapel Lane ☎ 028-9024 9166)

Butcher
● Owen McMahon

Owen McMahon's butcher's shop is small and traditional
and packed with great meat, the work of a creative crew of
charcutiers. Their sausages are amongst the very best – try
the Lincolnshire and the Cumberland to get a taste of real
expertise – and in addition to the excellent quality of their
beef, lamb and pork, they also sell many rare breeds of
meat, including wild boar and ostrich. (3-5 Atlantic Ave
☎ 028-9074 3525)

Restaurant
● Porcelain

The first-floor dining room of the groovy Ten Square hotel
has always had a fondness for Asiatically-accented cooking –
ceviché of salmon with wasabi; steamed hake with Asian
greens and and a lemongrass beurre blanc, food that under
chef Alistair Fullerton was beautifully realised. Mr Fullerton
has moved on to the company's new Ballymena destination,
Galgorm Manor, which makes that a space to watch, whilst
it is likely the changes in Porcelain will be smoothly navigated. (Ten Square, 10 Donegall Sq ☎ 028-9024 1001
www.twnsquare.co.uk — Open Breakfast, Lunch & Dinner)

Shop
● Sawer's

It may be a small shop, but what Sawer's doesn't have isn't
worth wanting, and from fresh fish to every manner of jar,
tin and packet, it is all packed into this little vestibule of a
shop. Excellent staff means that after decades of service,
Sawer's remains a vital part of the centre city. (Fountain
Centre ☎ 028-9032 2021)

Shop & Café
● Smyth & Gibson

S&G has a really ace café upstairs above all the sharp shirts and stuff in which the shop specialises. A short but utterly apt menu makes agony of choosing: the smoked chicken salad with Caesar dressing? The goat's cheese with roasted red pepper vinaigrette? Salad of beef tomatoes with buffalo mozzarella and pesto? Savoury tart with bacon? And then: the lemon drizzle or the coffee and chocolate crunch? The delivery of the food is as sharp as the cut of the shirts. (Bedford Street ☎ 028-9023 0388 — Open Day-time)

Shop
● Still

Maurice and Sharon Rankin's shop has all the home-ware gear you crave, from fab kitchen goods to beautiful bespoke furniture. A considered aesthetic is revealed by everything chosen for the home by this couple, an echo of the Dutch De Stilj group of artists, sculptors, architects and designers, whose aim was to find laws of equilibrium and harmony that would be applicable to life and society as well as to art. "Be Still", they suggest. Try telling that to your credit card. (11 Castle Lane ☎ 028-9023 0494 www.stillforlife.com)

Restaurant
● Sun Kee

Having made the long march all the way across the street to the old Manor House premises, the legendary Sun Kee just keeps right on serving the most delicious, authentic Chinese cooking, and doing so with great energy and charm. Stiff competition exists all around it, but the local favourite remains just that: the local favourite. Great service, great value, great fun. (Donegall Pass ☎ 028-9031 2016 — Open Dinner, closed Fri)

Restaurant
● Suwanna Thai Restaurant

Suwanna is a busy Thai restaurant and offers a rare stab at authenticity from a cuisine that is frequently traduced in other Thai addresses. Service can get woozy when it gets very busy, but this is a modest, ambitious ethnic restaurant. (Gt Victoria St ☎ 028-9043 9007 — Open Dinner)

Restaurant
● Tong Dynasty

Oliver Tong's superb Chinese restaurant is home-from-home for many of Belfast's resident Chinese community, which tells you just what you need to know about the authenticity and sharpness of the cooking here. The glorious hot pots, of eel, lamb, minced pork or salted fish, arrive bubbling in spicy liquors, but it's the beef flank with turnip that is our current fave. The seafood stew is great, the vegetable cookery is real. If you are nervous about unusual ingredients, then ask the staff to choose, and you will get a splendidly balanced, dazzling dinner that you will talk about for months afterwards, or at least until you get back to TD. The dim sum here is amongst the very best in these islands. (82 Botanic Ave ☎ 028-9043 9590 — Open Lunch & Dinner)

Restaurant
● Zen

Eddie Fong's mega-buck Japanese restaurant is a mega-bling address, and anyone old enough to remember the 1960's James Bond-Steve McQueen cool style will just love this unrestrained temple of va-va-voom! The Japanese food is the best bet, with sushi and sashimi well presented, and tempuras are crisp and light, dishes such as duck with mango alternate between degrees of sweetness. Staff alternate between absolute sweetness and something less sweet. (55-59 Adelaide St ☎ 028-9023 2244 — Open Lunch & Dinner)

East Belfast

Restaurant
● Alden's

Alden's is a beaut of a restaurant, a match for any other in Ireland. The combination of Cath Gradwell's intelligent, expressive cooking, and Jonathan Davies' understated service, makes for a template of distinguished individuality and professionalism. Ms Gradwell's cooking does the savvy and the sublime in equal measure: great lamb's kidneys and liver with sage and onion mash, or it might be perfect grilled scallops with black beans and a sesame and chilli crisp, and then on to desserts that are all the more potent for being so restrained and unshowy. The room is gorgeous, and it's a great date restaurant. (229 Upper Newtownards Rd ☎ 028-9065 0079 — Open Lunch & Dinner)

Shop & Tea Rooms
● S.D. Bells

A classic and very classy tea rooms and tea shop sells the fine blends and brews of Belfast's great old tea blenders. (516 Upr Newtownards Rd ☎ 028-9047 1774 — Open Day-time)

Restaurant
● Bennett's on Belmont

Holywood heroine Colleen Bennett's hip new eaterie at Belmont is a heaven-sent address for folk in east Belfast, who no longer have to drive to Holywood to enjoy the punky, assured modern food that is Ms Bennett's signature. In Bennett's the food is fast in style but slow in ethos; burger with celeriac remoulade! Submarine roll with roasted pork loin and gherkins! Salvation! Real fast food! Her excellent frittatas are here, packed with juicy, ripe ingredients, desserts are spot on and so are the coffee and the prices. (4 Belmont Rd ☎ 028-9065 6590 — Open Day-time)

Café
● Café Mocha

CM has the so-familiar nouveau pauvre style of MDF minimalism and plaster walls, and it's a key address in this part of town. (Cregagh Rd ☎ 028-9046 9982 — Open Day-time)

Wine Merchant
● Compendium Wine Merchants

Neil Groom's wine shop – the boutique part of the Russell's Cellars chain - is a beaut of a shop, where the buying power of the parent is translated into brilliant wine choices from all over the globe. If you love wine, you really can't live without Compendium, and Mr Groom's genuinely witty and funny wine notes are a joy. Incidentally, it is not as difficult to find Compendium as you might think: ask for the justly celebrated Ulster Weavers shop, and keep on driving around the corner. (Alanbrooke Rd ☎ 028-9079 1197 www.compendiumwines.com)

Belfast Chippers

· *The Bethany* A favourite chipper on the East side of town. Pristine red, white and blue colour scheme, and there is also a sister branch of The Bethany on the Cregagh Rd. (246 Newtownards Rd ☎ 028-9045 4498)

· *Fryer Tuck* Tuck into cod and chips made with the Fryer's special batter, and chips fried in dripping. (89 Bloomfield Rd ☎ 028-9047 1921)

· *The Golden Chip* The chip cognescenti rate the potato, onion and spice pasties. (12 Comber Rd, Dundonald ☎ 028-9048 0979)

· *Long's* Fantastic old-style in Athol St, and don't be put off by the slick fast-food style of Donegall Pass, for Long's do serious fish and chips. (39 Athol St ☎ 028-9032 1848, Donegall Pass ☎ 028-9024 1644)

· *Manny's* Big – like seriously big – portions are Manny's speciality. (241 Antrim Rd ☎ 028-9035 1504)

· *Raffo's* Famous for their Belly Buster Burger, half a pound in weight! (174 Anderstonstown Road ☎ 028-9062 4854)

· *The Silver Leaf Café* Fresh fish and tasty, home-made, traditional pasties. (15 Belmont Road ☎ 028-9047 1164)

· *The Sphinx* Great felafel and real lamb kebabs, and a genuinely hot chilli sauce. (74 Stranmills Rd ☎ 028-9068 1881)

· *The Willow* A legendary chipper, established in 1921, and run by the Spence brothers, Bill and Martin. The Willow has a great community feel, and they wrap take-aways in newspaper! (52-54 Calvin St, Beersbridge Rd ☎ 028-9062 4854)

Laganside

Hotel
● The McCausland

The McCausland has been taken over by the hotel chain, Malmasion. Can we ask that they redesign their new Belfast branch with lots of Charles Rennie Mackintosh design signatures, as they did in Glasgow? The Malmasion style of livening up icon buildings has never seemed as potentially promising as here. (34-38 Victoria St ☎ 028-9022 0200)

Market
● Saint George's Market

The traditional Friday market has taken over from the Saturday market as the most exciting shopping of the week, but make sure to get here early for the best fish, and look out also for fresh pasta from Tomasso, good things from the Olive Tree company, baking from Darko Markjovic. All during the week, the market has some dedicated stores where you can find excellent breads from Martin Millar such as griddle breads and Paris buns, fab local vegetables from Philip McKee and fine meats from Greenmount Farm. (May St, Fridays, Saturdays am)

Restaurant
● Tedford's

There is creative and sophisticated food to be found in Tedford's – crispy squid in chilli and lime marinade with dressed salad and a red pepper mayonnaise; baked halibut with crab and chive mash and grainy mustard cream; sea bass with tomato and basil butter. Pre-theatre meals offer great value for money. (5 Donegall Quay ☎ 028-9043 4000 — Open Lunch & Dinner)

Lisburn Road

Delicatessen
● Arcadia

Willie Brown's deli is packed to its rafters with deli foods, and in an age of incessant fashion-following, how nice that Arcadia continues to sell old-style local deli specialities: check out those salads. (378 Lisburn Rd ☎ 028-9038 1779)

Shop
● Camseng

Camseng sells all the weird and wonderful Asian gear your
wok cookery needs. (1 Lwr Windsor Ave ☎ 028-9066 9200)

Delicatessen & Café
● Cargoes

Mary and Rhada's benchmark café has been one of the
most consistent and inspiring addresses in Belfast for more
than a decade. The simple love of food this lively pair and
their crew exhibit is intoxicating, and the sharpness of the
Mediterranean-accented food is a thrill: tart of aubergine,
goat's cheese and semi-dried tomato; pasta with superb
pesto; great Moroccan orange and almond cake. The shelves
are packed with good foods that show a discrimination
equal to the cooking. (613 Lisburn Rd ☎ 028-9066 5451 —
Open Day-time)

Wine Bar
● Chelsea Wine Bar

This popular media and sportsmen's watering hole isn't
much to look at, but the cooking is rock solid and packs
'em in for pan-fried haddock with dauphinoise potatoes,
fishcakes with good salad leaves, lamb tagine with chilli-
flecked couscous and great desserts. The food in the CWB
is the benchmark other superpubs should try to emulate.
(346 Lisburn Rd ☎ 028-9068 7177 — Open Day-time)

Butcher
● Coffey's

Although it doesn't have the stellar profile of some
Northern butchers, Coffey's has an enthusiastic and creative
crew preparing and experimenting with their meats, and it's
an address where you can see and enjoy some real respect
for the art of charcuterie. In particular, Coffey's is a great
address for game and other seasonal rarities.
(380 Lisburn Rd ☎ 028-9066 6292)

Restaurant
● Shu

Shu is a eclectic mixture of food styles and design styles,
with sashimi offered alongside French brasserie classics
such as steak and chips. It ought to be difficult to make it
work, and yet the crew here has made it work for several

years now, and in doing so have pleased many punters with some tasty, imaginative cookery that is never lacking in either conception or execution. (253 Lisburn Rd ☎ 028-9038 1655 www.shu-restaurant.com — Open Lunch & Dinner)

Café Bar
● Taps

Queues out the door have been a feature of Taps ever since they opened the doors of this café-bar and its tapas specialities. Questions of authenticity are irrelevant: they do what they do really well, from dainty quail's eggs on Serrano to punchy patatas bravas to the lovely bolsitas, pastry parcels with spinach and raisins. Speedy service, great buzz, and we expect Ferran Adria to drop in any day now. (479 Lisburn Rd ☎ 028-9066 3211 — Open all day)

Café & Traiteur
● The Yellow Door

Simon Dougan understands how to make delicious food, and that has quite simply been the axis of success on which the Yellow Door operation has been founded. His food knows how to be pleasing: soulful soups; good pastries and breads; dishes with a serene but savoury edge. Whether you just want to grab a sandwich or linger over lunch at an outside table, the YD understands what you want, and the way you want it. Clever. (427 Lisburn Rd ☎ 028-9038 1961)

Ormeau Road

Asian Supermarket
● Asia Supermarket

The Asia is not just the best ethnic shop in the country, it's one of the very best shops in the country, full stop. Restaurateurs are here, buying by the pallet. Locals are here, buying by the basket, and the ambience is clamorous and glamorous and utterly exhilarating. Food lovers stock up with necessities, then make a proper morning of it by going across the street to Forever Chinese for tiny dim sum. (189 Ormeau Rd ☎ 028-9032 6393)

Pub Grub
● The Errigle Inn

Step into the Oak Lounge and you step back to the 1930's, but when the cooking hits the table in the Errigle you know you are back in the 21st century. A fine crew knocks out ace food at brilliant prices: perfect pâté with caramelised onions; loin of lamb with oven-dried tomatoes with potato and chive salad; char-grilled pineapple with chilli syrup. (312-320 Ormeau Rd ☎ 028-9064 1410 — Open Day-time)

Chinese Traiteur & Bakery
● Forever Chinese

Real dim sum, served with fizzy pop drinks, is the FC's recipe for success: prawn dumplings, chilli beef wontons, pork spring rolls; stewed chicken's feet all measured out with skill and smiling charm. A rite of passage for any food lover. (1 Agincourt Ave ☎ 028-9059 3543 — Open Day-time)

Restaurant
● Macau

The gentle and loquacious George from the Sun Kee now has his own tiny but wildly popular restaurant. Pork dumplings, salt-chilli prawns and some Sun Kee favourites such as duck and orange or char siu and monkfish as well as excellent vegetables such as moreish kai lan means the eight tables are always bunged with locals and local Chinese. BYO wine is another reason to go to Macau. (271 Ormeau Rd ☎ 028-9069 1800 — Open dinner)

Delicatessen
● Olive Tree Company

Conor McCann knows how to make the Olive Tree look and feel like a feast for the senses, so there are masses of good foods piled high for your delectation. Upstairs, the lovely Med ingredients become punchy, tasty food: omelettes with Comte cheese; spinach tagliatelle with butternut squash; salad of feta and dolmades. Smart, fun and, with only five tables, intimate. (353 Ormeau Rd ☎ 028-9064 8898)

Shop
● The Vineyard

The Vineyard is a real Aladdin's cave of a shop, and the more you look, the more you find on each visit. There are more than 100 varieties of wine sold in the shop and if making cocktails shakes your moneymaker, they stock 60 vodkas and all the gear necessary to create splendiferous hangovers for all your friends. (375-377 Ormeau Rd ☎ 028-9064 5774)

Restaurant
● The Watermargin

Here's how big The Watermargin is; the managers have to wear ear pieces to keep control of the 250 diners who can be packed into this converted church at the Ormeau Road end of Donegall Pass. It's big, noisy, and great fun, and that's before you find yourself in one of the karaoke rooms: bring on Bill Murray singing "More Than This"! For food lovers, the Watermargin is a must, because they serve all the weird stuff your Asiatic attitude craves: pork intestine; crispy duck feet, frog's legs. Once you have sorted out the weirdos from the wimps, it makes for great eating, and the wimps can have chow mein and lemon chicken. (159-161 Donegall Pass, off Ormeau Rd ☎ 028-9032 6888 — Open all day)

Cookery School
● Who's Cooking

Students of cookery should check out Elizabeth Kennedy's website www.whoscooking.co.uk for details of a complete range of cookery classes. From kids to corporate, beginners to gourmet, Elizabeth's classes are good value for anyone who wants to learn to cook better. (Amber Lodge, 184 Mealough Rd, Drumbo ☎ 028-9082 6229)

University District

Restaurant
● Beatrice Kennedy

There is no fashion following in Beatrice Kennedy, and thank the stars for that. Named after the lady who once inhabited the house, BK offers solid, classic, flavourful cooking with a conservative modern twist, and service is polite and proper. (44 University Rd ☎ 028-9020 2290 — Open Dinner & Sun Lunch)

Café & Pizzeria
● Café Renoir/Café Renoir Pizza

Café Renoir and its next-door pizza restaurant are beacons
of good things. Whether it is a funky sandwich, a fry-up or
just a cup of coffee, this is a restaurant that takes care of
the details, and thereby ensures that the big picture comes
across focused and successful. The café has a stylish but
understated interior with warm earth tones and lots of
wood, and it's always a pleasant place for a solo breakfast or
a gossipy lunch with food that has true flavour. Next door,
whilst purists might initially balk at some of the pizza combinations offered in CF Pizza, for their weird, around-the-
world-in-80-pizzas titles aren't reassuring, rest assured that
the crisp pizza bases are true, and the simpler pizzas, such
as the Istanbul which successfully marries spinach, goat's
cheese and caramelised aubergine and a drizzle of herby
yogurt, are knockout with flavour. Service is slick and
friendly, value for money is spot on. (95 Botanic Ave
☎ 028-9031 1300 — Open Lunch & Dinner)

Restaurant
● Rain City

Rain City now has a sister branch at the Junction One
Village, on the Ballymena Road, Antrim, whilst the original
packs in the punters on the Lower Malone Road. In a fast
food nation, which is what Northern Ireland often is, the
RCs are a godsend, for they offer accessible food – pizzas,
fish 'n' chips, burgers, pastas – but they do it right, and their
determination to show that using high-quality ingredients
can ennoble these dishes and make them good to eat,
whilst simultaneously being good for you, is the sort of self-
less determination more places need to copy. That is a lofty,
valuable ambition, and one that is too often overlooked by
cooks with too much ego and zero social conscience. Good
food and a good food culture, family-friendly, fair prices. Just
the sort of place Dublin needs. (33-35 Malone Rd ☎ 028-
9068 2929; Junction One International Shopping Outlet,
Ballymena Rd, Antrim ☎ 028-9442 7959 — Open Lunch &
Dinner)

Wine Shop & Café
● Wine & Co

Wine & Co has a second branch with a busy restaurant at
The Maypole in Holywood, and both the Holywood and the

Stranmillis addresses have always been home to a interestingly varied and well-selected choice of wines. In Holywood, you can choose a bottle from downstairs in the wine shop to take to drink in the restaurant upstairs with lunch or dinner. (54 Stranmillis Rd ☎ 028-9068 2407; Holywood branch: 57 High St, Holywood ☎ 028-9042 6083)

Ice Cream and Sweeties

· *Archie's Ice Cream Parlour* Mrs Desano's shop is a classic, and you can even get jelly with your ice cream! Fabuloso! They have been scooping out the cones and sliding out the sliders since 1938, and little has – thankfully – changed since. The shop stays open 'until the ice cream runs out!' (344 Newtownards Rd ☎ 028-9045 1608)

· *Vanilla's* Margaret Garland's sweetie and ice cream shop is a wee beauty. (131 Falls Rd ☎ 028-9031 0588)

· *Aunt Sandra's* There are fantastic, warm, sugary aromas to be enjoyed in Jim and David Moore's sweetie factory, originally started by their Aunt Sandra. They make their own yellow man (see it bubbling away in big vats in the workshop), fudge, nut brittles, candy shapes and boiled sweets, and buy in handmade Belgian chocolates. And kids! Don't miss the 'smelly feet' lollies! Yukerooyumola! (60 Castlereagh Rd ☎ 028-9073 2868)

· *The Chocolate Room* Christine Brittain makes a mean hot chocolate – smooth, thick, made with milk or plain chocolate beads: this is as serious a hit of hot chocolate as you can get outside of Turin. Beautiful handmade chocolates from Ireland, Belgium, France and Germany are for sale, with an admirable concentration of quality in every department. (529 Lisburn Rd ☎ 028-9066 2110 www.thechocolateroom.com)

County Antrim

pot still whiskey, yellowman, dulse, sausages, craft brewing,
Glenarm salmon, Antrim potatoes...

Ballycastle

Fishmonger
● **Morton's**

This local fishmongers is well respected in the area as a
source of good fresh fish, with ling, lythe and wild salmon
caught locally for sale, along with other specimens from
County Down. (30 North St, Ballycastle ☎ 028-2076 2348)

Delicatessen & Coffee Bar
● **The Park Deli**

Ann Marie McCaughan's deli has a coffee bar with Illy coffee, cured deli meats and salads, and shelves with some
attractive deli foods. There is also a small dining area at the
rear, which opens on Friday & Saturday nights for a good
value evening menu. There is a winning sharpness about The
Park, and service is brisk and polite. They also offer a catering service. (5 Quay Rd, Ballycastle ☎ 028-2076 8563—
Open Day-time & Fri & Sat Dinner)

Butcher
● **Wysner Meats**

Jackie Wysner's shop makes one of the great Irish black
puddings – light, beautifully made, and quite delicious. And
the same can be said of everything in this pristine butcher's
shop, all sold with confident modesty by charming staff.
Next door, the Wysner's Restaurant serves familiar food in
a cosy, informal setting, but they can rise to some serious
cooking. (18 Ann St, Ballycastle ☎ 028-2076 2372)

Ballyclare

Organic Farm
● **Ballylagan Organic Farm**

The impressive raison d'être of Tom Gilbert's Ballylagan
Farm is to grow, produce and sell as comprehensive a range
of organic foods as possible in their farm shop. The shop
also stocks dried goods, and a range of imported fruit, all of
certified organic standard. In addition, they operate what

Tom calls a 'home delivery system', where customers call in their orders each week. Check out their website and enjoy Tom's *Irregular Rant* column. (10 Ballylagan Rd, Straid, Ballyclare ☎ 028-9332 2867 www.ballylagan.com — Open Fri afternoon, Sat all day)

Butcher
● **Errol Jenkin's Butchers**

Errol Jenkin's busy shop pulls in the punters at lunchtime for good cooked food-to-go, and all the skilfulness and creativity of a member of the Elite Association of Butchers is found here. (41 Main St, Ballyclare ☎ 028-9334 1822)

Ballymena

Farmhouse Cheese
● **Causeway Cheese Company**

Damian and Susan McCloskey's Drumkeel is the only farmhouse cheese made in Northern Ireland, and you will see its distinctive hexagonal shape – reminiscent of the stones at the Giant's Causeway – on sale at farmers' markets. It's a mild cheese, pale white under its yellow wax overcoat, slightly crumbly in texture, and if you have the patience to mature it, the cheese gets interesting after 15 months. (Loughgiel Millennium Centre, Lough Rd, Loughgiel, Ballymena ☎ 028-2764 1241)

Guesthouse & Restaurant
● **Marlagh Lodge**

Robert and Rachel Thompson made a mighty reputation for their splendid, shy hospitality and, in particular, Mrs Thompson's fantastic cooking, when they ran the Moat Inn, in Donegore. Now transplanted to Ballymena, they are well on their way to being regarded as the most distinguished purveyors of hospitality in Northern Ireland. (Moorfields Rd, Ballymena ☎ 028-9443 3659)

Chutneys & catering
● **Minor Events**

Virginia Maxwell's chutneys are made from fresh vegetables and wild fruits, and they are wildly imaginative creations – carrot and ginger chutney; damson with cardamom chutney;

spicy onion relish. You will find them in local shops such as Osborne's of Ballymoney, Sean Owens' deli in Magherafelt, Jake Patterson's herb farm at Ballyvoy, as well as by mail order. Virginia also operates a catering service, Minor Events. (Ballymena ☎ 028-2766 6394)

Bushmills

Hotel
● The Bushmills Inn

The Bushmills is a well-respected 30-bedroom hotel with lots of open fireplaces burning peat, and striped antique pine throughout. They serve generous comfort food. (9 Dunluce Rd, Bushmills ☎ 028-2073 2339 www.bushmillsinn.com — Open Lunch & Dinner)

Distillery
● The Old Bushmills Distillery

Irish Distillers organise tours of the gorgeous Bushmills Distillery, open from Mon-Fri 10am-midday, Mon-Thurs 2pm-4pm, and no reservations are necessary except for groups. (Bushmills ☎ 028-2073 1521)

Carnlough

Hotel
● Londonderry Arms Hotel

The O'Neill family's pretty, ivy-clad hotel dates back to 1848. It's a lovely place to stay, with tasteful Georgian rooms that are well maintained, and is especially valuable as a stop for afternoon tea – check out that home-baked buttery shortbread! (20 Harbour Rd, Carnlough ☎ 028-2888 5255 — Open Day-time)

Carrickfergus

Gastro Pub
● Joymount Arms

Johnny Ritchie, a talented cook who has made the running

in several addresses, heads up the crew in the Joymount Arms, producing excellent pies, fresh salads, smart platters of ploughman's lunches, and the desserts from Johnny's brother are truly ace. (17 Joymount St, Carrickfergus ☎ 028- 9336 2213 — Open Day-time)

Cushendall

Fishmonger & Shop
● Dalraida VG Store

Harry McAlister follows in the footsteps of his forefathers and continues the 500-year-old family tradition of selling magnificent wild salmon from this wee shop. Visit between May and September to buy the fish during the season, and while you are at it, get hold of some crab and lobster. (Dalraida Ave, Cushendall ☎ 028-2177 1496)

Potatoes
● Glens of Antrim Potatoes

GOA are a family-owned firm of potato packers who work with a group of local growers. Michael McKillop and his family take their role as custodians of the land very seriously indeed, and have recently launched the Glens Organics label of organic potatoes. Look out for the GOA spuds in the major multiples. (118 Middlepark Rd, Cushendall ☎ 028-2177 1396 www.goapotatoes.co.uk)

Dunmurray

Restaurant
● H_2O

Between Tesco and Maxol is where you will find H_2O, and it is also where you will find good cooking. Slow-roasted duck with cherry and red wine compote; seared scallops and Parma ham with lobster jus; Lebanese chicken with farika; smoked haddock with caramelised onion mash and, best of all, a fabulous baked Alaska that beats the band. This is well-considered cooking that marches to its own beat and doesn't waste time or energy following fashion. How did Dunmurray get so lucky? (Kingsway House, Kingsway, Dunmurray ☎ 028-9030 9000 — Open all day)

Glenarm

Farmed Salmon
● Northern Salmon Company

The NSC of Glenarm have cracked how to breed fish of superlative quality, animals whose muscle development is superb, with the result that the flavour of these farmed salmon is excellent. The secret lies in the location which their fish pens enjoy, with strong tidal waters ensuring the fish have to work hard. The fresh and smoked fish are widely available in supermarkets. (Glenarm ☎ 028-2884 1691)

Glengormley

Delicatessen
● Country Harvest Delicatessen

Country Harvest is an enormous deli selling everything from wholefoods, pastas, jams, cheeses, Asian ingredients, and an incredible selection of things bottled in jars, through to a huge range of fruit and vegetables. (The Tramways Centre, Glengormley ☎ 028-9083 9338)

Butcher
● The Quality Food Shop

David Thompson's butcher's shop features all the expert prepared meats and delectable, delicious sausage skills you find in the Elite Association of Butchers shops, and his sirloin beef is hung for at least three weeks. (7 Ballyclare Road, Glengormley ☎ 028-9083 2507)

Lisburn

Market
● Farmers' Market, Lisburn

A small-but-interesting farmer's market takes place in Lisburn each Saturday, just down the hill from the square. It's a chance to get farmhouse cheeses from Trevor Irvine, always in impeccable condition, as well as some other interesting stuff from people like Offbeat Bottling of Bangor, whose jams and chutneys are excellent. Then, up to the square to Javaman for a coffee. (Lisburn Sat am)

Brewery
● Hilden Brewing Company

Seamus Scullion is the great pioneer of craft brewing in
Ireland, and has been patiently brewing his brews since
1981. The company brew three beers: Hilden Ale, a dark
pale ale; a red beer, Molly Malone, and the especially fine,
critics' favourite Great Northern Porter, a cracking porter.
You can enjoy them in the pub just outside Hilden, and in a
few other locals. (Hilden, Lisburn ☎ 028-2884 6663)

Portrush

B&B
● Maddybenny Farmhouse

Rosemary White's legendary farmhouse is a favourite return
destination for many visitors to the north coast. The house
is particularly renowned for monumental breakfasts, where
seemingly every manner of breakfast food is on offer. In
addition to the accommodation in the house, there is also a
series of self-catering cottages, and a busy equestrian centre
in the grounds of the farm. (18 Maddybenny Park, Portrush,
Coleraine ☎ 028-7082 3394
accommodation@maddybenny22.freeserve.co.uk)

Wine Bar & Restaurants
● The Wine Bar, The Harbour Bistro, Coast

George McAlpin's trio of Portrush addresses is a radical
threesome. The Wine Bar – formerly The Ramore – sees
McAlpin doing nothing less than re-inventing the idea of fast
food. This food does come at you fast – you are shown a
seat, order at the bar and pay upfront – but this is not the
fast-food cliché. The burgers are real, the fish dishes are
alluring, and there are good chicken and vegetarian dishes
and fresh salads. Downstairs, in Coast, the same ingredients
get whirled out with pizza and pasta as the staples – cal-
zone with bang-bang chicken; rigatoni with chilli steak and
pepper cream and tobacco onions – whilst in the Harbour
Bar the same ingredients turn up again, this time abetted by
grander cooking such as roasted lamb shank, steamed baby
turbot or Peking panco prawns. If we must have fast food,
then let it be fast food in the Wine Bar-Harbour Bar-Coast
format. (Portrush ☎ 028-7082 4313 — Open Lunch &
Dinner)

County Armagh

Armagh apples, gammon, Armagh potatoes,
wild boar, saddleback bacon, meat pies . . .

Armagh

Butcher
● **A Flanagan & Son**

David Flanagan's shop has been selling meat since 1931, and
in common with most members of the Elite Association of
Butchers, there is an impressive deli side of the operation.
Hunt down their own cured gammons, where the brining
spices are prepared in house, and the meat cured for four
days. Beef is hung for three weeks, and most of it is sourced
from their own farm, from breeds such as Limousin and
Blond Aquitaine. (1 Scotch St, Armagh ☎ 028-3752 2805)

Barnhill

Apple Juice
● **Barnhill Apple Juice**

Look out for the splendid juices of Ken Redmond, of
Barnhill Apple Juice; these are fine brews, some even spiced
with cinnamon and spiked with elderflower or red berried
fruit. (Barnhill ☎ 028-3885 1190)

Craigavon

Charcuterie
● **Moyallon Foods**

It is more than a decade since Jilly Acheson first introduced
wild boar to the family estate in Armagh,
and combined an interest in rare breeds
with exemplary animal welfare. The out-
come of such pioneering work has been
the creation of speciality foods of benchmark quality: wild boar; dry-cured saddleback bacon; Moyallon venison pies; wild boar and apple
sausage; smoked chicken fillet, and the sweetest bit is that
the Moyallon range of meats are cheaper than the foods
sold in the supermarkets. (Crowhill Road, Craigavon ☎ 028-
3834 9100 www.moyallonfoods.com)

Killeavy

Restaurant
● **Annahaia**

That excellent chef, Michael Rath, surfaces in a new destination, and immediately begins to make waves. Annahaia is a
hot ticket, serving a seven-course tasting menu in a beautiful
modern room. The cooking has real class: piccata of veal
with parsley butter; tempura of red mullet with shrimp
cream; sweet spring vegetables; monkfish with coriander
cream, and the balance between the courses is mightily
impressive. Manager Ardal O'Hanlon has enough cool for a
fleet of restaurants, and South Armagh just got put on the
map. (Slieve Gullion Courtyard, Killeavy ☎ 028-3084 8084
— Open Dinner)

Lurgan

Butcher
● **John R. Dowey & Son**

John Dowey's shop is both butcher's shop and delicatessen,
with many of the breaded and prepared products they
make also sold as cooked and ready-to-go foods in the deli
section. Excellent pies and fresh salads, and even organic
fresh eggs, complete the picture of a shop that has all you
need, backed up by informed expertise and knowledge typical of the best craft butchers. (20 High St, Lurgan ☎ 028-
3832 2547 jrdowey@aol.com)

Portadown

Wine Merchant
● **Ell's Fine Wine**

Ell's is a fast-moving wine merchant, with 700 wines for sale,
both in its retail and wholesale operations (the wholesale
side is dealt with as R&R Wines), and their areas of expertise such as Australia and Portugal are unearthing some star
finds. Look out also for fine sauvignons from New Zealand
and good-value wines sourced direct from France.
(42 Dobbin Rd, Portadown ☎ 028-3833 2306
rrwines@hotmail.com)

Butcher
● T. Knox & Sons

Barry Knox prepares his beef the traditional way, boning it by hand in the shop, and it will have been hanging for all of three weeks before it is finally trimmed, sliced and presented for sale. But don't overlook their excellent prepared food, such as the wonderful pies – minced meat, steak, steak & kidney, to name just three – because they even make their own pastry for the pies, a move that is typical of the care shown in this shop. (388 West St, Portadown ☎ 028-3835 3713)

Delicatessen & Patisserie
● Yellow Door Deli & Patisserie

Simon Dougan's cooking and baking is robust and tasty, and he has an instinct for succulence in his food that is truly pleasing. There is no conceit about his work: flavour and savour are the names of the game, and that is what you get. The daytime cooking at the Yellow Door is splendid: imaginative breakfasts such as warm blueberry pancakes with maple syrup or hot bacon and egg ciabatta; delicious lunches such as stuffed pork and green apple chutney sandwich complement smart main dishes such as seafood parcels with white wine and dill sauce. The food-to-go would persuade you to hang up your own apron: superb venison pies; fish parcels, duck confit, rare roast beef; and a fab selection of salads are echoed by choice bottles and their own chutneys and jams. A one-stop shop for food lovers. (74 Woodhouse St, Portadown ☎ 028-3835 3528)

Restaurant
● Yellow Door's Rugger's Bistro

The Diner's Club at the Portadown Rugby Club is local hero Simon Dougan's restaurant outpost, with the sort of yummy cooking that is Dougan's signature: duck confit with Puy lentils and crispy pancetta; rib-eye steak with caramelised onion mash, merlot jus and chanterelles; marinated chilli mushrooms. Simon also makes a big effort for rugger kids, with tempura chicken, and bangers and mash will be Moyallon sausages and real mash – 'proper food for kids'. (Portadown Rugby Club, Bridge St ☎ 028-3839 4860 — Open Dinner Wed-Sat, Lunch Fri-Sun)

County Down

Dundrum Bary oysters, Eriskay, Tamworth & Saddleback
pigs, Irish Moile & Dexter beef, Finnebrogue venison,
Portavogie prawns, champ, dressed crab...

Ardglass

Restaurant
● **Quayside Restaurant**

Joan, Jonathan & Linda Cochrane are fish merchants turned
fish shop owners, and their piscine knowledge shines
through in scrummy dishes such as dressed crab served in
the shell, fabulous fried fish such as cod, whiting, haddock,
plaice and scampi, and really ace hunky chips fried in dripping, and food lovers choose from the specials board. (The
Harbour, Ardglass ☎ 028-4484 1444 — Open Day-time)

Ballynahinch

Shop
● **Brennan's Garage**

People come to Brennan's to buy petrol (it's a garage),
organic foods (good for you), garden gear (it's a garden
shop), the newspaper (it's a newsagent); household stuff (it's
a grocery), booze (it's an off licence). Then, having gotten all
the necessities, they order one of Brennan's milky, caramelly,
sugary vanilla ice creams, and it puts the world to rights.
(149 Newcastle Rd, Seaforde ☎ 028-4481 1274)

Café
● **Ginesi's Café**

Ginesi's famous fish & chip café is always full of food lovers
who pile in here as much for the charm of Gillian and
Romano as for the super fried fish and the good Ulster
fries. (34 Main St, Ballynahinch ☎ 028-9756 2653)

Banbridge

Smokehouse
● **Drumgooland Smokehouse**

Suzanne Smyth's interesting smokery has already assembled
an impressive range of smoked products, from duck to a

very fine water-smoked chicken to salmon and on to smoked garlic and smoked eggs. These are useful and practical foods and, as the perfect complement, daughter Ciara has begun to make a fine range of imaginative dressings. (4 Gargarry Rd, Ballyward, nr Banbridge ☎ 028-4056 0720 www.drumgoolandsmokehouse.co.uk))

Butcher
● M.A Quail

The signs in the window spell out the trusted provenance of the meat Jim Quail sells, even before you step in the door of this lovely shop, with the names of the local farms and farmers who are his sources of meat proudly displayed. It's a typically enlightened and thoughtful gesture from an enlightened and thoughtful shop. Quail's is a place that understands the cultural impact of food just as much as its sociological, environmental and culinary impact, and artfully sourced, prepared and presented meat and other fine foods are just what you find in Quail's. (13-15 Newry St, Banbridge ☎ 028-4066 2604)

Home Bakery
● Windsor Home Bakery

Gordon Scott's excellent home bakery has an aim that is true: "We see our strength as traditional food producers – in many ways, we are the 'old' housewife of 20-30 years ago" explains Mr Scott. What that means is food cooked with good ingredients, from breads and cakes to cooked food-to-go from their hot kitchen, all marked by care and a determination for deliciousness. There is a second shop in Banbridge, at 30 Bridge Street, and other Windsors at 5 High Street, Lurgan, and 5 Smithfield Square, Lisburn. Only terrific. (36-38 Newry St, Banbridge ☎ 028-4062 3666)

Bangor

Delicatessen
● Spice

The range of breads, cheeses and international goods has always given the busy Spice an advantage over any other food destination in supermarket-saturated Bangor. It's an advantage that has been maintained over the last couple of years here, by a helpful and knowledgeable crew who enjoy their work, and there are always excellent things to be discovered. (7 Market St, Bangor ☎ 028-9147 7666)

Restaurant
● Coyle's

Ian Morrow's cooking in the upstairs restaurant of Coyle's pub is a major boost for Bangor, for here is food with style and polish: scallops with parsnip purée and leeks; cod with Portavogie prawn butter and parsley mash; lamb's liver with grilled polenta and date vinaigrette. A great wine list from Febvre, cracking service, great value for money, and a place to watch carefully. (44 High St, Bangor ☎ 028-9129 0362 — Open Lunch (bar food) & Dinner)

Butcher
● David Burns Butchers

Brian and George Burns shop never rests on its capacious laurels. Famed for great sausages, great meats, and great service, this crew is forever trying to get better. Just sample their own cured bacon for a superb example of how this questing for new frontiers keeps David Burns Butchers at the cutting-edge of charcuterie. An essential address, and a trail-blazing team. (112 Abbey St, Bangor ☎ 028-9127 0073)

On top of their game

Fishmonger
● McKeown's Fish Shop

This legendary and lovely old-style fish shop (check out that cool 1960's façade!) is where every smart food lover buys their fish in Bangor. The wet fish is always in pristine quality, and they do some nice smoked salmon come Christmastime. (14 High St, Bangor ☎ 028-9127 1141)

Preserves
● Off Beat Bottling Co

Funky jams and some excellent chutneys are the offbeat production of the Off Beat Co. Check out the banana jam, and the ratatouille chutney in particular for a taste of something quite deliciously different. You will find the Off Beat jars in good shops throughout the country. (51-52 Enterprise House, Balloo Ave, Bangor ☎ 028-9127 1525)

Restaurant
● Shanks

Robbie Millar has been at the cutting-edge for longer than any other contemporary Irish chef and, today, his food has all the fire and panache that first set Shanks apart from the posse. Potato and onion soup with a tortellini of kassler and cabbage is a dazzling start, some seared scallops with cauliflower purée shows Millar keeps re-inventing and reinterpreting his signature dishes, whilst his assiette of duck has such sublime and serene textures that it is a thrill. The dishes offered on his mid-week value menus are just as exciting – crispy pork belly with spiced couscous, tomato jus and mango salsa is a beaut of a dish – and the good value should convert those who think of Shanks as pricey. Benchmark in every detail. (The Blackwood, Crawfordsburn Rd, Bangor ☎ 028-9185 3313 www.shanksrestaurant.com — Open Lunch & Dinner)

On top of their game

Comber

B&B
● Anna's House

Anna Johnson's house is a cult address. The house is gorgeous, the gardens are gorgeous, and Anna's cooking, using her own organic ingredients from the garden, is as good as domestic cooking gets. Ken's breads complete a little picture of perfection. (Tullynagee, 35 Lisbarnett Rd, Comber ☎ 028-9754 1566 www.annashouse.com)

Rare Breed Farm Shop
● Pheasant's Hill Farm Shop

Janis and Ian Bailey's rare breed shop is a peach, a place to find rare breed pork from rare animals such as Eriskay, Tamworth, Saddleback and Berkshire. Beef might be Belted Galloway, Irish Moile or Dexter, and there is excellent lamb. Free-range chickens, great ducks, Finnebrogue venison, Drumgooland smoked foods and Irish cheeses complete the picture of a truly radical shop with a fabulous, singular aesthetic. Brilliant. (3 Bridge St Link, Comber 028 9187 8470 – Open Day-time)

Crossgar

Wine Merchant
● James Nicholson Wine Merchant

For every wine merchant in Ireland, achievement is measured by the benchmarks set by Jim Nicholson and his team at their elegant shop in Crossgar. Standards of sourcing of wines and of service to the customer are established here, and are then repeatedly bettered by a crack team who never stay still. Whether you are buying a case of summer quaffers, or spending a wagonload of money on en primeur selections, Nicholson's will see you right every step of the way. The high standards enjoyed throughout wine shops in Ireland can be traced back to the example set by this genial man for 25 years. (Killyleagh St, Crossgar ☎ 028-4483 0091 www.jnwine.com)

On top of their game

Donaghadee

Restaurant
● Pier 36

Margaret and Denis Waterworth are enthusiastic about their food, and their bonhomie and youthfulness make 36 a great place. They barbecue salmon on mesquite; layer pancetta between French toast; make a cassoulet with fine Moyallon wild boar; bake good Mom'n'Pop desserts along with excellent breads from the Rayburn. Simple, charming. (36 The Parade, Donaghadee ☎ 028-9188 4466 www.pier36.co.uk — Open Lunch & Dinner)

Downpatrick

Venison
● Finnebrogue Venison

Denis Lynn farms only red deer on the 600 acres of Finnebrogue, and slaughters before the animals are 18 months in order to obtain a milder, more tender meat: this is not the wild, chewy, gamey venison we associate with long-simmered stews, but a lighter, more consistent style of game which is raised as naturally as possible. Finnebrogue have created a range of venison sausages in collaboration with Andy Rea of Rain City, and new packaging for their retail line will see this assured and ambitious endeavour winding up on more and more dinner plates. This is a dynamic enterprise that bodes well for farming and also our own health. (Finnebrogue Estate, Downpatrick ☎ 028-4461 7525 www.finnebrogue.com)

General Store
● Hanlon's

Hanlon's old-style general store has a little bit of everything – a fish counter with fresh fish; local vegetables; Irish cheeses; groceries; wholefoods and some good quality baking ingredients – and the nifty male staff dressed in their blue overalls and grocers' hats are just the ticket. (26 Market St, Downpatrick ☎ 028-4461 2518)

B&B
● Pheasant's Hill

Janis and Ian Bailey have opened a farm shop to sell their exemplary rare breeds meat and organic vegetables in Comber, but Pheasant's Hill remains their base, home to a superb small-holding and also a fine B&B which, thanks to those molly-coddled pigs, serves one of the best breakfasts known to man. (37 Killyleagh Rd, Downpatrick ☎ 028-4461 7246 www.pheasantshill@dnet.co.uk)

Dundrum

Restaurant
● The Buck's Head

Alison and Michael Crother's brilliant restaurant is a true Northern Irish address. Whether you come here for a cracking Sunday lunch, or for a high tea, or for a celebratory dinner, the style and manner of how they work is quite unique. It's an open, friendly, feminine style, from cosy cooking through cosy comfortable rooms in which to enjoy lovely food: tempura oysters with chilli, sesame and soy; lemon chicken with tagliatelle with fennel purée; honey roast gammon with parsley sauce and champ, and the desserts are ace. (77 Main St, Dundrum ☎ 028-4375 1868 — Open Lunch & Dinner)

B&B
● Carriage House

Maureen Griffith's lovely house is right next door to the
Buck's Head, and indeed before opening here Maureen ran
the bar. Her instinct for hospitality and her eye for design
have created a smashing house, and it's a superb base for
getting the best out of the Mourne Mountains and the many
attractions in this gorgeous part of the country. (71 Main St,
Dundrum ☎ 028-4375 1635
www.carriagehousedundrum.com)

Oyster Fishery
● Dundrum Bay Oyster Fishery

Members of the public can buy oysters and mussels from
the fishery and, on occasion, clams are also for sale;
spaghetti alle vongole here we come! (5 The Quay,
Dundrum ☎ 028-4375 1810 — Open 8am-4.30pm Mon-Fri)

Gilford

Restaurant
● Mill Street Restaurant & Bar

Mill Street is extra-whacky, the sort of theatrically
overblown interior that wouldn't be out of place in SoHo
or Sydney. But, here it is in Gilford, a little hamlet that is
increasingly becoming the centre of the universe. Sea bass
with green beans and vanilla, garlic and white wine cream;
venison with blueberries, shallots and red wine jus; tempura
of oysters with fresh tomato juice; mussels with cayenne
and coconut jus are the sort of modern-Aussie cooking
that they pull off with gas in the tank, though desserts have
yet to be sorted. Mega-bling fun. (14 Mill St, Gilford ☎ 028-
3883 1166 — Open all day)

Restaurant
● The Oriel

When Barry Smith and his crew in The Oriel achieved stellar status from well-known guide books in
2004, the fascinating thing was not the volume of congratulations their achievement
garnered. Instead, it was the volume of
carping that Mr Smith received. Here was a

On top of their game

chef, allegedly unknown, who had suddenly exploded onto the scene with a wallop. As so often, the criticism was mean, and lazy, and ill-informed. If the critics had listened to local gossip, or even read those books – like the Bridgestones – that have covered Mr Smith's ascent since he took over in Gilford, they would have known that expectations for this team were high, and getting higher. Like well-trained athletes, Mr Smith and his team were steadily raising their game. No sudden arrivals. No explosions. Just hard graft, and focus.

Indeed, Mr Smith has such a fine crew nowadays that he spends much of his time at front of house, able to confidently leave the cooking to a crack young team. The food in the Oriel is a sublime meditation of the art of cooking. Even better, it remains hungry with determination. (2 Bridge St, Gilford, nr Banbridge ☎ 028-3883 1543 — Open Lunch & Dinner)

Groomsport

Wine Merchant
● Classic Wine

Robert Neill's excellent wine shop is as welcoming to visit as the owner is knowledgeable, a twin peaks offering that we like to see in the wine world. The range is only excellent, and look out in particular for the Vinus and the Step Road range. (49 Main St, Groomsport ☎ 028-9147 8982)

Helen's Bay

Organic Vegetables and Box Delivery
● Helen's Bay Organic Farm

Organic grower John McCormick is one of the great potato experts in Ireland, and a conscientious and principled grower who has used his box-delivery system to introduce countless people to the brilliant, distinct quality of his work. Benchmark spuds are simply one thing he does superbly, for all the produce coming out of Helen's Bay is brilliant. Sign up for that delivery today. (Coastguard Ave, Helen's Bay ☎ 028-9185 3122)

Hillsborough

Bistro
● The Plough Bistro

The Plough is a very successful enterprise where Derek
Patterson oversees a sharp team who ferry out good cook-
ing to local punters and visitors to pretty Hillsborough. The
same company also operates Barretro and The Pheasant, at
Annahilt. (The Square, Hillsborough ☎ 028-9268 2985 —
Open Lunch & Dinner)

Hilltown

Chipper
● The Hilltown Chippy

Paul Smith fries the best chips we've ever eaten. He uses
Cyprus spuds, he uses beef dripping, he uses 24 years' experience at the fryer, and with these he makes magic: big,
square, deep golden brown, crispy, dry, chips, with a great
taste of potato, and absolutely no greasiness. The fish is
good, with a crisp and crunchy batter, but those chips: wow!
Hilltown is the chip capital of the western world. (Take out
only.) (Main St, Hilltown ☎ 028-4063 8130)

Holywood

Café
● The Bay Tree

Thanks to Sue Farmer's superb cooking, The Bay Tree is a
destination address for food lovers, despite its simplicity
and modest size. The daytime food is as good as it gets: dill,
egg and tuna mousse with toasted brown bread; melted
goat's cheese salad with Puy lentils and warm toasted walnuts; excellent cheese and spinach flan, and desserts are fantastic. Then Friday night brings out the exactitude of good
cordon bleu cooking: beef olives with roasted root vegetables; cod with capers and sherry vinegar; confit of duck with
lentils and orange and onion chutney. Smashing. (118 High
St, Holywood ☎ 028-9042 1419 — Open Day-time and Fri
Dinner)

Café
● Cafe Kino

This modern café on the main strip of Holywood does some interesting and well-conceived food. (81 High St, Holywood ☎ 028-9042 5216)

Farm Shop & Bakery
● Camphill Organic Farm Shop & Bakery

Rob van Duin's excellent breads are just one reason to visit the superb Camphill shop and café, where you will also find pristine local organic vegetables, and rarities such as bio-dynamic cheeses from Donegal and very fine organic eggs. (Shore Rd, Holywood ☎ 028-9042 3203)

Kitchen Shop
● La Cucina

This nifty kitchenware shop has a sister branch at the Fairhill Shopping Centre in Ballymena (Unit 15, ☎ 028-2565 8800). Both are havens for food lovers who want the best brands of cooking equipment, so head here for all the Global knives, Bodum whatsits and sugarcraft esoterica. (63 High St, Holywood ☎ 028-9042 2118)

Restaurant
● Fontana

Colleen Bennett's upstairs restaurant has been newly made over, proving once again that this chef is as sharp an interior designer as she is a cook. With a partner restaurant in East Belfast – Bennett's on Belmont – focusing more on informal food, it has allowed the Fontana crew to get real funky with the Mediterranean comfort food that is their foundation, through some lovely improvisations with Pacific Rim ideas and combinations that show the kitchen at its food-fixated best. (61a High St, Holywood ☎ 028-9080 9908 — Open Lunch & Dinner)

Restaurant
● Sullivan's

Simon Shaw runs a reliable and extremely popular neigh-bourhood restaurant, where the modesty of the décor, the staff and the cooking is just right. (Tasty food, and very keen prices are the signature. (2 Sullivan Pl, Holywood 028-9042 1000 — Open Lunch & Dinner)

Butcher
● Orr's Butchers

This is a great store in which to find choice Northern Ireland foods such as Sprott's bacon, along with a host of other good foods, and some excellent meat and choice comestibles. (56 High St, Holywood ☎ 028-9042 2288)

Kilkeel

Brewery
● The Whitewater Brewing Co

Whitewater is the largest micro-brewery in Northern Ireland, producing 12 different cask-conditioned ales and a lager, Blonde. Kerry and Bernard Sloan's brewery has a 15 barrel brew length, and fermenting capacity of 2000 gallons per week. Peter McCullough is the brewer, and you should look for the Whitewater brews in good pubs throughout the country, including the Crown and the Botanic in Belfast and the Hillside in Hillsborough. (40 Tullyframe Rd, Kilkee ☎ 028-4176 9449)

Kircubbin

Restaurant & Bar
● Finnegans Restaurant & Bars

Don't judge a restaurant by its appearance, especially Finnegan's. If you do, you won't walk in here, and even if you walk in you might walk straight out again. But, stay awhile, and enjoy some spirited cooking. Go for the local specialities: crab salad; Portavogie prawns with lemon butter; duckling with sage and thyme, and then some gooey apple pie. Now, doesn't Finnegan's look a million dollars?
(Main Street, Kircubbin ☎ 028-4273 8282 — Open Lunch & Dinner)

Restaurant
● Restaurant Paul Arthurs

RPA is one of County Down's showcase restaurants. Paul Arthurs has a background in the meat business, and as a cook has a particular affinity with fish, so he has most everything covered. Superb raw ingredients get a rich but simple treatment: rib-eye with café de Paris butter; summer vegetable risotto; potato gnocchi with saffron cream and tomato, and desserts are superb. There is also a chipper downstairs, which is excellent, but the real glories are upstairs in this colourful, zesty restaurant. (66 Main St, Kircubbin, ☎ 028-4273 8192 — Open Lunch & Dinner)

Millisle

Pottery
● **Eden Pottery Centre**

Eden is a little-known pottery, with a shop housed in a for-mer school, just up the hill from the centre of Millisle. Why their work isn't known nationally is a mystery to us, for their spongeware has a tactile delicacy, and a gorgeous use of colour, that we think is only brilliant. What's more, the prices are very keen indeed, so the Eden work isn't merely covetable and collectable, it's mercifully affordable. (218 Abbey Road, Millisle ☎ 028-9186 2300 eden.pottery@virgin.net)

Moira

Butcher
● **McCartney's of Moira**

What you find in George McCartney's pristine shop, in the centre of pretty Moira, is a butcher's shop right on top of the game: meat sourced and presented with the finest artisan skills; the highest grades of beef animals from the Clogher Valley, all grass fed; the highest confirmation lambs from Foyle Meats. Onto this template, McCartney's brings a level of skill and creativity which is daunting to behold and delicious to enjoy; more than 30 varieties of sausage, all superb, and all hand-linked in the traditional way; a fantastic array of prepared meats; beautiful pies, lasagne made with the finest beef and freshly made pasta made in the kitchen, all of these served with wit and charm by the team of 14 butchers. Outstanding. (56-58 Main Street, Moira ☎ 028-9261 1422 — Closed Monday)

On top of their game

Newcastle

Restaurant
● Zest

Zest's cooking comes out of an Ulster-Scots tradition of cookery that has been all-but-neglected in Northern Ireland. The young team here cook Cullen Skink, that masterly Scots soup of finnan haddie, onions and potatoes, and their rosemary-and-oat-crusted supreme of chicken is a spot-on tribute to Scottish cooking techniques, as is a Cranachan parfait that modernises a lovely traditional idea. Hugely promising, and affordable as you can bring your own wine. Zest also operates as a standard daytime café. (22-24 Main St, Newcastle ☎ 028 4372 5757
— Open Day-time)

Newry

Italian Restaurant
● I Sapori

Sean McMahon's restaurant is as authentic as Italian food gets in the North. Start with some good pasta, then move on to something as simple as grilled lamb with garlic, parsley and lemon juice, or sea bass with crisp, thin potato slices, and you will swear you are somewhere north of Naples and south of Rome. Great service, good value. (16/17 The Mall, Newry ☎ 028-3025 2086
— Open Dinner)

Newtownards

Guesthouse
● Beech Hill

Victoria Brann's elegant house is just off the quiet Ballymoney Road, and very handsome, whilst the interior is crisp and cosy. Ms Brann is a professional to her fingertips, which means everything is done with exactitude and style. The presence of Shanks and Fontana and other good restaurants nearby means one doesn't have to travel far to eat superbly. (23 Ballymoney Rd, Craigantlet ☎ 028-9042 5892, beech.hill@btinternet.com)

Vegetable Shop
● Homegrown

Homegrown is a benchmark vegetable shop where you will find the best local vegetables sold at their very peak of perfection. This shop is a beacon of what can be, could be and should be: local foods in a local shop for local folk. Margaret Whyte has won the respect of her devoted customers by sticking to what she knows, and by being selective and astute. It is a treat to shop in Homegrown. (66b East St, Newtownards ☎ 028-9181 8318)

Coffee & cakes
● Knotts Cake & Coffee Shop

This self-service café and bakery is hugely popular with the decent folk of 'Ards, who love the cakes, the sweet squares and the fresh cream buns. But there is savoury cooking also – beef olives; stuffed pork; pastry pies served with turnips and champ. Sandwiches are soft and squidgy, packed with cress, and great old stagers such as coronation chicken sandwich get a respectable outing. (45 High St, Newtownards ☎ 028-9181 9098 — Open Day-time)

Farm Shop
● McKees Produce

In McKee's, you can buy local meat, sauces, fresh bread, cakes, meringues, home-made preserves, free-range eggs and chickens, all in the knowledge that everything is local – 99% of what they sell here is sourced in Northern Ireland. This is the food that Colin and Linda McKee feed their family, and we can feed ours, with confidence. It makes so much sense: why is it so rare? (28 Holywood Rd, Newtownards ☎ 028-9181 3202. www.mckeesproduce.co.uk)

Kitchenware
● Presence Tableware and Cookware

Presence is one of the best kitchenware shops in the country, and a present from Presence is just what food lovers dream about, for all the icon brands are here: Staub, Gaggia, Dualit, Wusthof Trident, Bodum, Legonart, Rosenthal, Alessi. They also sell very glam glass and tableware from many leading brands, so your new Baulthaup or Johnny Grey kitchen can be kitted out in just one visit to Presence. (37 High St, Newtownards ☎ 028-9182 0222)

Portaferry

Hotel
● **Portaferry Hotel**

John Herlihy's Portaferry Hotel has always offered seafood that is served just as simply as food lovers crave – Portavogie Prawn Tails in Garlic Butter; Pan-fried Scallops with Bacon and Garlic; Dundrum Bay Oysters with Shallot and Balsamic Vinegar Dressing; fresh lobster with salad and lashings of mayo – and good meat and sweet cooking joins the fish dishes, in an institution that has endured for more than three decades. (The Strand, Portaferry ☎ 028-4272 8231 www.portaferryhotel.com — Open Lunch & Dinner)

Restaurant
● **Quarterdeck Restaurant @ Fiddler's Green**

The Quarter Deck restaurant is operated by the three McCarthy sons, and the cooking is cautiously creative: rib-eye of beef with silky champ and roasted garlic gravy; slow-roasted shoulder of lamb with new potatoes and apple and rosemary chutney; hip dishes such as Peking duck with noodles and hot chilli tomato sauce, or Thai tiger prawn curry with bak choi and jasmine rice. Don't miss the homemade, comfort desserts such as apple and rhubarb crumble. (The Square, Portaferry ☎ 028-4272 8393 — Open Lunch & Dinner)

Warrenpoint

Restaurant
● **The Duke Restaurant**

Ciaran Gallagher is a chef who seemingly manages to please almost everyone, from fuel merchants who want surf 'n' turf or chicken Maryland, to food lovers who head upstairs for grilled turbot with wilted bak choi and prawn bisque cream or grilled tuna loin with mango and spiced guacamole, or fine bourgeois blowouts such as lobster in brandy and cream. Ambition is matched by a level of culinary execution that evades many young chefs. At midweek, the value for money is fantastic. (7 Duke St, Warrenpoint ☎ 028-4175 2084, www.thedukerestaurant.com — Open Dinner)

County Fermanagh

black bacon, farls, millionaire's shortbread,
the Ulster Fry, wheaten sodas, smoked lamb...

Enniskillen

Home Bakery
● Leslie's Bakery

Leslie's is yet another of the proud artisan bakeries that
happily survive so splendidly and successfully in Northern
Ireland, producing superb quality, distinctive, regional breads
for happy customers. Get your farls and fadge and millionaire's shortbread here. (10 Church St, Enniskillen
☎ 028-6632 4902)

Butchers
● O'Doherty's

Pat O'Doherty's shop is one of those addresses that, no
matter how much of a detour and no mat-
ter how much extra time it involves to
get into the centre of Enniskillen, you
will always find yourself making the
effort in order to get your hands on the
superb Black bacon, sausages and burgers
that this most singularly creative artisan creates. In fact, we
not only make the detour: when we get here we also order
some of the splendid meat pies they make, ask for them to
be heated up, and have an O'Doherty's picnic in the car
with the kids as we tootle along to wherever it is we
should have been several hours ago.
Mr O'Doherty is best-known for two particular products –
his homemade burgers and his celebrated black bacon – but
the truth is that it is invidious to single out these two products, superlative as they are, for everything that is made by
this team, with the quiet, diffident Mr O'Doherty guiding
them along, is as good as it gets. The sausages seem to be
able to spring endless changes in flavours, offering new lines
every time you turn up. The meat is of ace quality, just as
one would expect, whilst the specialist items, such as the
smoked lamb, show a butcher who revels in the challenges
of interpreting and creating exciting new charcuterie
flavours, textures and tastes. However far it is to travel, a
trip to O'Doherty's repays tenfold. (Belmore St, Enniskillen
☎ 028-6632 2152 www.blackbacon.com
pat@blackbacon.com)

Restaurant
● Restaurant No 6 & Café Merlot

All manner of changes have been taking place in Enniskillen, as Gerry Russell has moved from The Gallery to Restaurant No 6, situated upstairs above Enniskillen's oldest pub, Blakes of the Hollow, and where a strong food and wine offer has been assembled, and where Mr Russell's signature fusion cooking can be seen in its potent form. Smoked duck is served with bean sprouts, coriander, chilli and mint, a perfect risotto is powerfully flavoured with chorizo, whilst king prawns in ketaifi pastry – which could stand on their own right – are used to add more oomph! to a lovely dish of roast turbot. The sister Café Merlot has lighter fare, but it is no less ambitious – Asian pork with spring greens, egg noodles, lemon and soy; penne with Cashel Blue cheese and avocado salsa. Smart rooms, good prices, and one to watch carefully. (Blakes of the Hollow, 6 Church St, Enniskillen ☎ 028-66320918)

Lisbellaw

Cookery School
● Belle Isle Cookery School

Liz Moore has the energy and drive to make a success of the ambitious cookery school, just one element of the beautiful Belle Isle estate, a singularly gorgeous destination with fantastic self-catering accommodation. Liz has created an impressively large series of courses, ranging from one-day courses on vegetable cookery to special coeliac classes, and there are family cooking days, outdoor entertaining for men, Christmas cookery, and lots and lots of courses that ring all the changes of the seasons in order to focus on seasonal foods and seasonal dishes.

In addition to the school, Belle Isle offers self-catering accommodation in the luxurious courtyard apartments and in cottages, and groups can also rent the castle for family parties and get-togethers. This is an ambitious, top-of-the-market project, and one looks forward to seeing how it will develop in the coming years. (Lisbellaw ☎ 028-6638 7231 www.irishcookeryschool.com, www.belleislecastle.com)

County
Londonderry

Oatcakes, sausages, fondant fancies, batch bread,
gammon, scotch eggs, meat pies...

Aghadowey

Organic Farm
● Culdrum Organic Farm

Brian Wallace's organic farm offers splendid organic produce, everything from fruit and vegetables to saddleback
pork and real chickens who lay real eggs produced to
IOFGA standards. Click onto www.culdrum.co.uk and you
will discover all about the splendid foods grown and produced in Culdrum, and also how to get your hands on
them. (31 Ballylintagh Rd, Aghadowey, Coleraine
☎ 028-7086 8991 www.culdrum.co.uk)

Castledawson

Home Bakery
● Ditty's Home Bakery

Robert Ditty's brilliance lies in his ability to meld the experience of a traditional craft bakery, with
more than thirty years' experience, and
to mix this with a restless ability to
craft superb new products to keep the
animus of Ditty's driving ever forward.

On top of their game

This animus has led him to found the Artisan
Bakers of Northern Ireland, a new guild which is doing for
bakers what the Elite Guild has been doing for the butchers
of Northern Ireland. Members meet to share knowledge,
swap ideas, and collaborate in sourcing and supplying ingredients.

In truth, however, Robert Ditty leads by example: his
breads, cakes and biscuits are superb, his shops are superb,
and everything works because this most cerebral man
understands the cultural impact of what he is doing, of what
he is creating, and preserving. These artisan bakeries are life-
affirming, for they bring life and soul to communities. (44
Main St, Castledawson ☎ 028-7946 8243;
dittybky@aol.com)

10 CULINARY
RADICALS

1

MYRTLE ALLEN
— enobling Irish cooking

2

ROD ALSTON
— articulating organics

3

JOSEF FINKE
— conceptualising organic branding

4

SIMON PRATT
— quality in numbers

5

PAUL RANKIN
— radical restaurateur and educator

6

SHERIDAN'S CHEESEMONGERS
— revolutionising cheesemongering

7

TOBY SIMMONDS
— fighting for market rights

8

VERONICA STEELE
— the first artisan Irish cheesemaker

9

DR PATRICK WALL
— sanity in bureaucracy

10

PETER WARD
— country store gourmet

Claudy

Butcher
● O'Kane Meats

It says all you need to know about Michael and Kieran
O'Kane that, in the last four years, they have
won the prize for best sausage making in
Northern Ireland on three occasions. The
fierce level of competition for this prize
means that the winner is always richly

On top of their game

deserving, but three out of four is some sort of
amazing result. But an amazing result is what you always get
in O'Kane's, whether you are buying a pound of sausages,
some of their excellent cooked food, or a rack of lamb, for
the quality of everything is superlative. (69 Main St, Claudy
☎ 028-7133 8944 www.okanemeats.com)

Coleraine

Restaurant
● The Water Margin

Tony Cheuk's popular Water Margin has a second, bustling
outpost in Belfast, on Donegall Pass, but the original
remains a firm favourite in the North West, a great big busy
room at the boathouse, looking over the water. Part of the
fun is the sheer scale and hustle and bustle of the room, but
the cooking is also spot on, and whilst the menu offers all
the standard Saturday night-specials for conservative tastes,
the secret is to tell them you want the real thing, and then
they will do it for you. (The Boathouse, Hanover Pl,
Coleraine ☎ 028-7034 2222 — Open Lunch & Dinner)

Derry

Restaurant
● Brown's

A stylishly-designed brasserie, housed in a pretty terrace on
the edge of the city, Brown's is a rock-solid professional
restaurant that looks after the local business crowd by day
and the local community by night. Ivan Brown's cooking has

great character: fennel and lime marinated sea bass with chilli chick peas and baby plum tomatoes; crisp roast duckling with stuffed cabbage and crushed grape juice; char-grilled fillet of rare breed beef with kohlrabi puree; lasagne of smoked haddock with a garden pea and vermouth cream. At lunchtime things are simpler, to be as swift as possible for folk who want a quick bite. The mix of style, affability and good food in Brown's is more than all right. (1 Bonds Hill, Derry ☎ 028-7134 5180 — Open lunch & dinner)

Self-Service Restaurant and Bakery
● The Leprechaun

This excellent bakery has a modern, understated self-service restaurant that the locals flock to for lasagne and chips, sausage roll and salad, and good cups of tea. They also sell a range of delicatessen products, displayed on huge wooden tables. (23 Strand Rd, Derry ☎ 028-7136 3606 — Open daytime)

Limavady

Artisan bakery
● Hunter's Bakery

Shaun Hunter's excellent bakery is a member of the dynamic Artisan Bakers Guild of Northern Ireland, so you can expect the same cutting-edge creativity allied to a rich historical appreciation of baking that characterises the Guild members. (5-9 Market St, Limavady ☎ 028-7772 2411)

Delicatessen
● Norman Hunter & Son

Ian Hunter's shop wins awards for its produce and for its style and service on a seemingly never-ending basis. Year after year, it tends to be a competition as to who will come second to this gifted bio-chemist and butcher, who has brought new glories to a family firm that can trace its history back 160 years. All the meat is aged on the bone, whilst the complementary deli and vegetable sections are just as ace as the butchery division. (53-55 Main St, Limavady ☎ 028-7776 2665)

On top of their game

Organic Fowl
● Keady Mountain Farm

The Mullen brothers, Michael & PJ, bring their superb organic produce to the Friday Farmers' Market in Belfast, but you can also order Christmas turkeys and other organic specialities such as chicken, ducks, geese and eggs from the farm. (Limavady ☎ 028-7776 4157)

Restaurant
● The Lime Tree

Everyone loves The Lime Tree because Stanley and Maria Matthews look after everyone and make sure that they get just what they want. You can tell how smart Stanley is by the fact that he sources his meat from Ian Hunter's butcher's shop in the town, so Sperrin lamb with Moroccan spiced sauce, or that Saturday night special of sirloin steak with peppercorn sauce will be exactly that: special. The family-run style of the Lime Tree is charming and Maria's service – with Stanley's assistance – makes for a destination one is always glad to return to. (60 Catherine St, Limavady ☎ 028-7776 4300 www.limetreerest.com — Open Lunch & Dinner)

Fish and Chips
● McNulty's Fish and Chips

Brian McNulty's acclaimed chip shop has been frying since 1945, using fish from Atlantic waters and potatoes imported from the Fens area of England, all cooked carefully in vegetable oil. Lots of fresh ingredients means you get fish and chips the way they should be. (84 Main St, Limavady ☎ 028-7776 2148 — Open Day-time, Lunch & Dinner)

Maghera

Butchers
● McKee's Butchers

In recent years McKee's has built a mighty reputation for their meat pies, for the simple reason that they use meat from their own animals, make their own pastry in their own factory, and so you get the ideal set up for creating superb flavour and texture. Fattening a lot of their own charolais and limousin cattle as well as buying from local farmers, and then hanging the beef for three weeks also leads to superb meat, and at Christmas time McKee's will even hang the beef for as long as a month. Oh, and don't miss the scotch eggs. (26 and 78 Main St, Maghera ☎ 028-7964 2559)

Magherafelt

Artisan bakery
● **Ditty's**

Robert Ditty's bakery and café in Magherafelt is just as busy and just as benchmark as their Castledawson address. Unmissable. (33 Rainey St, Magherafelt ☎ 028-7963 3944 dittybky@aol.com)

Restaurant
● **Gardiners Restaurant**

Sean Owens is one of the most media-visible chefs and pro-prietors in the country, and his high profile has succeeded in putting Gardiners out-of-the-way location onto the map for out-of-towners. The restaurant is in a converted rugby club that has been extensively made-over, and the menu is packed with mid-Ulster variants of global standards – hummus, Caesar salad, Thai dishes, spag bol, and so on. But the hummus is fresh, satisfying and well made, the spag bol has good al dente pasta and a rich meat sauce, and a creamy casserole of pork with potato rösti has tender meat and golden baby mushrooms infused with rosemary. Desserts such as Bailey's ice terrine and stuffed baked apple are very well executed. (7 Garden St, Magherafelt ☎ 028-7930 0333 — Open Dinner)

Pork Charcuterie
● **Moss Brook Farm**

Trevor and Irene Barclay have become some of the best known artisans, selling their superlative pork products to a devoted audience at the St George's farmers' market in Belfast. Food lovers who would like to get their hands on some of the best sausages, bacon, gammons and hams you can eat can buy direct from the farm, and it is well worth the trip to buy this accomplished and very dis-tinctive charcuterie. (6 Durnascallon Lane, Magherafelt ☎ 028-7963 3454)

Supermarket
● JC Stewart

This brilliant supermarket is the Harvey Nichol's of mid-Ulster, a shop which is both superbly designed and which is packed with superb produce. In fact, it is unfair to call it a supermarket, for unlike the big, boring chains, it is individual, idiosyncratic and interesting, and there is a true sense of the culture of food to be seen and enjoyed here. Worth the detour. (1 Union Rd, Magherafelt ☎ 028-7930 2930)

Portstewart

Butcher
● JE Toms & Sons

Fine pies are the trademark of Alan Tom's choice butcher's shop on the seafront at Portstewart. The shop has a particular reputation for barbecue-prepared meats, but there is skill aplenty here in every division, not least – as you would expect – with superlative sausage making. Service is brisk and polite, and don't leave without some steak & kidney pies: these are fab. (46 The Promenade, Portstewart ☎ 028-7083 2869)

Cult Choice Artisan Bakers

Northern Ireland's artisan bakers are home bakers, people continuing the tradition whereby an accomplished baker would convert the front room of her house into a shop, and sell her breads and cakes. production was hand-made, local, regional, and individual. That tradition has died out almost everywhere in these islands, but not in Northern Ireland. The tradition survives, and is growing stronger, getting better.

And these proud, accomplished bakers know they are onto a good thing, so they have created the Artisan Bakers of Northern Ireland, to work together, to share knowledge and expertise. Look for the logo, as you buy your millionaire's shortbread, your fondant fancy and your batch loaf.

County Tyrone

Ayrshire milk, bramley apple juice, porridge with Black Bush, fadge, Sperrin lamb, Sperrin Sheep's Milk...

Castlederg

Dairy
● Erganagh Dairy

The Erganagh dairy milks its own herd of Ayrshire cows and this milk is worth hunting down in good shops, for its clean, elegant flavour is very pleasing, and the butter, buttermilk and yogurt the dairy also produce are extremely interesting. They also bottle sheep's and goat's milk from neighbouring farms. (29 Erganagh Rd, Castlederg ☎ 028-8167 0626)

Cookstown

Restaurant
● Otter Lodge

Otter Lodge has a pleasant interior which impresses with its clean and simple attitude. A blackboard announces the menu of the day: breaded king prawns, cheesy garlic bread, deep-fried brie with a mango dressing, classic prawn cocktail, along with staples such as lasagne, and it's nicely achieved home cooking, at keen prices. (26 Dungannon Rd, Cookstown ☎ 028-8676 5427)

Sheep's Milk & Ice Cream
● Sperrin Valley Sheep Products

Sidney Creighton milks a flock of 150 sheep and his Sperrin Valley company produces pasteurised sheep's milk, and the fine Sperrin Valley Ice Cream, a pale ice cream which has a very nice consistency, and a distinct but fairly mild taste: this is an ice cream for everyone to enjoy. You can find it for sale in good specialist stores throughout the country. (20 Drummond Rd, Cookstown ☎ 028-8676 6366)

Dungannon

Apple Juice
● Cumwins Apple Juice

This excellent apple juice can be found in and around Dungannon – it's served for breakfast at Nora Brown's

Grange Lodge, for example – and the farm also sells bramley apples and eating apples as well as cultivated blackberries. (Cornamuckla House, 60 Bush Rd ☎ 028-8772 4637)

Potatoes
● Dungannon Farmers' Market

The Dungannon farmers' market is held on the first Saturday of each month in the car park of Tescos, and before you start thinking what a philanthropist the supermarket chain is, bear in mind that research in the U.K. has shown that farmer's markets benefit every business in the towns where they are held. So Tesco aren't being kind, they are simply being clever. In the market, look out for Breda Treanor's home-grown vegetables, Joan Bird's tray bakes, Linda Haycock's eggs that are as fresh as daisies, with great golden yolks, Lorna Robinson of Cloughbane Farm whose beef is matured for 28 days and comes from Angus-Limousin crosses. You will also see Ken Redmond's fruit juices; organic produce from the splendid Culdrum Farm; fresh mushrooms from Declan McKeever; good spuds from Ian Brownlee and lots more. (Meadow Centre, Tandragee Rd, Portadown, first Saturday am)

B&B
● Grange Lodge

Grange is a pretty Georgian house set in mature gardens, whilst the interior is country-cottagey and intensely detailed, with animal ornaments, pot pourri, tapestry cushions, satin-edged towels and antique furniture, all the result of dedicated collecting, by Ralph and Nora Brown. Dinner is served dinner-party style, with only one choice available, and is modest country cooking, whilst breakfast features the ritual of the Black Bush porridge: overnight-cooked porridge oats are anointed at the table by Ralph Brown who pours cream, crunchy cane sugar and a drizzle of Black Bush onto the steaming bowlful, and that is before a fine breakfast with Nora's potato bread, excellent bacon and eggs, Cumwin's apple juice and lashings of hot tea. (Grange Rd, Dungannon ☎ 028-8778 4212 grangelodge@nireland.com)

Bar & Restaurant
● The Indigo Bar & Restaurant

The Indigo's best-selling dish is tempura chicken with sweet chilli, aioli, and fries, which gives a precise indication of the sort of multi-cultural magpie cooking on offer in Dungannon's most popular restaurant. Main course portions are big, big: homemade desserts such as warm apple strudel, are well-delivered. (10 Gortmerron Link Rd, Dungannon ☎ 028-8772 7121 — Open Lunch & Dinner)

Country House
● Stangmore Country House

Ann and Andy Brace's comfortable country house is a member of the Tyrone Good Food Circle, and admirably uses many local foods, sourced from the farmers' market and from local farm shops, on the menus. So, you can enjoy Cloughbane Farm lamb with sweet and sour aubergine, or Sperrin Valley ice cream with home-made shortbread. The rooms are cosy, and service is chatty and genuinely warm, which explains why the house is so popular with locals. (65 Moy Rd, Dungannon ☎ 028-8772 5600 www.stangmorecountryhouse.com)

Potatoes
● Wattle Tree Wines

Martin Forker's company imports a range of Australian wines from boutique wineries, with five wineries in Victoria and Western Australian supplying a range of more than 20 wines. There are some real crackers: the Montara New Wave Riesling is a beauty, its punky character covered with finesse; the Gloucester Ridge sauvignon blanc; the Eastern Peake chardonnay reserve. His trump card, however, comes in the shape of two incredible stickies, as the Aussies call their sweet wines: the RL Buller Fine Old Muscat and the RL Buller Fine Old Tokay are awesome wines — lush, vis-cous, packed with flavours of sultana, tea, and figs, with a perfect balance between sweetness and lightness. And, joy of joys, they are affordable. (P.O. Box 1475, Dungannon ☎ 028-8776 9206 info@wattletreewines.co.uk)

Fivemiletown

Creamery Cheese
● Fivemiletown Creamery

The mild Ballybrie is the best known of the Fivemiletown Creamery range of cheeses, although the smoked Ballyoak and the blue-veined Ballyblue are increasingly popular. The cheeses are all very mild in flavour, and do look out also for Cooneen, their goat's milk brie. (14 Ballylurgan Rd, Fivemiletown ☎ 028-8752 1209 clairemadine@fivemiletown.com)

Omagh

Butcher
● Mr Eatwells

Joe McMahon's famous shop is not just a butcher's shop of benchmark standards, for Joe's row of shops on Campsie Road also comprises a small bakery with a hot food bar, and a chip shop. Hugely popular for sausages – more than 20 varieties – and for barbecue specials, there is also fine Angus beef, and great service. (16 Campsie Rd, Omagh ☎ 028-8224 1104)

Cult Choice Sea Vegetables

Perhaps it was the use of the term Sea Weeds — an unworthy title if ever there was one — that has held us back from appreciating that Sea Vegetables are one of those Irish foods with enormous potential. The greatest potential is, firstly, for our own use of a series of sea vegetables — dilisk, carageen moss, kombu, spaghetti de mer, kelp — that are harbingers of health, pure foods packed with goodness, as people who have continued eating dulse in Northern Ireland have always known. Artisans have already harnessed these foods to flavour cheeses, including the Causeway Cheese Company in Ballymena, and to create exciting new foods, such as tapenade of sea vegetables, or smoked dilisk. But sea vegetables have infinite uses in the culinary arts, from seasoning fish, to dressing new potatoes, to fining beer. And there is potential to market and export our sea vegetables to many other countries. All we need do is collect them, and remember that they are not sea weeds: they are Sea Vegetables. (Dolphin Sea Vegetable Company, Dunmurry ☎ 028-9061 7512 www.irishseaweeds.com)

INDEX